Mark Glancy is originally from New Orleans, Louisiana. He has lived in Britain since attending the University of Lancaster as an undergraduate student and now teaches American and British film history at Queen Mary University of London. He is the author of *When Hollywood Loved Britain: The Hollywood 'British' Film, 1939–1945*, *The 39 Steps: A British Film Guide* and is co-editor of *The New Film History: Methods, Sources, Approaches*.

HOLLYWOOD
AND THE AMERICANIZATION
OF BRITAIN
FROM THE 1920S TO THE PRESENT

MARK GLANCY

I.B. TAURIS

LONDON · NEW YORK

Published in 2014 by I.B.Tauris & Co Ltd
6 Salem Road, London W2 4BU
175 Fifth Avenue, New York NY 10010
www.ibtauris.com

Distributed in the United States and Canada
Exclusively by Palgrave Macmillan
175 Fifth Avenue, New York NY 10010

ISBN: 978 1 84885 407 9

A full CIP record for this book is available from the British Library
A full CIP record is available from the Library of Congress

Library of Congress Catalog Card Number: available

Typeset by Newgen Publishers, Chennai
Printed and bound by CPI Group (UK) Ltd, Croydon, CR0 4YY

This book is dedicated to my parents,
Eileen Brener and Luke Glancy

Table of Contents

List of Illustrations

Acknowledgements

The research for this book was undertaken with a grant from the Arts and Humanities Research Council. I am grateful for this support and also for a period of sabbatical leave provided by the School of History, Queen Mary University of London.

Over the course of writing this book, I have benefited from opportunities to present and discuss my research as it developed. An invitation to speak at the Joint Neale and Commonwealth Fund Conference at University College London, on the topic of Anglo-American relations and film, planted the seed that later grew into this book. I am grateful to the organizers, and particularly to Adam Smith, for this source of inspiration, and also to members of the audience for their comments and questions. Similarly my thanks are extended to the organizers and audiences of the *Going to the Pictures* symposium convened by the Raphael Samuel History Centre, and the *Researching Cinema History* symposium convened by the British Universities Film and Video Council in tandem with Portsmouth University. I have gathered valuable feedback through presenting papers in the postgraduate seminar series in Cinema and Television History at De Montfort University; in Sport and Leisure History at the Institute of Historical Research; in the School of English Literature at Newcastle University; in Film Studies at the University of Southampton; in the Centre for Research in Media and Cultural Studies at the University of Sunderland; and in the American History seminar series at Queen Mary. The International Association for Media and History (IAMHIST) conference, held at Aberystwyth University in 2009 was another source of useful feedback, and I especially want to thank Steve Chibnall, Peter Krämer and Anne Morey for their comments on my paper. The Film History seminar series at the Institute of Historical Research in London has been a source of valuable guidance and advice on more than one occasion, and I am grateful to my friends and colleagues there for making the seminar a lively and supportive forum.

Parts of Chapter 2 were originally published in 'Temporary American Citizens? British Audiences, Hollywood Films and the Threat of Americanization in the 1920s', *Historical Journal of Film, Radio and Television* 26/4 (2006); and parts of Chapter 8 were originally published as 'The War of Independence in Feature Films: *The Patriot* and the Special Relationship Between Hollywood and Britain', *Historical Journal of Film, Radio and Television* 24/4 (2005). I am grateful to the journal's editor, David Culbert, and to its referees for their comments and suggestions.

The staff in the British Film Institute's library have been exceptionally helpful, patient and even cheerful over the course of many research days with them. My thanks go to them for answering innumerable queries and requests with a smile.

Philippa Brewster at I.B.Tauris and the series editor, Jeffrey Richards, have been both encouraging and very patient indeed. Thanks are also due to James Chapman, Mark Connelly, Adrian Garvey, Matt Jacobsen and Kiki Sarna for listening to my ideas, sharing their ideas, or, as and when it was necessary, telling me to get on with it, get over it, or simply forget about it for a moment.

I am especially indebted to Sue Harper and to Roger Law, who read the manuscript and offered insightful, detailed and frank comments on it. This book is much better for their input, and of course its faults rest with me alone.

Finally, this book is dedicated to my parents, Eileen Brener and Luke Glancy. There are more reasons for this dedication than I could ever hope to list here. Given the topic at hand, I will thank them for Americanizing me and for not objecting, over the years that followed, as at least some of that influence was undone.

General Editor's Introduction

In 1999 Mark Glancy made a major contribution to film history when he published *When Hollywood Loved Britain* which examined the heyday of the 'Hollywood British' film. He has now provided its counterpart, an equally significant study which might have been called *When Britain Loved Hollywood* but is instead called *Hollywood and the Americanization of Britain*. In this book he analyses the appeal of Hollywood films to British audiences and the sometimes heated debates and cultural anxieties stirred by their popularity. He rejects the simplistic interpretation summed up by *Daily Express* film critic G. A. Atkinson in 1927 and frequently echoed thereafter that millions of Britons have become, because of films, 'temporary American citizens' who 'talk America, think America and dream America'. He argues for a much more nuanced and sophisticated interpretation taking account of class and gender differences among film audiences, consumer choice dictated more often by aesthetic rather than ideological consideration and the development of and alterations in taste patterns.

Drawing on a wide range of sources – among them fan magazines, popularity polls, box office returns, reviews and the trade press – he charts the reception in Britain of American films through a series of case studies. He discusses the popularity of Rudolph Valentino who should be seen from an international rather than an American perspective as his most successful Hollywood films, set in Spain, Russia, Argentina and North Africa, were distinctively un-American. He charts the reaction of the British to the arrival of the talkies and the debate about accents which it sparked, a debate in which upper-class English accents received as much criticism as

obtrusively American ones. He examines the censorship controversies around gangster films in the 1930s and juvenile delinquency
films in the 1950s. He analyses the different responses of critics and
audiences to *Gone With The Wind* and the way in which British audiences, themselves enduring a war, found something to identify with
in a story about a war in the previous century. He looks at westerns
which have famously been described as America talking to itself
about its history and its values and finds that their popularity with
British audiences particularly of children and young adults, owed as
much to the visual appeal of the wide open spaces and the performance of rugged masculinity and the chivalric code as to American
history. He discusses *Grease* and the way in which British audiences in the 1970s and after appropriated an idealized view of 1950s
American high school culture. He concludes by examining the
British response to the violently anti-English *The Patriot* and finds
the response far from uniform. Altogether, this study adds up to a
complex, multi-dimensional account of how the cultural products
of one country (the United States) found a place in the cinema culture and popular consciousness of another (the United Kingdom)
in many varied and sometimes unexpected ways.

Jeffrey Richards

Introduction

This book is a history of British cinema that is not focused on British films or filmmakers. Instead, it is concerned with audiences and especially the reception of Hollywood feature films in Britain. It is unusual in that it does not approach the popularity of Hollywood films as a problem: it is not an account of government attempts to intervene on behalf of the British film industry; it does not investigate the business practices or diplomatic negotiations that gave rise to Hollywood's pre-eminence; and, although it acknowledges the opinions of cultural elites, its primary purpose is not to rehearse their largely hostile views on the topic. These issues have been explored elsewhere.[1] Rather, this book investigates the appeal of Hollywood films, as well as the issues and controversies raised by them, over the course of nearly 100 years. At the core of the book, and the research process that has informed it, is an interest in audience tastes, preferences and attitudes, and a curiosity about the meanings and pleasures that British audiences have found in Hollywood films. To what extent are Hollywood films regarded as foreign films? Does their popularity reflect a cultural affinity with the United States? How can we ascertain the meanings and significance that audiences found in them? Are there distinctive taste patterns in the rankings of Hollywood's box office hits and misses in Britain? And to what extent do taste patterns alter according to the age, class, gender and region of audiences? In pursuing these questions, Hollywood's prominence is considered as neither a problem nor a cause for celebration. It is instead approached as a central fact of British film history and yet one that has received relatively little attention from historians.

It was in the period between 1910 and 1912 that American and British journalists began to comment on the rising popularity of

American films abroad and in Britain especially. At this point, Hollywood (both as a place and as a synonym for the American film industry) was unknown, and so these reports referred directly to American films and wondered why they travelled so easily, and why they had assumed an advantage over French, Italian and British films. Their success in Britain was particularly noteworthy partly because the country had a large and eager cinema-going public, and also because London was a major international film distribution centre. At this point, there was no notion of a 'special relationship' between the two countries (either in political or cultural terms) to explain the phenomenon, and no alarm was registered about the possibility of films 'Americanizing' audiences; their popularity was assumed to be merely a passing fad. It was, of course, only the beginning. During the First World War, and as cinema-going became a routine part of the social life of most Britons, Hollywood's dominance increased dramatically. Admissions figures would rise and fall over the years, but cinema-going remained the nation's pre-eminent leisure-time activity until the mid-1950s. Since then, watching films has not been centred so exclusively in cinemas, but their availability on television, VHS, DVD, Blu-ray and the internet has ensured that they have never ceased to be a popular form of entertainment. Indeed, it is likely that, on average, more films are watched in Britain today than in the heyday of cinema-going in the 1940s.[2]

Throughout all of these periods, formats and settings, Hollywood films have been what most Britons think of when they contemplate seeing a film. My point is not that British films are insignificant or that audiences do not appreciate them. It is that the history of British cinema need not be solely concerned with British films and filmmakers. Indeed, as Geoffrey Nowell-Smith observed as long ago as 1985, the popularity of Hollywood films with British audiences constitutes a 'hidden history of cinema in British culture'.[3] An intriguing glimpse into that 'hidden history' was revealed in 2005 when the British Film Institute published its ranking of the 'the UK's 100 most popular films'. Based on a tally of tickets sold, and stretching back to include films released in every decade since the 1930s, this ranking of box-office winners was full of surprises. Some of these pertained to British films: who would have guessed that the most successful of all British-made films was *Spring in*

Park Lane (1948)? It was surprising, too, to see which Hollywood films, from *Gone with the Wind* (1939/40) in first place to *The Matrix Reloaded* (2003) in one-hundredth place, attracted the largest number of cinema-goers.[4] This glimpse into the film preferences of many generations of cinema-goers is in part what inspired this book, but the focus was never intended to be limited to box office hits alone. Audience preferences at any juncture are more diverse and fragmented than that would suggest, and of course the margins can be as interesting as the mainstream. Hence, this book focuses on the reception of a range of Hollywood films in Britain, including films that played in 'picture palaces' and 'flea pits', and films that met with favour as well as films that met with opprobrium.

That this 'hidden history' of British cinema has attracted relatively little scholarly attention can be attributed to several factors. Within the field of Film Studies, highly theorized, abstract concepts of spectatorship have diverted interest from the study of actual audiences, their specific and multifarious responses, and the interplay of contextual and textual factors that bear upon the meaning and impact of films. Film historians, meanwhile, have traditionally circumscribed studies of films, filmmakers, production organizations and regulatory bodies within national boundaries; transnational approaches have only recently come to the fore.[5] The concept of national cinema, too, is one most often explored with reference to the films produced rather than the films watched in a country; or, as Andrew Higson has commented, the concept is 'used prescriptively rather than descriptively, citing what *ought* to be the national cinema rather than describing the actual cinematic experience of popular audiences'.[6] Another key factor in making this 'hidden history' appear less than compelling is the long and deep association between Hollywood films and Americanization. This association is entirely negative. It has fuelled the idea that Hollywood's predominance is not based on audience choices but on the economic power of American film corporations, and by the fear that feature films serve as a form of propaganda for American values and ideology. Thus, it casts Hollywood films as unwelcome, foreign intruders, and blames them for holding back the development of both the indigenous film industry and an authentic film culture.

During the peak decades of cinema-going, the link between Hollywood and Americanization was pervasive among Britain's political, social and cultural elites. It was taken for granted that film was a powerful medium, and one that could shape the outlook and interests of audiences. The rise of Hollywood appeared to be an unfortunate and dangerous predicament of the modern world; one that threatened to undermine traditional social hierarchies and values. Britain was not alone in these concerns. In the interwar period, as Victoria de Grazia has argued, the appeal of American popular culture, and especially the cinema, led elites across Europe to question 'whether old world states still exercised sovereignty over their citizens' leisure'.[7] In Britain, however, the issue of Americanization through films rang particularly resonant alarm bells. The shared language was one reason for this. When British children mimicked the American English they learned from films, it confirmed many of the worst fears about Hollywood's influence. Another reason was the British film industry's struggles. While other European countries countered Hollywood's dominance with protectionist measures, the measures taken in Britain were not as aggressive or effective. Importantly, the rise of Hollywood also played into a narrative of national decline in Britain. This came into sharp focus after the First World War and as the United States emerged as an undoubted world power.[8] As we shall see, Hollywood served as a useful target for the resentments that stemmed from the USA's displacement of Britain at the centre of the world stage.

The concept of Americanization therefore casts a long shadow over the study of Hollywood films and British audiences. It has obscured the idea that audiences are able to make choices and to find their own meanings and pleasures in films, and it has diminished the scope for research in this area. Two early and valuable efforts to redress this were Helen Taylor's *Scarlett's Women: Gone with the Wind and Its Female Fans* (1989) and Jackie Stacey's *Star Gazing: Hollywood Cinema and Female Spectatorship* (1994).[9] These ethnographic studies were groundbreaking for engaging sympathetically with actual audiences and their views of popular films. Both studies focus on the written recollections of women film fans. In Taylor's study, the appeal of a single film (and the novel on which it is based) is considered, while Stacey's study concerns the impact of Hollywood glamour amid the postwar austerity of the 1940s and 1950s. More recently, Annette Kuhn's *An Everyday Magic: Cinema and Cultural Memory* (2002), has focused on men and women's memories of cinema-going in the 1930s, utilizing oral accounts. Kuhn's approach differs from Taylor's and Stacey's in its emphasis on the 'everyday' nature of cinema-going as a routine, social activity (as opposed to the significance of individual films or stars).[10] However, each study asserts the importance of analysing specific audience responses, and each investigates how meaning and impact varied according to the identities and circumstances particular to British viewing contexts. In these respects, they represent a significant shift away from the concept of passive spectators and a shift towards research into transnational film reception.[11]

This book, unlike the studies conducted by Taylor, Stacey and Kuhn, explores contemporaneous responses to film rather than audience memories. As time passes, using memory as a source becomes less viable for studies that include audiences from the peak years of cinema-going. Different sources and a different methodology are needed. Hence, a wide array of sources is used here to study the reception of Hollywood films in Britain: audience surveys and polls; film fan magazines; film trade papers; pressbooks and other forms of publicity; fan reviews posted on internet sites; critical reviews; and accounts of films and related issues in a wider body of periodicals. These are analysed to provide what Janet Staiger has described as 'an historical explanation of the event of interpreting the text'. In *Interpreting Films: Studies in the Historical Reception of American Cinema* (1992), Staiger rejects the long-held critical aim of arriving at the intended, preferred or correct reading of film. In reception studies, meaning is understood to be determined in large part by context rather than text, and it is subject to a confluence of factors: the cultural, social and ideological discourses surrounding a film at the time of its release; the expectations set by marketing, publicity and critical reviews; and the socially constructed identity of viewers. Reception studies therefore do not seek an essential or intrinsic meaning, but aim to explain how a range of meanings were generated by a single film. Importantly, while much of the research and analysis for a reception study is empirically based, Staiger asserts that interpretation remains crucial as a means of moving beyond data and evidence, and explaining the interplay of text and context.[12]

While my own research and analysis is informed by these methodological precepts, there are two provisos to register. First, Staiger expresses a strong wariness towards audience research materials such as surveys, polls and fan magazines on the grounds that they cannot be construed as 'raw data' because they are 'bound within an apparatus of perpetuating the pleasure of the cinematic institution' and are therefore subject to mediation and distortion.[13] The point is a valid one, and I am not claiming that such sources represent an open window on the world of popular film culture. However, it is possible to use such sources, with their original purpose and potential bias in mind, and to treat them critically. Furthermore, for the purposes of this study, I have found that it is *necessary* to use such sources. The public discourse on cinema in Britain, especially during the peak years of cinema-going, was largely hostile, and many of the most prominent and easily accessed historical sources (e.g., Hansard, *The Times* and other broadsheet newspapers) offer mainly disparaging views of Hollywood films and of cinema-going more generally. In this context, less prominent sources (such as fan magazines) are vital for providing an alternative viewpoint and one more representative of wider public opinion. Put another way, modern British historians have long employed letters to the editor of *The Times* as a representation of the 'bush telegraph of middle England', whilst acknowledging that such letters may be edited, or chosen for publication because they offer views that are extreme or in service to the paper's editorial policy.[14] Reception studies must surely use fan magazines such as *Picturegoer* in a similar way, as the 'bush telegraph' of cinema-goers, but without losing sight of the potential for mediation and distortion.

The second proviso is that both Staiger and another pioneer in film reception studies, Barbara Klinger, emphasize the value of diachronic reception studies (studies that show how a film's meaning changes over time) over synchronic reception studies (studies centred on a single time, usually the time of a film's initial release).[15] Klinger has commented that reception studies centred on a film's first release are 'stuck in synchrony' and therefore 'sidestep the big question', which concerns the 'the radical flux of meaning brought on by changing social and historical horizons over time'.[16] My own approach, however, is centred mainly on the period of each film's initial release in Britain, and it seeks an understanding of the encounter between specific films and historically located audience groups. Moreover, understanding why British audiences chose to see Hollywood films involves some consideration of the films themselves and the pleasures that were found in them. This is not intended as a rejection of the ideal of destabilizing textual meaning. That, of course, is an inherent aspect of transnational reception studies. As Richard Maltby has observed, cultural products are often shorn of their complexities when they leave their culture of origin. Specific points of reference and a deeper cultural resonance are likely to be lost in another, host culture. They may appear simplistic or crude in this newly simplified state, but they are also open to reinterpretation.[17] Transnational reception studies therefore must aim to situate films within the 'cultural matrix' of the host country, and this is an endeavour that involves additional contextual concerns. How did attitudes to the film's country of origin affect its reception in the host culture? How did the host country's censorship regulations and procedures affect the film? What qualities set the film apart from the host culture's own films? What did critics regard as noteworthy about the film's origins? Answers to these questions are necessary to provide what might be termed the 'back story' of a transnational reception study, and they take precedence over diachronic perspectives.

As the research questions suggest, a key part of situating a film is finding its place within the host country's 'cinema culture'. Michael Hammond has argued that this is crucial to ascertaining 'how audiences were encouraged to make sense of the films they saw and in turn how "the cinema" ... was seen to be affecting audiences'.[18] Examining a film's place within the distribution and exhibition system is therefore important, and so too is any evidence regarding its marketing and publicity. Analysis of pressbooks and film posters, for example, can reveal the film distributor's strategy: who did they imagine the audience for this film to be, and on what terms would the film appeal to them? Audience responses to individual films, meanwhile, pose particular challenges. Throughout much of the twentieth century, audiences left little evidence behind and, as previously noted, their responses were subject to the interests of gatekeepers who had a vested interest in what was published. In recent years, audience responses have become much more readily available on the internet, but here the stumbling blocks are the issues of identity and authenticity that arise in a forum that has so few gatekeepers. Nevertheless, it is possible to identify websites that require contributors at least to indicate their location – a crucial element in studies of transnational reception – and therefore to engage with this very substantial source of audience responses. More traditionally, two other sources have been used in relation to audiences. One is box office information. A figure for a single film is not especially enlightening in isolation, as it reveals little about audience opinions. However, as separate studies by Sue Harper, Julian Poole and John Sedgwick have demonstrated, box office information on a broad swathe of films, carefully located in terms of time and place, can be more useful because this allows for taste patterns to emerge.[19] Another traditional source used to gauge audience responses is critical opinion. No single critic's opinion of a film can be taken as representative of wider audience views, and even a multitude of critical opinions are not helpful if they belong to the same critical fraternity or write for periodicals aimed at the same readership. It is a range of critical opinion that is needed, from periodicals aimed at a variety of readerships, so that the distinctive elements of each can be identified and compared. If we think of a film's reception as the sum total of responses that a film generated, within specific temporal or geographical borders, research for reception studies is an attempt to retrieve as many of those responses as possible: to identify, scrutinize and explain the responses and to analyse the terms and the tone employed to evaluate films.

Investigating the reception of Hollywood films in Britain is, of course, no small task. It involves tens of thousands of films, released over many decades, and watched by millions of people. This book is therefore based around case studies of films, genres and stars that represent key time periods, distinctive audience groups, and box office hits and misses. Chapter 1, however, is not a case study but an examination of the concept of Americanization. My interest here, and throughout the book, is not to prove or disprove that Hollywood films have been the agents of Americanization;

the concept is too nebulous to be absolutely confirmed or denied. In this chapter my interest is instead to determine how and why Americanization became so closely identified with films, and to investigate the extent to which issues of nationality figure in popular film preferences. Chapter 2 is the first of the case studies. It pursues one of the central themes of this book – that Hollywood was the home of an international film industry rather than a specifically American film industry – by examining the reputation of the most popular star of the 1920s, Rudolph Valentino. His appeal, to women in particular, is investigated using fan magazines to examine the terms in which film fandom could be expressed in this decade and the anxieties that surrounded it. Chapter 3 concerns an aspect of British film history that hitherto has received little attention from historians: the arrival of the 'talkies' and the impact that they had on audiences. Alfred Hitchcock's *Blackmail* (1929) is often considered to be the country's first 'talkie', but only because this film was made in Britain. Many more Hollywood talkies were released in Britain before *Blackmail*, and this chapter compares responses to them in trade papers, critical reviews and fan magazines as a means of gauging how 'talking' weighed upon perceptions of the strengths and weaknesses of both Hollywood and British films. Chapter 4 focuses on the British Board of Film Censors and how its policies shaped perceptions of Hollywood films and British films, considering in particular the gangster films of the 1930s and the terms on which they were censored, as well as critical and audience views of this controversial genre. Here, another important theme emerges, relating to the different cultural tasks that Hollywood and British films performed. While British films were charged with representing the nation, Hollywood films were often granted greater licence and as a result could address a wider range of audience needs and interests.

Chapter 5 centres on Britain's most popular film, *Gone with the Wind* (1939/40), and examines its release during the Second World War. The hostile reception this film received in the film trade and from many critics makes a striking case for the need to use audience survey materials. One might suppose, from the initial trade and critical responses, that *Gone with the Wind* was regarded across Britain as a laughably irrelevant film. Audience responses, however, allow us to piece together another side of the conversation surrounding this film, and thus to understand how a film centred on the American Civil War proved to be powerfully compelling for Britons caught up in a war much closer to home. Chapter 6 traces the evolution of the western genre, as British audiences saw it, in several stages: from the 'Wild West' shows of the 1880s, to Hopalong Cassidy's popularity in 'B' films and on television, to the most popular of all westerns with British audiences, *The Big Country* (1958/59). This chapter questions why British audiences should find this most American of all genres appealing; an approach that involves considering qualities of the genre itself. It also examines the genre's capacity to move through a succession of different exhibition formats and explores how its 'domestication' in these formats influenced the meanings and pleasures associated with it. Chapters 7 and 8 are case studies of films that fared very differently with audiences. Chapter 7 considers how marketing and merchandising campaigns figured in the success of *Grease* (1978) and how this musical, centred on the American high school of the 1950s, became a family favourite for generations of British audiences. Chapter 8 investigates the controversy surrounding *The Patriot* (2000), a film that broke a long film tradition of portraying the War of Independence in neutral terms. The responses of political columnists, film critics and internet reviewers are compared to determine the extent to which national sympathies figured in its failure at the British box office.

Thus, the case studies proceed in roughly chronological order, and they are weighted towards the middle decades of the last century, when anxieties about Americanization were strongest. Each chapter utilizes an array of historical reception sources, and each reflects upon the strengths and weaknesses of the sources employed. The chapters are also intended to reveal aspects of British cinema history that have received little attention in historical accounts centred on British film and filmmakers alone. This points to one of the most significant, if least recognized, manifestations of Americanization in relation to cinema: the history of Hollywood is most often written with regard only to American audiences and the impact that films made in the United States. Yet there are more diverse histories, in which Hollywood films are central but American responses are not. This book seeks to redress this particular manifestation of Americanization by illuminating key moments and issues in the reception of Hollywood films with British audiences.

There are just a few points to be clarified before proceeding. Ascribing a year to film titles can be done on a variety of grounds: the year of production, the year of the premiere in the USA or, with British cinema, the year of either the premiere or the general release in Britain. As I am writing about American films, I have decided to use the year of the US premiere and, wherever there is a difference, to add the year of the film's British premiere. Hence, the designation of *Gone with the Wind* (1939/40) reflects that it was first shown in the USA in 1939 and first shown in Britain in 1940, while the designation of *Grease* (1978) reflects that it was first shown in both the USA and Britain in 1978. Another point of detail is that I am spelling Americanization with a 'z' rather than an 's'. This is not in deference to American spellings, but represents the spelling in the *Oxford English Dictionary*. Finally, it seems only fair to acknowledge to readers that I was born and raised in the United States, and that, although I have lived over half of my life in Britain, my origins are bound to have affected my perspective on the topic at hand. Having lived in both countries is also, of course, a strong factor in my interest in the topic, and one that I hope has inspired rather than skewed my thinking. But that is something that readers will have to decide for themselves over the course of the chapters that follow.

1 'Temporary American Citizens': Audiences and Americanization

In the four quarters of the globe, who reads an American book? Or goes to an American play? Or looks at an American picture or statue? What does the world yet owe to American physicians or surgeons? What new substances have their chemists discovered? Or what old ones have they analysed? What new constellations have been have been discovered by the telescopes of Americans? What have they done in mathematics? Who drinks out of American glasses? Or eats from American plates? Or wears American coats or gowns? Or sleeps in American blankets?

Sydney Smith, *The Edinburgh Review* (1820)[1]

The advent of the United States of America as the greatest of world powers is the greatest political, social and commercial phenomenon of our times. For some years past we have all been more or less dimly conscious of its significance. It is only when we look at the manifold manifestations of the exuberant energy of the United States, and the worldwide influence which they are now exerting upon the world in general and the British Empire in particular that we realise how comparatively insignificant are all other events of our time.

W.T. Stead, *The Americanisation of the World* (1902)[2]

The plain truth about the British film situation is that the bulk of our picturegoers are Americanized to an extent that makes them regard the British film as a foreign film, and an interesting but more frequently irritating interlude in their favourite entertainment. They go to see American stars. They have been brought up on American publicity. They talk America, think America, and dream America. We have several million people, mostly women, who, to all intent and purpose, are temporary American citizens.

G.A. Atkinson, *Daily Express* (1927)[3]

Sydney Smith's commentary on the insignificance of the United States (in the first quotation above) seems almost inconceivably remote. It is now difficult to imagine a world in which the USA had made so little impact. In 1820, however, Smith insisted that the only true source of pride for Americans was that 'they are a recent offset indeed from England' and therefore they could claim that 'they are sprung from the same race with Bacon and Shakespeare and Newton'.⁴ Less than a century later, W.T. Stead (in the second quotation above) urged his fellow Britons to face up to 'the Americanisation of the world'. Stead predicted that Americanization was 'the trend of the twentieth century' and argued that Britain could maintain its status as a world power only if it agreed to some form of union with the United States. He also advised that Britain would have to adopt the American model of democracy if it hoped to match the innovations and ingenuity of American manufacturing and commerce. To underline this latter point, Stead listed the many recent American products and inventions (including the automobile, elevator, light bulb, sewing machine and telephone) which, at the turn of the century, had become integral to the everyday lives of most Britons.⁵

Both writers overstated their case. The United States was not quite as insignificant as Smith claimed. His argument was made for the readers of the learned *Edinburgh Review* and in response to a book that listed the country's achievements in too proud a manner for his liking.⁶ Stead, by contrast, was a crusading and outspoken journalist who admired the USA for its modernity and egalitarianism, but made far-fetched claims about the need for, and the potential of, a union between the two countries. Nevertheless, the vast chasm between Smith and Stead's statements offers an illustration of the fundamental and dramatic change in the relative standing of the two countries over the course of the nineteenth century. Importantly, for the purposes of this study, the change occurred long before anyone thought of accusing films of selling American values or products to the world. At the time Stead was writing, in 1902, Hollywood was little more than a farming community on the outskirts of Los Angeles, growing oranges and avocadoes, and the 'Americanisation of the world' was apparently able to proceed without its contribution.

Twenty-five years later, in 1927, the connection between Hollywood and Americanization was regarded as a fact of modern life. G.A. Atkinson's comments in the *Daily Express* (in the third quotation above) have been quoted by film historians ever since not because he was the first to argue that cinema-goers were 'Americanized', and certainly not because his was an unusual or extreme point of view.[7] Rather, Atkinson's comments have served as a neat summation of the pervasive view of British cinema-goers: they were so enthralled by Hollywood films, and Hollywood films were so intrinsically American, that audiences must have lost some element of their own national identity in order to enjoy them so much and so often. Or, as Atkinson put it, Hollywood films transformed British audiences into 'temporary American citizens', who 'talk America, think America, and dream America' outside of the cinema. This was an elitist perspective on cinema insofar as it expressed disdain for popular tastes, but the presence of these comments in a mass circulation daily newspaper indicates that they had a common currency. In fact, as the film critic for the *Express* newspapers and for the BBC, Atkinson was regarded the country's 'most powerful film critic', and he regularly asserted that Hollywood films posed a 'menace' to Britain.[8]

Atkinson was correct in pointing out that Hollywood films dominated in British cinemas, and he was correct in observing that British cinema-goers' expectations of what feature films could and should be had been shaped by Hollywood. In terms of film style, narrative form, production values and the emphasis given to stars, Hollywood had set the standards for popular cinema. It is quite a leap, however, to suppose that the films made in Hollywood were vehicles for American ideology, and another leap again to assume that audiences appreciated them, or were subject to them, in this way. Yet these ideas run throughout commentaries about popular films during the peak years of cinema-going. Moreover, it is not clear when the ideas faded away, or indeed that they have entirely faded away. In time, the concerns surrounding popular tastes shifted to other, newer media, but the idea of Hollywood's powerful influence is still revived on occasion, and especially to support concerns about a particularly objectionable film or films.

The sections that follow therefore consider the roots of the association between Americanization and the cinema, as means of ascertaining why this association took hold and how it was popularized. Through examining broad taste patterns, the chapter also questions the extent to which an appreciation of Hollywood films necessarily entails a cultural affinity with the United States. Did British audiences really 'talk America, think America, and dream America'? And if not, what pleasures did they find in Hollywood films?

Americanization, Britain and the cinema

Within the United States, the term 'Americanization' has most often been used to describe the process of acculturation that immigrants underwent; that is, the process of learning the customs, manners, values and language of 'mainstream Americans'. It was 'something the native middle class did to immigrants', and it is associated most strongly with the late nineteenth and early twentieth centuries, when immigration reached unprecedented levels and nativists were keen to assert their cultural authority.[9] In Europe, and throughout much of the twentieth century, the term also referred to the exercise of American influences. Here, too, it was customs, manners, values and language that were at stake, but in European contexts these influences were not sanctioned by cultural authority figures. Instead they rose 'from below' and specifically from the proliferation of American popular culture among working-class communities. American influences were held to be both dismal and threatening by cultural authorities, who conceived of Americanization as a 'zero-sum game', in Rob Kroes' phrase, in which any measure of American influence resulted in a correlating measure of 'de-Europeanization'.[10] Yet this 'zero-sum game' had not always been the rule in Britain. Prior to the First World War, Americanization did not have exclusively negative connotations. *The Times*, for example, first used the term as early as 1849, when the impending Americanization of the territories of New Mexico and California was welcomed.[11] There was also wide support in the British press and among the public for the USA during the Spanish–American War of 1898.[12] In contexts such as these,

Britain and the United States were perceived as sharing an Anglo-Saxon culture that was being more widely disseminated through the United States' expansion, and Britain was seen to benefit from a widening realm of cultural influence.

There was less enthusiasm for the idea of Americanization taking place within Britain itself. During the presidential election campaign of 1868, reports about political corruption and the excesses of the press in the USA led *The Times* to consider the future Americanization of Britain as 'something to be dreaded'.[13] Signs of increasing American influence in the British Empire, and especially in Australia and Canada, were also reported with a sense of foreboding.[14] Beyond *The Times*, and when considering industry in particular, some commentators asserted that a measure of Americanization would be useful to the British economy. Unlike W.T. Stead, the *Daily Mail* journalist F.A. Mackenzie did not foresee a future union between the two countries, but in his book *The American Invaders* (1902), he observed that Britain had been invaded by American products at least partly because the two countries shared a language and 'common ways of life'. Mackenzie argued too that British manufacturers would regain their own markets only if they learned to emulate American methods.[15] Thus, Americanization was variously dreaded, accepted enthusiastically, or regarded as an economic necessity, but in all of these visions it was seen as an inevitable future. The United States was not Britain's cultural 'Other', then, but represented the recognizable and seemingly unstoppable forces of modernity.

Both McKenzie and Stead observed that, in 1902, American products had become remarkably commonplace in Britain. As part of a larger argument about the complacency of British industry, McKenzie used shoe manufacturing as an example and commented that while American boots had been 'practically unknown' a few years earlier, they were now 'the most prominent display in our show shops from Dover to Aberdeen'.[16] Stead cited a litany of examples as a means of demonstrating that, at every point in the day, the 'average man' uses American products as a part of his daily routine: from the sheets that he slept on to the clothes he wore, the foods he ate, the cigarettes he smoked, the trams and lifts that he rode in, the typewriter that he used in his office and the 'liver pills' he took in the evening. All were likely to have originated in the United States.[17] Neither writer thought to question whether these products had any impact on their users: wearing boots, riding in a tram and taking liver pills were not thought to influence values or outlook. Stead allowed that his average man might see an American musical comedy at the theatre, but he did not suggest that there was anything alarming in this. Importantly, though, his 'average man' was male and (as the routine of his daily life indicates) also middle class and middle aged. His patriotism and his sense of national identity were therefore considered constant and impenetrable, and it was never imagined that consumer choices could undermine them.

It was very different in the 1920s. Americanization became so inextricably linked with films that no one seemed to recall that the issue had ever been discussed without reference to the cinema. Of course, other American influences (including jazz music and styles of journalism and advertising) were noted too, but cinema was different because, in this decade at least, Hollywood films overwhelmingly predominated in British cinemas. In the years just before the First World War, American films had constituted 60 per cent of the films shown, but during the war they filled the gap left by the decline in production of British, French and Italian films. By 1917, they constituted 90 per cent of the films shown and the interest they generated among cinema-goers was abundantly apparent in film fan magazines. It was apparent, too, when film stars occasionally visited Britain. In 1920, the behaviour of the crowds greeting Mary Pickford and Douglas Fairbanks in London 'appalled' *The Times*: 'The crowd was enormous. It consisted chiefly of women. They did not stand and cheer like an ordinary crowd. Instead their curiosity overcame their manners and they made one wild rush to get a look at Miss Pickford.'[18] Charlie Chaplin was also 'mobbed' on a visit to London in 1921.[19] On such occasions, enthusiasm for films and stars effectively spilled out of the cinemas and on to the streets, where it bewildered the older, upper-class observers who did not share the new enthusiasm for films. A columnist in the *Express* contrasted the crowd's enthusiasm for Chaplin with the indignation felt by 'florid gentleman in their clubs' who could not understand 'all this tosh about a film actor'.[20] Initially, more sympathetic observers assumed that Hollywood's predominance was an unfortunate consequence of the war, and one that would pass as the economy returned to a peacetime footing. By the early to mid-1920s, however, British film production was declining rather than increasing. There were no signs of recovery and yet the 4,000 cinemas throughout the country's villages, towns and cities were testimony to the central place that cinema-going had in the leisure time of many, if not most, Britons. That British films should have so little value, even in their own home market, seemed to be symptomatic of a national malaise and a sign of Britain's declining stature in the post-war world. It was also a sign of the United States' concurrent ascendancy in world affairs – in diplomacy, trade and culture – that Hollywood should now be the world's film capital, with cinemas across the globe eagerly awaiting its output.

Cinema-goers, of course, chose to see Hollywood films. They chose to wear the fashions they saw in them, to read about stars in fan magazines and sometimes to adopt the stars' mannerisms and expressions (and later, characteristics of their speech too). Cinema was a more immediate and intense medium than its predecessors (for example, music hall, variety and theatre) and its enthusiasts enjoyed that it broadened their horizons and introduced them to a vast repertoire of stories, personalities, places, ideas, goods and styles. While most cinema-goers may have wished for a healthier British film industry or for more appealing British films, they did not fear the influence or effect of the films they saw. It was the country's elites – leading figures in politics, the arts and business – who assumed that Hollywood films were being imposed upon cinema-goers and that they had neither the means nor the inclination to resist them. Among the elites, as Ian Jarvie has commented, concerns about films and Americanization cut across political and party lines.[21] In their thinking, films were not at all like the boots or liver pills discussed so casually by Mackenzie and Stead. They took for granted that film was a powerful medium for propaganda; an idea that gained credence when governments used film propaganda during the First World War.[22] They took for granted, too, that audiences were inevitably influenced by films. The keenest cinema-goers were not the prosperous, middle-aged, middle-class men that Stead imagined using an array of American products or seeing an

American stage musical. It was predominantly women, the young and the working class or lower middle class who went to the cinema most often, and their patriotism and mental fortitude were not so easily assumed.

If we recognize that the anxieties around Americanization and film were largely confined to elites, we must also recognize that the idea was not their invention or delusion. It was, in fact, an idea promoted by Hollywood itself. In 1922, the newly formed trade organization, the Motion Picture Producers and Distributors of America (MPPDA), launched a public relations campaign aimed at quelling domestic criticism of Hollywood. From the perspective of the United States' own Protestant, middle-class establishment, Hollywood did not represent American values at all: it was an industry owned and operated largely by foreign-born Jewish businessmen; it was plagued by scandals, such as the recent, notorious Fatty Arbuckle case; and its films embodied cosmopolitan values at odds with middle-American sensibilities. Hence, the MPPDA set out to 'Americanize' the industry's image. Prominent film industry figures such as the MPPDA president Will Hays and the director D.W. Griffith promoted the industry as a patriotic one by promising that its films would 'sell America' to the world. As Hays expressed it, 'Every film that goes from America abroad, wherever it shall be sent, shall correctly portray to the world the purposes, the ideals, the accomplishments, the opportunities, and the life of America'.[23] The MPPDA also promoted the idea that Hollywood's international reach had a beneficial effect for the wider American business community. This was the thinking behind the expression, 'trade follows the film'; that is, wherever Hollywood films were shown, the demand for American goods swiftly rose.[24] In Britain, these arguments were readily accepted. Indeed, they were so readily accepted that it is worth examining the various interests that employed these ideas and the uses that they found for them. These interests can be divided into four categories – political, economic, cultural and intellectual – but these are overlapping rather than discrete categories.

In political terms, the concern over Hollywood and Americanization arose in tandem with the trebling of the electorate, as the franchise was extended in 1918 to include all men over the age of 21 and all women over the age of 30, and then extended again in 1928 to include all women over the age of 21. Britain's elites suspected that the uneducated masses, who were now eligible to vote for the first time, were volatile and open to manipulation and propaganda.[25] This apprehension could be directed at the press and radio too, but film raised specific concerns because the production sector was largely under foreign control. The British Board of Film Censors (beginning in 1913) offered one means of combating unwelcome influences, and it did not shy away from political censorship. Revolutionary Soviet dramas such as *Battleship Potemkin* (1925) and *Mother* (1926) were not approved for public screenings. Yet in some respects, American films may have represented a greater challenge for the censors. As Jarvie has commented, many American films rejected the notions of social deference and knowing one's place and promoted more egalitarian values of individualism, ambition, wealth and glamour.[26] Within a single film, such values were not overtly subversive or obviously censorable. It was their cumulative effect that was worrying. In 1927, an editorial in *The Times* brought together these concerns in a frank appraisal of the 'false values of the film'. It was a 'public danger', *The Times* argued, that the cinema continually promoted the importance of 'wealth, luxury and notoriety' to ordinary people. This was likely to cause resentment among 'the many newly enfranchised and slightly educated minds'. The answer was not censorship, because it was the repeated insistence on these values that caused the problem and not any single, excisable representation of them. The answer, according to *The Times*, was to promote British values by strengthening the British film industry.[27]

The economic concerns were twofold. A general concern related to the idea that 'trade follows the film'. The expression was a modification of 'trade follows the flag', which had been a governing principle of nineteenth-century imperialism. Hollywood therefore seemed to represent a twentieth-century form of imperialism, but one that seduced rather subjugated the colonized. A corollary to 'trade follows the film', boasting that for every foot of celluloid exported from the USA another dollar of export trade in American goods was generated, was never proved but it seemed to offer authoritative evidence of the power of film. Both expressions were widely quoted in Britain.[28] They offered a useful explanation for Britain's declining share of world trade; one that implied that the quality, cost or appeal of British goods was not at issue. The real issue was the power of films. The second and more specific economic concern related to the relative size and strength of the two film industries. Hollywood had a much larger domestic market under its control. Films could pay back their costs there, and then be sold at discounted rates abroad, with the foreign earnings from countries such as Britain offering filmmakers pure profit. Furthermore, aggressive business practices such as 'block booking' and 'blind bidding' were cited as reasons for Hollywood's predominance in British cinemas. Both the general concern about trade and the specific concerns about Hollywood's economic power suggested that the British film industry should be given government protection: as a means to bolster wider trade and as a means for British films to compete with their powerful rival. The assumption behind these economic concerns was that, given a level playing field, British films would prove as appealing to audiences as Hollywood films; that is, the predominance of Hollywood films stemmed from the industry's corporate power rather than the appeal of the films themselves. This idea has proved to be particularly enduring.

The cultural concerns centred on Hollywood's idealized portrayal of the United States. Films – then and now – often portray the USA as a modern, optimistic, consumer-oriented culture, while both film narratives and the publicity surrounding stars emphasize the capacity for ordinary individuals to transcend their circumstances and achieve personal fulfilment. British audiences could scarcely fail to register that this culture appeared more affluent, egalitarian and democratic than their own. The effect, it was supposed, was to 'sell' audiences on America itself. In 1925, Lord Newton warned the House of Lords that Hollywood films represented an advertisement for the USA:

> The fact is, the Americans realized almost instantaneously that the cinema was a heaven-sent method for advertising themselves, their country, their methods, their wares, their ideas, and even their language, and they have seized upon it as a method of persuading the whole world, civilized and uncivilized, into the belief that America is really the only country which counts.[29]

Newton (a former diplomat, MP and Paymaster-General) thus suggested that the influence was intentional, and part of a coordinated plan to boost American cultural prestige abroad. Yet at the same time he was concerned that, with its sordid tales of adultery or crime, Hollywood denigrated the authority of white people in the eyes of non-whites, and so loosened the ties that bound the British Empire. However inconsistent these ideas may seem, others echoed them. Within the British film industry, production interests stood only to gain from concerns over Hollywood. Thus, when the British National Film League was launched in 1923, the chairman of Gaumont-British Pictures, A.C. Bromhead, spoke of film as a weapon. It represented 'a great new power', he told an audience of officials and dignitaries, warning them that 'the nation which has no films of its own will become inarticulate in a world sense'.[30] Within the decade, British films would receive a measure of protection in the form of the Films Act of 1927, but granting protection proved to be a more straightforward endeavour than making films that fulfilled expectations of a culturally authentic national cinema and attracted large audiences. Hence, when the legislation was reviewed (for the Films Act of 1938), there was less optimism about British films, but concerns over the power of films as a form of cultural propaganda persisted in the debates.

Not all concerns about Hollywood and Americanization led inevitably to support for the British film industry. The intellectuals who expressed concerns over Americanization were hostile to film as a medium, and therefore saw no solution in British films. The intellectual critique of Americanization represents a 'tangled tradition', as Duncan Webster has observed, but its various threads can be traced back to concerns about mass culture that arose in the nineteenth century, and in relation to popular fiction, journalism and advertising.[31] All were implicated in what become known as the 'levelling down' of cultural standards. In Britain, this school of criticism was closely associated with the Cambridge literary critics F.R. Leavis and Q.D. Leavis, who were outspoken in their disdain for the democratization of culture and in their view that elitist tastes and values must be vigorously asserted and defended. For the Leavises, the term Americanization brought together a cluster of inter-related modern phenomena – consumerism, egalitarianism and mechanization – that resulted in a culture of mediocrity.[32] In his influential essay, 'Mass Civilisation and Minority Culture' (1930), F.R. Leavis set out his case against Hollywood. Film was not a medium that allowed audiences to exercise their critical faculties. Rather, it was an 'insidious' medium that had a 'potent influence' over audiences, forcing them to 'surrender, under conditions of hypnotic receptivity, to the cheapest emotional appeals'. Thus, it weakened minds and led to a further erosion of literacy.[33] At the heart of Leavis' thinking was the assumption that the mechanized age, hastened by the American enthusiasm for progress, had replaced an earlier social order in which cultural life was more humane, complex and intellectually rewarding. This idea – that a bland consumer culture was supplanting older and more distinctively national cultural forms and practices – was taken up later by Richard Hoggart in *The Uses of Literacy* (1957).

Richard Hoggart was not interested in venerating Shakespeare and Wordsworth, as F.R. Leavis had been, and he was not interested in the 'cultivated minds' that Leavis sought to protect. Hoggart took an ethnographic approach to the working-class culture of his own childhood in Leeds during the interwar period. Although he acknowledges the perils of romanticizing the past, Hoggart nevertheless portrays the traditional cultural life of the working class as vibrant, participatory and built around the shared values and customs of local communities. In the post-war era, however, the survival of this authentic culture was under threat by the 'shiny barbarism' of American popular culture, as well as home-grown imitations of it. He argued that the working class was more susceptible to Americanization because their sense of the past was not so strong. Hence, they were more willing to admire the new, the fashionable and the seemingly progressive, and to succumb to the 'myth world' which they associate with 'American life'.[34] Film was not his prime concern. By the mid-1950s, rock music, low-brow fiction and comic books were also considered to be at the forefront of the Americanization of Britain. However, he shared Leavis' contempt for cinema-going and his conception of it as a passive and mindless activity; he referred, for example, to the 'warm dark super-cinemas' as venues in which audiences were as docile as 'minnows in a heated pool'.[35] Hoggart differed from Leavis, though, in his concern for the working class and particularly in his view that popular culture would sap the masculinity of young working-class men, encouraging 'an effete attitude to life' in them.[36] Here, too, passivity was at the core of the problem. The 'juke-box boys', as he called them, were readily identifiable by their 'American slouch' as they sat in cafes with a 'stare as desperate as Humphrey Bogart'.[37] His prescription for more active and traditional pastimes, such as darts, choral singing, brass bands and pigeon breeding, was designed not only to maintain an authentically British culture, but also to reassert a masculine vitality in the face of the American threat.[38]

One more key voice should be added to the 'tangled tradition'. In a 1946 essay written for the *Tribune*, a weekly paper affiliated with the Labour Party, George Orwell offered brief but revealing comments on Americanization. His essay, 'The Decline of the English Murder', laments that newspaper accounts of 'perfect' murders had become a thing of the past. Orwell locates these as a fixture of the pre-war tabloids, involving respectable people who commit murder (typically killing their spouse) with 'the utmost cunning' and in order to hide some shameful secret (typically adultery). Now, Orwell regretted, the 'depth of feeling' and richly detailed schemes found in such stories were gone, and murders had become merely 'pitiful and sordid'. His thoughts were prompted by the wartime 'cleft chin murder' case in which a US Army deserter and a 'partly Americanized' English girl had robbed and murdered people at random. Orwell attributed the greed and brutality of the case at least in part to the 'false values of the American film', thereby echoing *The Times* editorial (discussed above) of nearly 20 years earlier.[39] Thus, his comments demonstrate the strange bedfellows that anxieties about Americanization and film could bring together. Politically, the Right disliked Hollywood because it feared that the working class would be infected with the egalitarian ethos of American culture, while the Left disliked Hollywood because it lured the working class towards consumerism and away from an authentic and traditional 'culture of the people'.[40] Across the political spectrum, the popularity of Hollywood was regarded as a threat to a truly indigenous culture and there was widespread agreement that films had a powerful effect on audiences, causing them to 'surrender', to 'slouch' and even to commit murders with no 'depth of feeling'.

Beyond Americanization

The concept of Americanization as an imposed and unwelcome cultural force no longer holds sway in scholarly circles. Arguments about the broad impact that cultures have on one another moved on to concepts of cultural imperialism (in the 1970s and 1980s) and globalization (since the 1990s).[41] Meanwhile, scholars interested in understanding the meaning and significance of American cultural products as they cross national boundaries are less likely to think in terms of economic coercion or of passive consumers, and more likely to consider the processes at work as products are introduced to new cultures. The concept of 'cultural transmission' highlights the idea that what is transmitted is not necessarily received intact. It is likely to be sifted through, rejected in whole or in part, or transformed for use in a new culture. Richard Pells, for example, has argued that intellectuals and government officials, who detested the influence of American media on their citizens, overestimated the role that media plays in the lives of people. People are influenced by 'the events of their childhoods, by how their parents raised them, by the opinions of their peers, by their experiences at work, and by the environment in which they live'; influences that run far deeper than watching films or television. Furthermore, people are sceptical about the ideas and information they gain from the media and they have the capacity to 'take from American culture whatever they want and need at any particular moment'.[42] Pells' concerns range from fast food to theme parks, but the concept of consumers selecting what they want and need and using it for their own purposes is one that is central to transnational reception studies of films.

Beyond scholarly circles, and in wider public discourses, film's capacity to influence audiences no longer raises the alarm that it once did. Film is a relatively old medium, and such alarm usually focuses on new media and its unknown effects on an up-and-coming generation. Additionally, in the wake of the 9/11 attacks it is difficult to sustain the notion of the Americanization of the world. Other cultures and ideologies have proved to be resilient to American culture and products, despite their ubiquity. Within the scope of this study, though, it is important not only to examine the factors that gave rise to fears about Americanization and film, but also to explore the extent to which they were based on mis-guided or exaggerated ideas about both films and audiences. A first step in this direction is to acknowledge that the elites who raised concerns about Hollywood had little experience of cinema-going or interest in popular films. They viewed the popularity of films in general, and Hollywood in particular, from a distance and through a class lens that obscured more than it revealed.

The idea of film as a 'hypnotic' medium, which causes its audiences to 'surrender', is one that ignores the social aspects of cinema-going. Annette Kuhn's study of 1930s cinema-goers highlights the extent to which films were viewed sitting alongside friends or family, in well-known neighbourhood or city centre cinemas, and as part of a larger day-to-day existence that was likely to have a direct bearing on the meaning and pleasure of the experience:

> For the majority, going to the pictures is remembered as being less about films and stars than about daily and weekend routines, neighbourhood comings and goings and organising spare time. Cinema-going is remembered, that is, as part of the fabric of daily life.[43]

In the mid-1940s, Rachael Low made similar observations about contemporary cinema-goers at the time when admissions were at a peak. She commented that for many, cinema-going represented 'an institutionalised night out', meaning that people went to the cinema not so much to see a particular film but to get away from their home or their work, to see friends and, especially for the young, to find a social space of their own and one suitable for 'courting' couples. For Low, this was regrettable. She wished audiences were more interested in the merits of individual films and that they treated film as an art form.[44] Nevertheless, her comments reinforce the historian A.J.P. Taylor's definition of cinema-going as the 'essential *social* habit of the age'.[45] The social dimension could be intrusive. Christine Geraghty's research into post-war cinema-going reveals a range of complaints that audience members had about one another: babies crying, adults snoring and anyone talking or eating noisily.[46] It is important, too, that in cinemas feature films were likely to be accompanied by a newsreel, a cartoon or a comedy 'short' and a second feature. These cinema programmes usually ran as a 'continuous performance', with audiences entering and leaving when they saw fit (sometimes midway through the feature). In this light, the significance of the feature film is diminished and the conditions of viewing are hardly those of 'hypnotic receptivity'.

Elitist concerns about Americanization and film also assume that Hollywood was essentially a national cinema, and one that promoted a coherent and approved concept of Americanness. This was far from apparent in the United States. In the 1920s, the very fact that the MPPDA worked to 'Americanize' the industry points to Hollywood's outsider status in the USA. Subsequently, there have been many campaigns against the industry. Hollywood has been accused of subverting the country morally (e.g., in the Legion of Decency's campaign in the 1930s) and politically (e.g., the House Un-American Activities Committee investigations of communist subversion in the 1940s and 1950s), and books such as Michael Medved's best-selling *Hollywood vs. America* (1993) have portrayed the entertainment industry as a 'poison factory' that aimed to undermine the country's 'traditional values'. As Richard Maltby has argued, 'the place of motion pictures in American domestic culture has been a constant site of contestation and debate'.[47] For all the films that seem to celebrate a wholesome American way of life, such as the small town films of the *Andy Hardy* series, or musicals such as *Meet Me in St Louis* (1944) and *Oklahoma!* (1955), there are others that expose the country's social problems. The perils of Prohibition, for example, have been a mainstay of the gangster film since the 1920s.

The debates about films within the United States serve as a reminder that national culture is not a monolithic entity but a set of competing groups, interests and outlooks. A country's elites prefer to conceive of national culture from a 'top down' vantage point, with political institutions, business activity and cultural identity arranged 'vertically' within national borders and under their control.[48] As Richard Collins has argued, though, the rise of mass culture allowed for audience tastes to be constituted 'horizontally' and across national boundaries. In this arrangement, the vibrancy of American popular culture united working-class audiences as a world audience. The USA was a natural home for the world's popular culture partly because of the entertainment industry's drive to maximize profits by satisfying audiences, but also because a country with such a diverse population, including many immigrants, served as a 'microcosm' of the wider world. In this respect, the internationalism of Hollywood – as opposed to the idea that it was an intrinsically American industry – was crucial to its success outside the USA.[49]

A key aspect of Hollywood's internationalism can be attributed to the fact that the industry was largely 'invented' (to borrow Neal Gabler's term) by Jewish showmen, many of whom had backgrounds in various retail trades. They approached filmmaking with the aim of giving the public what it wants, and their own background as first- or second-generation immigrants gave them a keen sense of working-class tastes and aspirations.[50] In Hollywood, the 'movie moguls', as they became known, were able to develop not just a powerful filmmaking industry but also a distinctive filmmaking culture – one dedicated to popular tastes. Their geographical isolation was important, too. Today, nearby Los Angeles is the second largest city in the United States and it is just five hours flying time from cities on the east coast. In the 1920s, however, Los Angeles was a smaller and a more remote city: the east coast was a three day train journey away. As Victoria de Grazia has argued, Hollywood's remote location made it very different from European film production centres. These were located in or near capital cities such as Berlin, Budapest, London, Paris, Rome and Vienna, and this meant that they could not develop a filmmaking culture free from the snobberies of the capital city (for example, the higher status given to theatre as an art form) and the influence or intervention of government officials. Thus, by virtue of its remoteness, Hollywood was able to develop a film culture in which beauty, talent, screen charisma and box-office returns had a legitimacy that was not overshadowed by middle-class concerns about artistry and respectability.[51] New arrivals to Hollywood were known to complain that it was a provincial, quiet, 'one industry community', without realizing that this was an integral part of its success.[52] And there were many new arrivals, from all over the world, who were drawn to this far-flung outpost by its power, resources and rewards.

The result was that Hollywood (as an industry) became the world's film capital and not simply the capital of the American film industry. The question remains, however, as to whether the popularity of Hollywood films 'sold' America to British audiences. It is easy to imagine, for example, that during the peak years of cinema-going a film fan in the North of England would be more familiar with the New York skyline than with the London skyline; that films showing a wide availability of consumer goods in the USA would make audiences envious; and that a fascination with glamorous stars would invest the USA itself with glamour. The scarcity of evidence concerning audience tastes and views makes it difficult to address this question in a comprehensive manner. Remarkably, for all the debates about the impact and influence of Hollywood films, real audiences were seldom considered or asked for their views. For the elites who regretted the rise of mass culture, the cinema-going public's tastes were too debased to be relevant or meaningful. In 1925, for example, Lord Newton's argument on behalf of British films dismissed the idea that public taste should govern the type of films that cinemas show: 'If our people are content to witness perpetual rubbish, let it, at any rate, be English rubbish in preference to American rubbish.'[53]

Audience preferences and the Snow White taste pattern

More nuanced views of audience tastes and interests were slow to emerge. Beginning in the 1930s, however, interest in gauging opinions about cinema-going habits and audience views began to gather pace, and although many of the surveys and polls that emerged were sporadic and limited in scope, clear taste patterns and attitudes are discernible when looking across them. Furthermore, when comparing these surveys with more recent evidence of audience tastes, continuities can be found in British preferences, particularly where Hollywood films are concerned. The most significant of the early studies was conducted in 1938 by Mass Observation, an organization which sought to conduct 'anthropology at home' rather than in faraway, foreign locales. 'Cinema-going in Worktown' was a survey involving 559 respondents, who were identified in terms of age and gender, and asked about their cinema-going habits and preferences. The survey was conducted in Bolton, Lancashire; a northern, industrial town far removed from elitist or metropolitan ideas about the

cinema. Bolton was chosen for its ordinary, working-class character, but Mass Observation was attuned to distinctions among these
average or ordinary audiences. The survey forms were issued not
only in the town's sleek, new, upmarket Odeon cinema, but also in
the smaller, less expensive, 'family-oriented' Crompton cinema and
the inexpensive, 'down-market' Palladium cinema. The location of
these cinemas, their ticket prices and their décor offer approximate
indications of the social class of their audiences, with the Odeon
and Crompton likely to have lower-middle-class and upper-work-
ing-class audiences and the Palladium likely to have working-class
audiences.[54]

The survey asked several questions, but the question that
prompted the fullest comments was, 'Which are the best films,
British or American, or are they both the same?' The responses to
this question offer a means of gauging attitudes to film nationality a full decade after the Films Act of 1927 bolstered British filmmaking. In total, 63 per cent of the respondents said that American
films were best, 18 per cent preferred British films and 19 per cent
thought they were the same. There were small differences along the
lines of age and gender on this issue; the young were more likely
to favour American films and women were slightly more likely
to favour British films. The most striking difference can be seen
along class lines. The preference for American films was strongest
among the working-class audiences of the Palladium: 75 per cent
preferred them, while 15 per cent had no preference and only 10
per cent preferred British films. By contrast, audiences at both
the Crompton and the Odeon were more favourable to British
films. At the Crompton, 59 per cent preferred American films, 23
per cent had no preference and 18 per cent preferred British films.
At the Odeon, 60 per cent preferred American films, 19 per cent
had no preference and 21 per cent preferred British films.[55] As we
shall see in Chapter 3, these findings accord with smaller surveys of
audience opinion in the 1930s, which indicate that the preference
for American films was particularly pronounced among working-
class audiences, and British films appealed most strongly to lower-
middle- and middle-class audiences. These class differences were
pronounced in Bolton, where a dislike of British films was often
expressed with references to their 'stilted' and 'affected' qualities;

qualities that could be used to describe the middle classes themselves. In each of the three cinemas, British films were characterized in this way. They were said to be 'wooden', 'lacking in pep',
'devoid of humour and wisecracks' and 'too stilted and stagey'; and
their actors were said to 'talk soft', to 'seem too stiff' and to have
a 'mincing, affected, stagey manner'.[56] As the references to their
'stagey' quality suggests, many comments associated British films
with the theatre, which served as shorthand for their middle-class
orientation and limited production values. They were criticized for
being 'stunted and too artificial', 'very crude and limited in scope',
and they needed 'more action and naturalizing'.[57] 'Why dont [sic]
they spend a bit of money and get some proper scenery?', a 19-year-
old man at the Palladium asked.[58]

American films were praised for having the opposite qualities,
and for many in Bolton they served as a stick with which to beat
British films. This was partly an issue of class orientation. Stating
that American films had 'more pace', 'stars [who] act like real men'
and 'quicker action' went hand-in-hand with the idea that they
were more 'natural' and 'realistic'.[59] But it was also an issue related
to escapism. Many of the commentators went to the cinema seeking 'an excursion into the world of make-believe', 'something bright
to cheer us up'; and they liked films that 'relieve the monotony',
'enable folk to forget for an hour or so the worries and cares of
existence' and 'make one forget for awhile the hum-drum of everyday life'.[60] Realism and social relevance were anathema to these
audiences. 'The critics may say I am easily pleased', an 18-year-old
woman at the Odeon said, 'but to think that for a few coppers,
one can enter the world of make believe and leave behind all the
worries and cares; well I say: "Long live the films!"'[61] Their preference for Hollywood was thus based on an aesthetic choice: they
sought glamour, spectacle, adventure and exoticism in the cinema.
Furthermore, Hollywood's geographical distance was a huge advantage for audiences seeking escapism. As a 19-year-old man at the
Palladium put it, 'When you have spent a dull dreary day in the
spinning room you want to see some open air life as you usually get
in a Western'.[62]

The resentment that simmers within some of the comments
about British films suggests that Bolton audiences did not like

seeing a middle-class, home counties image of England projected as representative of the nation, but it does not suggest a special affinity with the United States. In fact, the enthusiasm for Hollywood films was qualified by complaints about their American qualities. Accents figured strongly in this. Eight years after the first talkie was shown in Bolton, many audiences did not like the American accents that they characterized as 'Yankee drawl', 'nasal drawl' and 'twang'.[63] American slang was also scorned, especially by the audiences at the Odeon.[64] There were complaints too about films that had culturally specific subjects, and especially 'social problem' films ('Of what interest are they to the British people?'), and films extolling the nation's virtues ('too much Yankee doodle pip').[65] It is also apparent that, when respondents discuss films that they like, British stories predominate. For all of the complaints about British films, the most frequently admired film was *Victoria the Great* (1937), a slavishly patriotic, British-made biopic of Queen Victoria. Many of the others – including *Lives of a Bengal Lancer* (1935), *Mutiny on the Bounty* (1935), *The Charge of the Light Brigade* (1936) and *Lost Horizon* (1937) – were British stories filmed in Hollywood.[66] All of these feature charismatic stars, plenty of action and adventure and an element of exoticism through historical or faraway settings.

These findings fit with a conclusion that Mass Observation reached several years later about audiences and the 'unreality' of films. The 'Report on Opinion on America' was written in March 1942.[67] By this time, and as a result of the war, Mass Observation was a larger operation, which conducted more extensive public opinion surveys on a variety of war topics. This report, based on a national survey conducted soon after the United States entered the war, compared the most recent national survey with earlier surveys about British public opinion towards the USA, and it also considered the source of people's 'ideas about Americans'. The findings would surprise anyone who thought that a steady diet of Hollywood films had made the public think more favourably about the USA. It showed that people relied mainly on newspapers, magazines and the radio for their 'ideas' about the country.[68] Their opinions therefore tended to fluctuate with war events. In October 1940, when Britain 'stood alone' in the war, only 27 per cent of the public had a 'favourable' opinion of the USA, but in April 1941, after the commencement of Lend-Lease aid, 60 per cent of the public expressed a 'favourable' opinion.[69] Very few people said that they got ideas about the country from the cinema, and the report made it clear that these findings were not anomalous. 'Over and over again', the report stated, 'and in our investigations over the past four years', surveys focusing on the cinema had shown that its 'importance in influencing people has been much over-estimated in the past':

> People look upon films as a form of *entertainment* and as a process of *unreality* ... They do not regard them as representing America but as representing a sort of dream stereotype from America. Hollywood as much represents America to the average Britisher as Blackpool represents Britain to the average Lancastrian. Both are fun and escape, excitement and incredibility. They are interludes from the routine of living.[70]

The preference for Hollywood films, therefore, lay in their entertainment value and in their removal from the realities of everyday life, but there was no evidence to support the idea that they were an effective advertisement either for or against American values and ideas.[71]

Further evidence concerning British film preferences reinforces the importance of 'entertainment' and 'unreality' in what can be termed the Snow White taste pattern, after Walt Disney's film. Box office figures on films released before the 1970s are scarce, but several studies indicate that *Snow White and the Seven Dwarfs* (1937/38) was the most popular film of the 1930s in Britain and that it still stands as one of the country's all-time box office champions.[72] It has several characteristics in common with other films that have attracted extraordinary audience numbers. First, the film's setting is far removed from a real or specifically locatable time and place. The story's origins as a folk tale are referenced with a 'once upon a time' opening scene, and a 'Mitteleuropa' atmosphere is conveyed by the visual design, but no exact time or place is ever mentioned. Together with the instantly hummable musical score, this encourages viewers to enter the 'world of make believe' that Bolton's cinema-goers found so attractive. Second, the film's imaginative, fantastic, spectacular qualities are an intrinsic part of its identity and appeal. The quality of the animation, sound effects and colour made it a landmark film in its day. As Walt Disney's first animated feature film, it was also the subject of considerable 'hype', and audiences would have been well aware that it was a state-of-the-art production, made at a cost ($1.5 million) that was out of bounds for British films.[73] It affirmed the idea of cinema as an escapist medium and also Hollywood's reputation for providing the most opulent forms of escapism. Third, the story follows a classical narrative structure (of conflict and resolution) that is imbued with populist values (a young, innocent individual overthrows an older, established, corrupt power). Bolton's cinema-goers were unlikely to find a middle-class bias in a story that is egalitarian (Snow White is a princess yet she is a keen cleaner and a homemaker for the dwarfs), anti-elitist (the queen is defeated) and optimistic (in the happy, romantic ending). Of course, these narrative qualities were not the invention of Hollywood, but Hollywood deployed them so briskly and cheerfully that they appeared natural, inoffensive and – crucially from a British perspective – unworthy of the censor's attention.

The Snow White taste pattern is not limited to the 1930s but is discernible in wider rankings of Britain's biggest box office hits. The 'ultimate film chart' compiled by the British Film Institute ranks the country's 100 all-time box office winners over the years 1936 to 2005, using the inflation-proof method of counting the number of tickets sold for each film in the UK.[74] It surprised many to see three British films in the top ten (see Table 1.1), but the popularity of *Spring in Park Lane* (1948), *The Wicked Lady* (1945) and *The Seventh Veil* (1945) testifies to the importance of women as a cinema-goers in the 1940s (each is a 'woman's film') and also to the appeal of films that addressed – however obliquely – the wartime upheavals in class and gender relations. Among the remaining seven films in the top ten, all are Hollywood films but five are not set in the United States. These five include the musical *The Sound of Music* (1965), *Snow White and the Seven Dwarfs*, the science fiction film *Star Wars* (1977), Disney's animated *The Jungle Book* (1967/68) and the disaster film *Titanic* (1997/98). Each of the five films is set outside of the present-day: in the past, in a story-book never-never land, or in an inter-galactic future. Each involves lavish spectacle: in the form of animation, special effects, or, in the case of *The Sound of Music*, dramatic shots of Austria's mountainous landscape. And

Table 1.1 The UK's top 10 films according to tickets sold (1935–2005)

Rank	Film title	Release year	Number of tickets sold	Nationality
1	*Gone with the Wind*	1940	35 million	USA
2	*The Sound of Music*	1965	30 million	USA
3	*Snow White and the Seven Dwarfs*	1938	28 million	USA
4	*Star Wars*	1978	21 million	USA
5	*Spring in Park Lane*	1948	20. 5 million	UK
6	*The Best Years of Our Lives*	1947	20.4 million	USA
7	*The Jungle Book*	1968	19.8 million	USA
8	*Titanic*	1998	18.9 million	USA
9	*The Wicked Lady*	1945	18.4 million	UK
10	*The Seventh Veil*	1945	17.9 million	UK

Source: Ryan Gilbey (ed.), *The Ultimate Film: The UK's 100 Most Popular Films* (London: British Film Institute, 2005), p. 5.

each story centres on a naively rebellious youthful outsider who struggles against a more powerful, corrupt authority figure. Of the two remaining films in the top ten, which are set in the USA, *Gone with the Wind* does not stray far from the Snow White taste pattern: it is set in the past, its production values are opulent and its young heroine (as we shall see in Chapter 5) has no regard for conventional, middle-class social norms. That leaves *The Best Years of Our Lives* (1946/47), a film that would seem to be exactly what some Bolton residents disliked, an American 'social problem' film. However, its story had an unusual significance for British audiences. This is partly because it invested epic importance into a common problem of the time, post-war readjustment. But it is also because a large portion of the audience would have had some contact with the 3 million American service personnel stationed in Britain during the war. From a British perspective, *The Best Years of Our Lives* was the story of what happened to those men who were 'over-sexed, over-paid and over here' once they went back over there.

Beyond the top ten, the Snow White taste pattern runs throughout the 100 films ranked on the 'ultimate film chart'. Two-thirds of the films are defined as 'US films', but what is most striking is that so many of the films are international in scope. *Dr Zhivago* (1965/66), for example, is labelled as a US film, but it has an Italian producer (Carlo Ponti), a British director (David Lean), stars who are Egyptian (Omar Sharif) and British (Julie Christie) and a story set during the Russian Revolution.[75] Among the other US films, there are numerous science fiction films, animated features and biblical epics. Hollywood's own treatment of British stories figures prominently, too. These are often criticized for their lack of authenticity – and Dick Van Dyke's Cockney accent in *Mary Poppins* (1964) is legendary in this regard – but it did not stop audiences from seeing *Mary Poppins*. Some 14 million tickets were sold.[76]

The Snow White taste pattern persists in more recent box office figures. This can be seen in another ranking: the ten films that have earned the highest-ever box office grosses in Britain (see Table 1.2). This favours more recent films because it is not an inflation-proof ranking; it points to the ten most popular films of the last 15 years. Of the ten films, six are international co-productions, signalling Hollywood's position as the world's film capital and not simply the USA's film capital. Only one film is set in the USA, and *Toy Story 3* (2010) is an animated feature made by the Disney subsidiary Pixar Films. The other films include the current box office champion, *Avatar* (2009), a 3-D film that brought a new degree of spectacle and exoticism to its representation of life in the distant future and on a faraway planet. *Avatar* also stands as the top-earning film in the USA and many other countries, but elsewhere on the list there are some points of difference between UK and US film tastes. The *Harry Potter* and *Lord of the Rings* films have been very successful in both countries. However, when their rankings in the UK and US are compared, it is clear that these films, based on novels by British authors and featuring a roll call of the country's leading actors, have a greater appeal in the UK. Similarly, when *Casino Royale* (2006) revived the *James Bond* series, its impact was greater in Britain than in the USA. The most striking distinction however, can be seen in a

Table 1.2 The UK's top 10 films according to box-office earnings (through 2011)

UK rank	Film title	Year	UK box-office total	Nationality	US rank
1	*Avatar*	2009	£ 93.4 million	USA	1
2	*Toy Story 3*	2010	£ 73.4 million	USA	11
3	*Harry Potter and the Deathly Hallows Part 2*	2011	£ 73.1 million	USA	16
4	*Mamma Mia!*	2008	£ 69.2 million	UK/USA	252
5	*Titanic*	1998	£ 69.0 million	USA	2
6	*Harry Potter and the Philosopher's Stone*	2001	£ 66.1 million	UK/USA	31
7	*Lord of the Rings: The Fellowship of the Ring*	2001	£ 63.0 million	NZ/USA	33
8	*Lord of the Rings: The Return of the King*	2003	£ 61.1 million	NZ/USA	18
9	*Lord of the Rings: The Two Towers*	2002	£ 57.6 million	NZ/USA	23
10	*Casino Royale*	2006	£ 55.5 million	Czech/UK/USA	190

Source: UK Films Council. Online. Available at <sy09.ukfilmcouncil.ry.com/?id=41121/>. More recent (post-2009) figures and US figures: Box Office Mojo. Online. Available at http://boxofficemojo.com/.

comparison of the UK and US rankings of *Mamma Mia!* (2008). This distinction stems from the fact that the Abba songs that feature so strongly in this musical were not as popular in the USA as they were in Britain. The stage version of *Mamma Mia!*, which debuted in London and remains a long-running favourite, also made less impact on Broadway. In the UK, the appeal of *Mamma Mia!* fits well within the parameters of the Snow White taste pattern. The story is set in neither Britain nor the USA, but on a Greek island. The holiday island atmosphere has little cultural specificity and the time period is vaguely placed. Although it does not feature animation or special effects, the island's stunningly bright blue skies and seas are spectacular. The campy musical numbers and dance routines also enhance the film's inviting sense of 'make believe'. And, like *Snow White*, the story centres on an outsider, mired in the drudgery of housework, who is reawakened and given the prospect of fulfilment in the ending. The woman (Meryl Streep) may be much older and more experienced, but in this sense *Mamma Mia!* can be seen to reinvent *Snow White* for baby boomers of advancing years, at least insofar as it rejects the notion that ageing must turn women into bitter, jealous crones.

Understanding the meanings and impact these individual and highly popular films have had cannot be achieved through brief comments such as these. In the chapters that follow, more detailed research and analysis is employed in the case studies of individual films, stars and genres. The preceding comments on the most popular films have been made as a means of highlighting a broad taste pattern that has dominated in Britain over many decades. This taste pattern suggests that the success of Hollywood films with British audiences is not related to their American origins. The Motion Pictures Producers and Distributors of America promoted the idea that films could sell American ideas and products, but this was part of a strategy to protect the industry from its domestic critics. British elites promoted the connection between films and Americanization for different reasons. Some considered Hollywood films as a marker of the modern age, which threatened to undermine traditional social and cultural hierarchies. Hollywood films were resented and scorned because they were the most prominent manifestation of the triumph of mass culture and the simultaneous rise of the United States as a world power. Others could see nothing of value in popular films, and assumed that their audiences were dupes. They imagined that audiences had fallen prey to an insidious medium, capable of diminishing their humanity and vitality. The concept of Americanization was also used as a reason for promoting British film production, and in this respect it had some success.

Films, however, are an unlikely conduit for 'Americanization'. In the past, watching films was a social activity, shared with friends and neighbours in cinemas that served as familiar, communal spaces. More recently, films are likely to be watched privately, and on television or computer screens, but seeing them on smaller screens and in the more intimate comfort of a home is hardly likely to enhance their power and influence. Then as now, watching films is one of many leisure activities that people enjoy, and the assumption that it has an overriding influence is unproven. Indeed, the American qualities of Hollywood appear to be a significant drawback as far as many British audiences are concerned. The dominant taste pattern highlights the appeal of films that transcend national or cultural specificity, that transport audiences into the past or the future and that thrill them by demonstrating the medium's capacity for spectacle and fantasy. Hollywood has been better situated to make films along these lines because early in its history it secured a large domestic and international market, and this has enabled film production on a scale scarcely known in smaller countries. Moreover, the industry's size and success has reinforced its own international character, drawing filmmakers from around the world, including British filmmakers.

Finally, and most importantly for this book, identifying taste patterns reinforces the idea that audiences pick and choose among the many films released. Hollywood films are not imposed on audiences. Rather, they are released to a public that occasionally embraces them wholeheartedly. More often they succeed modestly, find a niche audience, or fail miserably. The most interesting aspects of transnational reception reside in these choices, in investigating how and why they were made, and the responses that followed. A key aspect of this research is seeking an understanding of the pleasures that films offered and an understanding of how specific Hollywood films – made thousands of miles away and for a wide array of international markets – so frequently satisfied the specific needs and interests of British audiences.

2 'For the Purpose of Pleasing Women': British Fan Culture and Rudolph Valentino

Now one thing never to be lost sight of in considering the cinema is that it exists for the purpose of pleasing women. Three out of every four of all cinema audiences are women. I suppose all successful novels and plays are also designed to please the female sex too. At any rate the overwhelming, apparently meaningless, and immensely conventional love interest in the bulk of films is certainly made for them.

Iris Barry, Let's Go to the Pictures (1926)[1]

That women are the chief patrons of the kinema is a fact as patent as it is easy to explain. It is too often their only relaxation, their one chance of mental expansion. Man's work, his pleasure, even his necessity for getting somewhere every day in pursuit either of business or sport, enable him to touch life at a far greater number of points than do women.

Marjorie Williams, 'The Woman Patron' (1925)[2]

It was a Monday and therefore a new picture. But it was also washing day, and yet the scattered audience was composed almost entirely of mothers...Tired women, their faces sheened with toil, and small children, penned in semi-darkness and foul air on a sunny afternoon. There was almost no talk. Many of the women sat alone, figures of weariness at rest. Watching these I took comfort. At last the world of entertainment had provided for a few pence, tea thrown in, a sanctuary for mothers, an escape from the everlasting *qui vive* into eternity on a Monday afternoon.

Dorothy Richardson, 'Continuous Performance' (1927)[3]

The public debate about the cinema in the 1920s was, in one sense at least, deafening. Amid the cacophony of voices that entered into discussions about the cinema – those calling for support for the British film industry, warning about the loss of trade and prestige

that would befall any country without a film industry and expressing anxieties about Americanization – there was very little heard
from the audiences who actually went to the cinema. We know
that, despite the negative public discourse on cinema, cinema-
going had a pre-eminent place in the everyday life of many British
people. Throughout this decade, when the population was approximately 45 million people, admissions ranged between 500 million
and 1,000 million per year, and it was estimated that just over one-
third of the population went to the cinema at least once a week.[4]
There is no doubt, too, that audiences mainly went to see American
films. Hollywood reigned supreme in British cinemas during the
1920s and even the institution of the films 'quota' in 1928 did little,
initially, to diminish that. Yet we know little about the experiences
and preferences of these millions of people and the pleasures that
they found in their regular visits to the cinema.

Iris Barry was among the most influential British film critics of
the decade and in her groundbreaking book on cinema she claimed
(in the first quotation above) that three out of four audience members were women. This was probably an exaggeration; other sources
indicate that on average audiences were 60 per cent women and 40
per cent men.[5] Nevertheless, the association was strong and Barry
was not alone in linking the predominance of women among film
fans with the sentimental and formulaic nature of Hollywood films.
Barry's view was that filmmakers underestimated the taste and intel-
ligence of audiences. Writing for the *Daily Mail* and other publications, she fought against the cinema's poor reputation by setting
out the parameters of good taste.[6] Both Barry and another significant female critic of this period, C.A. Lejeune of the *Manchester
Guardian*, wrote for readers who, as Lejeune put it, were 'inclined to
take their cinema a little seriously'; that is, an audience interested
in cultivated rather than popular tastes.[7] They could admire a select
set of Hollywood films, and particularly those made by noted directors such as D.W. Griffith, Charlie Chaplin and Ernst Lubitsch,
but they were more likely to extol the virtues of French, German
and Swedish cinema.

Other women who commented on cinema-going focused not so
much on the merits of individual films as on the appeal of the cinema itself. The cinema was heralded for giving new opportunities to

women outside of the home. In *Kinematograph Weekly*, the journalist Marjorie Williams argued (in the second quotation above) that it was domestic drudgery and 'the sight of too familiar crockery and furniture' that prompted women to go the cinema more often than men and regardless of what was showing. A woman's duty as house-wife and carer was routine, hard work that was best alleviated by leaving the home.[8] The author and journalist Dorothy Richardson echoed this in an article for *Close Up* in 1927 (in the third quota-tion above). Recounting her experience of an afternoon matinee in a run-of-the-mill north London cinema, Richardson observed that the cinema was a 'sanctuary for mothers', who took a respite from their domestic obligations while their husbands worked and their children were at school. The most memorable aspect of the experi-ence for Richardson was not seeing the film but seeing the 'shining eyes and rested faces' of the women as they watched the screen. In her evocative words, the cinema had enabled the women to leave their day-to-day cares behind and find 'eternity on a Monday afternoon'.[9] Decades later, the historian A.J.P. Taylor made a similar point (albeit in a different style), when he argued that in the 1920s, and especially for the lower-middle class, the cinema changed the pattern of everyday life and created a new opportunities for leisure. This had a greater impact on women than men because, while men had always enjoyed 'football matches and other public pleasures', the realm for women's leisure had been more restricted.[10] They might go to the church or to the pub with their husband or boy-friend, but the cinema was a venue that they could attend without a male escort. Furthermore, they could expect the programme to cater to their expectations and tastes. The cinema offered a new kind of social space to women, one that was both respectable and dedicated to their enjoyment.

The association between women and the cinema was so close that some argued that watching feature films involved pleasures that were inherently feminine. Silent films in particular were thought to be suited to the tastes and disposition of women. Virginia Woolf, writing in the *New Republic*, commented in 1926 that the cinema was at its best when it avoided words (including intertitles) and pursued feelings through visual means alone. She saw the medium's greatest potential in developing some 'secret language, which we feel and see, but never speak'.[11] Several years later, when silent cinema had given way to 'talkies', Dorothy Richardson developed this line of thinking further. Silent cinema, she argued, prized feelings over words; it was characterized by 'having more intention than direction' and 'more purpose than plan'. For Richardson, this marked the silent era as the medium's feminine phase.[12]

It should be noted that, like Iris Barry and C.A. Lejeune, commentators such as Dorothy Richardson, Marjorie Williams and Virginia Woolf were quite tentative in their contemplation of the medium. As well-educated and middle-class women, they could not wholeheartedly endorse a form of entertainment that was predominantly appreciated by the lower classes and therefore encumbered with the limitations of popular taste. In this era, the cinema's supporters spoke of the medium's potential and its future, and many felt obliged to preface their comments on the cinema with an admission of its present weaknesses. The tone of Dorothy Richardson's writing indicates that, for all of her sympathy with the weary mothers of north London, she is neither one of them nor in need of the succour that she supposed popular cinema offered to them. Virginia Woolf acknowledged that 'at first sight ... the art of cinema seems simple, even stupid' and looked forward to its development. And while Marjory Williams' column in *Kinematograph Weekly* was dedicated to explaining the tastes of 'the woman patron' to the (male-dominated) film trade, she too frequently drew a line between tastes she approved of and those she did not. Even the cinema's supporters could offer only qualified support and enthusiasm for the medium.

In order to locate voices more sympathetic to popular cinema-going among women, it is necessary to look beyond both mainstream and elitist publications, and to consider film fan magazines. *Picturegoer*, *Picture Show* and *Girls' Cinema* focused squarely on their readers' enjoyment of films, and in this respect they provided a truly unique forum for British film fans; one in which the tastes and preferences of ordinary cinema-goers were given precedence. In this chapter, then, the fan magazines will be analysed to ascertain the terms on which ordinary British cinema-goers appreciated American films generally, and the films of Rudolph Valentino in particular. Valentino was the decade's most popular star, and the fan magazines covered his career extensively. Furthermore, his stardom raises some particularly pertinent issues. The first of these centres on perceptions of his films' nationality. As an Italian actor working in Hollywood, his films were not necessarily perceived first and foremost as American. The second concerns the critical criteria with which his films were considered. British responses to Valentino's films and his stardom demonstrate the terms by which films and stars could overcome the stigma of popularity and receive serious attention from critics. The third contrasts his reputation in the United States with his reputation in Britain, allowing an exploration of the extent to which the reception of films was governed by distinctive cultural values and assumptions.

British fan magazines

The primary function of the fan magazines was to provide a specifically British forum in which to consider and discuss the pleasures of cinema-going. One means of achieving this lay in the editorial policy and writing style of the magazines. Following the example of the burgeoning number of women's magazines in this era, the fan magazines adopted a writing style that fostered a sense of community among their readers and made them feel welcome.[13] Eschewing the elitism and the often elaborate prose style of 'quality' newspapers and periodicals, the fan magazines were written in a strikingly informal and friendly manner, and one designed to put readers at ease rather than to impress or educate them. Their competitions and letters pages encouraged readers to correspond and interact with the magazine's writers and its other readers. Competitions abounded: readers were invited to write poems about their favourite stars, to pose for photographs dressed in costume as a star, or to relate their own cinema-going experiences or their opinions on a specific theme. These were just a few of the more common competitions, all of which prioritized the readers' experiences and their involvement with the medium. The prizes were often no more than a shilling, but they were usually given to a number of entrants rather than a single winner, and in many instances the name and home town of every entrant was printed in the magazine. Letters pages also built a sense of participation. Each magazine had at least a few of these as regular features, with headings such as 'What do you think?' inviting readers to express their opinions about films and stars. There were also pages in each magazine devoted to answering readers' questions about films and stars. It is likely that the greatest factor in building a sense of community among the readers, however, was the sheer enthusiasm for cinema-going that is evident in each magazine.

Fan magazines were by and large averse to reporting salacious gossip or scandals about stars. That was the stuff of tabloid newspapers, many of which were intent on portraying Hollywood as the Sodom and Gomorrah of the 1920s. The fan magazines steadfastly maintained a positive and upbeat tone, and promoted the virtues and benefits of cinema-going. In 1921, an editorial in *Picturegoer* defined the cinema for its readers as 'the greatest place in the whole wide world' and proclaimed cinema-going to be an enjoyable and educational pastime.[14] One of the most commonly cited benefits of cinema-going, according to all of the fan magazines, was that it expanded the horizons of audiences. This was not merely a matter of offering housewives a vista beyond their crockery. As another *Picturegoer* editorial explained it, feature films were educational because they revealed 'lands afar and other people and other ways of life as it is lived in other places'. They led to personal improvement because they showed their audience 'some way of beauty in home or life, some courtesy, some example for self-betterment'.[15] Similarly, when *Girls' Cinema* ran a contest entitled 'Why I Go to the Pictures', the five winning respondents gave explanations such as 'to widen my outlook on life', and '... to learn and see a lot more of the world than would otherwise be possible'.[16] Such responses can be taken as an indication of the magazine's editorial policy; out of hundreds of entries to the contest, these were the voices selected for quotation. Nevertheless, the editorial stance was itself illuminating. It offered a response to the cinema's lofty critics, who dismissed cinema-going as a mindless pursuit, and it lent a form of legitimacy to the taste for escapism and the 'world of make believe' that was so prevalent among film fans.

Throughout the 1920s, the primary interest of the fan magazines was Hollywood. This is not to say that they lacked a sense of patriotism for British cinema. Each consistently gave assurances that British films were emerging from their doldrums and that British stars were as good as any. Yet it is readily apparent that Hollywood fascinated the magazines' readers. Their attitude toward the United States itself was far more ambivalent. In 1921, *Picturegoer* endorsed a measure of Americanization as one of the educational benefits of cinema-going:

> Already we know Texas as well as we know Barking Creek. We know what the Sante Fe railroad is, and how to eat grapefruit, and all about New York and 'Los' and the Great North-West. We can say 'sure thing' as easily as we can say 'not 'arf'. We are partly American. And it is the part of us that should have been American years ago![17]

This is a remarkable statement for the 1920s, and it marks a wide gap between attitudes toward the USA in the fan magazines and in most other British periodicals. However, even in the fan magazines such overt enthusiasm for all-things-American was rare. Furthermore, as the decade progressed, a strong undercurrent of film nationalism emerged out of the various campaigns and proposals to protect the British industry. Attitudes to Hollywood stars did not change – the fascination continued unabated – but attitudes towards Hollywood as an industry, and towards the USA generally, cooled noticeably. A statement such as 'we are partly American' could not have been made so lightly later in the decade. For the most part, the fan magazines were careful not to let their enthusiasm for Hollywood appear to be an enthusiasm for the USA. One means of drawing a distinction between the two was to refer to Hollywood as 'the film capital', or 'film land' or even as 'the film colony'. This made it seem like an international outpost for filmmakers rather than a specifically American city or industry, and of course the term 'colony' had a resonance for the British.

The notion that Hollywood was more international than American was not altogether incorrect. In the late silent era, Hollywood sought and maintained its success abroad by recruiting filmmakers from around the world, and by filming stories that were not specifically American in their appeal. Hence, southern California's 'film colony' became the home of *émigré* directors such as Ernst Lubitsch, Mauritz Stiller, Victor Seastrom and Erich Von Stroheim. And many of the most lavish productions drew upon the western world's best known literature, historical figures and legends for their subject matter. Even a quintessentially American director such as D.W. Griffith made films set in London's East End slums (*Broken Blossoms*, 1919/20) and in Paris during the French Revolution (*Orphans of the Storm*, 1921/22). Among female stars, there was a strong foreign presence, led by *femmes fatales* such as Greta Garbo and Pola Negri. Mary Pickford, known as 'America's Sweetheart' in the United States, was the 'World's Sweetheart' abroad. The American star Douglas Fairbanks enjoyed a run of box office hits – taking the lead roles in *The Three Musketeers* (1921), *Robin Hood* (1922) and *The Thief of Bagdad* (1924) – without playing an American character. Similarly, the American John Barrymore played the British roles of *Dr Jekyll and Mr Hyde* (1920), *Sherlock Holmes* (1922/23) and *Beau Brummel* (1924). Meanwhile, the British-born Charlie Chaplin undoubtedly brought his own experiences of the south London slums to *The Kid* (1921), even if the setting was an unidentified (and seemingly unidentifiable) city in the United States. Yet no star was more international than the Italian-born Valentino. His film career was entirely based in Hollywood and although he played Frenchmen, Arab sheiks, Spanish bullfighters and a Russian guardsman, among many other nationalities, he seldom played either an American or an Italian. Nationality, according to Hollywood, was not a fixed and restrictive quality, but one that could be assumed, enjoyed and discarded.

Over the course of the decade, cinema buildings increasingly reflected this concept of nationality as a masquerade. The number of cinemas in Britain actually declined in the 1920s, but this was because many small and humble venues were replaced with large-scale, lavish 'dream palaces', which were as far removed from everyday life as the films themselves.[18] When *Picture Show* ran a cover story extolling 'the glamour of the East' in 1923, it was referring to recent Hollywood films such as *The Sheik* (1921/23), *The Young Rajah* (1922/23) and *One Stolen Night* (1923), but it might just as well have been referring to the increasingly exotic designs for cinemas built in the 1920s. The Majestic, the Alhambra, the Pavilion, the Palace, the Regal and the Imperial were fitting names for venues that were decorated as Venetian palaces, Egyptian temples, Assyrian ziggurats and Chinese pagodas. As Jeffrey Richards has commented, they were appropriately exotic settings in which to see 'Garbo romancing, Fairbanks swashbuckling or Valentino sheikhing'.[19]

British fan magazines favoured this international strain of Hollywood. These films and stars received the most prominent coverage in the magazines: in photographic collages, in articles based on 'the making of' a film and in the short story versions of films which regularly appeared in each magazine. However, the magazines focused more on stars than on individual films. Biographical sketches, interviews, photographs and lifestyle features displayed a seemingly endless fascination with every aspect of the stars' professional and private lives. Most of all, the stars were admired for their youth, their beauty and their lifestyle. The Hollywood lifestyle was represented as one that freed its inhabitants from the constraints of national culture, from the boundaries of social class and from the limitations of economic hardship. This was not identified as an American lifestyle, but one that belonged to the 'film colony', where the glory of youth, wealth and glamour overwhelmed conventional lifestyle determinants. This emphasis on stars and lifestyle, together with the many advertisements aimed at women, made the fan magazines unpalatable to dedicated cineastes and perhaps to men generally. Alfred Hitchcock would later recall that in the early 1920s, when he was a young film enthusiast and not yet a director, he always read the trade papers and never the fan magazines.[20] It is not clear whether he was attempting to disassociate himself from their feminine appeal or their emphasis on celebrity. It is likely that the two were linked and that, for many men, fan magazines were either avoided altogether or represented a guilty pleasure.

Picturegoer

Each of the fan magazines had its own identity and appealed to a specific readership. This cannot be demonstrated with reference to exact statistics, because before the 1930s circulation figures were rarely audited and publishing houses did not release their own figures. However, the likely readership of each magazine can be gleaned from advertisements, letters from readers and editorial comments. It is overwhelmingly apparent that *Picturegoer*, *Picture Show* and *Girls' Cinema* were aimed primarily at female readers. Indeed, it is likely that the Odhams publishing firm launched *Picturegoer* in

1921 and that the Amalgamated Press launched *Picture Show* and *Girls' Cinema* in 1920 and 1921, respectively, because advertisers were seeking new ways of reaching women who had some spending power, and magazines oriented toward the cinema offered one key avenue.[21] Apart from gender, there are also identifiable differences in the age and class of each magazine's readers. *Picturegoer* was the most distinctive in these respects. In the 1920s, *Picturegoer* was targeted at relatively affluent women, who were either single or newly married and enjoyed cinema-going as one part of a modern and aspirational lifestyle.

In 1921, an editorial in *Picturegoer* envisaged its readers as people who live 'not on the hill with the apple blossom waving, but in a place like Acton or Ashton-under-Lyne, Blackburn or Bow'.[22] This definition fits with the earliest available circulation data, from the 1930s, which suggests that *Picturegoer* was sold mainly in England (only 6 per cent of its readers were in Scotland and a mere 3 per cent in Wales), and especially in the metropolitan areas of the Southeast, the Midlands and the Northwest.[23] The 1930s figures also indicate that the majority of readers had incomes that placed them in either the lower-middle class or the top-earning sector of the working class; that is, people who did not live 'on the hill' but in a modestly afflu-ent suburb or town.[24] Thus, many readers of *Picturegoer* fell within what has been termed the 'new middle class' of the interwar period. This upwardly mobile class emerged from the increasing num-bers of managerial, clerical and service industry jobs. In the inter-war years these professions were comparatively unscathed by the unemployment and hard times that affected workers in traditional industries such as coal, cotton, ship-building and steel. Members of the 'new middle class' were distinct from the traditional working class because of both the nature of their work and their lifestyle: they were more likely to own their homes, to live in one of the many semi-detached homes built in this period and to have a significant amount of disposable income. Yet they were also distinct from the established middle class because they had less social standing and fewer attachments to traditional institutions such as the Church, the army and public schools. Members of the new middle class were 'more Americanized, more mobile, [and] less attached to older class cultures', according to the historian Ross McKibbin.[25] They were also much more likely to be regular cinema-goers, and this combination of a love of cinema and a flourishing culture of consumerism is readily apparent in the pages of *Picturegoer*.

Many of the advertisements in *Picturegoer* were illustrated with pictures of young, single women, who are seen working in offices, wearing fashionable clothes and attending the better class of the *palais de dance*. These women bear all the signs of the 'flapper': they have bobbed hair, they wear dresses cut in the 'schoolboy shape', and they go out in the evenings unchaperoned.[26] The image was one of emancipation and independence, and advertisers mobilized it to sell clothing, beauty products, and career training courses.[27] Another type of advertisement, selling detergents and home furnishings, was aimed at a slightly older female reader. An ad for Lux, for example, pictures two more mature women, walking leisurely across a tree-lined and sunny golf course, with their golf clubs in hand.[28] Even if they are discussing washing powder, in terms of gender and economic status this was a decidedly modern and aspirational image for women of the 1920s. By far the greatest number of advertisements were for facial powders and creams, hair care products and other cosmetics, all of which promise access to the glamour and beauty embodied by the film stars whose pictures figure prominently elsewhere in the magazine.

In his *English Journey*, J.B. Priestley commented that one feature of the 'new England' of the interwar years was the reverence paid to film stars. Priestley noted that film stars had replaced the British aristocracy as the subject of widespread hero worship.[29] *Picturegoer* provided ample material with which to worship this new aristocracy. As the title suggests, this was a magazine for people who went to the cinema rather than one about specific films, and in the 1920s its emphasis was more on the lifestyles of the stars than their films or their acting abilities. The greatest attention was paid to glamour; full-page glamour photographs are a central feature of most issues. Biographical sketches, as well as generously illustrated features on the stars' homes, their fashions, cars, pets and pastimes, portrayed the stars in terms closely associated with the British aristocracy and upper classes. Photographs reveal that many live in homes modelled on country estates; mock Tudor mansions stand amid extensive grounds. Inside, the homes are furnished with antiques or artefacts acquired on international travels. Fashion spreads show them wearing clothing associated with high society (notably furs and evening dress). Lifestyle features indicate that they spend their spare time playing sports associated with the middle and upper classes (riding, golf, tennis), tending to their exotic pets and 'motoring' (at a time when car ownership in Britain remained a luxury for the few). What marked the aristocracy of stardom as different from the traditional British aristocracy was its accessibility. The stars, in most cases, were born in humble circumstances, and the fan magazines gave prominence to their rising fortunes. In many cases, articles offered their real names, foregrounding the idea that they had reinvented themselves and that their lifestyle was acquired rather than inherited. Equally, stardom was often represented as a matter of good luck rather than innate talent, signalling that it was open to everyone.

Christine Gledhill has argued that the American star system represented a 'radical democracy' for British audiences in the 1920s, and one that was remarkable for both its presentation of social mobility and its revelations about private lives.[30] The effect was to diminish boundaries between the extraordinary and the ordinary – in both economic and social terms – and to suggest that wealth, glamour and beauty were available to everyone who sought them. *Picturegoer* played a significant role in this. Its articles teased readers with the idea that they could become, or at least associate with, stars. One, entitled 'You Must Have a Hobby' advised readers that, if they wanted to become a star, they should acquire a trademark pastime with which to distinguish themselves.[31] Another, 'If the Stars Come To Your Party', gave advice on what would be expected in precisely that scenario.[32] Most strikingly, the articles and advertisements portrayed consumerism as the primary means through which ordinary people could achieve the personal expression, self-improvement and fulfilment that was portrayed as an integral part of the experience of stardom. A regular feature entitled 'Film Stars at Home' consistently discussed the décor of the stars' homes as extensions of their personalities. While the magazine's readers would have had a much more limited budget, the interest in home decorating would not have seemed at all foreign in the new suburbs of Acton or Ashton-under-Lyne.[33] It should be noted, too, that this feature would not have looked out of place in *Ideal Home* magazine, which was another Odhams publication and one that was often promoted in *Picturegoer*. 'The Film Fashion Plate' was also a regular feature. This consisted of a collage of photographs showing Hollywood stars wearing the latest and most expensive fashions and furs. These must have represented unattainable luxuries to most readers, but the photographs are not far from advertisements for fashionable clothes that were actually available in Britain. These were touted as being stylish and yet inexpensive.[34] Advertisements for items such as 'Eastern Foam Vanishing Cream' and Eram-Khayyam cigarettes, meanwhile, pursued a similar line of Orientalism to that seen in cinema designs and many prominent films of the time, promising that the 'glamour of the East' could be found in the most routine, inexpensive and widely available products.[35]

If *Picturegoer* fuelled the aspirations of its 'new middle class' readers, it also mediated the distance between the fantasy of Hollywood and the reality of British life. Hollywood glamour was celebrated, but it was depicted as utterly foreign and something that could be imported only in a diminished or compromised form. The distinction between the image of Gloria Swanson dressed 'wondrously in white fox furs' and an advertisement for a 'dyed squirrel coat' on sale in London, or between high quality silk and 'inexpensive *crêpe de chine*', anchored the magazine in ordinary life, just as the frank and everyday opinions expressed on the letters pages counterbalanced the magazine's all-embracing optimism. This is an important qualification to Gledhill's observation that Hollywood represented a 'radical democracy' for British fans, at least as far as the fan magazines are concerned. The distance between Hollywood and Britain was always maintained, and as a result the prospect of social levelling was effectively diminished. British stars, for example, were seldom portrayed as having the enthralling, carefree and wealthy lifestyle of Hollywood stars. It is notable too that while British stars often advertised ordinary products such as cigarettes, cold creams and even the humble house dress, Hollywood stars never did. There may have been very practical reasons for this, but it nonetheless indicated that Hollywood represented the gold standard for glamour, and it was all the more admirable for being out of reach.

It is occasionally apparent that the editors of *Picturegoer* would have preferred to raise the tone of the magazine, lifting it above the fascination with Hollywood stars and lifestyles and into a discussion of British and European directors and films. A few articles pointed in this direction, including those promoting European cinema ('The Art of Abel Gance'[36]), explaining filmmaking techniques ('The Way of a Film Editor'[37]), as well as a few features centred on a single praiseworthy film. But the editors were not fully confident in their ambitions. They never abandoned altogether the focus on celebrity, and so an appreciative article on 'a weird film from Germany', Fritz Lang's *Metropolis* (1927), sat alongside the well illustrated feature 'Lucky Dogs! Pets of the Stars'.[38] The letters pages offer a few more glimpses of editorial unease concerning the emphasis on celebrity and fandom. When one reader wrote to express disinterest in stars and their private lives, his letter was given an enthusiastic 'welcome' by the editor. Conversely, the deluge of letters concerning Valentino drew some disdain. When they first started to arrive, in 1923, the editor responded with bemusement to the 'hundreds of eulogies crowding my desk', exclaiming 'Oh! How you girls love Rudolph!'[39] But by May 1925, after two years in which this level of enthusiasm persisted, the editor was reduced to asking, 'can you not think of something else besides Rudolph?'.[40] Even the editor of *Picturegoer*, it seems, could occasionally lose patience with popular film culture. The other fan magazines, however, had no uncertainties about their readers or their mission.

Picture Show

Picture Show and *Girls' Cinema* were published by the Amalgamated Press, a branch of Alfred Harmsworth's publishing empire, which began as a publisher of comic books in the 1890s. After the First World War, Amalgamated made concerted moves into the fan magazine market, launching *Boys' Cinema* in 1919 and then both *Picture Show* and *Girls' Cinema* in 1920. Like the comic books, each was published on low-quality paper. At a cost of two pennies (in pre-decimal currency) per weekly issue they were also significantly less expensive than *Picturegoer* (published monthly at one shilling per issue). The advertisements in *Picture Show* are markedly different from those in *Picturegoer*: there is little that can be termed aspirational.

Many centre on the testimony of married and middle-aged women, who affirm the efficacy of inexpensive, quasi-medical tonics that promise relief from a wide variety of ailments, some of which can only be referred to euphemistically ('maternity weakness', 'brain fag', 'kidney weakness' and 'wasting' among them). This points to a readership that could not easily afford medical care, and, together with the lack of advertisements for consumer luxuries, it suggests that *Picture Show* had a largely working class readership.[41] There were more photographs than in *Picturegoer*, and fewer and shorter articles. *Picture Show* was also more likely to focus attention on a single recent film, although this was done by printing several pages of photographic stills rather than through any form of critical assessment.

There were similarities between *Picture Show* and *Picturegoer*. The greatest attention was given to Hollywood's international films and, while stardom was not so closely linked with consumerism in *Picture Show*, the notion that Hollywood represented a dream to which anyone could aspire was strongly apparent. A cover story on 'Working girls who found world fame in films', for example, emphasized the chance nature of stardom and revealed that major stars such as Mabel Normand, Anna Q. Nilsson, Bessie Love and Pola Negri had been typists and shop girls before they became famous.[42] One regular feature was a monthly profile of a specific star, which was printed on a single page lined with small, close-up photographs of the star demonstrating a range of facial expressions or moods. 'The Expressions of Rudolph Valentino', for example, shows Valentino with a range of facial expressions captioned as 'a dude', 'enquiry', 'trustful', 'repose', 'interested' and 'his smile'. This emphasis on an actor's versatility and craftsmanship was drawn directly from the English stage tradition, as seen in acting manuals and handbooks dating back to the nineteenth century.[43] But in *Picture Show* these demonstrations of an actor's versatility did not prompt a consideration of technique or method. Typically, the feature on Valentino discusses his appeal as a 'type' rather than his acting. The various other stories on Valentino similarly demonstrate his ability to assume a variety of guises. One issue features a collage of photographs of Valentino on the cover, showing him cooking spaghetti in one photograph, dressed only in a loin cloth as a Native American in another and wearing the riding attire of an English gentleman in the third (Figure 1). But the emphasis is on his wide-ranging personality rather than his range as an actor; the headline is 'Rudolph Valentino off the screen: a pen picture of the man he is'.[44] As we shall see, however, while the fan magazines themselves were reluctant to discuss Valentino's acting skills, their readers entered such discussions with enthusiasm.

Competitions were numerous, but by far the most prominent was the 'Doubles' competition, which asked readers if they were 'the double' of a specific star and offered a prize for the photograph

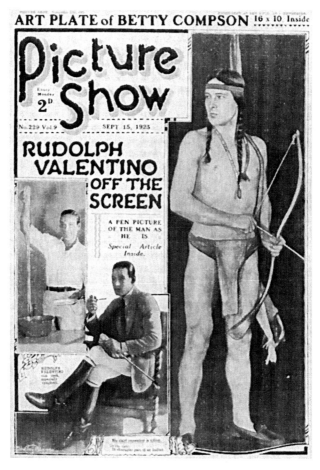

Figure 1   On the cover of *Picture Show* (15 September 1923) Rudolph Valentino's 'powers of disguise' were demonstrated

that demonstrated the best likeness.[45] Photographs of the winners and several runners-up were printed in the magazine and, more often than showing any innate physical resemblance, they reveal the fans' extraordinary attention to the star's make-up, hairstyle, clothing, jewellery and demeanour. These were intensely studied, particularly by young women, and then adopted with apparent pride. At first glance, such photographs might seem to demonstrate the fans' close identification with stars, to the point that they could 'become' an American star such as Lillian Gish or Edna Purviance. It is as close as one might come to finding photographic evidence to support G.A. Atkinson's accusation that films turned British cinema-goers into 'temporary American citizens'. Yet further contemplation leads to a very different conclusion: the photographs reveal the fans' awareness of the construction of the star image. These fans are enjoying the sense of masquerade that was such a central feature of popular cinema culture in this period and which featured so strongly in Valentino's career. In the competition, they are taking as much pleasure in exposing the masquerade as they are in recreating it. Furthermore, the photographs reveal a fan culture that was centred on the active participation of fans: their inside knowledge and cunning awareness of the film industry and its representational forms. They could toy with star images, compare one likeness over another and even construct and don the costume of a star themselves. Thus, even as they admired Hollywood, they appear to have been attuned to its artifice rather than mesmerized by it.

Girls' Cinema

Competitions, letters pages and short articles also abounded in *Girls' Cinema*. It was promoted as the 'ideal paper for girls' and in many respects it serves as a general interest magazine for adolescent girls rather than a film magazine. Its short stories, for example, included 'Tilda the Torch Girl' ('a charming story of a torch girl in a picture palace') and 'A Gay Time with a Miser's Gold' (the story of a 'pretty draper's assistant' who inherits £500) and, unlike the short stories that were featured each month in *Picturegoer* and *Picture Show*, neither was based on a film. Also unlike *Picturegoer* and *Picture Show*, none of the letters pages in *Girls' Cinema* was devoted solely to readers' opinions of films and competitions were not always film related. Instead, readers' dreams were interpreted, their handwriting analysed and their horoscopes revealed. There was an 'agony aunt' column, too, and a fascination with clothing and hairstyles that at times overwhelmed the discussion of film. All of these features, together with the chatty tone of the writing, mark *Girls' Cinema* as a typical woman's magazine of the period, albeit one aimed at a younger age group. It had little advertising, which reflects the limited spending power of adolescents in this era, and, in keeping with lower production values generally, the magazine featured far fewer photographs. What it lacked in photographic evidence, however, it more than compensated for with its intimate discussion of the stars' lives.

Rather than reporting from Hollywood in a straightforward journalistic style, *Girls' Cinema* often offered its news in columns such as 'Fay's Chat' and 'Letter From Dorothy'.[46] In each of these, the columnist was identified as a young British woman (Fay or Dorothy, respectively), and she addressed the reader directly, writing in a casual and conversational tone and yet revealing the most exciting events in the 'film colony'. Throughout these pieces, the stars themselves are portrayed as friends of Fay and Dorothy and so, by extension, they are friends of the readers as well. Once again, then, the emphasis is on the egalitarianism of Hollywood. Fay's Chat, for example, informed readers of how 'Rudy' (Rudolph Valentino) met his wife at a costume party, revealing this as though it happened next door and to new acquaintances.[47] Letters from Dorothy, meanwhile, often recounted the writer's first-hand interactions with the stars; in a typical week, for example, she might take tea at Pickfair with 'Doug and Mary' (Fairbanks and Pickford).[48] As the reference to tea suggests, the articles are built on the notion that the stars are very nearly British but happen to live in a distant utopia of wealth, beauty and fulfilment. Occasionally, Dorothy's comments overtly acknowledged the distance between Hollywood and Britain:

I am distinctly envious of screen actresses in Hollywood for one reason, Fay. They are able to purchase the most wonderful homes with as much ease as I purchase a new frock. What wouldn't I give to be able to buy and furnish to my own ideas a little nest for myself just on the outskirts of London.[49]

Yet envy of Hollywood did not equate with admiration for the United States. One columnist commented on seeing many American tourists in London over the summer of 1923 by observing that the girls looked 'typically American with their large heads [and] rather fuzzy hair' and complained that 'they persist in the ugly fashion of wearing black stockings with brown shoes'.[50] Similarly, a profile of Rudolph Valentino assured readers that he spoke 'perfect English, without a trace of Americanisms'.[51] *Girls' Cinema*, even more than *Picturegoer* and *Picture Show*, demonstrates the very selective way in which fans appreciated Hollywood and admired film stars, placing both within the context of their own values and interests.

Valentino: a Hollywood star

Common to all of these fan magazines was a fascination with Valentino that went beyond that shown to any other star in the 1920s. *Picturegoer* printed his 'travel diaries' over the course of 14 issues in 1923 and 1924 and, in one of the few popularity polls conducted in Britain in this era, its readers voted him their favourite star in 1925. *Picture Show* featured Valentino on its cover four times in 1923 alone, and it regularly devoted a full page to a publicity portrait or a still from one of his films. *Girls' Cinema* ran Valentino's life story ('written by the star himself') as a serial spread over five issues in 1923, and articles about his upcoming films and his private life were a feature of nearly every issue in the mid-1920s. The letters pages of all three magazines were also regularly filled with queries and opinions regarding Valentino. His appeal spread across the spectrum of these magazines' fans, from style-conscious adolescents to aspiring office workers and middle-aged matrons.

In many respects, Valentino's image was custom-made for the British fan culture that had developed in the early 1920s. He enjoyed six major box office hits in Britain, beginning with *The Four Horsemen of the Apocalypse* (1921/22) and ending with the release of his last film, *The Son of the Sheik* (1926).[52] None of these six films is set in the United States and most are based on foreign source material. *The Four Horsemen of the Apocalypse* was his first significant role in a major production. An adaptation of a bestselling novel by the Spanish author Vicente Blasco Ibanez, it is set in Argentina and France during the First World War. This was followed by an adaptation of Ibanez's *Blood and Sand* (1922) set in Spain. The bodice-ripping melodrama of *The Sheik* (1921/23) is based on a notoriously racy bestseller written by the British author E.M. Hull and set in the Arabian desert. *Monsieur Beaucaire* (1924) is an adaptation of a novel by the American author Booth Tarkington, but the story is set in eighteenth-century France and England. *The Eagle* (1925) is based on a story by poet Alexander Pushkin and set in Russia during the reign of Catherine the Great. *The Son of the Sheik*, his last film, offers a return to the desert in another story based on Hull's characters. Of course, this kind of internationalism bears little resemblance to the travelogue or instructional film. As newspaper critics took pleasure in pointing out, neither the countries nor the time periods are rendered accurately or even realistically.[53] Despite the claims made in *Picturegoer* editorials, then, popular films such as these were hardly educational. Rather, the exoticism of these films mobilized escapist fantasies of personal reinvention. Valentino captivated his fans not only with the wide range of roles that he played, but also with his ability to cross the boundaries of time, class and nationality. Furthermore, he flattered his fans by suggesting (in films as well as publicity photographs) that his masquerades were performed for their enjoyment. Valentino's image was itself a marker of the new power of women as consumers.

It was widely known that the star was an Italian *émigré* from a relatively humble background, that he arrived in the United States penniless, and that he found work in films largely by chance. These were the cornerstones of his often-told life story. But his admirers were more interested in his 'power of disguise' (as one letter to *Picture Show* described it) than his real background.[54] The characters of his most popular films change identity as easily as they change their clothes. In *The Four Horsemen of the Apocalypse*, he is first seen dressed as an Argentine gaucho and dancing the tango in a seedy Buenos Aires nightclub. When he moves with his family to France, he soon becomes a nightclubbing Parisian playboy, tenderly attending to the wealthy older woman with whom he has fallen in love. Then in the final reel, he redeems himself by enlisting and dying in uniform on the muddy battlefields of France. In *Blood and Sand* he is the bullfighter Juan Gallardo, whose rise from rags to riches is signalled by his acquisition of a regal and intricately detailed toreador's costume. As Ahmed Ben Hassan in *The Sheik* he abducts an English heiress and forces her to live as his wife in a remote desert. Yet any sense of brutality or danger is undermined by his strikingly androgynous outfit. This sheik is groomed to perfection: his turban is loosely wound around his head and frames his face like a woman's hair; his robes are multi-layered and flowing; they fall open to reveal a low-cut shirt, tight breeches and knee-high boots (Figure 2). Hence, it is no surprise that the abducted heiress falls in love with him, and no surprise that he is ultimately revealed to be European by birth and not an Arab at all. In *Monsieur Beaucaire* he is the Duke de Chartres, an eighteenth-century dandy who, in a quest for true love, flees court life at Versailles and poses as a mere barber in Bath. In *The Eagle* he is a guardsman to Catherine the Great, but her unwanted affections prompt him to shed his uniform and become the masked bandit of the title, a Robin Hood figure who protects the weak from the powerful. Finally, in his last film, *The Son of the Sheik*, he has two roles: he reprises his role as the now ageing and authoritarian Ahmed Ben Hassan and also plays Hassan's rebellious and romantically tormented son.

These roles demonstrated to fans that Valentino himself was able to transcend the boundaries of identity through clothing and

Figure 2   In the title role of *The Sheik*, Rudolph Valentino is an eager and strikingly androgynous lover

make-up. This fitted well within a fan culture that celebrated the transformation of others (that is, shop girls who turned into stars) and one that encouraged readers of fan magazines to transform themselves – through make-up, hairstyle and poses – into their more glamorous 'double'. It also fitted well within a consumer culture that embraced Orientalism as its prime signifier of luxury and sensuality. Valentino never disguised himself as an accountant or an insurance salesman. His trademark was his exoticism, and this was derived largely from ornamentation; each costume is an elaborate ensemble of trinkets and embellishments. Most of all, Valentino fitted perfectly with a popular film culture that was dominated by women, or at least gave priority to their interests and desires. It was widely recognized that he was unlike the other leading men of the era. Douglas Fairbanks, for example, was athletically masculine; he climbed, leapt and performed any number of daring physical feats to save his heroines.[55] Two other major stars, Wallace Reid and Richard Barthelmess, were admired for their good looks, but they were inadvertently handsome. The difference with Valentino was that his exhibitionism was far more sexually charged and his attractiveness was not inadvertent but by design (in terms of flamboyant costumes and make-up). He was admired not for his strength and certainly not for his wholesomeness, but for his beauty and sensuality. It is notable, too, that while the other leading men of the era played characters who were emotionally restrained and straightforward, Valentino's characters betrayed an intense romantic ardour and a complicated sexuality that could swing from dominance to submission.

One of his trademarks, which occurs in nearly all of his films, involves him kissing the hand of the film's heroine, smelling her handkerchief, or revelling in the aroma of a flower that she had been holding (Figure 3). In each case, he lingers at the moment of contact, submerging himself in the action and taking a fetishistic pleasure in it. He therefore seems to return the fascinated attention that women in the audience paid to him, presenting himself as the object of their gaze and demonstrating his own ability to be fascinated beyond reason or rationality.[56] A newspaper advertisement for *The Sheik* – in which he ardently carries away a supine Agnes Ayres – also showed him to be entranced with desire for her. He is defined as 'a lover with a heart as hot as desert sands',

Figure 3   In *Blood and Sand*, Juan Gallardo immerses himself in a handkerchief thrown to him by a fan

a phrase which neatly combines his passion with the exoticism that
set him apart from conventional codes of sexual conduct.[57] He is
represented as an acceptable source of pleasure for women and as a
figure of beauty presented for their pleasure. This is apparent, too,
in the publicity photographs taken of Valentino together with his
second wife, Natacha Rambova. In one head-and-shoulders shot,
Valentino and Rambova appear naked and utterly self-absorbed as
they gaze off camera together, apparently entranced by the beauty
of their own reflections. Rambova is slightly above him, though,
and because she leans into him, she appears to be the dominant,
controlling presence. In another portrait, the couple sit in front of
a roaring fire in what appears to be a drawing room, but while she
reads intently, Valentino sits at her feet, the very model of uxori-
ous devotion (Figure 4). It is little wonder that *Picture Show* printed
each photograph as a full-page portrait and on special, high-quality
paper.[58] Even Marjory Williams, the usually restrained commentator on the 'woman patron' in *Kinematograph Weekly*, admitted that
'always attractive to the girl and the grey-haired woman alike is the
image of a lover at the feet of the woman he loves'.[59]

Valentino's appeal to women was a constant point of discussion
in the fan magazines, where phrases such as 'his charming allure',
'smouldering fires' and his ability to convey 'unutterable things'

Figure 4   This publicity photograph of 'Mr and Mrs Rudolph Valentino', by Russell Ball, was printed over two pages of *Picture Show* (5 April 1924, pp. 12–13)

served as euphemisms to describe his sexual appeal.[60] On the letters page of *Picturegoer*, fans frequently commented on his good looks in terms that emphasized his foreignness; his appeal lay in his 'varmint-street-araby' qualities, according to one.[61] In these comments, it becomes clear that Valentino's 'ethnic' appearance was crucial in granting women the right to express their desire for him. More traditional, Anglo-Saxon images of masculinity did not allow for similar responses, and at least some of Valentino's fans rejected the other stars for that very reason. As a letter from a reader in Birmingham explained, women 'are tired of the everlasting "sons of the soil", registering nobly in every "close-up". Rudolph is the personification of romance we longed for but thought dead.'[62] Another reader enthused that 'Romeo could learn a lot about loving from Rudy'.[63] As striking as these comments are, the ideas expressed were an integral part of Valentino's appeal in other countries too, and particularly in the United States. There were other elements of Valentino's reception and reputation in Britain, however, that were much more specific to the British context, and these explain why, at the height of his fame, Valentino was admired as an actor in Britain and not just as a matinee idol.

Valentino: a British actor

Valentino was a phenomenally popular star in the United States, but his fame there was much more controversial and divisive than it was in Britain.[64] He was one of the best known Italian immigrants in the USA at a time when nativist feeling was strong and directed against immigrants from southern and eastern Europe. His overtly eroticized image as a 'Latin lover' fed anxieties about miscegenation and racial purity that were a scarcely concealed part of the public discourse on immigration. Although for many he was the 'great lover of the screen', he was at times derided by American fan magazines and newspapers for his supposed effeminacy. Reams of bad publicity were generated by scandals involving his private life (two divorces and an arrest for bigamy) and his attempt to free himself from a long-term studio contract. The American reaction against him was often histrionic: when an editor of the *Chicago Tribune* noticed that a face powder dispenser had been installed in a men's washroom, he denounced Valentino, blaming him for the nation's 'degeneration into effeminacy'. Hollywood, the editorial explained, was the 'national school of masculinity', and as a Hollywood star Valentino was considered to be a representative of the USA but also a standard bearer for its values. Under the weight of this kind of scrutiny, his fame stirred crosscurrents of hostility and anxiety, and he was seldom taken seriously as an actor by American critics. His performance in his first major film role, *The Four Horsemen of the Apocalypse*, received wide praise, but the subsequent scandals and controversies undermined his reputation as an actor and the sexually charged melodrama of *The Sheik* further reduced his status to the level of a pin-up.[65]

In Britain, by contrast, discussions of Valentino's ethnicity and masculinity did not resonate so strongly. Some British journalists, who were aware of Valentino's reputation in the United States, commented after interviewing him that they were bewildered by the allegations of effeminacy; they saw no evidence of it.[66] This could be attributable to differing conceptions of masculinity and to a less rigid sense of gender boundaries. It may also be that British critics felt no need to question the moral implications of his stardom; as an Italian actor working in American films, Valentino had less bearing on Britain's sense of national identity and direction. There was, however, another important factor governing Valentino's British reputation: he benefited from a long delay in the release schedule of his films. In the USA, the premiere of *The Four Horsemen of the Apocalypse* took place in March 1921 and *The Sheik* followed in November 1921. While these films thrilled Valentino's new legions of admirers, his fame was tainted by a series of scandals. His first divorce in November 1921 and his arrest on bigamy charges in May 1922 were widely covered in the American press and brought forth revelations that called his reputation as a 'great lover' into question. For example, at a time when American audiences were enthralled by the lusty tango sequence in *The Four Horsemen*, and then by his strutting confidence as *The Sheik*, it was revealed in court that his second marriage had not been consummated and that, on the wedding night, his new bride had made him sleep outside and on the porch. These and other revelations made the newly famous star a tabloid sensation in the United States, but in Britain the release of both films was delayed for over a year, and this proved highly advantageous to Valentino's reputation.[67]

The delays stemmed from concerns over *The Four Horsemen of the Apocalypse*. Ibanez's novel was a part of a first wave of reflection on the experience and meaning of the Great War. Its story offers a curious combination of bitterness toward the Germans, pride in victory, morbid pacifism and religious mysticism. The head of Metro Pictures, Marcus Loew, produced the film on an epic scale and distributed it in his own theatre chain in the USA. In Britain, Metro's films were normally distributed through the British firm Jury's, but Jury's had no enthusiasm for *The Four Horsemen* in 1921. The distributor feared that, so soon after the war, British audiences would reject a war film, and especially one that did not place their own country's involvement at the centre of the story. Furthermore, the film's ending, in which Valentino's Julio is killed in battle, was regarded as too depressing. Marcus Loew therefore decided to distribute the film in Britain himself. He made careful arrangements to present it as a 'super film'; that is, a high-prestige release that played exclusively at a single, large theatre in each major city rather than making the rounds of numerous ordinary cinemas.[68] The London premiere, in August 1922, was 17 months later than the New York premiere, but Loew had secured a home for the film at the Palace Theatre, an imposing venue that had originally served as the home of Richard D'Oyly Carte's Royal English Opera House. There, it played to packed houses for six months and earned considerable critical kudos. James Agate, for example, commented in the *Tatler* that this film demonstrated that the medium had 'at last found its artistic feet' and admitted that the final scenes had 'caught me by the throat'.[69]

The long delay in the British release of *The Four Horsemen of the Apocalypse* meant that Valentino was little known in Britain during the period when courtroom revelations about his private life were making tabloid headlines, and so the scandals did not have the impact that they had in the United States. It was important too that all of Valentino's subsequent films were held back from release until *The Four Horsemen* had appeared; presumably, both of the studios involved (Metro and Famous Players-Lasky) predicted that his films would be more valuable in its wake. Four major releases followed *The Four Horsemen* in rapid succession: *Camille* (1921/22), *The Conquering Power* (1921/22), *The Sheik* and *Blood and Sand* were released between September 1922 and January 1923. British audiences were thus able to assess Valentino's range as an actor in several films released over a comparatively brief period of time and to consider them without the weight of scandal that tarnished his reputation in the USA.

In February 1923, as the wave of Valentino films spread from London to the provinces, the editor of *Picturegoer* commented that 'the rave over Rudy is in full swing'.[70] Yet many of Valentino's admirers did not consider themselves to be caught up in a mere 'rave'. Readers responded to the editor by prefacing their praise for Valentino with statements such as, 'I'm no silly flapper', 'I am not a hysterical flapper', 'I am not a fan, but ...', and then arguing that it was his acting that they admired and not simply his appearance or personality. Valentino was, as various letter writers put it, 'a genius', 'an artist to his fingertips' and 'the greatest actor the screen has ever known'.[71] Both *Picturegoer* and *Picture Show* were apparently ill-prepared to deal with this line of thinking; they preferred to discuss the star as a 'type', offering biographical details, descriptions of his home, as well as comments about his popularity and news of his upcoming films. *Girls' Cinema* had similar interests – with even more attention to his costumes and coiffure – but on at least one occasion an article acknowledged that Valentino was more than a mere heartthrob:

> Rudolph Valentino is the fashion of the moment in the film firmament, and there is no likelihood of him slipping from public favour, for he is undoubtedly as clever as he is fascinating. He has been called the 'perfect lover' of the screen. It must also be added that he is a perfect actor as well, who is so thoroughly in harmony with his work that he lives every role he takes.

This article also took the opportunity to define Valentino's talent as neither typically American nor Italian. He had 'curbed the natural Italian tendency to expression with his eyes, hand and body' and he had also 'curbed' the qualities of 'friendliness' and athleticism that characterized 'the majority of stars in California'. This left him with a 'natural warm-heartedness' that was held in check beneath 'a veneer of reserve'. As the reference to 'reserve' indicates, this assessment of Valentino's appeal came very close to defining him as an Englishman, and also as an actor worthy of the West End stage.[72]

Critical assessments of acting in the 1920s had evolved from a Victorian stage tradition, which judged performances on the basis of an actor's gestures, traits and mannerisms. These were considered demonstrative evidence of an actor's craft and the means through which character could be conveyed. The best performances, according to the standards of the time, were located somewhere 'between restraint and passion'. As Christine Gledhill has observed, neither restraint nor passion was valued on its own; restraint could appear to be a lack of expression or inhibition, while passion could appear excessive or undisciplined.[73] It was therefore the interplay of these qualities that was valued and, in the right measures, the combination of restraint and passion could convey both the essence of a character and an actor's authority over the performance. Critics, in effect, wanted to see both a manifestation of a character and the actor's skill in constructing it. Valentino was one of the few Hollywood stars to benefit from this critical perspective. The common criticism of film acting was that stars played the same character type over and over again, but Valentino's range – in contemporary and costume films, playing characters of many different nationalities and playing characters who undergo marked transformations in dress and manner – was readily apparent. The fine balance between the recognized presence of the star and his performance of a masquerade was itself a close approximation of the balance between restraint and passion. In reviewing *Blood and Sand*, for example, the critic for *The Times* stated that audiences would recognize Valentino ('the young actor now familiar through his performance in *The Four Horsemen of the Apocalypse*'), and noted that the role was a challenging one because the character began as a 'young cobbler' but became 'the idol of Spain'. Valentino's mastery of this role lay in his controlled performance:

> He is remarkably restrained in a part where restraint might have been least expected, but there is no doubt about the brilliance of his performance. He conveys exactly the character of the young hero, and some of the facial expressions, fleeting as they are, grip the attention in a remarkable way … This film is well worth seeing, if only as a study of efficient film acting.[74]

According to the prevailing critical criteria, this was high praise indeed, and the sort usually reserved for revered West End stage performers rather than mere film stars.

Critical standards were very different in the United States. As Gledhill has described it, American critics prized 'acting from the heart' and an admirable performance conveyed 'the illusion of the first time'.[75] That is, an actor should seem to be experiencing the role rather than constructing it and the performance should seem spontaneous and sincere rather than rehearsed or studied. In the best performances, then, the boundary between actor and character was blurred, and the audience came to associate one with the other. These markedly different critical contexts had profound implications for Valentino's reputation. The reception of *Monsieur Beaucaire* in the United States and in Britain provides a particularly striking example. In the USA the film was disliked by critics and fans alike, and Valentino's performance was the primary issue. In the American context, the star's portrayal of an eighteenth-century dandy was assumed to be an expression of his own personality and many Americans looked askance at both royalty and refinement. The *New York Times* argued that Valentino's performance was marred by vanity. Other American critics jeered that the star was 'dolled up … in white wig, silks, lace and satin knickers', and letters to the fan magazine *Photoplay* expressed discomfort with what they assumed to be Valentino's new screen persona. As Emily W. Leider has observed, the film 'tripped emotional switches' in the United States and 'people felt called upon to take a stand as if [Valentino] were running for office'.[76] In Britain, however, *Monsieur Beaucaire* was 'hailed with rapturous delight by [Valentino's] legion of admirers', according to *Picturegoer*, which attributed this film with propelling Valentino to the top spot in its 1925 ranking of Britain's most popular film stars (Figure 5).[77] On the letters page of *Picturegoer*, fans expressed both high praise and some dissatisfaction regarding Valentino's acting in *Monsieur Beaucaire*, but both his admirers and detractors discussed his acting rather than his personality.[78] British critics were almost unanimously in favour of the film. It was acclaimed as 'Mr Valentino's success' in *The Times*, which praised his 'distinguished performance'; the *Scotsman* observed that 'Valentino acts with sureness and grace'; while the *Daily Mirror* declared of Valentino that 'the screen idol reveals himself as a genuine actor' and considered *Monsieur Beaucaire* 'one of the best films London has seen for a long time'.[79]

British critics did not admire all of Valentino's films. His performance in *The Sheik* could hardly be characterized with a term such as 'restraint' and, although that film was extraordinarily popular, it met with derisory reviews.[80] Nevertheless, in the four years between the premiere of *The Four Horsemen of the Apocalypse* in August 1922 and his death in August 1926, there is every indication that Valentino enjoyed not only wide popularity but also considerable respect and admiration in Britain. He was an 'idol' to many, but he was also a genuine actor in the eyes of those who had no interest in idols. One sign of his status is that the royal family made no secret of their enjoyment of his films. During the long run of *The Four Horsemen* at the Palace Theatre, every member of the royal family except King George himself went to see the film, and it was announced that they gave it an unqualified endorsement.[81] This was an unusual distinction for a Hollywood film, and it was all the more remarkable given the national sensitivities surrounding the First World War.

Figure 5   *Picturegoer* hailed the arrival of *Monsieur Beaucaire* on the cover of its October 1924 issue

A year later, *Monsieur Beaucaire* was chosen for a screening in the ball-room at Sandringham as part of the birthday celebrations of Queen Alexandra (the queen mother). On this occasion, King George was present.[82] Members of the royal family were also expected to attend the London premiere of *The Eagle* alongside Valentino himself, who had travelled from California for the occasion. The royal family's plans were cancelled, however, because of Queen Alexandra's death a few days earlier, on 20 November 1925.[83]

   Valentino's trips to Britain were another important factor in establishing his distinctive British reputation. On his first trip, in August 1923, he arrived in the midst of a bitter and protracted contract dispute with his studio, Famous Players-Lasky, which prevented him from making any films for more than a year. He was seeking more money and more control over his films, and he represented the dispute as a battle for his own artistic freedom and against the philistinism of the Hollywood studio system. In the

United States, these criticisms were seen as ingratitude: how could a young *émigré*, who had achieved the American Dream so swiftly, resent the industry that brought him success? As Miriam Hansen has observed, Valentino's hostility to Hollywood appeared to be 'hypocritical and unprofessional' and symptomatic of an immigrant's 'failure to adapt to American ways'.[84] When Valentino's critique of Hollywood was heard in London, however, it was music to the ears of many British critics. His comments lent credence to the view that Hollywood was little more than a factory town, sustained by unfair business practices, and they flattered audiences with the idea that they were eager to see more intelligent films. Only the industry's crass executives stood in the way of this progress.[85] The British fan magazines softened Valentino's comments, but others delighted in them.[86] The *Daily Express* critic G.A. Atkinson was Valentino's least likely admirer, but Atkinson relished the star's criticisms of Hollywood and decided after hearing them that he was indeed a young man with 'artistic sensibilities'.[87] In exile from Hollywood, Valentino could win over even the most sceptical Britons.

His second visit, in November 1925, did not leave such a good impression. He came to London to make a personal appearance at the premiere of *The Eagle* and thousands of eager fans waited outside the Marble Arch Pavilion to see him. Their numbers were so strong that they had to be restrained by the police, and Valentino himself had difficulty making his way past them and into the cinema. Once inside, he introduced the film to thunderous applause. 'See if you like the film first', he admonished the audience. When the screening had finished and he had accepted more applause, he avoided the crowds in front of the cinema by going up to the roof, crossing to the roof of a neighbouring building and then going down to a back alley where he could depart unscathed. The headline on the *London Evening News* the next day was 'Mob Scenes at Kinema', and the article described a 'surging mass' of women, 'screams' and 'sounds of crashing glass as advertising boards were pulled to the ground by those clambering to get a better view' of the star.[88] 'Women Besiege a Cinema' was the headline in the *Daily Express*, and the accompanying article described the women as a mix of 'flappers', the middle-aged and the elderly; implicitly, then, those not preoccupied by women's traditional duties as mothers and wives. And in *Kinematograph Weekly*, Marjorie Williams observed that Valentino had an 'irresistible feminine appeal' but she scorned the 'hysterically minded' women who allowed their 'feelings to run riot' at the premiere.[89] These views of the cinema and its effect on the public were informed by a critique of mass culture: that it exploited the most impressionable members of society, stripped them of their humanity, and turned rational individuals into a hysterical mob. Valentino's popularity among women, however, enabled commentators to explain the power of cinema with specific reference to the 'weaker sex'. This association was established early in his career in the USA, but in Britain it had been counterbalanced by his reputation as an actor. The London premiere of *The Eagle* was the beginning of a marked shift in his reputation in Britain and one that would prove overwhelming because of the circumstances surrounding his death.

Valentino's death

Terms such as 'hysterical', 'besieged' and 'riot' were not uncommon in discussions of Valentino. Even those who admired him as an actor acknowledged that his extraordinary fame was a peculiarly modern phenomenon. For the most part, though, it was American fans who were considered to be 'completely crazy' about Valentino and especially American women, who were said to throw their jewellery at him when he made a public appearance.[90] The scenes of mayhem in New York following his death on 23 August 1926 therefore seemed like a fitting climax to a career characterized by hysteria. News of the events in New York filled every major British newspaper. Each told the same story, which came from wire reports, with headlines such as 'Vulgar spectacle', 'Wild scramble at bier', 'Crowds out of control' and, most pointedly, 'Dead Film Actor: Women's Strange Behaviour'.[91] The story was that the day after the 31-year-old Valentino died, unexpectedly and from peritonitis, tens of thousands of people gathered outside of the funeral parlour in midtown Manhattan. The crowds waited for hours, and at times in the rain, for a chance to view the body, and when the doors finally opened there was a surge forward that descended into a riot. The funeral home's windows were broken and its parlour was torn asunder. Women, who were said to be in the majority, reportedly became hysterical as mounted police tried to force the crowds back. Dozens were injured in the melee and the streets were littered with shoes, umbrellas and torn clothing. When order was eventually restored and people were allowed to file past the body, the disrespect of many in the crowd reportedly shocked observers. 'Heartless', 'giggling', 'morbid' women and girls applied their make-up and chattered as they filed past the body. The callous were accused of stealing mementoes of the occasion from the funeral parlour. The tearful were assumed to be publicity-seekers 'shamming' their sorrow for the journalists. One girl was said to have hidden an onion in her handkerchief in order to prompt her tears for the camera.[92]

At the very least, these reports were exaggerated and distorted; one commonly made claim – that the disturbance outside the funeral home was the worst riot in New York City's history – was patently ridiculous. It is worth noting, too, that the newsreel footage of the events bears little relation to the newspaper accounts: there are crowds outside the funeral home, but the mourners file into the funeral home in an orderly and calm manner. Some footage does indeed show a crowd that becomes unruly, but only because mounted policemen are charging into it. At any rate, throughout the footage the crowds consist mainly of men.[93] Of course, it was hardly the fault of the British press if American journalists filed exaggerated reports of events in New York City. What is interesting, in the British context, is the prominence these stories received in the press and the use that editorialists made of them: the 'scenes at the bier' demonstrated, once and for all, the harmful influence that cinema had upon women. At least one local British newspaper drew a distinction between local reactions to Valentino's death and the events in New York: 'there were no noisy demonstrations of sorrow by Bolton girls', the *Bolton Evening News* reassured its readers.[94] In the national papers, however, the argument was repeatedly made that reactions to Valentino's death betrayed universal truths about the cinema. The *News of the World* claimed that the events revealed that films could 'warp weak and untrained minds'.[95] The *Yorkshire Evening Post* declared that films ruin marriages because 'husbands fail to live up to the dream standard created by wives out of visits to the pictures'.[96] On the editorial page of the *Daily Express*,

James Douglas pointed out that Valentino had been twice married but died alone, thus revealing his reputation among women as a great lover to be 'a cheap and meretricious fantasy'.[97] It was a full seven months later that the same newspaper's film critic, G.A. Atkinson, argued that cinema-goers ('mostly women') 'talk America, think America, and dream America', but his observations were undoubtedly influenced by coverage of Valentino's death. The news stories from New York were perfectly suited to those who considered the cinema to be a powerfully influential force, and one that encouraged women to be 'hysterical flappers' rather than traditionally demure, housebound, dedicated wives and mothers.

In the midst of such reports Valentino was repeatedly referred to as 'the sheik' and as a 'matinee idol' and it was implied that his only admirers were lovesick fans. Thus, coverage of the events in New York quickly overwhelmed Valentino's British reputation as an actor and an artist at odds with Hollywood. Instead, he became symptomatic of Hollywood and the very embodiment of its pernicious influence. Of course, contemporary British cinema-goers did not necessarily accept these arguments. When *The Son of the Sheik* was released two months after the star's death it became an immediate box office hit, and re-releases of his earlier films played to packed houses up and down the country throughout the autumn of 1926.[98] A memorial plaque was installed at London's Marble Arch Pavilion, and his waxwork became the most popular exhibit at Madame Tussaud's. For several years, *Picturegoer* and *Picture Show* continued to print photographs of him and stories about his death. Two memorial associations were formed in Britain, and each dedicated itself to the defence of the star's name and reputation. Even some 40 years after his death, the most dedicated members continued to ask newspapers to commemorate the anniversary of his death and, when interviewed, they continued to insist that he was a talented actor rather than a mere matinee idol.[99] In this last endeavour, however, his admirers were fighting a stubborn battle against the tide of popular memory.

Valentino's reputation in subsequent decades was not informed by the quality of his films or his performances. Silent films were seldom revived once 'talkies' became the norm, and so within a few years his body of work was confined to the archives and rarely retrieved. The popular memory of Valentino was instead informed by the weight of controversy surrounding his stardom in the United States; that is, by the accounts of scandals relating to his private life and his untimely death, which were told and re-told in the years after his death until they became a standard part of Hollywood's folklore. By 1949, a commemorative article in *Picturegoer* – the very magazine where readers once insisted they were not hysterical fans – could recall Valentino only as a star whose death made 'women throughout the world weep' and 'fling themselves prostrate over his bier'.[100] This image was also popularized by scandal-mongering books such as *Hollywood Babylon* (1975) and it overwhelmed the less salacious but more distinctive perspectives on Valentino that had prevailed in Britain during the star's lifetime.[101] To uncover British responses to Valentino is to reveal a star who was once taken much more seriously and, more importantly, a history of Hollywood films that acknowledges their varied reception in the wider world. These histories can tell us not only about film preferences, but also about the cultures that received the films. Contemplating Valentino's films, his image and the discussions that surrounded them in Britain, reveals a culture at the dawn of a consumer age. This was a time when the 'purpose of pleasing women' (to return to Iris Barry's comment) had an increasingly high profile, but women's tastes, interests and disposition as consumers were often viewed contemptuously. The discourses surrounding Valentino's stardom were informed by both sides of this phenomenon. In death, his stardom became a cautionary tale and a means of questioning women's taste and discernment as consumers. But during the peak years of his career, he attained that rare status of being both a film star and an admired actor. His reputation suggested that popular film tastes were not necessarily lamentable, and that the pleasures women found in cinema-going might involve more than escaping from the familiar sight of crockery and finding sanctuary in the dark.

3 'Two Countries Divided by a Common Language': The Arrival of the Talkies

We have really everything in common with America nowadays, except, of course, language.

Oscar Wilde (1887)[1]

I shall be inclined to fear that the 'talkies' are more likely to turn British audiences into 'Twangies' than to impose on the American public the English tongue, pure and undefiled.

Mrs Belloc Lowndes (1928)[2]

England and America are two countries divided by a common language.
usually credited to George Bernard Shaw (exact origin unknown)[3]

The arrival of 'talking pictures' is one of the best known legends in the folklore of Hollywood. The story has been kept fresh by the perennial popularity of the musical *Singin' in the Rain* (1952), which, through the screeching voice of Jean Hagen and the mellifluous singing and graceful dancing of Gene Kelly, portrays the transition from silent films to 'talkies' as a predestined triumph. It is a legend informed by the American success ethic, showing the overthrow of a corrupt older star and the rise of young, genuinely talented stars. Equally, it is a story of the industry's inventiveness, the triumph of technology and the public's appetite for novelty.[4] Hollywood was adept at creating such legends out of its own history and portraying itself as the embodiment of American dynamism. But where do audiences outside of the United States stand in relation to such legends? Is *Singin' in the Rain* a part of their history too, or are there other, more culturally specific accounts of this moment in film history?

Certainly, no British film portrays the arrival of the talkies with the verve of *Singin' in the Rain*, but Noel Coward's *This Happy Breed*

(1944) does offer a brief, nostalgic glimpse of this transitional moment. In the midst of Coward's saga of ordinary family life, set between-the-wars and in a lower-middle-class suburb of London, young Violet Gibbons goes to see *The Broadway Melody* (1929) with her boyfriend, Sam. This is clearly a chance for Sam to show off: he pays advanced prices and even opts for the more expensive seats. Yet once they are seated in the crowded theatre and watching one of the film's brassy song and dance routines, he observes that 'I can't understand a word they're saying', to which Violet responds, 'Neither can I, but isn't it wonderful?' If this is not quite the stuff of legends, it nevertheless encapsulates the ambivalence with which the earliest talking films were greeted: British audiences were intrigued by the new technology, but many found the sound of the voices bemusing. Indeed, it is likely that George Bernard Shaw's often quoted observation – that a common language can be more divisive than unifying – was never so apparent as in the late 1920s, when Hollywood's first talkies were released throughout Britain.

From Hollywood's perspective, Britain's status as the most popu-lous English-speaking country outside the United States meant that it was the most promising foreign market for the talkies. They were hardly likely to appeal in the other major foreign markets (most in Europe or Latin America), and so Britain was confidently chosen to be the first market beyond the USA and Canada to receive the talkies. This optimism belied the fact that the common language had evolved along separate paths for some 300 years. Ever since the Pilgrims departed for the new world, American English had been mixed with the language and speaking styles of Native Americans and with successive waves of settlers from other countries, and it had developed its own words, idioms, accents and syntax. By the 1920s, the American forms of the English language were distinct from British forms, and they would have been quite unfamiliar to most ordinary Britons. While many American soldiers had been transported through Britain during the First World War, the vast majority were on their way to France and their interaction with the British public was far more limited than it would be in the next war.[5] Otherwise, travel between the two countries was rare and it was reserved almost entirely for the wealthy. Radio was in its infancy: the BBC began broadcasting in 1922, and home radio ownership grew steadily, but American programmes and performers were uncommon in this first decade. Sales of gramophones and records soared in the 1920s and American jazz was particularly popular, but singing voices rarely convey the cadence and tone of everyday speech. Moreover, the singing voice and the speaking voice are not judged in same manner; different criteria apply. There was little, then, apart from travelling American music hall performers, to prepare British audiences for the voices that they would hear in the talkies.

Responses to the earliest talkies demonstrate how alienating voices could be, and there was noticeably less enthusiasm for them in Britain than there had been in the United States.[6] The different responses are apparent (albeit at the most general level) in cinema admissions figures. In the USA, cinema admissions had been running at a rate of approximately 50 million per week in the mid-1920s, when silent films were the norm. Then, between 1927 and 1930, as talking films pushed silent films to the margins of the American exhibition sector, admissions swept upward to a weekly rate of 80 million per week.[7] In Britain, the comparable period is 1928 to 1931, because the conversion to sound occurred roughly one year later than in the USA.[8] Over this period, as more and more talkies were released, admissions to British cinemas drifted downward from a level of 20 million each week in the mid-1920s to 17 million each week by the early 1930s.[9] This does not necessarily represent a wholesale rejection of the talkies. The swift downturn in the economy at the outset of the decade undoubtedly had a major influence on cinema admissions too (in the USA admissions also plummeted in 1931 and 1932). Nevertheless, the flat level of cinema admissions in Britain suggests that the arrival of the talkies brought less enthusiasm and more difficulties than it had in the United States.

In order to move beyond the general level and locate both the prevailing currents of opinion and the lesser crosscurrents, it is necessary to look in more detail at two specific groups and account for their reactions to key films. The first group is a loose coalition of film critics and representatives of the British film industry; grouped together here as film nationalists. Their responses to the arrival of the talkies in the autumn of 1928 must be considered in relation to the new British 'quota' system (instituted through the Films Act of 1927), which promised to raise the fortunes of British films and, by implication at least, to lessen Hollywood's dominance. In their positions as leaders and spokespersons for the domestic industry, it is perhaps predictable that the film nationalists framed discussions of the talkies in terms of the threat or opportunity that they offered to the country's own filmmakers. What is more remarkable is how quickly the ground shifted beneath them and the pace at which their views had to change in order to keep up with events. The second group is popular audiences, whose responses evolved rapidly during the first year of talkie releases. An element of film nationalism is apparent among popular audiences too, but so too are divisions along the lines of class and regional identity. Ultimately, these divisions proved the most significant factor in determining audience preferences, and by 1930 distinctive and long-lasting taste patterns had emerged. Despite the many public pronouncements against them, audiences gradually accepted the talkies. Indeed, among the cacophony of the disgruntled and disapproving, it is even possible to locate some enthusiasm for them.

Film nationalism

Although Hollywood legend tells us that Warner Brothers' *The Jazz Singer* (1927/28) was an overnight and record-breaking success when it was first released in New York on 6 October 1927, and that it spurred an immediate and industry-wide 'talkie revolution', film historians tell a less dramatic story.[10] This first, feature-length film with dialogue did not instigate an *immediate* rush to produce more talkies. It was not until *The Jazz Singer* had performed well nationally, and subsequent talking films had also opened well, that Warner Brothers moved wholeheartedly into the production of talkies. Still, most American cinemas were not yet wired for sound in 1928 and so Warner Brothers continued to make silent versions of its talking films. Other Hollywood studios followed Warner's lead, in most cases tentatively at first but with more vigour once they too enjoyed some success with the new technology. It was more than a year later, and in the wake of the enormous box office success of another Warner Brothers musical starring Al Jolson, *The Singing Fool* (1928), that it became apparent that the film industry was undergoing a significant transformation and one that was likely to put an end to all silent film production in Hollywood.[11] Many American critics, meanwhile, were willing to praise some of the early talkies, but they also routinely complained about bad vocal delivery, static camera set-ups, obvious microphone placement, poor sound technology and any combination of these early faults.[12] The 'talkie revolution', it seems, was settled through a long series of skirmishes rather than one blazing battle.

If Hollywood's response to the steadily growing success of the talkies can be characterized as guarded optimism, the British industry's response was open scepticism. Observed from afar, the popularity of talking feature films seemed to be a purely American phenomenon and one that might never cause more than a ripple on British shores. This sense of detachment grew over the course of the long delay between the release of films in the United States and in Britain. As in the USA, *The Jazz Singer* was the first feature-length film with dialogue to be shown. It opened in London on 27 September 1928, nearly a full year after its New York debut, with a high-profile premiere at London's Piccadilly Theatre and then a four-week run at this large (1,200 seat) venue. Other talkies followed in its wake, but they arrived slowly. Warner Brothers had leased the Piccadilly Theatre for several months and it served as the studio's showcase for a selection of talkies that demonstrated how sound could be used in a variety of genres. *The Jazz Singer* (a musical) was followed by the horror film *The Terror* (1928) in October, by the comedy *The Home Towners* (1928) in November, and then by the courtroom drama *On Trial* (1928) in December. In the meantime, only two further talkies appeared in the capital. Both were musicals: Universal's *Melody of Love* (1928) began a long run at the Rialto (Piccadilly Circus) in November, and in the same month Warner Brothers' *The Singing Fool* began an even longer run at the Regal (Marble Arch). For several months, then, the talkies were confined not only to London, but also to the city's West End. None was shown outside London until *Melody of Love* played in Manchester in December 1928.[13] Glasgow and Birmingham did not see a feature-length talkie until *The Singing Fool* arrived in February and March of 1929, respectively, and many smaller cities did not receive their first talkie until the summer of 1929.[14]

Silent films, meanwhile, continued to play as usual throughout the country and so it was easy for the film trade to dismiss the talkies as a novelty item. Throughout 1928, the Cinematograph Exhibitors Association (CEA) steadfastly advised its members to stick with silent films. The talkies may have some novelty value, the CEA admitted, but they were likely to alienate regular customers, and so the expense of wiring a cinema was deemed to be too risky.[15] The industry's production sector received similar advice from the leading trade papers. In the week before *The Jazz Singer* was released, an editorial in *The Bioscope* described the American push for the talkies as 'premature and misguided' and it applauded the British trade for adopting a 'critical attitude' toward them. 'It would have been easy', the paper argued, 'to whoop up enthusiasm and start running after the talkies, but running, if it is in the wrong direction, is a poor way of saving time.'[16] Three months later, *Kinematograph Weekly* observed that silent films would continue to be popular for the foreseeable future, and 'therein lies the chance for the British studio'.[17] It would be many months before either paper changed its thinking.

The industry's scepticism went hand-in-hand with the critics' disdain for the talkies. *The Jazz Singer* itself roused neither admiration nor condemnation. Critics were perhaps understandably preoccupied with comparing the film to a live performance. The Piccadilly Theatre, where it was first shown, had previously been used for stage musicals. When comparing this first 'talking' screen musical with a live stage musical, critics generally found the screen version to be lacking, although many recognized that the new technology had potential.[18] *The Jazz Singer*, however, is a hybrid rather than a true talkie; it is mainly a silent film, with several musical sequences and just a few lines of dialogue. It was not until *The Terror* was released four weeks later that the floodgates of critical scorn opened. *The Terror* had been released much more recently in the United States, and there it was considered a state-of-the-art talkie in the autumn of 1928. It was 'all-talking' and had no silent sequences or intertitles. Even the credits were spoken so that the written word could be banished altogether. In Britain, Warner Brothers may have thought that, following so closely on the heels of the pioneering

Jazz Singer, this most modern of talkies would impress upon critics and audiences alike the rapid development of the talkies in the space of just one year. The studio may also have thought that a film based on a story by Edgar Wallace, Britain's most popular and prolific author, would have a strong appeal in his native country. But Warner Brothers misjudged the critical mood. The decision to give *The Terror* such a high-profile release actually intensified the hostility of the critics, who perceived the film – and by extension all talkies – as an affront to the nation.

Some criticisms of *The Terror* merely concerned the limitations that the new technology imposed on the medium: the placement of microphones made the staging dull and predictable; the emphasis on dialogue inhibited camera movement; and, in the pursuit of vocal clarity, the dialogue itself was delivered at a snail's pace. Here, too, comparisons with the stage were made, and not least because *The Terror* had also been staged in a West End theatre only a few months earlier. In this context, *Kinematograph Weekly* found the film so inferior that it alleged that 'even a second-rate touring company' could have mounted a more competent production.[19] The greatest scorn centred on the vocal performances of the actors. Although the film maintained its story was set in England and featured English characters, American actors predominated in the cast and, inexplicably, they used their own country's accents and idioms. The result, as far as London's critics were concerned, was an extended string of anachronisms. A Scotland Yard inspector, for example, was played by an American actor (Joseph Girard) who used American police jargon. The audience at the premiere reportedly greeted the film with frosty laughter and, at the end of the screening, there was none of the applause customary at such occasions. Edgar Wallace's son, who attended the premiere in place his father, could find no kind words to say about this high-profile film and was overheard remarking that his father's reputation had been irreparably tarnished.[20] The London correspondent for the *New York Times* explained the offence caused by asking his American readers to imagine a British-made western in which one cowboy says to another, 'I say old chap, lend me a bob to buy some fags'.[21] However, it was not just the gaffes that caused dismay. The peculiar combination of a British setting and American voices raised the prospect of American speech supplanting British speech altogether in films, as Hollywood's new technology overwhelmed the native film industry. British critics responded with patriotic fury. *The Times* took umbrage at each 'metallic Americanism' and described the cast as 'shouting giants, who, with their rough tongues, make little attempt to speak English'.[22] In *Kinematograph Weekly*, the 'mechanized American accents' were described – disparagingly – as 'amazing', and *The Bioscope* considered that the American voices were so unpleasant that they promised a good future for what its critic termed 'English-speaking stars'.[23]

The Terror offered the first instance in which British audiences heard an established silent film star's speaking voice. The star of *The Jazz Singer*, Al Jolson, had not made any feature films before this first talkie and so his screen voice was unlikely to surprise or offend audiences. In fact, he was already a popular recording artist and the talkies offered a new medium in which to enjoy his musical performances. *The Terror* was a different matter. The lead star was May McAvoy, a dainty beauty who had prominent roles in high-profile silent films such as MGM's epic *Ben Hur* (1925/26) and Lubitsch's *Lady Windermere's Fan* (1925/26). Unfortunately, at least as far as British critics were concerned, McAvoy's New York accent did not match her delicate appearance. Writing in the *Tatler*, the film critic James Agate described McAvoy as a 'delicious little person whose silent miming I could watch for hours'. Upon hearing her voice, however, he declared that 'five minutes of that accent would drive me into the street, for the salutary, precautionary reason that ten minutes of it would drive me to Bedlam'.[24] In the *Observer*, C.A. Lejeune was more restrained in her initial review of *The Terror*; she advised her readers not to judge the talkies on the basis of this one 'crude' film. Years later, however, when Lejeune recalled the arrival of the talkies, McAvoy and *The Terror* figured prominently in her recollections. The incongruous sight and sound of the 'flower-like' McAvoy opening her 'rosebud lips' and speaking the inelegant line, 'Say, Pop, can't you hear that turrible oirgan?', still haunted Lejeune decades later.[25]

In the wake of *The Terror*, Reginald Whitley of the *Daily Mirror* observed that 'a sledgehammer attack on the talkies is now in full swing'.[26] A film that was – to British critics at least – so laughably bad held out the promise that the talkies might lead to Hollywood's doom and to Britain's ascendancy in the league of film-producing nations. According to this view, the talkies gambled with Hollywood's two greatest assets, its star system and its international distribution network. If the gamble failed, and *The Terror* suggested to critics that it would, Hollywood would be bankrupt and the British industry, newly bolstered by the 'quota' system, could fill the void. G.A. Atkinson unreservedly promoted this line of thinking. In the autumn of 1928, he poured scorn on the earliest talkies and concluded his columns in the *Sunday Express* with defiant declarations such as 'the talkies are moribund', 'the talkies make silents eloquent' and 'there is no evidence that Britain wants the talkies'. He predicted that if British producers shunned the talkies and continued to make silent films, their films would be welcomed by domestic audiences and also by 'the thousands of American theatres that do not and may never show talkies'. Hollywood was 'voluntarily resigning its leadership of the film world' and committing 'commercial suicide' by rushing into the production of talkies. This, in his eyes, 'has practically made a present of the film producing industry to Britain'.[27] Atkinson was not alone in his views. In April 1929 *The Times* commented that the talkies were 'intolerable' and complimented the British film industry for turning its back on them. Two months later the same paper revisited the topic to observe that 'even film fans' would not remain content to see 'entertainment so crude and incompetent as that which has lately been imported for them'.[28] In the following month, the *Telegraph* also predicted that 'the small but discriminating portion of the public' which rejected the talkies would 'soon become a majority'. The *Telegraph* went further in alleging that the talkies were actually a plot devised by Hollywood to undermine the British industry, just as it was finding its feet in the wake of the Films Act.[29] Cinemagoers were therefore exhorted to resist them on the grounds of both patriotism and good taste.

National newspapers such as the *Express*, *The Times* and the *Telegraph* saw it as their role to prescribe socially appropriate attitudes, and to draw lines of distinction between acceptable and unacceptable cultural forms. The talkies were therefore bound to trouble them; by giving prominence to unfamiliar and unrefined

accents, they defied the newspapers' own sense of cultural authority. It is more remarkable that the alarm raised by the talkies was
not limited to the national newspapers, but could also be found in
Kinematograph Weekly and *The Bioscope*. These trade papers were primarily concerned with the business of film production, distribution
and exhibition. Nevertheless, during the first six months of 1929
their editorial policy was imbued with cultural misgivings about
the talkies. In March, *Kinematograph Weekly* advised film producers
that 'the silent film, especially of British make, has a terrific future'
and in April it warned exhibitors not to be 'stampeded' into the
'talkie panic'.[30] In May, *The Bioscope* admitted that the industry was
in a 'temporary state of chaos' because of the talkies, but reminded
its readers that silent films remained 'an excellent proposition' and
that 'no greater mistake could be made than to suppose the silent
film dead'.[31]

These comments (and many more like them) were made in prominent editorials and by regular columnists, while on the back pages
of these papers – buried amidst minor news items – there was growing evidence that the first wave of talkie releases was drawing huge
crowds. The Al Jolson musical *The Singing Fool* was a phenomenon:
it ran for 15 weeks in London's West End, lasting from November
1928 to March 1929, and when its national release began in January
1929, reports from up and down the country indicated that it was a
record-breaking success. In Glasgow, 430,000 tickets were sold at
its first five-week engagement.[32] In Manchester its initial engagement lasted for 14 weeks and in Birmingham for eight weeks, and it
broke box office records in Bristol, Cardiff, Croydon, Gloucester,
Leeds and Norwich.[33] MGM's *The Broadway Melody*, released in
May 1929, was another huge success, selling over 600,000 tickets
at the Empire, Leicester Square, over the course of a nine-week run
and earning some £3,000 each day that it played at that one venue.
British critics had given *The Broadway Melody* dire reviews, but
MGM fought back by running full-page advertisements in the trade
papers, featuring photographs of the long queues of patrons outside
the Empire.[34] *Lights of New York* (1928/29), *Noah's Ark* (1928/29), *In
Old Arizona* (1929) and *The Wolf of Wall Street* (1929) were other early
talkies that did well in both London and the provinces.[35] Only *The
Terror* goes unmentioned in these reports of early talkie successes.

While these films attracted audiences to the largest cinemas in metropolitan areas, the great majority of cinemas continued to resist the new technology. By the end of 1929, only 22 per cent of the country's cinemas were wired for sound.[36] Film producers remained intransigent too. In his autobiography, Michael Balcon admitted that during this period he and other British filmmakers 'thoroughly deceived themselves' and 'steadfastly refused to believe' that the silent film was dead.[37] There are two explanations for the willingness of these producers to heed the critics and ignore their instincts as showmen. One is that the noisy din of the talkies embarrassed the industry's leaders. In the 1920s, silent cinema had attained a measure of respectability, but critics prized the elements of cinema that made it a distinctive medium; that is, the visual qualities of *mise en scène* and montage. The talkies, with their emphasis on dialogue, threatened to rob the medium of its primary claim to artistry. Furthermore, with their love of wisecracks and popular music, the talkies were regarded as vulgar by British film producers and executives, who – by contrast with their Hollywood counterparts – had middle-class sensibilities. They feared that this disreputable new form of cinema was likely to set back the cultural status of the medium by some 25 years, to a level not seen since the penny gaffs. The second, closely related explanation is that the talkies stirred strong currents of nationalism, which were both hopeful and anxious. The talkies represented both the encroaching presence of American culture in Britain and the possibility that this might be resisted. 'For years we have had to tolerate American stories and ideas', the editor of *Kinematograph Weekly* complained, 'and now they are going to inflict their dire language on us.'[38] Such resentment was not limited to the film nationalists, but extended into popular audiences as well.

Popular audiences

In Donald Crafton's analysis of American responses to the talkies, he reminds readers that 'while the fanzines were speaking *for* an audience, they were also speaking *to* that audience'.[39] They set the agenda, determining which topics would be discussed and the terms of the discussion. This cautionary note is equally important to any consideration of the British fan magazines, and the evidence that they offer of reactions to the talkies among cinema-goers, because the two publications that gave the most column inches to readers' comments were those that were at first decidedly against the talkies. One was *Picturegoer*. At the outset of the 1920s, *Picturegoer* was characterized by an all-embracing enjoyment of popular cinema-going, but later in the decade it became self-conscious in its appreciation of the cinema. Editorials and other forms of commentary were much more likely to draw distinctions between good and bad taste, and more often than not Hollywood was regarded as the capital of bad taste. This could take the form of mocking humour. In 1927, for example, the magazine invented a columnist named Lola De Twaddle, a crass starlet who reported her adventures in Hollywood. One column recounted her attempt to adapt Charles Dickens' novel *The Old Curiosity Shop* for the screen under the new and improved title of *Love's Purple Passage*.[40] But the humour could also turn ugly, and on occasion it gave way to anti-Semitism. Another article referred to Hollywood's studio executives as 'Hebraic nitwits' and mocked them for interfering with the work of British authors.[41] The sentiments underlying both columns – centred on the superiority of British culture over Hollywood's commmercialism – fitted well with the magazine's support for British cinema in this period and the hopes that were attached to the new 'quota'. It was a far cry, though, from the magazine's earlier and more populist stance.

The other fan magazine was the newcomer *Film Weekly* (1928–39), which had a similar readership and tone to *Picturegoer*.[42] Wartime necessity would eventually lead the two magazines to merge and become *Picturegoer and Film Weekly* in 1939, but long before the merger these magazines seemed natural bedfellows. Like their rivals (the most significant of which remained *Picture Show*) both routinely featured Hollywood stars on their covers and ran a continuous stream of articles centred on the stars' lifestyles and consumer habits. This ensured that each had a wide readership. However, *Picturegoer* and *Film Weekly* featured more editorials and other forms of commentary than other fan magazines, and their content was often critical of Hollywood and the commercial imperatives of the studio system. This was a means of courting a more discerning film fan: one who appreciated *some* Hollywood films but also thought that many films were inconsequential, and that British cinema (given a chance) might raise the tone and quality of popular films.

Both *Picturegoer* and *Film Weekly* responded to the arrival of the talkies by insisting that these films would not be acceptable to British audiences and that their eventual demise represented an opportunity for British cinema. Indeed, *Picturegoer*'s opinions would not have been out of place in the *Express*, *The Times* or the *Telegraph*. An editorial published in May 1929, entitled 'The Peril of the Talkies', took little account of their box office success:

> Most American talkies … will alienate altogether thousands of kinema patrons. The chief reason is that they are definitely foreign. American movie magnates, drunk with instantaneous success at home, have not yet fully realised what they have done. They have largely destroyed the greatest and most valuable attribute of motion picture art – its internationality.[43]

Film Weekly showed more willingness to take account of public opinion when it conducted a poll in July 1929 to ascertain its readers' opinions about the talkies. The editor, however, highlighted the results that suited the magazine's longstanding view that 'the public still wants silent films'. That 90 per cent of respondents did not want silent films to be 'eliminated completely', for example, was offered as proof that 'public feeling at the present time certainly supports my frequent contention that the silent film is far from dead'. Less prominence, meanwhile, was given to the finding that 45 per cent of respondents stated a preference for talking over silent films and 62 per cent said that their interest in talkies was increasing.[44] A more general editorial bias was apparent, too. New talking stars such as Al Jolson, for example, rarely received the coverage given to silent stars.

The magazines' letters pages offer a wider range of views, but the editorial influence must be taken into account here as well. Both *Picturegoer* and *Film Weekly* offered cash prizes for letters to the editor, thus setting a financial incentive for readers to appeal to the editors' sensibilities. In May 1929, *Picturegoer* specifically asked for 'your views on the talkies, or the "squawkies" as some people unkindly call them', and in the following month a first prize of two guineas and a second prize of one guinea for the 'best letters' was introduced.[45] A plethora of letters about the talkies ensued. In this first wave of responses, there were two dominant strands of thought. One echoed the opinion voiced in intellectual journals such as *Close Up*; that cinema was primarily a visual medium and the talkies' emphasis on dialogue undermined the medium's artistic dimension. Or, as one prize-winning letter put it:

> The great appeal of the screen is that it presents motion pictures with a capital 'M'. The action of a talking picture is slowed down to allow the actors time to talk, and in consequence the story drags until there is little motion left ... Give me the silent drama, with soft orchestral music, and no talking.[46]

The other strand was wholly preoccupied with the vocal qualities of established stars. Richard Barthelmess and Pauline Frederick were among those silent stars whose voices were deemed unsuitable by some fans.[47] Responses to Mary Pickford's voice, meanwhile, were similar to the reactions James Agate and C.A. Lejeune had to hearing May McAvoy for the first time. Pickford, like McAvoy, was a petite star, and by 1929 she had been playing naive, juvenile roles for nearly 20 years. Fans expected her to have 'a sweet voice like a bell', as one letter explained, and so it could only be an unfortunate surprise to hear a voice that was 'something like a fog-horn'.[48]

These letters suggest that audiences had grown accustomed to imagining the voices of silent film stars and attributing them with any vocal qualities that they found appealing. The arrival of the talkies took away this imaginative dimension and replaced it with voices that – initially at least – British audiences found alienating. The silent era's conception of nationality as a matter of masquerade was swept away, and many Hollywood films and stars were suddenly and unmistakably American. Thus, comments about American accents abounded on the letters pages and, in this first wave of responses, they were overwhelmingly negative:

> To sit and hear a voice which sounds as though its owner has very bad catarrh or some nasal defect is hardly my idea of an afternoon's enjoyment.[49]

> Oh that American twang! All very well for a comedian, but most irritating in a hero or heroine.[50]

If only these American artists would take a course in elocution … I think the raucous American accent is dreadful.[51]

The reaction against American accents was often coupled with a distaste for the noisiness of the earliest talkies and a sense that dialogue had taken films out of an ethereal, highly stylized realm and placed them instead in more ordinary, modern and urban settings. Musicals such as *The Singing Fool* and *The Broadway Melody* are set in New York City, and they portray brash and noisy vigour as intrinsic qualities of big city life. (*The Broadway Melody* was exuberantly advertised as '100% All Talking! All Singing! All Dancing!') For some silent film fans, who may have preferred an orchestra to jazz and a Ruritanian setting over Forty-Second Street, it was all too noisy. Two letters in *Film Weekly* made the case against the brash new settings and sounds of Hollywood:

American talkies up to the present have only been rather thin musical comedies … [with] a plentiful supply of lewd wisecracks, suggestive scenes and sloppy, unnatural sentiment … Picturegoers are getting tired of hearing Americans bawling, nasally and incoherently, from the screen.[52]

A couple of shrill-voiced common chorus girls, a hundred or so damsels garbed in beads, a sickly theme song, a lot of incomprehensible back-chat and slabs of penny novelette sentiment, that's all the 'great' American talkie has achieved so far … We have had no beauty of scene or atmosphere – no beauty of characterisation.[53]

Both *The Singing Fool* and *The Broadway Melody* had their defenders, but praise in their direction was most often aimed at the performances of individual stars (notably Al Jolson and Bessie Love) rather than the films as a whole.[54]

In the second wave of responses to the talkies, hostility towards American accents continued, but the talkies were no longer dismissed altogether. Rather, it was now assumed that British cinema would benefit from the talkies, because audiences were bound to reject American accents in favour of British (and more specifically English) accents. Alfred Hitchcock's *Blackmail* was pivotal to this transformation. *Blackmail* went into production as a silent feature, but in April 1929, as *The Singing Fool* was breaking box office records throughout the country, Hitchcock and his studio (British International Pictures) decided to make a parallel version of the film that would have some dialogue sequences. The talking version was completed and rushed to a trade show by 21 June 1929, whereupon critics and filmmakers alike gave it a rapturous reception.[55] The claim on the film's poster – that this was 'the first full-length all-talkie made in Great Britain' – was not true (Figure 6). It was not quite the first and it was not 'all-talking', but *Blackmail* suited the mood of the moment so perfectly that no one seemed to notice or care about these fabrications.[56]

Hitchcock made a film that challenged objections to the talkies from a range of different perspectives. For the more intellectual

Figure 6   The poster for *Blackmail* implored audiences to 'see and hear it – our mother tongue as it should be spoken!'

critics, it was unimportant whether or not the film was 'all-talk-ing'; they appreciated the expressionist imagery and symbolism deployed in this visually stunning film. Furthermore, they admired Hitchcock's insistence that sound (and even talking) should be used imaginatively and not just to reproduce dialogue. The now-famous sequence in which the word 'knife' is repeated in a distorted and exaggerated manner on the soundtrack, as a means of conveying the heroine's disturbed mental state, was heralded in 1929 by the editor of *Close Up* as nothing less than a 'cinematic' use of sound. This was high praise indeed from this rarefied journal.[57] It was important to a wider array of critics that Hitchcock filled *Blackmail* with images of London, many of them shot on location in the city centre. The film begins, for example, with scenes of Scotland Yard's 'flying squad' racing through the streets of London, and it ends with another police chase through the British Museum. These scenes, and the sight of other London landmarks, gave the film an authenticity that was highly prized after the inaccuracies of *The Terror*. Scotland Yard, in Hitchcock's hands, was depicted with a documentary-style inter-est in procedure, setting and detail. Most importantly, for those who longed for an alternative to American voices, Hitchcock took great care to ensure that *Blackmail* featured English accents with clear, concise diction and tones.[58] This was no small task. When the film was put into production as a silent, the Czech actress Anny Ondra played the central role of Alice. Ondra's heavily-accented voice was obviously unsuitable for the dialogue scenes but, rather than re-making the entire film, it was decided that Ondra would silently mouth her lines of dialogue while the well-spoken English actress Joan Barry actually voiced them. In these early days before dubbing, when all sound was recorded live, this meant that Barry had to stand just out of view of the camera and synchronize her speech to Ondra's lip movements.

The painstaking ventriloquism was crucial to the film's accept-ance by the critics. Although Barry's accent is too middle class for a Cockney newsagent's daughter, neither this nor the 'doubling' of the voices troubled viewers in 1929. The more important fact, at this juncture, was that the voices heard in *Blackmail* had authenti-cally English accents and fine diction. This was crucial to the mar-keting of the film, too. Posters and advertisements for *Blackmail* exhorted audiences to 'see and hear our mother tongue as it should be spoken'. Critics wholeheartedly agreed. 'After the nasal voices imported from America', the critic for the *Daily Chronicle* averred, 'the English voices in *Blackmail* are like music.'[59] The *Daily Mirror* declared that it was 'a treat to hear the dear old Cockney accent and a few typically English "cheerios" and "rightos" instead of Bowery Slang', and even the *Newcastle Chronicle* overcame any regional bias about accents to approve of 'good English voices that do not sound like fog-horns'.[60] The majority of critics had no hesitation in declaring that the film was 'superior to many of America's best' (*Kinematograph Weekly*), 'ahead of any American rival' (*Morning Post*), 'far better than any Hollywood talkie' (*Evening Standard*) and many thought that it was the harbinger of good times to come for the British film industry.[61] The critic for the *Sunday Dispatch* summed up the enthusiasm in declaring, 'I assert that Britain's film chance is now. Alfred Hitchcock has proved it.'[62]

The fan magazines quickly dropped their support for silent films and fell into line with this new position on the talkies. According to *Picturegoer*, *Blackmail* was the first dialogue film not to deserve the label of 'shoutie' and it had 'thrown down the gauntlet' to Hollywood.[63] *Film Weekly* posed the question, 'are the talkies the birth or the death of British films?', and then cited the success of *Blackmail* as reason to hope that British films would thrive. 'Britain has at last received the chance to make her films and players world famous,' the editor declared. An accompanying cartoon predicted that British films would now be welcomed everywhere in the world except the United States: the drawing shows Uncle Sam hanging his head in humiliation at Britain's triumph.[64] Throughout the autumn of 1929, as *Blackmail* went on general release, the majority of letters printed in the fan magazines concurred with this new thinking. A letter to *Picturegoer*, for example, predicted that 'grumbling' about the talkies would soon cease:

> If one can judge this superb film [*Blackmail*] as an indication of what may be expected from British studios, then the talkies have come to stay ... Every word could be heard, since they were spoken in the proper King's English ... [W]ith British talkies we shall not regret the passing of the silent film.[65]

Another letter urged readers to see *Blackmail* as part of a 'buy British' campaign at cinemas. Not everyone agreed, but the patriotism stirred by the film meant that dissent was expressed carefully. One *Picturegoer* reader in Sheffield confessed 'with a sense of guilt' that she preferred *The Broadway Melody* over *Blackmail*; while a reader in Bournemouth agreed with just about everyone else in saying 'the accents ... were beautiful', but she reluctantly admitted that 'I did not like the film itself'.[66] Some fans and critics were also uncomfortable with the idea that a thriller – and one based around the sordid scenario of a rape, a stabbing and a blackmail attempt – should serve as Britain's ambassador abroad. The editor of *Picturegoer* regretted that 'there is no heroism' in the film.[67] A hostile review in the *Glasgow Herald* complained that this first British talkie was nothing more than the story of a 'silly little shop girl'.[68] And six weeks after his first review, G.A. Atkinson reflected on this issue as well, and came to the conclusion that the film was unsuitable because its 'sordid' and 'repellent' story would not 'improve any foreigner's opinion of England'.[69] Thus, even at a time of a heightened and defensive awareness of film nationalism, it was difficult to find any one film that represented the nation for all interested parties.

The third wave of responses to the arrival of the talkies demonstrated that British accents could be more divisive and alienating than American accents. *Blackmail* had benefited from its arrival in 1929, when many audiences were pleased to hear any British accent. By the end of 1930, however, nearly two-thirds of the country's cinemas were wired for sound and the number of British-made talkies was rising steeply.[70] It was at this point, as talkies became routine, that audiences grew increasingly impatient with the limited range of accents that they heard in British films. The editor of *Picturegoer* identified the problem as West End 'stage accents':

> In several British talkies of late I have been annoyed to hear 'stage accents'. You know the sort of thing: 'Listen, deah, I'm feahfully sorry' – 'Fawncy that' – 'How demnable', etc. Both male and female players are equally guilty of using this mincing English ... Even American nasal sounds are preferable to these terribly 'refaned' accents that masquerade as English. Dialogue should be uttered with vigour; it is not necessary to try and convince your listeners that you were at a public school.[71]

The problem for audiences, however, was not so much the link to the stage, but the fact that a southern, English, well-educated and upper-middle-class manner of speaking had become the standard for British films. Other accents were either under-represented or treated as deviations from the norm. As the decade progressed, working-class and regional accents were increasingly heard in supporting roles or in low budget films based around musical hall performers such as Gracie Fields, George Formby and Will Hay, and in both contexts they were often treated as comical. Audiences did not necessarily reject the films made by these performers; they were, in fact, quite popular. However, as John Ellis has argued, they disliked the ranking of accents that was established across films, in which the southern, middle-class accent could 'speak facts and emotions' and 'anything serious or important', but the accents of other regions and classes conveyed 'a limited understanding'.[72] This ranking mirrored existing cultural hierarchies – effectively bringing them into the cinema and placing them on the screen – and audiences resented it.

On the letters pages of *Picturegoer* and *Film Weekly*, readers from Scotland, Wales, the north of England and the East End of London began to use the word 'refined' as a term of abuse, spelling it (phonetically) as 'refaned' and 'refeened' to ensure that it was not mistaken as a term of admiration. A letter from a woman in Bethnal Green (in the East End of London) complained to *Picturegoer* that:

> ... practically all of our actresses deserve to be kicked out ... Even when their expressions are good one immediately loses one's sense of being carried away by the plot on hearing those ultra-refaned, grating tones. It is because most of our so-called actresses are pin-money girls. I am sure if the directors were to look among the genuine working classes they would find living, vital creatures, in short, real people ...[73]

A letter from Cleveland in Yorkshire similarly observed:

> All the films the British studios seem to make concern society people and their troubles; divorces and the life of the higher class ... Movie fans would much rather see someone like themselves than society dolls floating around in evening dress and drinking cocktails.[74]

Letters from Scotland were also outspoken and routinely hostile to British films. A man in Angus offered the following advice to filmmakers:

> The sooner British producers realise that the artificiality of speech is likely to hamper their dreams of a world market, the better for all concerned. The fault lies mainly with certain actresses recruited from the stage whose 'too – too – frightfully propah' accent (and lack of naturalness) is enough to damage the success outside England of any British film. There is English and English![75]

A woman from Glasgow made similar points more forcefully:

> Everytime I come away from a British film I say to myself, 'If that's what England is like, thank god I don't live in it'. Judged by these films, England is still in the feudal age … I have yet to see a hero who does not have at least a butler, valet and chauffeur to help him through life. When the producer does condescend to introduce 'lower orders' they are shown as illiterate, ape-like beings. Is it any wonder that the ordinary, hard-working citizen gives the 'refaned' films a wide berth and plumps for the more democratic American products? Wake up, British films. Open the drawing room windows and let in the sounds of the streets.[76]

Another letter, from Edinburgh, made it clear that it was not simply middle-class accents or settings that offended. The less refined Cockney accent could also be objectionable from a Scottish perspective:

> … it is high time British producers dealt in a sensible fashion with the speech of Cockney characters that are so prevalent in British films. It is even worse than the 'Oxford' accent, for whilst the latter is at least understandable, the Cockney dialect is baffling. No one objects to minor characters being Cockney, but surely the folly of making a film where the complete cast is made up of Cockneys is obvious to everyone.[77]

The common thread in these complaints is demonstrated most clearly in one last example. A *Film Weekly* reader in Wales offered that in his opinion, 'the best English is spoken in Cardiff'.[78]

Everyone, it seems, considered their own accent to be the most natural and unobtrusive way of speaking. Furthermore, at a time when British films were extolled on the basis of their nationality – that is, on the basis that they represented the nation's culture – audiences expected to see (and hear) their own way of life represented in them. Anything less provoked regional and class resentments.

Picturegoer and *Film Weekly* portrayed the problem as a lack of 'pep' and 'vigour', qualities that they attributed to voices (or found lacking in them), and linked this with other problems that the magazines and their readers identified in British films.[79] Complaints about the slow pace of British films, the emphasis on dialogue rather than action, the limited production values and the 'refined' actors were thus conflated into a single issue, the influence of West End theatre on British films. This explained why British cinema had a middle-class outlook, why actors seemed to lack the vigour of their Hollywood counterparts and why the dominant visual aesthetic appeared stage bound and unimaginative. It was a selective and simplistic explanation, but it stuck, and readers were ready and willing to join in the complaints.

The concept of a truly popular 'national cinema' for Britain thus became fraught with issues of class and regional identity. An article in Glasgow's *Evening Times* in 1932 summarized the complaints made by a local cinema manager about British films:

> As far as Scotland is concerned, there is no disputing the fact that British 'talkie' pictures have been a 'flop'. Many of his regular patrons stayed away if they saw that a British film was showing, while others took out their frustrations on the cinema itself. 'When we show bad British pictures', the manager revealed, 'the cheap-seat element produce a knife or razor and cut up the seats'.[80]

This is, of course, an extreme example, but throughout the 1930s various reports indicated that British films were appreciated most in the southeast of England and by middle-class audiences. In 1937, the London-based journal *World Film News* surveyed cinema managers throughout the country and found that those catering to middle-class audiences were 'generally satisfied' with British films; the films of Alfred Hitchcock and those with stars such as

Jessie Matthews and Anna Neagle were singled out as particularly appealing. However, the same survey found that exhibitors with working-class patrons found 'the majority of British films ... unsuitable for their audiences' and complained that they were too heavy with dialogue and lacking in pace and action. The issue here was not necessarily a preference for American accents, but a preference for 'films with tempo and action, stirring in their appeal, simple and straightforward in their treatment, and related to the lives of the people'.[81] The issue of accents, though, served as a shorthand for dissatisfaction with British cinema. Again, the most striking examples came from the East End of London and from Scotland. In the East End, one manager reported that 'they won't stand British pictures here at any price' and attributed this to their refined accents and slow pace.[82] In Scotland, a manager pointed out that British films actually should be called 'English films'; they seemed 'more foreign to his audience than the products of Hollywood, 6000 miles away'.[83] *World Film News* placed the blame squarely at the feet of British filmmakers; one article referred to Alexander Korda's London Films, and complained that filmmakers 'think in spectacles and history, but cast in Mayfair and forget [the audience in] Liverpool'.[84]

In the following year, Mass Observation's study of 'Cinemagoing in Worktown' asked cinema-goers in Bolton, Lancashire, 'which are best, American or British films, or are they both the same?' As we have seen (in Chapter 1), American films were preferred by nearly two-thirds of the respondents. In each of the three cinemas surveyed, a dislike of British films was expressed primarily in relation to accents. In this northern and industrial city, southern accents sounded 'mincing', 'effeminate' and 'soft', but here 'Oxford' was used as the marker of pretension rather the word 'refined' ('cut out the Oxford accent and speak more King's English', a 16-year-old girl at Bolton's Odeon instructed).[85] Remarkably, though, in the same survey there were also many complaints about American 'twang' and American slang. Older patrons and patrons at the upmarket Odeon in particular objected to the 'nasal drawl' and 'Yankee slang' heard in Hollywood films.[86] Eight years into the 'talkie' era, the issue of accents and language still provoked strong feelings among cinema-goers.

Nevertheless, the British fan magazines were able to identify two types of speaking voice that worked well with a broad swathe of audiences, and both were associated with Hollywood. The first was the hardest to pin down because it involved vocal personality rather than a particular, idealized accent. The voices of Greta Garbo and Gary Cooper, for example, reportedly won the favour of fans because Garbo's 'growl' and Cooper's 'drawl' expressed the stars' own personalities.[87] They fit with fans' expectations and so enhanced the stars' screen presence and impact. The other appealing speaking voice was defined as 'pure English'. It was attributed to both male and female stars. Among the women, it was the Canadian-born Norma Shearer and the Americans Ruth Chatterton and Ann Harding, who were said to speak 'pure English'. Interestingly, none was British and yet all played ladies of some grace and dignity; there was little or no 'twang' in their voices. Meanwhile, it is apparent that there was something alienating about British women's voices, although whether this was a cultural bias against women as actors or a vagary of the recording process remains unclear. By contrast, among the men, it was a trio of English-born actors – Ronald Colman, George Arliss and Clive Brook – who were considered to have the most appealing voices, and each was known for playing gentlemen.[88] Thus, the most appealing male voices were well spoken, but it was crucial that all of these stars worked in Hollywood, where their accents had taken on a transatlantic quality that effectively removed specific regional and class connotations from them. They spoke with enough polish to inspire admiration, but with an accent so indistinct as to avoid raising specific resentments. This meant that they had no exact, locatable place in the established social hierarchy of accents. Hence, their voices were often referred to as 'unaccented' and never attributed with 'refined', 'Oxford' or 'old school tie' qualities.

Ronald Colman and transatlanticism

Ronald Colman mined the transatlantic seam with the greatest and most significant success. His acting career began on the stage and, although he attempted to break into films, he found few opportunities in Britain.[89] He went to Hollywood in 1920, and by the middle of the decade he had emerged as a popular leading man. In the silent era, he was known for his dashing and rather swarthy good looks, and he was more likely to play a Latin lover than an Englishman.

His best known silent roles cast him alongside the Hungarian-born Vilma Banky in European costume melodramas such as *The Night of Love* (1927), *The Magic Flame* (1927/28) and *Two Lovers* (1928). Like many other established silent stars, Colman was reluctant to make his talking debut. He could not count on his accent being appealing or even acceptable; an English accent could easily convey too much 'class and culture' for middle-American tastes. Moreover, it would define him more narrowly than silent films ever had. Certainly, there would be less scope for him to play Latin lovers. Yet when he finally made his talking debut in *Bulldog Drummond* (1929), the film proved to be a watershed for both Colman and Hollywood. Samuel Goldwyn's adaptation of H.C. McNeile's popular detective story demonstrated that Hollywood could film British stories in a manner that would have wide appeal in both Britain and the United States. This was a welcome development – for Hollywood at least – after the recent misfire of *The Terror*.

Bulldog Drummond was an immediate hit when it was released in New York City in May 1929 and its success extended throughout the USA.[90] As Donald Crafton has commented, the film demonstrated that Colman had what was widely regarded as 'the best voice for the talkies'. It was a 'hybrid voice' rather than one that could be precisely located; one combining 'a British accent (but not too strong), clear enunciation, unstilted delivery, a distinctive voice, and a "natural" demeanour suited to the roles he played'.[91] In Britain, Colman's talking debut was eagerly awaited.[92] However, when *Bulldog Drummond* arrived in London in June 1929, many critics were still eager to cast aspersions on any Hollywood talkie, and so they noted that Colman's accent was as much American as English.[93] In the *Sunday Times*, for example, Sydney Carroll stated that 'Ronald Colman plays the title role like a full-blooded Yank'. With *The Terror* in mind, he labelled the film as evidence that 'the Americanization of English popular drama through the talkies continues'.[94] Audiences, however, did not appear to mind at all. The film played for no fewer than 21 weeks at its premiere engagement, at London's Tivoli cinema, a plush venue with over 1,500 seats.[95] Letters to *Picturegoer* confirmed the film's appeal. 'How much more delightful is Ronald Colman when one can hear as well as see him,' one observed; and another, emphasizing that 'I am *very* English', declared that *Bulldog Drummond* was 'the best talkie I have ever heard' and that 'Ronald Colman's voice is excellent'.[96] In fact, there were no complaints in the fan magazines at all, about either the star or the film, and in 1929 that was a significant achievement for a Hollywood talkie.

Bulldog Drummond knowingly satirizes the British disdain for the talkies. The first scene is set in London at the grand and formal 'Senior Conservative Club', an archetypally stuffy and smoky gentleman's club, and the camera lingers on a sign on its front door demanding 'Silence!' Inside, the club is filled with well-dressed men reading newspapers in absolute, deadly silence. When a slow-moving, elderly waiter drops a single spoon on the floor, one member angrily splutters, 'The eternal din in this club is an outrage!' Colman then appears and wryly responds with his first-ever on-screen line, 'I wish someone would throw a bomb to wake the place up'. Walking out of the room with a defiantly casual manner – with his hands in his pockets and whistling loudly as he goes – he thereby distinguishes himself from the rigid, humourless snobs of this gentleman's club. The scene can be taken as Hollywood's reply to British critics of the talkies: only stuffed shirts could object to a little sound. More importantly for Colman, the scene at once identifies him as a new breed of English gentleman; one who is free from pomposity and snobbery. His vocal intonation is warm rather than haughty, the cadence of his speech is laconic rather than clipped and his demeanour is relaxed rather than formal. The scenes that follow reinforce the idea that his character is no ordinary gentleman, but longs to break free of the refined Conservative Club. 'Romance, thrills and adventure' are what he wants, and his quest leads him to an everyday roadhouse, where he proves more than capable of defending himself in rough company. Hence, the film's advertising (Figure 7) could promise not only that *Bulldog Drummond* is 'a 100% talking drama', but also that it is 'packed with thrills' and that its hero is 'fiction's most reckless adventurer'.[97]

Like other debonair men-of-action who followed in his footsteps – Robert Montgomery, Robert Donat and William Powell to name but three – Colman moves through all sections of society with confident ease. He could handle himself in both Mayfair and Liverpool. In the ending, he not only defeats a sinister group

Figure 7   The British pressbook for *Bulldog Drummond* has a selection of advertisements that promote Ronald Colman's character as a gentleman hero who is also a 'reckless adventurer'

of foreign criminals but also saves the damsel-in-distress. All of this is achieved with a casual, suave manner that marked him as a new kind of hero. He was demonstrably masculine and tough, but also appealingly smooth, urbane and wry. His attitude was more tongue-in-cheek than stiff upper lip, and that gave him an appeal that extended beyond the middle classes. For Colman, the new persona enabled a remarkably extended career. The findings of the Bernstein Questionnaires (named after Sidney Bernstein and conducted in the chain of Granada cinemas that he owned) are among the few sources of information revealing the popularity of specific stars in this period. It was not a national survey and it was conducted irregularly (in 1927, 1928, 1932, 1934, 1937 and 1946–7), but the 1928 survey and the 1932 survey place Colman at number one as the country's most popular male star. He was the only major star to make the transition from silent to sound films without losing ground. In the subsequent surveys, conducted in 1934 and 1937, he maintained a place among the top ten male stars despite the fact that by the latter point he was 46 years old.[98]

Throughout the 1930s Colman continued to play in Hollywood films, and in his most popular roles he continued to play the English gentleman who was also eager to step outside the narrow confines of upper-class manners and conventions. He was the 'gentleman thief' of *Raffles* (1930), the civil servant-turned-soldier of *Clive of India* (1935), a cynical barrister who sacrifices himself for love in *A Tale of Two Cities* (1935/36), an Englishman abroad who impersonates a king in *The Prisoner of Zenda* (1937) and a prominent statesman who prefers the mythical kingdom of Shangri-La to the modern world in *Lost Horizon* (1937). Although it is located somewhere high in the Himalayas, Shangri-La closely resembles the utopian images of Hollywood that were so regularly seen in the pages of British fan magazines; it is a paradise of wealth, classlessness, sunshine and perpetual youth. Fuelled by this fantasy, *Lost Horizon* was the top box office film of 1937 in Britain.[99] Shangri-La was an appropriate home for one as transnational as Colman. He typified mainstream, popular film tastes in the 1930s and his films stand as prime examples of Hollywood's ability to film British stories in a manner that appealed far and wide. If the talkies had given a voice only to the likes of Ronald Colman, there would have been few objections to them.

The triumph of the talkies

Audiences became accustomed to the talkies within a relatively short space of time. In late 1928, responses to the Bernstein

Questionnaire found that less than half of those surveyed 'welcomed' the arrival of the talkies.[100] Yet just four years later, in the 1932 survey, the majority of audiences stated that they no longer wanted to see silent films at all; indeed, less than half would 'tolerate' seeing a silent film 'occasionally'.[101] By the time of the next survey, in 1934, the issue of silent versus talking films was not even raised. The talkies may not have led to a boom in cinema admissions, but within a few years they did become the unquestioned norm for the majority of cinema-goers. The effect on film tastes was less clear-cut, at least as far as nationality was concerned. In 1929, the pertinent question was, 'are the talkies the birth or the death of British films?' As we have seen, however, many audiences soon reconciled themselves to hearing American accents in the cinema and, after a period of some initial good will, British 'talkies' provoked considerable grumbling and resentment. For a moment at least, hopes for British cinema faded and the regrettable qualities of domestically made films were well rehearsed in the fan magazines and elsewhere. However, it is all too easy to generalize about the problems surrounding British cinema and to allow the grumbling and complaints to obscure the progress that was made in this period.

Arguably, British cinema benefited from the arrival of the talkies more than Hollywood did. British films were both more numerous and more popular in the 1930s than they had been in the 1920s. Furthermore, the genres that proved most popular – the comedy and the musical – flourished precisely because of the coming of sound. The talkies enabled British producers to turn to long-established entertainment forms, including the music and comedy of variety and the music hall. Many of the most popular British stars of the 1930s – including Tom Walls, Ralph Lynn, Jack Hulbert, Jack Buchanan, Jessie Matthews and the aforementioned Fields, Formby and Hay – entered into filmmaking as a result. As David Sutton has argued, these performers brought 'pre-cinematic modes of popular entertainment' to the screen; their films were 'essentially British' and far beyond the scope of Hollywood.[102] It was in this manner that a truly popular and indigenous cinema developed in Britain. By comparison, the high-profile productions of London Films, such as the landmark *The Private Life of Henry the Eighth* (1933), were both fewer in number and less consistently successful. Within

Britain, the smaller scale, less celebrated comedies and musicals proved to be the more sustained competition to Hollywood.

If this achievement was not celebrated at the time, it is because the rise of British cinema did not occur in the form or on the scale that was anticipated. The film nationalists had decidedly middle-class tastes and they were disappointed that so much of the new British cinema rose from the lowly cultural forms of music hall and variety. Their hopes were for a national cinema that was aesthetically superior to Hollywood, and not for one that seemingly imitated its model of popular stars and familiar genres.[103] The scale of British cinema's success was also disappointing to them. It was limited by the relatively narrow demographic appeal of, on the one hand, music hall and variety and, on the other hand, the West End theatre. Put bluntly, these pre-cinematic forms of entertainment did not travel well. Their 'essentially British' qualities meant that they had little export value. They were certainly unlikely to fulfil the *Film Weekly* cartoonist's fantasy of British films that would humble Hollywood in countries around the world. Another limitation was that they did not always travel well within Britain. A performer such as Gracie Fields, who brought to the screen the music, humour, accent and mannerisms of the northern, working-class music hall, found a far greater audience in her native Lancashire than in London or Brighton.[104] Conversely, films adapted from West End stage plays, such as the 'Aldwych farces' that starred Tom Walls and Ralph Lynn, were unlikely to have a strong appeal outside the realm of the English middle classes. Scotland and Wales, of course, were ill-served by all manner of British films; the notion of 'essentially British' should actually be 'essentially English'.

In the short term, audiences flocked to see Hollywood's early, blockbuster musicals such as *The Singing Fool* and *The Broadway Melody*. They were also eager to see films in which prominent stars made their talking debuts, but these were accepted on a film-by-film basis and, while talking undoubtedly enhanced the intensity of the best star performances, the judgements could also be harsh. Over the longer term, it is apparent that Hollywood lost market share. In 1926, British films had constituted only 5 per cent of all releases but by 1932 the figure had risen to 24 per cent.[105] The latter figure was above the level required by the 'quota' regulations, and therefore demonstrates that audiences had a genuine taste for British films. Henceforth, Hollywood sustained its market share at or around this level by adapting to the demands of British audiences. Disasters on the scale of *The Terror* were few and far between, and the carefully balanced transatlanticism of *Bulldog Drummond* served as a template for many years to come. Furthermore, as British films became more numerous, Hollywood films were able to serve as a culturally neutral cinematic space. British audiences found in them an alternative social landscape that was once removed from recognizable signifiers of class and regional identity. The speaking voice, which serves such a significant role in maintaining social and geographic boundaries, was a key factor in this. American accents were not always admired, but they were at least outside the hierarchies of British culture. Hollywood films were therefore more likely to offer a release – however temporary – from the specific realities of everyday life. The fact that the gentlemanly Ronald Colman, Clive Brook and George Arliss were the most popular male stars of the early talkie period indicates that British audiences did not want to stray far from their familiar cultural landscape. Yet their popularity also indicates that a small step beyond the immediately recognizable, the familiar and the everyday was a crucial one.

4 'Nothing Ever Happens in England': Keeping the Gangsters at Bay

My very expert and experienced advisers at the Home Office are of the opinion that on the whole the cinema conduces more to the prevention of crime than to its commission. It keeps the boys out of mischief; it gives them something to think about. ...In general, the Home Office opinion is that if the cinemas had never existed there would probably be more crime than there is rather than less.

Sir Herbert Samuel, Home Secretary, speaking in the House of Commons (1932)[1]

A fellow of an Oxford college no longer feels an embarrassed explanation to be necessary when he is recognised leaving a cinema. A growing number of cultivated and unaffected people enjoy going to the pictures, and frequent not merely the performances of intellectual film societies but also the local picturehouse, to see, for example, Marlene Dietrich ... The cinema is acquiring prestige.

Commission on Educational and Cultural Films,
The Film in National Life (1932)[2]

I go to the cinema for any number of reasons....I go to be distracted (or 'taken out of myself'); I go when I don't want to think; I go when I do want to think and need stimulus; I go to see pretty people; I go when I want to see life ginned up, charged with unlikely energy; I go to laugh; I go to be harrowed; I go when a day has been such a mess of detail that I am glad to see even the most arbitrary, the most preposterous, pattern emerge; I go because I like bright light, abrupt shadow, speed; I go to see America, France, Russia; I go because I like wisecracks and slick behaviour; I go because the screen is an oblong opening into the world of fantasy for me; I go because I like story, with its suspense; I go because I like sitting in a packed crowd in the dark, among hundreds riveted on the same thing; I go to have my most general feelings played on.

Elizabeth Bowen, 'Why I Go to the Cinema' (1938)[3]

The cinema's enthusiasts and admirers were more much more prominent in the 1930s than they had been in the previous decade. There were some important defenders of cinema-going, too. Sir Herbert Samuel's statement (quoted above) – that cinema-going was more likely to prevent juvenile delinquency than to cause it – was a particularly bold claim for a Home Secretary to make. It ran counter to pronouncements dating back almost as far as the medium itself, which blamed the cinema for any number of social ills and saw it as a particularly harmful influence on children. The most consistent and worrying accusation was that films glorified criminals, made heroes out of villains and taught the methods of crime to the young and impressionable. This notion was so widely perceived to be true that some magistrates were known to be lenient with young offenders who claimed their misdeeds had been inspired by the screen.[4] The Home Secretary was therefore breaking with a long tradition and a convenient one. Blaming crime films for juvenile delinquency had long served to distract attention from more complicated causes.

The improved public standing of films and cinema-going stemmed in part from the success of the Films Act of 1927. The increasing number of British films made and shown to appreciative audiences meant that the medium could no longer be regarded as utterly and thoroughly foreign. The talkies also raised the status of cinema. After the initial alarm over voices and accents had passed, films came to be seen as a more literary medium and therefore a more respectable one (especially for the middle classes). The Commission on Educational and Cultural Films (quoted above) recognized that films were a part of the 'national life' – so much so that even 'a fellow of an Oxford college' no longer felt embarrassed to be found at the cinema – and therefore called for better use to be made of the medium in education. The attitude of the newspapers changed, too. By 1930, film criticism was a prominent part of virtually every major newspaper, and sympathetic critics, following the lead of pioneers such as Iris Barry and C.A. Lejeune, replaced the haughty critics of the previous decade. G.A. Atkinson, for example, left his post at the *Daily Express* for the much smaller readership of the *Methodist Times*. The fact that cinema was the focus of intellectual film societies and journals (*Close Up*, 1927–33; *Cinema Quarterly*, 1932–5; and *World Film News*, 1936–8), also gave the medium an air of distinction. In the wake of Iris Barry's groundbreaking *Let's Go to the Pictures* (1926) there was an outpouring of books on the subject, ranging from the cultivated, lofty heights of Paul Rotha's *The Film Till Now* (1930) and Raymond Spottiswoode's *A Grammar of the Film* (1935) to the middle-brow ruminations of C.A. Lejeune's *Cinema* (1931) and Charles Davy's collection, *Footnotes to the Film* (1938). In the latter, Davy felt obliged to title his own chapter 'Are Films Worthwhile?', but the more significant chapter was surely Elizabeth Bowen's contribution (also quoted above). In 'Why I Go to the Cinema', the upper-middle-class novelist expressed her personal enthusiasm for cinema-going in unfettered terms.

For all the prestige that cinema had garnered, it had not completely broken free of its detractors. Alongside the enthusiasts and admirers of the 1930s there were also the anxious and the concerned. These were not critics, intellectuals or ordinary audience members, but the social authorities who represented civic, religious and educational organizations and institutions. Most were not against cinema-going or the medium of film *per se*. Rather, they thought that such a powerful and persuasive medium should not be left to the commercial imperatives of the film industry. Film, in their view, had enormous potential as an educational and uplifting force, and this could be used toward positive, pro-social ends if the medium was properly regulated and controlled.[5] In the 1930s, however, the most overt demonstration of the cinema's influence was the number of American words and expressions that had entered common daily usage in Britain since the arrival of the talkies. These tended to be short and snappy expressions – 'oh yeah', 'yep', 'OK', 'OK, chief!', 'it's all boloney', 'iz zat so?' and 'sez you' – and they appeared to offer demonstrable evidence of the Americanizing influence of films.[6] 'Sez you' was considered the most lamentable expression and it was often cited as the epitome of all that was disagreeable about Hollywood's talkies and their influence.[7] Just as 'refaned' had become a byword for the middle-class respectability of British cinema, 'sez you' became a form of shorthand for the slangy tone and streetwise ambiance of so many Hollywood films. This was partly because of its ungrammatical construction and imprecise pronunciation, but also because of the attitude that lay behind it. As a defiant retort to any authoritative command or statement, it seemed characteristically American in its informality and egalitarianism and, when it was used by British cinema-goers, it appeared that these values had triumphed over the more traditional British values of social deference and decorum.

The 1930s thus began as a decade of petitions, deputations, conferences and inquiries centred on the influence of films and, in some cases at least, on the perceived shortcomings of the British Board of Film Censors (BBFC). It was taken as self-evident that films were influential and that their influence was going from bad to worse. 'The tone of American films is deteriorating and it is likely to deteriorate still more,' a report for the General Assembly of the Church of Scotland warned in 1931.[8] In 1933, the Catholic Teachers' Federation complained in tandem of 'pictures which were calculated to injure the English of our children' and 'the influence of gangster and sex appeal films upon youth'.[9] In the same year, a joint conference of the Mothers Union, the National Council of Women, the National Federation of Women's Institutes and the Public Morality Council gathered to discuss the 'obvious' influence that the cinema had on youth.[10] Between 1930 and 1933 four city councils (Birkenhead, Birmingham, Edinburgh and London) embarked on major investigations into the effect cinema-going had on children.[11] In 1935 the Archbishop of Canterbury led a delegation of educators, church leaders and MPs to Downing Street to discuss the 'insidiously attractive qualities' of film and their 'potent influence on the public' with Prime Minister Stanley Baldwin.[12]

The talkies made the spectre of Americanization, and its direct link with Hollywood, seem more apparent than ever before, and its manifestations were noted up and down the country, and among adults as well as children. In 1937, the MP Reginald Sorensen (Labour, Leyton West) lamented the rise of American slang in the House of Commons, and used this as evidence of the need for a stronger films quota. He spoke not specifically about children but about 'the public' and 'those who attend cinemas in this country' when he urged fellow MPs to realize that the 'psychological influence' of films is 'comprehensive', and therefore 'more and more pictures of British life' were needed. 'The chief function of the cinema', he assumed, 'was to accomplish what I am sure will never be accomplished, or even attempted, in any other way – the annexation of this country by the United States of America.'[13] The concern for children therefore seems to have been only the tip of the iceberg, beneath which lay a much wider concern for the effects that films had on society as a whole, and on working-class adults in particular. This was seldom stated directly – a paternalistic concern for children was more defensible than an authoritarian desire to control the viewing habits of adults – but the distance between children and adults proved slippery, and comments on the ill effects of films often strayed into discussion of teenagers and adults. This is most apparent in the preoccupation with crime films as a cause of juvenile delinquency. In the 1930s, when high unemployment threatened social stability, juvenile delinquency was a major social concern, and the cinema was often held up as a poor influence on the young, teaching them the methods of crime and giving them criminal heroes to emulate.

Concerns about Hollywood's influence no longer applied to all or even most films. Few could object to the films of the gentlemanly Ronald Colman or the ladylike Norma Shearer, who, as we have seen, were consistently among the top stars of the decade. They represented a form of mainstream and genteel taste that was considered harmless. The problem lay at the margins, with *some* films and *some* audiences. The films were those that tested the boundaries of censorship; belonged to genres that portrayed a way of life deemed by some to be completely foreign; and featured stars who were considered objectionable by many cinema-goers but appealed to others. The problematic audiences were not the fellows of Oxford colleges or upper-middle-class novelists. They were not even the ordinary devotees of the 'picture palaces'. Rather, the concern was for the patrons of the cheaper 'flea-pit' cinemas, where children, the unemployed and the low-waged could wile away hours at a cost of just a few pennies. Here, genteel tastes did not predominate, and James Cagney was more likely to be on the bill than Ronald Colman. Above all, the problem lay with Hollywood's gangster films and their appeal to working-class audiences.

Little Caesar (1931), *Scarface* (1932) and many other tough films about life in America's modern cities startled British commentators, while Cagney's *The Public Enemy* (1931/32) was considered so disturbing that the BBFC held up its release for a full year, and then gave its approval only to a version that had been both renamed and heavily cut. Of course, many Americans considered gangster films to be objectionable too, as the Legion of Decency's protests against Hollywood films indicate. In Britain, however, concerns about the crime film took distinctive forms, and responses to them demonstrated differing opinions about Britain's readiness to resist or succumb to Americanization.

Censorship and social authority

In order to place the concerns over the cinema and Americanization into context, it is important to remember that radio – another mass medium that flourished in this period – had been placed entirely under the control of the BBC. From the 1920s, the BBC held a monopoly over domestic radio broadcasting in Britain and, under the leadership of the Director-General John Reith, the commercial imperative of 'giving the public what it wants' was considered less important than the paternalistic policy of 'giving it what it ought to have'.[14] Prescribing a preferred form of speaking was a key aspect of this. 'BBC English', as it soon became known, was associated with the upper- and upper-middle classes, and it became synonymous with the 'Oxford' accent that so many cinema-goers found unappealing. The rationale for 'BBC English' was that it would raise the standard of speech among the wider public: 'We are daily establishing in the minds of the public', announcers were told, 'the idea of what correct speech should be, and this is an important responsibility.'[15] There was another purpose. In an age of burgeoning media, in which the values of the many generally triumphed over those of the few, the BBC under Reith's leadership represented a rearguard action against the democratizing influences of mass culture. The American model of broadcasting, in which programmes were tailored to popular tastes and broadcasters had friendly personalities, was rejected. Instead, a lofty tone was established. BBC announcers were required to remain anonymous and to wear dinner jackets when broadcasting; anything else might breed familiarity.[16]

Programming was designed to raise rather than reflect audience tastes, and American programmes and music were largely kept at bay.[17] The Reithian philosophy held firm until the late 1930s, and although listeners were able to tune into 'pirate' radio stations (broadcast from ships) or to continental stations, the authoritative status and tone of the BBC made it clear that, on these shores at least, a culture of deference was maintained.[18]

Film was not so easily controlled. There was no single, visionary figure like the BBC's John Reith to govern the film industry, which, in any case, was not under monopoly control. Instead, the legal authority to censor films – either banning them or cutting particular scenes – rested (and still rests today) with local councils, which number in the hundreds. The BBFC had been created by the film industry as a means of streamlining the censorship process and simplifying the interaction between the filmmakers and the councils that might censor their products. Although it is not (and never has been) an official government body, and its income is drawn from the industry rather than the government, it has often seemed like a branch of the government. This is because, since the Board was formed in 1912, it has acted in consultation with the Home Secretary, and also because many of its leaders held government positions before taking up the reigns of censorship. T.P. O'Connor, president of the BBFC from 1916 to 1929, was a Liberal MP with a long record of service. His successor, Edward Shortt, who held the post from 1929 to 1935, had been Home Secretary in Lloyd George's coalition government. Lord Tyrrell, who held the post from 1935 to 1947, had been a Foreign Office official and a high-ranking diplomat prior to his appointment.[19] These figures lent an air of officialdom to the BBFC and, despite some notable exceptions, local councils were largely willing to follow its decisions: whether a film should be passed, whether cuts were necessary and whether it should receive a 'U' certificate (classifying it as suitable for audiences of all ages) or an 'A' certificate (classifying it as suitable for audiences over the age of 16 or younger persons if they are accompanied by an adult). The quasi-official status of the BBFC made it an easy target for the pressure groups that found censorship too lax, and from its very beginnings there were calls for stronger censorship and for a fully-fledged state censor. These calls were resisted, but the criticisms left the BBFC on its guard and always wary of the next controversy.

Under T.P. O'Connor's leadership, the BBFC made discreet attempts to address the issue of Americanization through films. One of the Board's most sweeping requests came in 1925, when it called for a ban on silent film intertitles that used 'terms and idioms that are not current in this country' as a means of protecting the 'beauty of our language'. Film distributors were instructed to re-write the intertitles of all foreign films, replacing foreign words, expressions or spellings with native ones. *Kinematograph Weekly* cast aside the polite euphemism of 'foreign' films and pointed directly to the American influence. The paper not only endorsed the BBFC's ban, but went further in arguing that Americans should not be allowed to write the intertitles for films screened in Britain.[20] The BBFC's concerns over the portrayal of crime were expressed less discreetly. Crime featured strongly in 'O'Connor's 43', a list of 43 prohibitions for filmmakers that was issued in 1917, and the prohibitions were enforced with a vigour that at times surprised the film industry.[21] One widely reported case involved a high-profile adaptation of Dickens' *Oliver Twist* (1922), produced in Hollywood by First National, which fell foul of the BBFC because of a scene in which Fagin (played by Lon Chaney) shows young Oliver (Jackie Coogan) how to pick pockets. This, the BBFC insisted, broke the prohibition against depicting 'the *modus operandi* of criminals'. Despite First National's protests – this was, after all, a well-known episode in a much-loved novel – the scene was cut for the British release.[22] In 1926, when the BBFC published a longer list of prohibitions, one of its seven sections was devoted entirely to crime, and 13 separate offences were listed.[23] The broadest of these were the already familiar 'methods of crime open to imitation', which stood alongside warnings against 'objectionable prison scenes', 'stories in which the criminal element is predominant' and stories in which 'sympathy is enlisted for the criminal'. These rules fitted well with the BBFC's middle-class values. The Board sought to maintain an image of the nation as deferential, law-abiding and staunchly moral. It enforced this by refusing to allow unfavourable depictions of British officials, institutions and professions; it rejected films that portrayed the police or other authorities as unjust or inept; it prevented all but the most innocuous representations of class or labour disputes; and it permitted crime films only if they focused on the detection of crime rather than criminal activities.[24]

O'Connor's successor, Edward Shortt, was no less vigilant. In fact, the number of feature films that were denied a certificate of release rose steeply during his term: whereas 37 films had been refused a certificate during O'Connor's last five years as president (1925–9), during Shortt's first five years (1930–4) no fewer than 106 films were refused.[25] This was not only a sign of Shortt's vigilance, but also a marker of the troublesome issues that arose during his presidency. There was an outcry over horror films and their supposed effects on children, which resulted in the introduction of an 'H' certificate in 1933. 'H' denoted the 'horrific' nature of films ranging from the eerie Danish film *Vampyr* (1932/3) to Universal Studios' campy *The Bride of Frankenstein* (1935).[26] The talkies also gave rise to new problems. With sound, it was more difficult to cut objectionable shots out of a film and maintain continuity on the sound track; as a result, talkies were more likely to be banned altogether. Another factor was that sound gave rise to greater opportunities for offence in the form of sound effects, wisecracks, double entendres and innuendo. As the film historian Sarah J. Smith has commented, with the talkies 'screen sex suddenly became more sexy and screen violence more violent'.[27] It is notable, too, that in this period Hollywood was in its so-called 'pre-Code' phase; a period that began with the establishment of the Hays Office Production Code in 1930 and ended in 1934, when protests by the Legion of Decency ensured that the Code was applied with more vigour. As Richard Maltby has argued, the idea that the Production Code was abandoned between 1930 and 1934 is more myth than reality.[28] Rather, the combination of the Wall Street crash and the ensuing economic crisis, together with the arrival of sound, created an environment for tough talking and streetwise films, with sound accentuating every outburst, gunshot and car horn. Stories of fallen women, cynical journalists, hard-bitten convicts and ruthless gangsters were told with a gusto that had little reverence for authority and considerable sympathy for the underdog. These were gritty films about modern and urban working-class lives, and they had few counterparts in British cinema.

At a time when the economy was in crisis and crime was perceived to be spiralling out of control, the gangster film was deemed
to be particularly troublesome. There is no doubt that the British
economy was in sharp decline: the unemployment rate reached
22 per cent in 1932 and, although there were wide regional varia-
tions, every region of the country suffered unemployment over
13 per cent.[29] Gauging the effect of the economic 'slump' on the crime
rate is a more complicated matter. The historian John Stevenson
has pointed out that there was 'no clear-cut parallel between unemployment and crime' in this period, and also that 'the worst years
of the inter-war depression ... appear not to have had a decisive
impact on total criminal activity'.[30] However, the fear of crime
was exacerbated by national and local newspaper coverage, which
gave the impression that Britain was 'in the grip of violent crime
of all kinds'.[31] Two kinds of criminal activity stood out as new and
alarming: organized crime and juvenile delinquency. Newspapers
portrayed the United States as an 'infinitely more violent and more
dangerous' country than Britain, as Andrew Davies has observed,
but they also sounded the alarm over the prospect of American-
style organized crime arriving in Britain. Glasgow was depicted as
the 'Scottish Chicago' in both Scottish and London-based newspapers, and the activities of its 'notorious gangs' were reported in bold
headlines.[32] Yet the parallels had little basis in fact. Prohibition had
made racketeering a tremendously lucrative business in the United
States. Without it, organized crime in Britain remained on a comparatively small scale, and confined mainly to racetracks and inner-
city protection rackets.[33] The weapons, too, were different. British
criminals tended to use the cosh, the knife or the razor; all potentially dangerous instruments, of course, but nowhere near so violent
and deadly as Chicago's weapon of choice, the machine gun.[34]

Juvenile delinquency was not new, but in the interwar years it
was on the rise, and much of this was attributable to an increase
in young men engaged in larceny and burglary. Furthermore, there
was a sense that criminals were not only younger, but also more callous, more disrespectful and more violent. Social commentators
focused on why crime had taken a turn for the worse. Was it the
brutalizing effect of the Great War? The economic downturn? The
opportunities that the motor car gave to criminals? Or was it that
the courts were too lenient?[35] Films provided a culprit that seemed

more obvious and direct. From the letters pages of *The Times* to the columns of the fan magazine *Picture Show*, the connection between crime films and real crime among juveniles was presented as a self-evident truth.[36] In this context, the Home Secretary's aforementioned 1932 statement, that cinema-going prevented crime and did not cause it, represented a brave (and lonely) stance against those eager to point the finger of blame at outside forces. In the House of Commons, the MP James Lovat-Fraser (National Labour, Lichfield) immediately disagreed with the Home Secretary and insisted that the gangster film was harmful to 'boys':

> They see burglaries, murders, and every kind of burglarious trick exhibited. The gangster is held up as a hero. The leader of the gangsters always scores, and he secures the sympathy of the boys. This influence steadily, year after year, exercised on an enormous number of unemployed, imperfectly educated boys, has undoubtedly affected the youth of this country very detrimentally.[37]

The statement offers an example of how slippery the distinction between adults and children could be when censorship was discussed: at first glance, the concern is for 'boys', yet a closer reading reveals that the 'boys' are already old enough to have been 'imperfectly educated' and to have become 'unemployed'. The reference to unemployment sheds light on the discomfort that these films posed. The combination of men and teenage boys left idle by unemployment, and films that threatened to awaken their aggression and channel it towards antisocial ends, was the real focus of concerns. Those who found no pleasure in gangster films assumed that there was nothing but harm in them; that their true purpose was to serve as a form of 'crime school'.[38]

The BBFC and British crime films

While the Home Secretary was willing to admit that films were not to blame for crime, the BBFC had to appear vigilant. Hence, when Edward Shortt addressed the Public Morality Council in 1933, he confirmed his audience's concerns about the influence of films and perhaps even added to them:

> [The cinema] is the greatest power for good or evil that we know in our country at present. I know of nothing to which loyal citizens should devote

> more wholehearted attention than to the proper regulation of this enter-
> tainment ... I do not think I am exaggerating when I say the real future of
> this country, the future of its people or their children and grandchildren,
> depends on the way we regulate the cinema today.[39]

In practice, however, the BBFC was not as prohibitive as Shortt's statement suggests. The Board was very strict with British films, but they were a minority of releases, and the standards applied to American films were looser and more liberal. For example, Warner Brothers attained an 'A' certificate for *The Crowd Roars* (1932), a racing track melodrama filled with exciting footage from the track and centred on a story (typical for its star, James Cagney) about a ruthless driver with a win-at-all-costs mentality. Yet when the British firm Hall Mark Films proposed a scenario entitled *Speed King*, it was flatly refused by the BBFC. This was not because *Speed King* borrowed heavily from the Hollywood film – it was essentially same story as *The Crowd Roars* but set at Wembley – but because 'there is a grave objection in this country to showing foul play taking place in English athletic and sporting events'. The BBFC went on to clarify that 'there would be no objection if the whole thing was staged in America', but a British setting for such 'foul play' was ruled out and the film was not made.[40]

The different standards were particularly pronounced in the crime genre. Many British crime films were made during the 1930s, but as the film historian Robert Murphy has observed, the 'whodunnit', with its 'bloodless and unemotional' stories, was the dominant type.[41] These films typically involved master detectives investigating ingenious and extraordinary crimes and they did not touch upon routine crimes, hooligans, slums and recognizable urban environments. Everyday crime, corruption and violence were left to Hollywood and to films set in the United States, and American social ills could not be seen to cross the Atlantic. An Edgar Wallace story entitled *When the Gangs Came to London*, depicting Chicago gangsters on the rampage in London and the inability of the Metropolitan Police to deal with them, was rejected when it was proposed as a film script in November 1932. The BBFC's response to the proposal stated its views plainly. Gangster films had only been given certificates because 'they were so obviously American':

In this country we do not allow our police to be shown on the screen as incompetent, or accepting bribes from criminals. We do not recognize 'Third Degree' methods, nor do we permit the suggestion that our police force would arrange for the murder of a criminal if they thought the evidence was too weak to secure a conviction. Wholesale machine gun murders in the streets of Chicago possibly are deemed to come under the head of 'topicals', but, in London, would be quite prohibitive. The idea of a junior American police officer being placed in actual, if not nominal, control of the whole of the Metropolitan Police is a situation that police authorities in this country would not allow to be shown on the screen. Nor would we allow a picture of a member of Parliament being murdered on the floor of the House.[42]

The boundaries between Britain and the USA must not become blurred, in other words, and British authorities and institutions must not be treated with the indignity that Hollywood inflicts upon American authorities and institutions. In subsequent years, further proposals for British crime films drew a similar response from the BBFC: *The Mail Bag Murder* (submitted in 1933) and a story entitled *Public Enemy* (submitted in 1935 and not related to the Warner Brothers film) were both declined on the grounds that they were set in Britain and yet treated crime in the manner of Hollywood gangster films.[43] Neither of these proposed British films was made.

The racketeering drama *Tiger Bay* (1934), featuring the Chinese-American star Anna May Wong as a hostess whose nightclub is targeted by racketeers, nearly met the same fate, but the producers agreed to change its setting from a London slum to a slum in an unnamed South American city. This made the film acceptable. Stories that took place 'amidst low and sordid surroundings' (as the BBFC described *Tiger Bay*) were permissible only if they were set far away, and not in Britain itself.[44] The BBFC held this line firmly for most of the decade. Hence, the censors refused to certify the low-budget, independently-made crime drama *The Green Cockatoo* (1940) when it was ready for release in 1937. This highly unusual film, modelled on American gangster films but set in London's Soho, reveals a criminal underworld centred around race tracks and backstreet nightclubs. Even if it is an uneven and uncertain gangster film, it is nevertheless startling to see today. This is partly because its sleazy urban environment was seldom seen in 1930s British cinema, and also because of its up-and-coming star, John Mills. In the war years, Mills would emerge as the screen's 'archetypal Englishman' and the 'definitive, stoical Everyman for a nation at war'.[45] But in *The Green Cockatoo* he is a second-rate song-and-dance man who carries a knife and uses it in self-defence. The BBFC did not approve, and the film sat on the shelf for three years. By the time it was granted a certificate, other low-budget crime films had begun to chip away at the BBFC's policies, and the war had lessened concerns about unemployment and wayward male aggression.[46] Nevertheless, anxieties around screen portrayals of Britain's own criminal underworld persisted, and after the war the BBFC would face extraordinary criticisms for allowing 'sordid' and 'brutal' crime films such as *Brighton Rock* (1947), *They Made Me a Fugitive* (1947) and *No Orchids for Miss Blandish* (1948).[47]

Before the war, the BBFC's policies were stifling for British filmmakers. Even criminal legends from the country's past were deemed unsuitable for the screen. Dick Turpin was one exception, but in films such as *Dick Turpin's Ride to York* (1922) and *Dick Turpin* (1933), the legendary highwayman – whose criminal career included cattle rustling, stealing horses, smuggling, housebreaking and robbing coaches – was portrayed as a dashing and gentlemanly figure. As Jeffrey Richards has observed, on screen Turpin was a figure like Robin Hood, a 'knight errant', who protected the weak and saved damsels in distress.[48] Criminals who did not fit with schoolboy adventure stories were considered unsuitable for the screen. In 1931, Gainsborough Films proposed filming *The Devil Man*, a biopic of the notorious nineteenth-century burglar and murderer Charles Peace, but this was rejected outright because it might encourage audiences to sympathize with this thoroughly disreputable character.[49] In 1932, Gainsborough also proposed *The Anatomist*, a story centred on the murders committed in the 1820s by Burke and Hare, who killed their victims so that they could sell the corpses to Edinburgh Medical College, but the BBFC advised the filmmakers that it would be better if the public forgot this 'ghoulish' story, and rejected the proposal.[50] In the same year, the BBFC allowed Twickenham Films to re-make Alfred Hitchcock's silent film *The Lodger* as a talkie – it was a safer prospect because it focused on tracking down a killer rather than on the killer himself – but the Board insisted that the killer must not be called 'The Ripper'. That would link the story to the all-too-real crimes of 'Jack the Ripper' in the 1890s.[51] George King's *Sweeney Todd, the Demon Barber of Fleet Street* (1936) was also likely to have been allowed because the story was fictional. Nevertheless, the censors insisted that the film must not show the barber murdering his patrons, and that no reference should be made to the patrons' remains being used in the pies made in a neighbouring shop. It was left to audiences familiar with this well-known Victorian melodrama to fill in the gaps of the story themselves.[52]

Just before he left Britain for Hollywood, in 1938, Alfred Hitchcock commented on the BBFC's policies toward American and British films in 1930s. He took the opportunity of his departure to complain that in the past the censors had thwarted his plans for more realistic British crime films:

> … it is a matter of the sugar-coated pill with films. I wanted to make an anti- capital punishment film where the prison governor revolts and refuses to hang his man. It's a stirring subject. But there would be difficulties with the censor. America can send over things of this sort, because the attitude here is that America can do what she likes with social subjects in her own country. In England this has to be left alone.[53]

His interest in making a feature film about the 1926 General Strike ('I saw in this subject a magnificently dynamic motion picture') was also 'vetoed' by the BBFC, according to Hitchcock.[54] However, the director could claim at least one significant victory. When making *The Man Who Knew Too Much* (1934), he wanted to recreate a real London gun battle, popularly known as 'The Siege of Sidney Street', which took place in the East End of London in 1911. The siege involved a gang of foreign criminals led by a Latvian revolutionary known as 'Peter the Painter'. When police surrounded their Sidney Street hideout, the gang began shooting and the Home Secretary, Winston Churchill, called out the Scots Guards to defeat them. A six-hour gun battle ensued, which ended only when the besieged house burned to the ground. These strange and mysterious events apparently captured the imagination of the young Hitchcock, who was 11 years old at the time and living less than a mile from Sidney Street.[55] Twenty-three years later, in 1934, he planned to include a similar scenario as one episode in *The Man Who Knew Too Much*, a spy thriller set partly in the East End. This would involve the foreign spies opening fire on the police when their backstreet hideaway is discovered, and a prolonged gun battle that ultimately leads to their deaths, but the story would be set in the present day and machine guns would be used rather than rifles. This raised alarm at the BBFC. In the wake of the talkies, 'cold blooded machine gun murders' had been added to the censors' list of prohibitions and, most importantly, machine-gun fire would make London seem too much like Chicago.[56] 'The censor wouldn't pass it,' as Hitchcock recalled. The BBFC insisted that machine guns must not be used, and a scene must be inserted in which it is made clear that London bobbies do not normally carry guns; the guns had to be supplied specially by a local gunsmith.[57] Hitchcock did as he was told, abandoning the machine guns and adding the requested dialogue, but otherwise the gun battle was filmed largely as he envisaged it. If the BBFC was less rigid in this instance, it was probably because *The Man Who Knew Too Much* was not a crime film but a thriller, involving foreign intrigue and fantastic events rather than local criminals and common offences.[58] In this guise, it offers a very rare instance of a 1930s British film featuring violent crime in a recognizably modern and urban setting.

Occasionally, British filmmakers proposed making gangster films set in the United States, but the BBFC was not comfortable with this either. Hence, a proposal for a screen version of Edgar Wallace's hit West End play *On the Spot* was deemed unacceptable even though it was set in Chicago and concerned an American gangster in the mould of Al Capone. An adaptation was proposed no fewer than five times between 1931 and 1937, but the BBFC rejected it each time.[59] The censors were not so squeamish when it came to films that sent up the gangster genre. British International Pictures' *Innocents of Chicago* (1932) told the story of an Englishman (played by Henry Kendall) who inherits a Chicago business and finds that it is a front for bootleggers. The critic for the *New York Times* disapprovingly regarded the film as a 'slavish imitation of Hollywood', but the BBFC would have noted crucial differences with the 'straight' gangster film.⁶⁰ The story was played as a broad farce and audiences were encouraged to laugh at gangsters rather than be enthralled by them. Most importantly, a clear boundary was maintained between the two countries by contrasting English innocence with American criminality. Similarly, in Gaumont-British's *Gangway* (1937), the musical comedy star Jessie Matthews played an Englishwoman abroad who finds herself caught up in the world of American gangsters. But this was another story that laughed at gangsters, and another one in which the contrast between the two countries was drawn in stark terms. This made *Gangway* permissible, machine guns and all.

There is a scene in *Gangway* when Jessie Matthews' character, the journalist Pat, talks to her young assistant, Joe (Graham Moffat), about the latest newspaper drama he is going to see at the cinema. Joe is depicted as a Hollywood-besotted youth, whose speech is littered with Americanisms and whose imagination is fired by Hollywood's representations of American life. In conversation, he and Pat speak of their longing for the fast-paced excitement of the United States ('you know you're alive there') and agree that 'nothing ever happens in England'. They then perform a kind of duet, listing the exciting events that they assume are commonplace in American life: 'gangsters … riots … fires … earthquakes … racketeers … floods … stick-ups … murders'. 'Gee, what a swell country to live in!', Joe concludes. The scene is played for laughs, but it inadvertently highlights the consequences of the BBFC's policies. By insisting that Britain must be portrayed as a decent, law-abiding and peaceful country, and at the same time granting far greater leeway to Hollywood films, the BBFC allowed American culture and society – at least as it is portrayed by Hollywood – to appear more compelling and vivid. The censors' narrow view of their own national life and character had the effect of making British films seem staid and rigid, while Hollywood's America was more exciting and, for some at least, more recognizably true-to-life.

The BBFC and Hollywood

While British filmmakers were told that films must concern the detection of crime rather than criminal activity, and while they were routinely refused permission to dramatize the lives of criminal legends, Hollywood films such as *Little Caesar* and *Scarface* were passed by the BBFC. Both films were widely recognized as fictionalized accounts of the life of Al Capone, America's most notorious contemporary gangster, and both films emphasize the rags-to-riches success of the gangster and his ruthless disregard for authority and conventional morality. Of course, the gangster hero comes to a bad end in the final reel – Hollywood's own censors made sure of that – but what is more noteworthy about these films is the dynamism of the outlaw. In both films this is immeasurably enhanced by the central performances. Edward G. Robinson as Rico in *Little Caesar* and Paul Muni as Tony Camonte in *Scarface* play their roles with a ruthlessness that makes them more compelling than any other character in the films. Arguably, even the moralistic endings are undermined by their charismatic performances. Robinson's final stagger into the gutter as he dies from a bullet wound, asking 'Mother of Mary, is this the end of Rico?' and Muni's dash into a hail of police bullets remain among both stars' most memorable screen moments. Yet the BBFC asked for only minor cuts to *Little Caesar* before granting it an 'A' certificate in February 1931, and in May 1932 *Scarface* received an 'A' certificate without any cuts (although this was a version that had already been through the censor's wringer in the United States).[61]

These were not unusual cases. Where Hollywood films were concerned, the BBFC served as a gatekeeper. It scrutinized the films after they had been made and when they were ready to be released in Britain, and so the Board's options were limited. It could ban a film altogether, but this was not done often (the 106 films banned between 1930 to 1934 were a fraction of the thousands the BBFC certified in this period). It more commonly asked for cuts, and these were usually minor. It could also ask for a change of title, in a manner that softened the original title or expressed a moralistic viewpoint toward the story. At the BBFC's behest, for example, Joseph Von Sternberg's seminal gangster drama *Underworld* (1927) was known to British audiences as *Paying the Penalty*; the Warner Brothers gangster film *Doorway to Hell* (1929) was released with the gentler title of *A Handful of Clouds*; and the same studio's *Blonde Crazy*, a comedy with James Cagney and Joan Blondell playing a pair of con artists, was renamed *Larceny Lane*, presumably to signal that the film was not a romantic comedy. Another measure was to insist that a foreword was placed at the outset of the film, explicitly informing the audience that the film depicted conditions or problems that had no parallel in Britain. This measure was used mainly on stories set within harsh or corrupt social institutions (such as reform schools and prisons), and it was the clearest expression of BBFC thinking on Hollywood films: they portray a completely separate social environment and have no relevance to British life.

There were two guiding principles behind the leniency afforded to Hollywood. One was that, while British films represented the nation and therefore had to reflect its values and moral principles, the BBFC had no responsibility over American films. That was the job of the Hays Office. The other was the belief that British audiences would recognize Hollywood films as foreign, and that they were more likely to be alienated than influenced by them. This belief was shared by many journalists and film critics, who labelled the tough new talkies as 'strong meat' films and openly wondered whether British audiences could stomach them. A prime example of the 'strong meat' trend was *The Front Page* (1931), a satirical comedy concerning press coverage of a man who has been convicted of shooting a policeman and is awaiting execution. A similar story in a British film of this period is unimaginable, and many critics, while admiring the film on its own terms, were dismayed by the disrespect with which the film portrays journalists, politicians and the criminal justice system. 'It is astonishing with what zest and care the makers of American films will pillory their own institutions,' the reviewer for *The Times* commented.[62] It was assumed that audiences too would be taken aback by the cynicism and the slang. *Kinematograph Weekly*, for example, commented that 'never was a picture so blatantly American' and warned readers of the 'many crude Americanisms' in the dialogue.[63] *Film Weekly* opened its review by stating, 'Do not be deterred from seeing this magnificent film by the fact that it is intensely American'.[64] *Picturegoer* noted the 'many Americanisms' in the dialogue and also observed that 'the Americans are apparently not afraid of laughing at themselves and in this [film] they haven't spared anything'.[65] Remarkably, *The Front Page* and another caustic newspaper drama, *Five Star Final* (1932), were regarded as truthful representations of a depraved American press, and reviewers asserted that nothing of the sort existed in Britain. 'Luckily', the reviewer for *Picturegoer* declared after seeing the wildly melodramatic *Five Star Final*, 'our newspapers over here have not reached the depths to which American "yellow" journalism has sunk.'[66]

Gangster films were also regarded as startlingly brutal yet truthful accounts of modern American life. Fox's *Quick Millions* (1931), with Spencer Tracy starring as a lorry driver-turned-racketeer, was praised by *Picturegoer* as a 'purely realistic and unromantic' portrayal of 'life as it is really lived by American gangsters'. The reviewer warned that this did not make for easy viewing: 'it is so 100 per cent American in outlook and speech that I have doubts as to whether a British audience will find it entirely to their tastes'.[67] *Kinematograph Weekly* concurred, noting that the dialogue is 'full of Americanisms', and that the film's 'appeal to the generality of English audiences is problematical'. In the same year, *Little Caesar* drew more positive reviews, largely on the basis of Edward G. Robinson's performance, but the idea that the gangster film was an accurate depiction of modern America recurred in its critical notices.[68] *Film Weekly* described it as 'true picture' and advised readers to 'see this film to know how Chicago lives'.[69] *Kinematograph Weekly* wondered whether 'the graft and intrigue are exaggerated' but nevertheless labelled it '100 per cent American in atmosphere and accent'.[70] A year later, *Scarface* drew praise for Paul Muni's intense performance as a volatile, psychotic gangster, but there were no indications that critics had become accustomed to the genre's violence. For *Kinematograph Weekly* the film was both 'truly American' and 'all too brutal'. The paper was still unclear whether 'this side of the Atlantic' would accept 'this type of entertainment'.[71] *Film Weekly* commented that 'many filmgoers' would find *Scarface* to be 'a revolting and nauseating production'. The reviewer was taken aback by the lawlessness: 'The gangster's tactics are so utterly outrageous in their complete defiance of law and order that they can only appear incredible to British eyes.' Similarly, the *Daily Express* reassured it readers that 'such things just could not happen in this country'.[72]

Not everyone was convinced that the gangster and his tough environment, as depicted in films, were so unfathomably strange, and that audiences would regard these films as representations of a distinctly foreign environment. Manchester City Council expressed its disapproval of the 'A' certificate that the BBFC gave to *Scarface* when it banned the film from local cinemas. The neighbouring city of Salford followed suit, explaining that the film was 'too thrilling' and had 'too much shooting' to be shown locally.[73] Beckenham and Birmingham councils also rejected *Scarface*.[74] These councils assumed that, for some of their residents at least, the films were not at all alienating, but had the potential to enthral audiences and possibly influence their behaviour and values. Thus, they rejected this central plank of the BBFC's policy toward Hollywood's gangster films – that they need not be banned because they were 'so obviously American' – and they overrode the BBFC's decisions.

Were British audiences vulnerable to American crime films? The difference of opinion on this issue, and the way the debate was conducted, surfaced most acutely in relation to MGM's prison drama *The Big House* (1930). Set in a grim and overcrowded American prison, *The Big House* tells the story of three inmates who share a tiny cell: two tough career criminals (Wallace Beery and Chester Morris) and one soft newcomer (Robert Montgomery). When the trio's escape plan goes wrong, a prison-wide riot ensues. A gang of the most hard-bitten inmates battles against the prison guards with machine guns, and the carnage ends only when army tanks arrive and are used against the inmates. At that point, the prison is in ruins and 50 people (including guards and inmates) have been killed in the mayhem. The film clearly broke a number of the BBFC's prohibitions, but in September 1930 the board granted it an 'A' certificate with the proviso that it should carry a foreword stating that it depicted prison conditions in the United States and that the events shown 'could not happen in this country'.[75] But 16 months later, when a riot broke out at Dartmoor Prison, it was widely alleged that the disturbance was a direct imitation of the events in *The Big House*.[76] Journalists used the film and its supposed influence to exaggerate the severity of the riot and to suggest that outside influences were to blame; the *Daily Mail*, for example, referred to the riot as an 'amazing reign of terror' that was 'without precedent in the annals of British prisons'.[77] Actually, the 'Dartmoor Mutiny' (as it became known) bore little relation to the events depicted in *The Big House*.

It did not arise as part of an escape plan, the prisoners had no guns, the army was not involved and there were no fatalities among either the prisoners or the guards. Moreover, it emerged later that the disturbance was sparked by a petty issue: the prisoners rebelled because their breakfast porridge was cold and watery.[78] Thus, it was not the inmates of Dartmoor who imitated Hollywood, but the press. The riot occurred on a Sunday morning and in one of the country's most remote prisons. Lacking real and immediate information, journalists turned readily to *The Big House* and its wildly dramatic scenario to fill in the gaps. Yet months after the more mundane truth had emerged, the 'Dartmoor mutiny' was still being discussed as an example of the American influences brought to Britain by Hollywood.[79] It seemed that, despite the BBFC's insistence, many people believed such things *could* happen, here, especially if films led the way. It was certainly easier to denounce Hollywood than it was to address issues relating to the harsh conditions in prisons as bleak as Dartmoor.

Cagney and *The Public Enemy*

While the BBFC was generally less alarmed by the potential influence of American films, the Board regarded Warner Brothers' *The Public Enemy*, starring James Cagney, as particularly harmful. Today, *The Public Enemy* stands alongside *Little Caesar* and *Scarface* as a trio of iconic films that defined the gangster genre in the early 1930s and influenced it thereafter. Yet where *Little Caesar* and *Scarface* passed through the BBFC comparatively unscathed, *The Public Enemy* was initially denied a certificate altogether. It was first viewed by Edward Shortt in June 1931, but it was two months before a decision was reached *not* to approve the film, and a further ten months before the board finally gave the film an 'A' certificate. In the interim, changes were made to *The Public Enemy*. These included a different title – it became the more damning and plural *Enemies of the Public* – as well as extensive cutting. The cuts were reportedly so severe that the story was made incomprehensible and the continuity ruined in places. Some speculated that the BBFC remained unconvinced that the film was suitable even with these alterations, but felt obliged to pass the film in June 1932 because *Scarface* had been granted an 'A' certificate in the previous month. Others remained unconvinced by the BBFC's decision: Beckenham Council banned *Enemies of the Public* even its reduced state.[80]

What, then, was so distinctively offensive and dangerous in *The Public Enemy*? At first glance, it breaks no more of the BBFC's prohibitions than *Little Caesar* or *Scarface*. Each of the films centres on the rise and fall of the central gangster character, and therefore breaks the prohibition against 'stories in which the criminal element is predominant'. Arguably, the three films break the prohibition on 'films in which sympathy is enlisted for the criminals'. Each details specific criminal activities, and therefore breaks the prohibition on portraying 'the methods of crime'. Each also includes machine guns used with rapid-firing abandon, murders committed in cold blood and an ineffectual criminal justice system. On the other hand, it also possible to claim that the three films ultimately demonstrate that crime does not pay: each culminates with the gangster facing a hailstorm of bullets, thus neatly combining violent spectacle with moral retribution. Furthermore, all three portray their gangster heroes as deeply flawed and, in each case, incapable of a fulfilled sexual relationship. In *Little Caesar*, Rico is seemingly in love with his handsome younger accomplice Joe (Douglas Fairbanks Jr) and becomes bitterly jealous when Joe leaves him for a woman and an alternative career as an entertainer. In *Scarface*, Tony Camonte is so consumed by an incestuous desire for his sister, Cesca (Ann Dvorak), that he kills his loyal accomplice Guino (George Raft) when he finds the two together. In *The Public Enemy*, Tom Powers' relationships with a range of women are peculiar to say the least, but in one of the film's most frequently noted scenes he attacks his girlfriend, Kitty (Mae Clarke), at the breakfast table by suddenly and violently smashing a grapefruit into her face (Figure 8). Of course, the genre's fans may not have regarded the gangster's peculiarities as flaws. For some, the gangster's homosocial lifestyle and lack of chivalry might have been further and welcome signs of their defiance of social norms.

Some aspects of *The Public Enemy* seem designed to placate the censors. The film arrived in Britain with a foreword already in place, explicitly stating that the story depicts 'a certain strata of American life' and that it is not meant to 'glorify' the criminal. Furthermore, the moral finale is delivered not just once but twice: first when Tom

Figure 8   In *Public Enemy*, Tom Powers (James Cagney) attacks Kitty (Mae Clarke) with a grapefruit at the breakfast table

Powers is shot by a rival gang and falls into the gutter declaring 'I ain't so tough'; and then again when, having inexplicably survived that shooting, he is kidnapped from the hospital by a rival gang and delivered back to his family home, wrapped up like a mummy. As his bound body falls headfirst and flat on to the floor of his family home, it is not clear what unspeakable things have been done to him, but it looks like a particularly nasty comeuppance. If the foreword and the ghastly denouement were not enough to placate the BBFC, it could cut the shots or scenes it found most offensive before it agreed to award a certificate. Eventually, such cuts would be made. A detailed record of exactly which scenes the BBFC cut has not survived, but two cuts were noted in the press. One was the breakfast scene in which Tom attacks Kitty with the grapefruit. This crude, misogynistic demonstration of Tom's temper was likely to offend many viewers. It strayed far from the chivalrous ideal represented by gentleman such as Ronald Colman, and of course the censors would regard it as open to imitation. The other cut was made to a scene after a gang leader has been accidentally killed in a riding accent and Tom goes to the stables to shoot the horse. The shot was heard but not seen in the original version, but the BBFC cut even the sound of the gunshot.[81] Yet these and other excisions could have been made when the film was first submitted to the

BBFC, so it remains to be explained why deliberations about the film continued for many more months.

The BBFC's wider disapproval of *The Public Enemy* was likely to have stemmed from the film's portrayal of juvenile delinquency. Unlike *Little Caesar* and *Scarface*, *The Public Enemy* depicts the gangster's childhood and therefore strays into the most sensitive issue surrounding gangster films: that they fuelled juvenile crimes, both by teaching the methods of crime and by portraying criminals as heroes. The film's early scenes show Tom and his future sidekick Matt as youngsters drinking beer, falling prey to a Fagin-like petty thief who encourages them to steal, being chased from a department store and, in their teenage years, robbing a fur warehouse. It is the film's pretence that these scenes are offered as a matter of sociological observation – that it is revealing the environment that gives rise to criminality – but there is no denying that these youthful crimes are also represented as exciting escapades. When Tom and Matt are chased through the department store, for example, they recklessly manoeuvre their way through middle-aged, overweight shoppers laden with goods and, when they unexpectedly come face to face with a slow-to-respond policeman, they quickly scramble on to the central section of the escalators and slide gleefully down to the next floor. Matt casually swats at a well-dressed gentleman's top hat as he slides past him and the camera lingers for a moment as the man awkwardly tries to retrieve his fallen hat. The scenes thus convey more boyish *joie de vivre* than sociological concern, and it is easy to imagine a youthful audience cheering the boys on. Later, when they are teenagers and they break into a fur warehouse, there is a comical edge to the scene: Tom accidentally reveals their presence in the dark warehouse because he stumbles across a large stuffed bear, which he shoots several times in a panic. Undoubtedly, the censors would have been appalled by what follows: they are chased from the warehouse by a policeman and, just out of view of the camera, they shoot and kill him. Here, too, the film lends some sympathy to the criminals: the policeman had already shot their getaway driver in the back and he was attempting to shoot them in the back when they turned on him. The censors also would not have failed to notice that, until the film's finale, a life of crime is seen to pay off handsomely: Tom and Matt gain smart clothes, fast cars, entry into exclusive nightclubs and their choice of girlfriends. Midway through the film, Tom chooses Gwen, effortlessly picking her up as she walks down the street and he passes by in his swanky new convertible car. If that wasn't bad enough, Gwen was played by Hollywood's latest and hottest sex symbol, Jean Harlow, and it is clear that this bra-less and brazen siren is immediately attracted by Tom's apparent wealth and status. Although it is later suggested that Tom and Gwen's relationship is never consummated (in one of the film's discreet references to Tom's sexual inadequacy), there is no denying that the film conveys the pleasures of youthful, fast living.

Another factor that made *The Public Enemy* different from *Little Caesar* and *Scarface* is that it offers no rightful authority figure as an alternative to the corrupt authority exercised by the gangsters. Both *Little Caesar* and *Scarface* conclude with the police killing the gangster. It may be a long time in coming, but the police finally prevail in the ending. In *The Public Enemy*, by contrast, the police are portrayed as passive bystanders, who observe gang activity but are apparently powerless to do anything about it, and no other pro-social characters are offered as alternative figures for audience sympathies. Tom's brother, Mike (Donald Cook) is an upstanding and dutiful citizen, but he is also unerringly dull and humourless, and Tom easily puts him in his place. 'That sucker? He's learning how to be poor,' Tom sneers, when he hears that his brother is attending night school to better himself. When Mike accuses Tom of murder, Tom compares his own criminal deeds with his brother's experiences in the Great War: 'You didn't get those medals holding hands with the Germans. You killed and you liked it!' In one version of the story, Mike was going to demonstrate more authority in the ending. When Tom's bound body is delivered to the family home, Mike would not stand by powerlessly, as he does in the film, but instead he would go on to retrieve grenades stored among his war mementoes and then go out to kill the gang members himself.[82] Curiously, this ending was used when *Enemies of the Public* appeared as a short story in *Picture Show*, but the film's ending (in the American and British versions) was abbreviated.[83] In the released version of the film, Mike does nothing but stand by as Matt's bound corpse falls to the floor. Thus, audiences are left with the knowledge that a rival gang has killed Tom and that gangsters have prevailed rather than the forces of law and order.

It is unlikely that, even if the filmmakers had included a moral alternative to Tom Powers and gangsterdom, the alternative could have challenged the appeal of James Cagney. This may have been the most significant problem *The Public Enemy* posed for the BBFC. The up-and-coming star was younger and more handsome than both Edward G. Robinson and Paul Muni. Moreover, while Robinson's Rico and Muni's Tony are overtly Italian in appearance and demeanour, Cagney's Tom is an Irish-American with an Anglo-Saxon appearance, and this was likely to bring him closer to home for many British audiences. In this regard, it is telling that the BBFC also insisted on cuts and a change of title when it saw Warner Brothers' *The Doorway to Hell/A Handful of Clouds* (1930/31).[84] This (now largely forgotten) film tells the story of the rise of an Italian-American gangster named Louie Ricarno but clearly modelled on Al Capone. The casting was very peculiar. Lew Ayres, the young and innocent hero of the Great War drama *All Quiet on the Western Front* (1930), was far too fresh-faced and clean-cut to play the sinister Louie. With Ayres in the lead, the film seems to suggest that gangsterdom is just another career option for bright, ambitious boys with nice smiles, and this was clearly a problem for the BBFC, which found gangsters less offensive if they were set apart by ethnicity, age and demeanour.

Cagney had a co-starring role in *Doorway to Hell*, as Louie's ruthless sidekick, and in this film, as in all of his roles, he was a uniquely charismatic performer who brought energy, confidence and humour to his portraits of ordinary working-class men. His physical assuredness, combined with his tough talk and cheeky demeanour, made him a natural hero for the young, urban, no-frills audience. He spoke in a street-smart patois that rejected deference or any values other than his own hard-boiled variety, while his body language was equal parts grace and swagger. When he is gunned down in *The Public Enemy*, his stumbling descent on a rain swept street is performed as a captivating dance of death. (Only Gene Kelly, in *Singin' in the Rain*, could make more of an urban rain dance.) Thus, even when dying in the gutter and admitting 'I ain't so tough', Cagney was capable of inspiring greater sympathy, hero-worship and imitation than any other gangster star (Figure 9).

Figure 9   Tom Powers dies in the gutter in *The Public Enemy*

The Public Enemy offered an early starring role to the up-and-coming Cagney. In his subsequent films, some of which were released in Britain while *The Public Enemy* was in limbo, Cagney continued to play the working-class hero of the pacy, contemporary urban dramas that were a Warner Brothers speciality in the early 1930s. His roles as a New York taxi driver who defeats a corrupt syndicate (*Taxi!*, 1931/32), a bell hop turned conman (*Larceny Lane*, 1931/32), an ex-convict who becomes a tabloid newspaper photographer (*Picture Snatcher*, 1933) and a cinema usher who becomes a Hollywood star (*Lady Killer*, 1933/34) place him, initially at least, in exactly the sorts of jobs working-class men might have, and then the films offer audiences the fantasy of seeing this ordinary man become extraordinary by means of guile, audacity and fisticuffs. His roles as a racing car driver (*The Crowd Roars*, 1932) and boxer (*Winner Take All*, 1932), meanwhile, place him in the sorts of jobs working-class men might fantasize about. Although he is on the right side of the law in some of these films, he seldom keeps both feet there. His stories involve telling the boss off and being sacked for it, fighting against vested interests and embarking on schemes and set-ups designed to earn some fast money. They almost always involve his rough and ready treatment of women; the grapefruit scene in *The Public Enemy* became a kind of trademark for Cagney. In some films, he simply slaps any woman who dares to annoy him (just as any man who crosses him gets a punch), but in *Lady Killer* he drags poor Mae Clarke – the actress previously subjected to the grapefruit – across the room by her hair when she refuses to leave his hotel room voluntarily.

Cagney was not to everyone's taste. The star and his films divided both critics and audiences. Sydney Carroll, the film critic for the *Sunday Times*, was his most prominent opponent. He disliked every Cagney film of this period. Reviewing *Larceny Lane* in January 1932 (when *The Public Enemy* had yet to receive a certificate), Carroll offered this advice to the BBFC:

> James Cagney is nothing short of a public menace. Mr. Edward Shortt, the film censor, should ban him sternly from every picture in which he is now appearing. For he makes rascality youthfully adorable and villainy extenuate. No one can throw such glamour over trickery, cheating and 'chiselling'. His antics on the screen are calculated to drive half the youth of this country into the commission of misdemeanours, if not larger crimes. I am sure of it.[85]

Not surprisingly, then, Carroll denounced *The Public Enemy* when it was released as *Enemies of the Public* in June 1932. He took the view that the film was both utterly 'alien' and yet also capable of 'corrupting' British youth:

> If ever a movie deserved total and absolute suppression, it is this one. It glorifies as despicable a bully, thief and murderer as any gangster in America ... All this may or may not be a faithful picture of a certain aspect of American life, but I cannot see the slightest justification for corrupting the youth of this country by the example of a successful desperado of such a disgusting type ... To the rubbish heap with such rotten, degrading, alien products, I say, and with all speed.[86]

Not everyone was so alarmed, though, and in fact Cagney had some supporters in unexpected places. C.A. Lejeune, who wrote for the middle-class readers of the *Observer*, rarely liked crime films, but she was profoundly impressed by Cagney's star power. In January 1932, she recommended *Taxi!* 'even if you are tired of racketeering films' because 'Cagney is worth it'.[87] In the next week, when *Larceny Lane* was released, she commented that 'I doubt if there is a better show-man on the American screen' and instructed readers that 'Getting to know Cagney should be a point of honour among filmgoers; he is the New Year's real find'.[88] Six months later, she had little enthusi-asm for *Enemies of the Public*, but still expressed some admiration for its star: 'Cagney is one of the few stars who give bone and blood to every part they touch, a fact that makes this orgy of a Chicago gun play even less edifying in practice than in theory.'[89] Cedric Belfrage, writing in the *Sunday Express*, was also an early admirer of Cagney, and one who previously defended him and his films against charges of 'vulgarity'.[90] With *Enemies of the Public*, however, Belfrage found that even after the censor's cuts, the film 'remains pretty gruesome' and suggested that it was likely to awaken thoughts 'which normally would not enter even the most depraved English crook's head'.[91] The British documentary filmmaker John Grierson, who regularly reviewed films for a variety of periodicals, was another of Cagney's admirers and also of Warner Brothers' gritty working-class real-ism. Clearly, Grierson's documentary interests were at work later in the decade, when he urged readers of *World Film News* to remem-ber that cinema 'began in the gutter' and it must not be given over to middle-class respectability; or, as he put it, Hollywood should not 'eliminate the Cagneys in favour of the Colmans' and it should not 'Colmanize Cagney himself'.[92] *Enemies of the Public* was one of the films that inspired this admiration. Grierson admired Cagney's performance, the script's interest in exploring the psychological underpinnings of the gangster and the film's representation of the environment from which the gangster emerges. His one caveat in recommending *Enemies of the Public* was that the BBFC's cuts had damaged the continuity of the film.[93] Other critics also observed that the BBFC had left the film 'very much a patched-up affair' (*Daily Express*), 'maddeningly muddled, in places almost unintelli-gible' (*Daily Telegraph*) and 'scrappy and disjointed' (*Film Weekly*).[94] *Kinematograph Weekly* noted that the film had obviously been 'heav-ily censored', but the writer was more concerned to warn that it nevertheless remained 'very strong meat' and that it 'should be seen personally by bookers' to ensure that it was appropriate for their patrons.[95]

Audience responses to *Enemies of the Public* were not recorded, but it is notable that the film does not figure at all in John Sedgwick's calculation of the 100 most popular films of 1932. Two of Cagney's other films appear in this ranking, but in rather lowly positions: *The Crowd Roars* at number 93 and *Winner Take All* at number 97.[96] Interestingly, these were the films in which he played a racing car driver and boxer rather than a conman or a gangster, suggesting the wider audience's discomfort with the crime genre. In that same year, *Film Weekly* explained that there were no half measures when it came to Cagney: 'you either like him or you hate him and that's that'.[97] This is the only conclusion to be drawn from the Bernstein Questionnaires of 1934 and 1937. The 1934 survey found that Cagney stood at number 25 in the ranking of the 50 most popular male stars, placing him above fellow tough guys Spencer Tracy (number 33), Paul Muni (number 36) and Edward G. Robinson (number 45). The more striking point, however, is that on the same questionnaire Cagney took the number one place in another category: the most *disliked* male stars.[98] When Bernstein repeated the questionnaire three years later, in 1937, Cagney's popularity ranking had moved up to number 17, and he remained at number one on the list of disliked male stars. The commentary accompanying the questionnaire explained the divergence of opinion: the majority of those who named Cagney as a favourite were men, while the majority of those who disliked him were women.[99] Who could blame women for disliking him? The star famous for the grapefruit scene and other violent indignities toward women was hardly likely to win their approval.

Class also played a role in attitudes toward Cagney. It is revealing that the ribald Mae West was the most disliked female star in both the 1934 and 1937 questionnaires.[100] Cagney and West make interesting opposites to stars such as Ronald Colman and Norma Shearer. By contrast with these mainstream favourites, the disliked stars were noted for abandoning decorum, gentility and good taste. This clearly discomforted a majority of the audience but also appealed to a significant minority. That Cagney's appeal could be located primarily with working-class audiences is apparent in the way the trade papers categorize his films for exhibitors, designating them as 'for the masses', or for bookings in 'industrial halls' and 'populous areas'; all euphemisms for working-class audiences and venues.[101] It is apparent too that *Picturegoer* and *Film Weekly*, both of which had a large contingent of lower-middle-class women among their readers, had little interest in the star and even less in the genre he was most associated with, the gangster film. Both magazines walked a fine line between their opposition to stringent censorship and their disapproval of the gangster genre, but readers' letters were less equivocal: 'Is it not about time that we turned from Chicago and its crime to something more pleasant?', a typical letter in *Picturegoer* asked in 1931.[102]

Like other Hollywood studio products, gangster films such as *Little Caesar*, *Scarface* and *Enemies of the Public* made their debut at large city centre 'picture palaces'. But crime films were unlikely to last for long in the pricey and plush sector of the exhibition market. They were more a prominent and recurrent fixture of the smaller neighbourhood cinemas, and particularly those in urban, working-class areas. Mass Observation's study of cinema-going in Bolton during the 1930s found little appetite for crime films in the city's upmarket Odeon or its family-oriented Crompton cinema, but crime was the favourite genre at the 'flea-pit' cinema, the Palladium, and it was the Palladium's male patrons who liked crime films best.[103] Similarly, when *World Film News* reported on cinema-going in the impoverished East End of London, it found that audiences in the area's ageing, outdated cinemas especially liked gangster films (they 'pack the house', according to one manager).[104] Historian Robert James' research into cinema-going in Portsmouth found that in that city, crime films (including *Enemies of the Public*) also played most frequently at a downmarket neighbourhood venue, the Queens Cinema, which was known for playing films on their third or fourth run. At the Queens, as James has described it, audiences paid low admission charges to see films featuring 'tough men and feisty women' in the leading roles.[105]

The appeal of the gangster

The gangster film offered its fans a world they recognized: one of crowded neighbourhoods and unsophisticated people, one in which people struggled to make a living, one where men were unlikely to get ahead through lawful means and one in which social structures and authorities were more likely to be criticized than celebrated. There was a cathartic release to be found in these films. Laws could be flouted, aggression acted out and authority challenged. There was also, perhaps, a comfortable safety in experiencing this catharsis in settings far from home – on the streets of Chicago rather than Portsmouth, or in the tenements of New York rather than those of Glasgow. The films' appeal to men is also revealing. These gangster films are masculine fantasies of empowerment, and they arrived at a moment when many men had been made redundant and idle. Little wonder, then, that the films raised the hackles of those who saw themselves as the voices of social authority. Part of the appeal of the gangster film was the fantasy of riding roughshod over that authority and all that it represented.

It is ironic that some prominent Americans lamented the release of Hollywood's gangster films abroad and regretted that these films would represent the United States to the rest of the world as a lawless, violent and chaotic nation. Joseph Kennedy, the American Ambassador to Britain in the 1930s, felt obliged to ask Britons not to judge his country by such films and he expressed his regret that they were shown at all.[106] Yet the gangster film and other 'strong meat' films did not necessarily give a bad impression of the USA. For some, Hollywood's willingness to portray American social problems and to question institutions was a sign of openness, while Hollywood's predilection for sympathizing with rebels and underdogs, and for investing the ordinary with extraordinary qualities, was a form of flattery. The 'tough and feisty' audiences at Britain's flea-pit cinemas would seldom find these qualities in their own country's films. In British films of the 1930s, working-class characters were likely to be at the centre of comedies rather than 'strong meat' dramas.[107] There was certainly no British Cagney.[108] The BBFC's policies ensured this, and working-class audiences in particular turned to Hollywood for relief from the middle-class respectability of so many mainstream British films.

This is not to say that working-class audiences turned away from their own culture and embraced American culture instead. Rather, they turned away from one strand of British culture that predominated in the country's films. In Hollywood films they found characters, situations, attitudes and manners that seemed closer to their own lives than those in many British films. What seemed like 'strong meat' to film critics was the stuff of ordinary life for less refined audiences. Furthermore, when audiences adopted the idioms they heard in these films, it was often a form of self-conscious mimicry rather than the passive absorption of foreign influences. American English could be adopted knowingly and for specific purposes, as the author Winifred Holtby observed when she described the character of Elsie, a young servant in the novel *South Riding* (1936), as 'trilingual': 'She talked BBC English to her employer, Cinema American to her companions, and Yorkshire dialect to old milkmen like Eli Dickson.'[109] Mimicking snappy, disrespectful Americanisms was all the more pleasing for being so open and unabashed, and for angering those who valued deference and decorum. The most disagreeable of all the adopted sayings, 'sez you', did not say anything that was new in British culture, but it said it with more verve and vigour, and that made it worth adopting and enjoying.

5 'The Minx's Progress': *Gone with the Wind* as Britain's Favourite War Film

We are not intentionally turning peace films into war films. It just happens. It would surprise the good folk in Hollywood no end, I fancy, to know how their gentlest offerings are being tinged with the colour of battle. What might surprise them less, for they are a sporting community, is the way the English public are extracting fun from the air raid warnings in cinemas. The matching of film dialogue with sirens is quite a game, I find, among the tougher element. Filmgoers compete for the most apt phrase heard in conjunction with a warning. One young lady ... came back delighted from an interrupted session of *The Blue Bird*. 'Let there be light!' said the Fairy on the screen – and there was light – house lights, and the manager making his announcement. My own family yesterday reported a riotous moment in the local show of *My Two Husbands*. The words 'all clear', it seems were thrown on the screen during a heated argument between Melvyn Douglas and Fred MacMurray over their legal status. The house appreciated it.

C.A. Lejeune, 'Are All Films War Films?' (1940)[1]

'Staff and public alike were marvellous and there was no panic. The kiddies particularly were splendid and I didn't even see one crying.' Manager Cyril Huxtable told the *Kine* this after his kinema at Brighton had suffered a direct hit on a Saturday afternoon, killing two adults and four children, and injuring some 20 others ... There were 220 people in the kinema at the time, most of them adults, and the film they were seeing was *It Could Happen To You*.

'Patrons Calm When Kinema Is Bombed', *Kinematograph Weekly* news from September 1940[2]

Young Tom Edison marked many people's first experience of bombing. Deanna Durbin's *Spring Parade* turned up in the same week as the Fire of London. *The Lady Eve* coincided with Hess' arrival in Scotland, and *That*

Uncertain Feeling, somewhat ironically, with the German invasion of Russia. While the Japanese were attacking Pearl Harbour, our cinemas were showing *Dumbo* and *Here Comes Mr Jordan*. *My Gal Sal* marked the turn of the tide in Africa. *The Magnificent Ambersons* slipped in quietly after we had landed in Sicily … ..

Guy Morgan, *Red Roses Every Night* (1948)[3]

Popular memory of the Second World War is now so tightly intertwined with Britain's own war films that it can be surprising to realize the prominent role Hollywood films played in the everyday life of wartime Britain. Decades later, it is likely to be one of John Mills' wartime roles – as the Cockney sailor of *In Which We Serve* (1942) or the quiet flyer of *The Way to the Stars* (1945) – that springs to mind at the mention of films and the war, or perhaps the heroic-yet-restrained performances of Jack Hawkins and Richard Todd in post-war war films such as *The Cruel Sea* (1953) and *The Dam Busters* (1954). During the war, however, Hollywood stars were much more likely to be found on Britain's screens and in the sights of the country's cinema-goers. As indicated in the quotations above – from C.A. Lejeune's film column in the *Observer*, from the news pages of *Kinematograph Weekly* and from Guy Morgan's recollections of the Granada cinema chain in wartime – Hollywood's films were so much a part of ordinary life that even the children's fantasy film *The Blue Bird* (1940), the frothy romantic comedy *My Two Husbands* (1940) and the routine potboiler *It Could Happen to You* (1940) could assume some wartime relevance. As Lejeune observed, the circumstances outside the cinema transformed the films. Morgan referred to films as the country's 'common experience' during wartime; they punctuated key war events and became inextricably bound up with them. A similar, but more personal, account of the way films permeated wartime experiences can also be found in Hazel Wheeler's memoirs, written from her diaries, of growing up in Huddersfield: seeing Charles Boyer in *Hold Back the Dawn* (1941) coincided with helping her grandmother with the blackout curtains; *Now, Voyager* (1942/43) arrived in the city at the same time as a shipment of oranges and a shortage of fish; and the appearance of the exotic Dorothy Lamour in *Beyond the Blue Horizon* (1943) led local factory girls to adopt the star's hairstyle, her heavy make-up and her air of 'sultry aloofness'.[4]

Of course it is perfectly understandable that, over time, Britain's John Mills and Richard Todd took precedence over Hollywood's Fred MacMurray and Dorothy Lamour in popular memory and in historical accounts of wartime experience. Mills and Todd starred in films that were aimed first and foremost at British audiences and films that portray actual wartime experiences. It is likely that their films represent the way many Britons would *like* to remember the national experience of war, if not their own experience of it. By contrast, Hollywood's connection with the wartime British audience seems in retrospect to be more ephemeral and extraneous. There were so many Hollywood films (hundreds were released each year) that it is now a challenge to locate the significant or noteworthy. Produced far away and with an American audience primarily in mind, Hollywood films may also seem to be mere escapism for British audiences, lacking the relevance and purpose of homegrown films. Yet this should not lead to the conclusion that they were irrelevant. Escapism should not be equated with meaninglessness. Audiences made choices between films that might be labelled as escapist, they expressed opinions about them, and these choices and opinions can be revealing. They can tell us something about an audience's disposition – its preoccupations, ambitions, desires and fears – that may be too troublesome or sensitive to be depicted in realist or straightforward terms. Indeed, given the upheaval and tumult of the war years, it may be that escapist films are *more* revealing about their audiences than films that represent wartime experience in a direct or officially approved manner.

It is with this understanding of escapism that the wartime popularity of *Gone with the Wind* will be explored. This was neither a sober British war film nor a routine Hollywood release. It was the most eagerly anticipated, the most controversial and arguably the most popular film of the war. Its story is set on another continent and in an earlier century, and it centres on a conflict that few in Britain knew much about, but the film ran and ran throughout the war years: first as a highly expensive 'road show' release, shown in selected cities in 1940; then on general release throughout the country in 1942, and then again as a high-profile re-release in 1944. It also had a record-breaking four-year run in London's Leicester Square, spanning the period of the 'phoney war' in 1940 to D-day in 1944.

This success prompted C.A. Lejeune to observe in 1942 that *Gone with the Wind* had become 'as much a part of the issue of London life in wartime as the foreign uniforms in the streets, the altered skyline, and the friendly square gardens now open to the casual strollers'.[5] But how and why did a story set during the American Civil War and Reconstruction period, and centred firmly on the experiences of Southern belle Scarlett O'Hara, come to resonate so strongly with British audiences? To answer this question, we must turn to contemporaneous responses to the film. For this most talked about of all films, there is a plethora of evidence: from those who wanted the film banned to those who made a fortune showing it; from snide to enthusiastic critics; and also from the cinema-goers who saw it in an array of different contexts as the war progressed. The weight of evidence alone testifies to the film's status and significance during these years, and it suggests that, alongside any of the heroic characters played by John Mills or Richard Todd, Scarlett O'Hara deserves a place as an icon of the British at war.

Excess and austerity

Although *Gone with the Wind* arrived in Britain at the tail end of the 'phoney war' period, which stretched from the autumn of 1939 to the spring of 1940, the war had already transformed everyday life. Conscription, mass evacuation, rationing and requisitioning were just some of the features of life in wartime that Britons already faced, and government-imposed austerity measures continued to pile up (in the week after the film's release further tax rises were announced on cigarettes, beer, cinema tickets and other pleasures). In this environment many commentators regarded *Gone with the Wind* as wholly inappropriate; in the tight grip of wartime it appeared excessive and wasteful. Everything about it was oversized. Margaret Mitchell's novel was 1,037 pages long. When it was published in 1936, it was translated into 18 languages and became a best seller around the world. In Britain, the first edition sold out even before publication and, to the surprise of many commentators, it remained a best seller for years, with 300,000 copies sold before the film was released.[6] Advance publicity for the film emphasized the extravagance of the production: the £1 million production cost, the running time of nearly four hours and the use of Technicolor (still relatively rare in 1940) were widely reported, and so too were other signs of producer David Selznick's largesse.[7] His 'search for Scarlett' involved a highly publicized talent-scouting effort in which 1,400 women auditioned for the part. A whole studio back lot was set alight and reduced to ash for a few short scenes depicting the burning of Atlanta. The press reported that this one film had not one but three directors: Victor Fleming and Sam Wood filmed 'principal scenes' simultaneously, while William Cameron Menzies shot 'background and atmospheric' material.[8] The world premiere in December 1939 was also widely reported in Britain: a public holiday was declared in the state of Georgia, and in the city of Atlanta the occasion was celebrated with a parade, fireworks and a formal ball. Just before the film arrived in London, it won eight Academy Awards, including the award for 'best picture' and most of the other principal awards. The London premiere was on an unprecedented scale. High-profile films normally made their debut exclusively in one major West End venue before going on general release, but *Gone with the Wind* had a premiere that stretched across three West End cinemas. The Empire Leicester Square, with 3,110 seats, was MGM's own lavish, showcase cinema. Its neighbour, The Ritz, had just 430 seats and was often used by MGM for extended runs or lesser features, but in this case it was used to add to the Empire's seating capacity. And the Palace Theatre at Cambridge Circus, with 969 seats, was another grand West End showcase that screened only the most prominent films.[9]

The premiere was held on 18 April 1940. This was, perhaps, the last moment in the war when a 'gala' premiere was still possible. The climax of the 'phoney war' had been reached just two weeks earlier, when Prime Minister Neville Chamberlain confidently declared that Hitler had 'missed the bus' (that is, lost the initiative in the war). By mid-April, the full extent of Chamberlain's misunderstanding was still coming into focus. The Germans were on the move in Norway, but the calamitous events of May and June – the German occupation of Belgium and the Netherlands, the evacuation of British troops from Dunkirk and the Fall of France – were at least a month away. Hence, on 18 April the red carpets could still be rolled out, and an array of notables could don evening dress for a glamorous event. Leslie Howard was the only cast member to attend, but many other film stars, including Leslie Banks, Robert Donat, Robert Montgomery and Conrad Veidt, were present. 'Society' was also out in force, represented most notably by Lord and Lady Louis Mountbatten, the Duke of Westminster and the Duchess of Marlborough. Remarkably, given the tenor of the times, the premiere also brought together the ambassadors of Belgium, China, Denmark, Hungary, Italy, Japan, Poland, Rumania and Spain. Numerous government officials attended. Winston Churchill, who would become Prime Minister just three weeks later, was there. So, too, were Sir John Anderson (the Home Secretary), Sir Kenneth Clark (head of the Films Division of the Ministry of Information), Sir Samuel Hoare (Secretary of State for Air), Sir Kingsley Wood (Lord Privy Seal) and others.[10] A last gasp of pre-war glamour was hard to resist, it seems, although Chamberlain himself stayed away.

David Selznick was apparently willing to bet that, even amid wartime austerity, the film's grandeur would spark the interest of British audiences. Advertisements for the initial London engagements read: 'The film which is so big it needs three West End theatres to accommodate it.'[11] That same grandeur, however, rankled many in the film industry and related professions.[12] *Picturegoer and Film Weekly* took a hostile view of the film even before the London premiere. In an article headlined 'The *Gone with the Wind* Menace', the magazine reported on the film's early box office success in the United States and expressed regret that Hollywood producers could not recognize this as a 'freak' and were instead 'frantically' trying to imitate it by planning lavish films with long running times.[13] The mocking tone fitted well with the editorial stance *Picturegoer and Film Weekly* had adopted since the outset of the war, in which Hollywood was ridiculed for its neutrality and its isolation from world events, while British filmmaking was regarded with stalwart patriotism, as a cause to be promoted and protected. A succession of headlines betrayed the magazine's wartime chauvinism: 'Keep the Home Cameras Turning', 'Call-up for Hollywood', 'Should the Boys Be Embarrassed?', 'Hitler Scares Hollywood's He-Men', 'Are Our Stars Slacking?' and 'Call up the Hollywood Britons'.[14] All of these articles appeared in the first nine months of the war, and they shared a strong sense of indignation that, while the war had disrupted filmmaking in Britain, many British filmmakers continued to work as normal in Hollywood. The targets were both numerous and prominent: just about everyone who had any success in British films during the 1930s was working in Hollywood by 1940. The exodus of talent had actually started before the war, when a financial crisis had brought the film industry to its knees. The number of features produced annually plummeted from a peak of nearly 200 in the mid-1930s to just 50 in 1940. Indignant commentators overlooked the fact that many filmmakers departed for Hollywood simply as a means of continuing to work, and suggested instead that the 'Hollywood Britons' had fled from their country in its hour of need.[15] At a time when the USA remained defiantly neutral, working in Hollywood was portrayed as being one step short of aiding and abetting the enemy.

Gone with the Wind figured in these criticisms because it became emblematic of all of Hollywood's excesses, and it stood as an infuriating reminder that the major studios were suffering little hardship as a result of the war. The film also figured because it featured two British stars in leading roles. Leslie Howard, who played Ashley Wilkes, returned to Britain immediately after the filming ended and thereby avoided any accusations of disloyalty. The other star was Vivien Leigh. Two years earlier, it had been a point of some national pride when she won the coveted role of Scarlett O'Hara, but Leigh stayed in Hollywood when *Gone with the Wind* finished filming, and this made her a target for the fan magazine's scorn. In January 1940, the magazine mocked-up a photograph of her in uniform as a WREN, and suggested that she should return to Britain to make films as a part of her 'national service' and on officer's pay of £240 per year.[16] In March 1940, an editorial asked, 'does she know there's a war on?', adding that 'perhaps it is easy to forget ... when one is sitting safely 6000 miles away basking in the warmth of the Californian sun and American applause'.[17] Later that month her plans to tour the United States in a stage production of *Romeo and Juliet* led the magazine to belittle her talent ('If Vivien Leigh is a great figure of the English theatre, it is time the English theatre was told about it') and also to refer to Laurence Olivier, her future husband and co-star in *Romeo and Juliet*, as 'Mr Scarlett O'Hara'.[18]

The other reason that *Gone with the Wind* became a target was that Selznick's proud boasts about its size and scale fitted well with snobbish perceptions of American cultural values: it was the large, the new and the expensive that Americans prized, while questions of quality, taste and tradition were disregarded. It was at one of the great crisis points of the war, in the last week of May 1940, and as the German advance through France reached the English Channel, that the most memorable put-down of *Gone with the Wind* was recorded. The actor-manager Sir Seymour Hicks, who was the head of ENSA (the service that provided entertainment to the troops), issued a letter to the press, drawing attention once again to the British actors working in the United States. His letter was partly aimed at Broadway and the actors 'gallantly facing the footlights' on the New York stage, but also at Hollywood where, he charged, the Hollywood Britons were making a new film called *Gone with the Wind Up*.[19] That phrase, so succinctly deflating the bombast of the title and the hype surrounding the film, became an instant catch phrase; and it has served ever since as a shorthand for the contrast between Britain, as it stood on the verge of the blitz, and a vision of Hollywood as a far-flung outpost of luxurious, cowardly isolation.

The campaign against *Gone with the Wind*

Film exhibitors might have been expected to welcome *Gone with the Wind*, if only for the rush of patrons it was likely to bring through their doors, but this was not the case. Once again, size was the crucial issue. Selznick and the film's distributor, MGM, insisted that a film of this length and status warranted a 'road show' release: it would play exclusively at select theatres, with highly priced seats, and advanced booking and separate performances (as opposed to the continuous performances that were the norm in most cinemas at this time). Exhibitors, however, were aghast at MGM's booking terms and stipulations. While in the past they had paid as much as 50 per cent of the box office revenues as the rental charge for high-profile films, MGM was demanding 70 per cent for *Gone with the Wind*.[20] Furthermore, the ticket prices were set at a minimum of three shillings and sixpence; four times the average ticket price of just over ten pence.[21] In return, MGM guaranteed each exhibitor an exclusive run of the film for a full year; it would play in only one venue in each city for that period. Remarkably, MGM also guaranteed exhibitors that they would not lose money in any single week that they played the film and that they would receive a profit of at least 10 per cent of the total box office revenue over the whole run.[22] Yet these guaranteed profits did not allay anxieties about the film. Exhibitors were in no mood for special conditions and unusual arrangements.

In 1940, there were few signs that the war would bring steep rises in cinema admissions. In fact, the beginning of the war had brought a government order closing all cinemas. With their city centre locations, their night time opening hours, and their hundreds (if not thousands) of closely-packed seats, cinemas looked likely to become death traps in the event of bombing. When the bombers did not come during the first weeks of the war, the order was gradually rescinded and within a month all cinemas had reopened, but it was not quite business as usual.[23] Opening hours were curtailed in some cities, the blackout put many people off going out at night and no one knew if cinemas would have to be closed again in future. Also troubling exhibitors was a steep rise in the entertainment tax (the amount paid to the exchequer on each ticket sold) that came into effect in the spring of 1940. In this climate, many hoped merely to stay open and retain their regular customers. Exhibitors therefore found the excitement surrounding *Gone with the Wind* easy to resist, and assumed that the high ticket prices would either alienate regular patrons or absorb too much of their leisure spending in one sitting. 'Cream for two weeks is not worth skimmed milk for fifty,' the Cinematograph Exhibitors' Association (CEA) warned it members, as it pressed home the point that this epic film was a luxury that Britain could not afford.[24]

Two days after the premiere, the CEA mounted a campaign urging its members, who controlled the majority of the country's cinemas, to boycott the film. The tone and tactics employed in this campaign demonstrate that there was more at stake than high ticket prices for a very long film. The CEA insisted that *Gone with the Wind* was the shape of things to come; that Hollywood would make ever bigger and more lavish films, and it would use these to justify charging increasing sums to exhibitors. The ultimate goal, the CEA alleged, was to bankrupt exhibitors so that the Hollywood companies could buy British cinemas at reduced prices. Having used the First World War as an opportunity to crush the country's film producers, the argument went, Hollywood was now using the Second World War to crush its exhibitors. *Gone with the Wind* was their proof.[25] A simmering resentment against American neutrality, and a much more specific resentment toward Hollywood's business-as-usual approach to the war, lay at the heart of this conspiracy theory. Hence, war-related rhetoric and references were employed to make the CEA's case. MGM was portrayed as a powerful foreign aggressor, while British exhibitors were cast as the beleaguered but defiant resistance. MGM's insistence on 'dictating' terms was referred to as the 'Hitler technique' and any exhibitor who agreed to the company's terms was a 'fifth columnist'.[26] The film itself was 'unsuitable' because it emphasized 'the horrors of war' too strongly for a nation actually engaged in war, according to the CEA. Meanwhile, at meetings, CEA members rallied one another by declaring 'We are fighting a battle for the people' and by likening their 'fight' against 'aggression and grab from America' to the war against German aggression.[27] The contrast between British austerity and American excess was also made in relation to MGM's chief executive in Britain, Sam Eckman, and his annual salary of £46,000. This, the CEA asserted, was 'greater than the sum of the entire British War Cabinet's salary'.[28]

The CEA printed 5,000 pamphlets, setting out its case against the film, and distributed them to its members, to the press and to members of parliament.[29] The press was largely sympathetic, and reports about the dispute reached well beyond the film trade papers and into magazines and daily newspapers.[30] The theatre and cinema employees union, NATKE, fell into line when it called upon the government to invoke defence powers to 'suppress' *Gone with the Wind*.[31] There were questions in the House of Commons, where the CEA drew cross party support. Sir Jocelyn Lucas (Conservative, Portsmouth South) asked whether, as a means of conserving the foreign exchange that was vital to the war effort, the Board of Trade could restrict the rental charges paid to American film companies. Neil Maclean (Labour, Glasgow Govan) put forth the CEA's argument when he asked, 'Is it not the case that when this war finishes cinemas in this country will be in the hands of the American producer, who has taken possession of the film production in this country since the last war?' John Wilmot (Labour, Kennington) asked for the Board of Trade to refuse to issue an import licence for the film 'unless a reasonable rental is charged'. The Parliamentary Secretary to the Board of Trade, Major Lloyd George, responded by pointing out that British exhibitors were being asked to pay no more for the film than their American counterparts, and, at any rate, the Board of Trade did not have the power to regulate film rental agreements.[32]

MGM was in a vulnerable position because, beyond Leicester Square, it had no cinemas of its own in Britain. In the United States, *Gone with the Wind* was released on the Loews circuit, which was affiliated with MGM, but in Britain the company would have to rent the film to unaffiliated exhibition outlets. The gala premiere was one means of attracting exhibitors' interest; reviews were another. Coverage of the film's release was overshadowed, however, by the CEA's campaign.[33] The three major national cinema circuits – ABC, Gaumont and Odeon cinemas – hesitated to book the film, standing back from the controversy and perhaps hoping that it would lead MGM to offer better terms and conditions. With the major circuits standing back, MGM turned to independent exhibitors, who rarely got to handle first-run films. In Manchester, the entrepreneur Harry Buxton stepped forward and booked the film into his 900-seat Gaiety Theatre, which had recently been converted from stage to screen entertainment. *Gone with the Wind* had its first screenings outside London at the Gaiety in May 1940, and over the next six months it also gained bookings from independent exhibitors in Aberdeen, Birmingham, Cardiff, Coventry, Dundee, Newcastle and Southport. The ABC circuit, meanwhile, agreed to book the film into just a dozen cinemas (in cities where independents had not come forward) during the summer of 1940, although not in the circuit's largest, city-centre venues.[34] The CEA responded to these bookings by taking its case directly to audiences. It printed posters and leaflets, distributing them in the cities where the film was booked, and it made trailers and slides that could be shown in neighbouring cinemas. All advised audiences to boycott the film until it was shown at 'normal prices'.[35] In Manchester, the effort to undermine the film was particularly intense – 500 posters went up and the trailer was shown in 100 local cinemas – but similar tactics were employed in other cities.[36]

In London, the CEA campaign had little effect on the box office. The strategy of selling the film as a special occasion for affluent audiences was a resounding success. Going to see the film at London's Empire, Palace or Ritz theatres was certainly no ordinary evening at the cinema. Ticket prices (which were as high as ten shillings and six pence) were set at the level of West End stage shows. They were designed to be reassuringly expensive; that is, to convince middle-class patrons, who visited the cinema selectively, that this was a cinematic event worthy of their attendance. The venues themselves reinforced a sense of exclusivity. The Empire was Britain's plushest cinema, and its gilded age elegance – with a vast foyer, sweeping staircases, elaborate chandeliers, deep carpets, gleaming mahogany and mirrored walls – was even more ostentatious than Scarlett and Rhett's Atlanta mansion.[37] The Palace was almost as lavish and, as a venue usually reserved for stage shows, it screened only the most significant films (such as *The Four Horsemen of the Apocalypse* in 1922). The Ritz was newer, smaller and situated in a basement, but it had a sleek Art Deco interior, with chromium-plated walls, and a reputation for attracting the smart set.[38]

In this rarefied London exhibition niche *Gone with the Wind* thrived. From its opening in mid-April 1940 it played at all three West End cinemas for five weeks, attracting nearly 250,000 patrons. It was pulled from the Ritz in late May, and then pulled from the Palace in early June.[39] It played on at the vast Empire, but by this time the ever-worsening war news had brought about 'the bleakest spell that the cinema in England has faced', according to C.A. Lejeune. Audiences in most cinemas were 'about as big as a parish sewing-bee', but *Gone with the Wind* was singled out as the one film still drawing 'fair-sized crowds' to its matinees in June 1940. No film, apparently, could draw audiences out at night, when the public's compelling need to hear the BBC's nine o'clock news broadcast brought 'death to the evening house'.[40] In mid-July, when West End ticket sales had surpassed 425,000, the film's run at the Empire ended after 12 weeks. Even then it did not leave Leicester Square but resumed running at the Ritz.[41] There, as Guy Morgan recalled, the blitz did not deter patrons from queuing to see the film:

> During the big blitz you went into Leicester Square early in the morn-
> ing, after a long night of bombing, and found the queues already circling
> the theatre. Sometimes customers had to climb over fire hoses to get to
> the paybox. 'I shall never forget', says one Londoner, 'the night the Café
> Anglais was hit. All hell was let loose that night. The corner block was down.
> A huge fire was blazing. Twenty or thirty engines were tearing around the
> square. There was still a long queue of people waiting to go into *Gone with
> the Wind*.[42]

Of course, it may have helped that the Ritz was 16 feet underground and therefore regarded as one of the safer venues in central London during the blitz.[43]

Outside of London, MGM attempted to hold the line on the minimum ticket price of three shillings and six pence, and in pro-vincial cities such as Aberdeen these prices set local records but had no apparent effect on demand.[44] The venues were not always as grand as the Empire and the Palace. The Gaiety in Manchester, for example, had struggled to find an identity since turning from stage to screen entertainment a few months earlier. The theatre had been refurbished, with new seats and carpets in honour of the film's arrival, and the industry watched with interest to see if the CEA campaign would deter patrons. It was noted, for example, that the CEA trailer, advising audiences not to pay high prices to see the film, drew cheers in nearby cinemas. Yet even the Gaiety's owner, Harry Buxton, was surprised by the extent of the film's success in Manchester: its run lasted for nearly six months and 200,000 tickets were sold.[45] Midway through the run, Buxton explained that the film's success was not attributable to routine cinema-goers or even local audiences: 'We have not touched the fringe of the average cinema public. It is the theatregoers that the film has so far attracted. We have had parties from as far afield as Leeds, Huddersfield and Crewe.'[46] The CEA campaign – which was the reason *Gone with the Wind* did not play in Leeds, Huddersfield or Crewe in 1940 – effectively gave the film a cachet it probably would not have had if it had shown widely on one of the major cinema circuits.

In fact, all of the independent exhibitors who took a chance on the film appear to have been amply rewarded.[47] Nevertheless, the CEA's campaign should not be regarded as a complete failure. As the film historian Allen Eyles has argued, the backlash against MGM's terms 'did enormously reduce the number of bookings [the film] received at this time'.[48] Outside of London, this long-awaited, high-profile film was reduced to playing either in independent cinemas that did not normally screen first-run films or in the second-tier houses of the ABC circuit. Furthermore, the film reached just 20 cities in 1940 and this meant that many cinema-goers were not able to see it on its initial release.[49] It was only in September 1942 that the film received a wide general release throughout the country. In the meantime – throughout all of 1941 and much of 1942 – the only screen in Britain that continued to show *Gone with the Wind* was the Ritz in London. Thus, for nearly two years Hollywood's over-sized epic was restricted to a single screen in a small basement cinema off Leicester Square.

Those who missed the film in 1940, either because it did not play in their city or because they could not afford the high prices, had a long wait for a wider release. When the general release finally began in September 1942, there was no further controversy about high ticket prices or rentals. The prices had come down – tickets now ranged from two shillings and nine pence to five shillings and six pence, and MGM charged a rental of 55 per cent – but they were still very high. The difference was that exhibitors had enjoyed a huge increase in cinema-going since 1940, and they knew the public was especially eager to see this much-discussed but elusive film. Advance word about its quality was overwhelmingly strong. Before the general release began, a survey in *Picturegoer* found that it already ranked third (behind *Goodbye Mr Chips* and *Mrs Miniver*) among readers' 'ten best films of all time'.[50] Film columnists regularly updated their readers on news of the general release.[51] And there was some dismay that troops serving in Egypt and Libya were able to see the film, and describe it in letters home, before their 'impatient' wives and sweethearts could see it in Britain.[52] The long period of anticipation, the high prices and lengthy

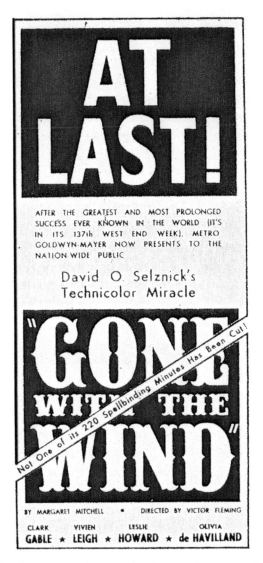

Figure 10   The long-awaited general release of *Gone with the Wind* was announced with this advertisement in *Picturegoer* (19 September 1942, p. 2)

running time ensured that, on general release, the film's arrival in provincial cities assumed an unusual importance and a sense of occasion.[53] Ironically, then, the CEA campaign was successful in restricting the film's 'road show' release, but this ultimately transformed *Gone with the Wind* into one of the much coveted luxuries of wartime, and people were willing to spend extra time and money to acquire it. Hence, an advertisement in *Picturegoer* announced the general release with the proclamation 'at last!' and the promise that 'not one of its 220 spellbinding minutes has been cut' (Figure 10).[54] As the leading trade paper described it, the film was in 'a class of its own' as a box office attraction, but it was only after the general release in 1942 and the re-release in 1944 that the millions of ordinary cinema-goers in Britain were able to see it.[55]

Critical responses

Before the premiere, before the CEA's campaign started and before the box office queues began to form, British critics sat down to watch the film in a trade screening held especially for the press. The critics fell into different camps. At one end of the spectrum were those who wrote for the film industry's trade papers and for the popular daily and Sunday newspapers, and therefore were concerned primarily with a film's ability to please audiences. It was these critics who gave *Gone with the Wind* its most positive reviews. 'Spectacular', 'phenomenal' and 'outstanding' were the adjectives sprinkled throughout the review in *Kinematograph Weekly*, which heralded it as 'the biggest box office attraction ever', and in *Today's Cinema*, the reviewer advised that the film had 'record-breaking box office possibilities such as are rarely offered to exhibitors'.[56] Where the former had only praise, the latter was concerned by the war scenes, which it thought would 'strike a little too closely at the heart of a nation at war'. This criticism, picked up and disseminated by the CEA, was also made in some popular newspapers. In the *Daily Mail*, Seton Margrave questioned the 'timeliness' of showing 'hundreds of wounded soldiers in simulated agony, especially the scene of the amputation of a leg without anaesthetic'; in the *Sunday Pictorial*, Dick Richards commented that 'for these times [the film] is too harrowing and gloomy'; in the *Sunday Express*, Isolene Thompson referred to the same scenes as 'very harrowing'; and in London's *Evening News* Jympson Harman commented that 'these are no times for scenes of whole streets cluttered with bodies of wounded men'.[57] Only Dick Richards disliked the film, though, and otherwise the popular critics praised the performance of the stars, the extent to which the film followed the novel and the use of Technicolor.

The popular critics consistently presented *Gone with the Wind* as a triumph for Vivien Leigh. 'This is the biggest part that was ever tackled by any actress in the fantastic history of motion pictures,' Paul Holt enthused to readers of the *Daily Express*, concluding that Leigh is 'superb' and 'the film is hers'. Similarly, Isolene Thompson declared that Leigh is 'so good she steals the film', while Seton Margrave said that she 'holds the picture securely in her hands'. Jympson Harman praised her performance as 'one of the most gripping character studies film has ever given to us'; in the *Daily Mirror*, Reginald Whitley stated 'you'll find her absolutely irresistible'; and P.L. Mannock of the *Daily Herald* assured readers that 'her first Hollywood role puts her in the front row of stars'. There was praise for Clark Gable too, but Gable's suitability for the part of Rhett Butler was so widely foretold that even a 'flawless performance' (as Margrave described it) was less noteworthy than Leigh's triumph. The film's fidelity to the novel also won unanimous approval from the popular critics. They assumed their readers knew the book and that they would resent any significant diversions from it. Referring to the film as a 'page by page' adaptation of the novel, as both Seton Margrave and Isolene Thompson did, aimed to reassure readers. The issue of Technicolor was not quite so clear-cut. Many British cinema-goers preferred their films in black and white, and some regarded Technicolor as gaudy and artificial.[58] But the colour in *Gone with the Wind*, these critics informed their readers, was used meaningfully: 'shots such as the mule teams against the scarred earth, and Scarlett O'Hara in her scarlet gown coming down the red stairs, are art', Ian Coster informed readers of London's *Evening Standard*. P.L. Mannock also referred to the 'vivid artistry' of the 'colour effects', and for Isolene Thompson the film was evidence that 'soon the cinema must adopt colour permanently'. Reginald Whitley, writing with the many women readers of *Daily Mirror* in mind, reported that colour added another dimension to the appeal of Vivien Leigh, showing her 'green eyes, narrow waist and pert features' to their best effect and also enhancing the 'lovely frocks' seen in the film.[59]

The limitation of popular reviews (at least for the film historian) is that they are generally shorter, less detailed and less stringent than the reviews found in the 'quality' press. The distinction between the two modes of criticism was discussed by Jympson Harman, the critic for London's *Evening News*. Critics writing for the popular press, he explained, can never be certain whether they are 'writing for a docker or a don'. Their mass readership meant that they were obliged to suppress personal opinions and instead scrutinize a film for any potential merit it might have. The critic might see a film and think 'heavens, how it stinks!', but he also had to consider 'is this the sort of thing some people like?' and tailor his review to popular tastes.[60] Critics writing for the quality press – an assortment of upmarket newspapers and magazines covering cultural, social and current affairs – had quite a different brief. There were likely to be more dons than dockers among their readers; or at least they would include a higher proportion of more affluent, better educated and older readers. These groups were not habitual cinema-goers, but instead chose to see individual films, and reviews helped them make their selections. The quality critics were therefore quick to dismiss a film if they suspected it was beneath their readers, and also eager to highlight a film of merit that might otherwise be overlooked. They wrote for an audience seeking opinionated views, and they did not shirk from providing them.

As the war progressed, the quality critics would become increasingly preoccupied with notions of realism and with championing a strain of British cinema that emerged from the documentary movement, but in 1940 these interests had yet to take centre stage.[61] At this juncture, the leading critics emphasized aesthetic qualities that were specific to film. The 'pictorial qualities' of a film were a primary concern, and so fidelity to a novel or play had no importance.[62] Acting was often commented on, but the criteria for judging film acting remained indebted to stagebound notions of an actor's craft, and Hollywood stars, whose appeal was attributed to charisma and glamour, were seldom admired. However, neither fidelity to the original source nor acting was the primary concern of quality critics; this was the director, and what was referred to as the 'director's vision'. Hence, when Dilys Powell of the *Sunday Times* defined her 'credo' as a film critic, she emphasized visual design, composition

and movement as the key aesthetic criteria, and also the importance of the director as the source of the film's 'integrity'. Twenty
years before the ascendance of the *auteur* theory, Powell confidently
commented that 'no work of art exists without betraying to some
extent the personality of the artist'.[63] Many others agreed with
her.[64] In practice, this meant that the quality critics often favoured
European films, whose directors they considered to be less bound
by commercial imperatives, as well as the British and Hollywood
films made by directors with a recognizable style. The concern for
individual artistry and vision made them wary of the idea of film as
a factory product, produced to entertain the masses. They therefore had little regard for Hollywood, the studio system, and any film
that appeared to be its crowning glory.

These critical values left little room for appreciating *Gone with
the Wind*. Victor Fleming, the credited director, was prominent
within Hollywood but his films were not considered to be distinctive. At any rate, this film was better known as David Selznick's
project, and producers were regarded as 'money men' rather than
creative artists. Money, of course, was something the film had in
abundance, but most quality critics treated the high production
values flippantly. Dilys Powell joked that the sweeping crane shot
that reveals the entire Atlanta train depot to be filled with thousands of dead or wounded Confederate soldiers looked to her like
'a bank holiday on Bournemouth beach'. Technicolor, too, was dismissed. 'The colour of the sky ... it seems ... is practically always
red', she complained.[65] Where some quality critics at least singled
out Vivien Leigh for praise, Powell found her performance 'almost
entirely without interest'. She described Clark Gable as having 'the
nonchalance of a touring vaudeville artist' (in other words, it did not
look as though he was trying very hard). In fact, Powell found the
film to be so unworthy of the hype surrounding it that she built her
entire review around an extended joke about an expedition team –
with members chosen for their 'hardihood, tenacity and powers of
resistance' – setting off on the long and arduous journey of watching the nearly four-hour film.[66]

MGM was not amused. The company soon punished Powell by
banning her from their trade screenings.[67] Her readers, however, were
delighted. Powell had a loyal following (referred to as 'Dilysians' by

one rival critic), and cartoonists and reviewers followed in her wake by reinventing her joke about the fortitude needed to survive a screen-ing of *Gone with the Wind*.[68] A reviewer for *Picturegoer and Film Weekly* commented that, before going to see the film, he and his wife:

> ….considered for a long time whether we ought to take with us a vacuum flask, sandwiches, cushions, fur coats and even a primus stove in case win-ter had set in by the time we came out. But the film doesn't seem so very long once you get used to it.[69]

In *The Bystander*, George Campbell dubbed the film the 'four-hour Colossus' and reported that he 'felt that I had seen a longish picture and could do with a longish Scotch' when he realized he had reached only the intermission.[70] Ivor Brown's review in the *Illustrated London News* was admiring enough to comment that 'If there were "seven wonders of Hollywood" this would be the first', but he added that 'four hours is a very real test of optical endurance' and 'it would do the public eyesight quite a deal of good to cut at least half an hour out of its later reaches'.[71]

Other quality critics were also concerned by the film's size, and particularly its status as an epic historical film, but this was not a joking matter. The historical genre raised acute sensitivities. One key issue was historical accuracy, but this was scarcely discussed in relation to *Gone with the Wind*. The American Civil War was not a widely studied topic in Britain, let alone one likely to spark debate among film critics.[72] The film's portrayal of slavery sparked objec-tions from the London Colored People's Association, which asked both the Home Office and London County Council to ban the film ('on the ground that it is insulting to the negro community'), but this protest met with no success.[73] A more pertinent issue was that historical films should be tales of progress and the people who made it; stories of the sacrifices made by altruistic and noteworthy figures. Such films were valued for the light that they cast on sig-nificant moments or prominent people from the past. *Victoria the Great* (1937) and *Nurse Edith Cavell* (1939) had demonstrated quite recently that critics readily accepted films centred on noteworthy women, so long as the women were eminent and virtuous. This is where *Gone with the Wind* fell short: why should a four-hour epic be centred on a woman of questionable morality and no apparent social or political importance? It bemused some critics and left others spluttering. In numerous reviews, the words 'hussy' and 'minx' were called into play:

> Given the right central character, all this might have made one of the greatest pictures ever seen. Alas, Scarlett O'Hara is just a hussy. She has courage and greed and a passion for the family land – qualities you find in peasants everywhere. She is too vulgar, too obvious and too stupid to hold the attention for four hours (Campbell Dixon, *Daily Telegraph*).[74]

> The one serious weakness about *Gone with the Wind* is that the story lacks the epic quality which alone could justify such a lavish outlay of time, talent, and production values. If the personal drama had been made subservient to the cinematic treatment of the central theme – the collapse and devastation of the Old South – the *Gone with the Wind* might have been a really great film (D.S., *Manchester Guardian*).[75]

> It is a matter of regret that a film conceived on such epic proportions should deal only with the life story of a hussy (E.P., *Monthly Film Bulletin*).[76]

> As a story it does not 'need' its length; it is merely a succession of incidents … it reveals nothing, it states nothing except the outlines of a comparatively commonplace character (R.M., *Punch*).[77]

> The plain fact is that what has thus been presented as a super-epic is the sordid personal story of a scheming, hard-hearted, ruthless Southern belle and a cynical war profiteer. A story, in short, which from its nature can have no sort of epic quality (George Pitman, *Reynolds' News*).[78]

> *Gone with the Wind* has not, never had, a theme quite big enough for its colossal size. It is simply the story of a minx's progress, and some of us may feel that Scarlett O'Hara, with all her charm, all her devilry, is not quite a great enough figure to motivate so vast a drama (C.A. Lejeune, *Sketch*).[79]

> This film has no justification whatever for lasting three hours and forty minutes … .Where the epic sweep of a nation at war with itself was required [the filmmakers] have lapsed into petty personalia (Basil Wright, *Spectator*).[80]

> This vast and rather overwhelming work takes the trivial story of a heartless girl and splashes it in crude, magnificent colours against a backdrop of civil war … If the subject had been worthy of the treatment that would indeed have been a film (Anthony Gibbs, *Sunday Chronicle*).[81]

One finds oneself wishing that the teller of the story would concentrate on history and cut the tiresome Scarlett out of it ... Since the Civil War is not the theme, what is? I can only suggest the minxishness of minxes ... No expense has been spared on the glorification of what housemaids call 'a little madam' (James Agate, *Tatler*).[82]

Here are three and half hours of ranting, roaring and much history, some of it very well done as spectacle, all centring around a little minx who means nothing to anybody from start to finish (John Coverdale, *Time and Tide*).[83]

Clearly, these objections were based in both class and gender distinctions: the *nouveau riche* Scarlett was not worthy of an historical film. Her story was the stuff of the 'woman's film': a critically denigrated genre that dealt with personal, intimate and emotional affairs rather than recounting significant public events. C.A. Lejeune was one of the few critics to define *Gone with the Wind* as a 'woman's film' and she acknowledged that the label brought with it lower expectations.[84] Of course, the film could also be labelled as a costume drama; that is, a fictional story set in the past, which is only loosely concerned with real events and people.[85] Yet respected costume dramas were usually based on classic literature rather than recent bestsellers, and Mitchell's novel (a commercial phenomenon but not a book noted for its literary merits) had no critical distinction to extend to the film.

When regarding *Gone with the Wind* as an historical film, the quality critics did not wilfully misread it. Its epic length and its status gave the film an air of authoritative or official history. Would the state of Georgia declare a public holiday for a mere costume drama? Would government leaders and foreign diplomats attend the premiere of a woman's film? Despite these markers of respect, however, the film itself betrays its willingness to depart from the conventions of the historical film in its opening moments. The first intertitles, for example, adopt a highly fanciful rather than an authoritative tone:

There was a land of Cavaliers and Cotton Fields called the Old South. Here in this pretty world, Gallantry took its last bow. Here was the last ever to be seen of Knights and their Ladies Fair, of Master and of Slave ... Look

for it only in books, for it is no more than a dream remembered. A civilization Gone with the Wind ...

The words appear against a backdrop of pastoral images, and as a
hushed and mournful rendition of 'Dixie' is heard on the soundtrack. This nostalgic and whimsical tone was the stuff of 'moonlight
and magnolias' folklore rather than history, and as a staple of many
other films set in the Old South, it would have been familiar to critics. The first scene continues in this vein. Opening with a view of
the imposing plantation house Tara, the scene shows the Tarleton
twins drinking mint juleps on the front porch, and speaking with
a slow and heavy drawl, while hound dogs laze in the sun behind
them. Scarlett's first lines of dialogue also suggest that the grim
reality of war will not be allowed to intrude on the drama:

> Fiddle-dee-dee. War, war, war. This war talk is spoiling all the fun at every
> party this Spring. I get so bored I could scream. Besides, there isn't going
> to be any war. ... If either of you boys says 'war' just once again, I'll go in
> the house and slam the door!

But of course Scarlett cannot slam the door on the war, and when it
arrives some thirty minutes further into the film, the tone changes.
The siege of Atlanta, for example, is prefaced with the words:

> Siege. The skies rained Death ... For thirty-five days a battered Atlanta
> hung grimly on, hoping for a miracle.

This informative tone is more typical of the historical genre and,
with the words printed over an illustrative image (in this case, Union
troops with their cannons trained on Atlanta and waiting to fire), a
sense of veracity is conveyed. A similar combination of intertitles
and images is used to preface scenes set at the time of the battle
of Gettysburg, Sherman's march through Georgia, and post-war
Reconstruction. If this change in tone and address discomforted
the critics, it was because the film refers to these moments of public or official history briefly, and merely as a means of punctuating
Scarlett's story. The image of Union troops waiting outside Atlanta,
for example, is a fleeting one. The soldiers and the wider story are

quickly left behind, and the film reverts to Scarlett and her attempts to cope with the imminent arrival of Melanie's baby. 'Real' history serves only a backdrop, and the film sets up a dichotomy between the public/male sphere and the private/female sphere which suggests that the latter is more vivid and compelling.

The dichotomy is demonstrated most strikingly in the film's epic crane shot, discussed so dismissively by Dilys Powell, which reveals Atlanta's train depot to be filled with thousands of dead and dying Confederate soldiers. In some respects, this shot fits well within the conventions of the historical film. It is a 'spectacular vista', which registers the importance of the historical moment in a display of extraordinary and excessive spectacle. In Tom Brown's definition, the 'spectacular vista' is usually associated with the world of men; that is, with the public history of wars, battles and grand achievements.[86] The crane shot at the train depot seems to meet these criteria: for a full 53 seconds, the camera sweeps up and back, leaving the tight focus on Scarlett and her personal story, and revealing a much broader canvas of war-ravaged Atlanta. At the climax of the crane shot, a tattered Confederate flag comes into the frame, thereby offering an historical explanation for the carnage that lies everywhere below it. Yet even in this moment of grand and public spectacle, the importance and centrality of Scarlett is scarcely diminished.

The scene begins as Scarlett makes her way through Atlanta, seeking Dr Mead to deliver Melanie's baby. When she arrives at the train depot, the camera remains fixed on her and for a moment the audience sees only her response to the multitude of dead and dying men, and not the men themselves. In a medium close-up, a look of amazement crosses her face, turning from disbelief to revulsion (Figure 11). Then the crane shot reveals what she has seen, but because it begins with her reaction, the experience of the moment remains bound up with her. Furthermore, even as the camera moves up and back (away from her), she remains at the centre of the frame, and many of the wounded men reach out to her, effectively pointing to her and emphasizing her presence (Figure 12). At the peak of the crane shot, the intrusion of the Confederate flag temporarily obliterates her, but this lasts for only three seconds, and it serves as a reminder that, beyond Scarlett, one will find only hopeless causes in this story (Figure 13). In the next scene, she is once again front

Figure 11   In *Gone with the Wind*, Scarlett (Vivien Leigh) observes the devastation of war-torn Atlanta

and centre. She finds Dr Mead, who mistakenly assumes that she has come to help him. 'You've got to come with *me*,' she insists, reasserting her own pre-eminence within the film. In *Gone with the Wind*, war is not a collective experience characterized by the good deeds and altruism of Dr Mead; it is a set of circumstances that affects individuals, and it means little beyond tragedy, danger, and the struggle to survive.

It is not surprising, then, that Dilys Powell disapproved of the film and mocked this scene in particular. In the spring of 1940, as Britain stood on the verge of sweeping historical events, the quality critics could only regard *Gone with the Wind* as an unfortunate precedent. The films they would admire over the coming years valued community over individuality, the dutiful over the rebellious, and restraint over excess; values almost completely at odds with Scarlett's story. In fact, the one character universally admired by the quality critics was Mammy.[87] Although the comments mainly praised Hattie McDaniel's robust performance, it is notable that the most positive comments related to this dutiful and undemanding character; the one who keeps her spirits up and never questions her small place in the grand scheme of things. By contrast, Scarlett's individualism and self-importance were regarded as ill suited to the historical film. Her story did not warrant epic treatment; minxes had no place in history.

Figure 12   Scarlett remains at the centre of the frame as the sweeping crane shot in *Gone with the Wind* reveals the thousands of dead and wounded Confederate soldiers around her

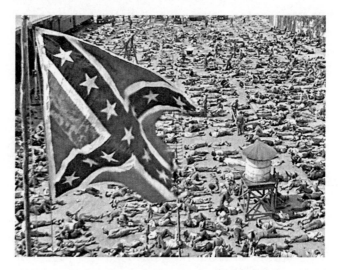

Figure 13   A tattered Confederate flag momentarily obscures Scarlett at the peak of the crane shot in *Gone with the Wind*

Audience responses

What can reviews of *Gone with the Wind* tell us about wider audience responses to the film? While critics for the trade papers and the popular press offer some indication of how and why the film may have appealed to audiences, their reviews were on the whole too swift and light to be fully revealing. The quality critics wrote at greater length, and with more concern for the aesthetic value and cultural standing of a film, but their carefully studied opinions seem (at least in this case) hostile to popular tastes. Indeed, the uniformity and the disdain that is apparent across the body of quality reviews suggests that they are reacting to something they find distasteful. Yet approached in this way, as a reaction, the common terms of their disapproval may be taken as enlightening. It suggests that these critics were aware of popular taste, and that they were engaging with and responding to it. Although their views represent a rebuke, they are nevertheless conversant with the tastes they seek to diminish. Thus, while asserting their own opinions, and designating the boundaries of cultivated tastes, they actually reveal a greater range of opinions than their own. This can be demonstrated with recourse to the available evidence on audience responses to the film, and with reference to publicity and other materials relating to the film's release.

Audience responses to the film feature significantly in the two most substantial surveys of wartime cinema-goers, Mass Observation's 1943 survey of 'favourite films' and the sociological studies conducted by J.P. Mayer in 1945.[88] Respondents to these surveys express themselves in very different terms, but two common threads are discernible. One is that, far from finding the lengthy running time to be problematic, respondents in both surveys found that it was a fundamental part of the film's ability to captivate and engross them. A 30-year-old man from Birmingham, working as a biologist, told Mass Observation that:

> I previously avoided going to see it under the impression that I could not stand a 4hr. film … So I went prepared to be bored and instead was amazed to find that the 4 hrs. seemed more like 1½ - 2.[89]

A similar (if more emphatic) response was reported to J.P. Mayer by a 14-year-old schoolgirl from Hampstead:

> I went to see the film soon after its first arrival in London and I have never enjoyed sitting for three hours more than I did then. In case I should be bored I took three bars of chocolate with me but I was so enthralled with the film I forgot to eat them – a thing which has never happened to me before.[90]

One of her classmates, another schoolgirl from Hampstead, attributed her enjoyment of the film to its length:

> As it was a long film you had time to catch hold of the spirit of it and you did not, as you do with some of the shorter films, come away from it with a feeling that you were not anything to the actors and feeling you were worlds apart from each other.[91]

Thus, the lengthy running time not only offered an opportunity for (extended) escapism but also, as further comments indicate, an opportunity to identify closely with a particularly compelling character.

Intense identification with Scarlett, particularly among women, is the other common thread linking the two surveys. It could be argued that this is a corollary of enjoying the film. Rarely has any film been so entirely dominated by a single character. She is in all but a tiny minority of scenes, and the vast majority pivot around her. This is done conventionally through close-ups and, at key points, more distinctively by showing her thin, feminine frame standing proudly against a dramatic landscape. In the most famous of these scenes, as she proclaims to the heavens that she and her family will 'never go hungry again', the combination of her defiant speech, her central position against a dawn sky, and the soaring musical score lend a weight and importance to Scarlett that few previous film heroines had been accorded. The critics may have regarded her as a lamentable subject for an epic, but audiences were clearly riveted by her.

Audience enthusiasm is not expressed unreservedly in the Mass Observation survey, in which 220 people discuss the six 'favourite films' they have seen over the previous year, but Mass Observation's respondents hardly formed a representative sample of the cinema-going public. In wartime, the keenest cinema-goers were those who went to the cinema at least once every week, and they tended to be young (less than 40 years old), working class or lower-middle class, and educated only to the elementary or secondary school level.[92] Mass Observation's respondents, by contrast, included a greater proportion of middle-aged and elderly people. Their occupations (writer, retired banker, research physicist, biologist, college lecturer, school mistress, etc.) mark them as well educated and middle class. And many of the respondents mentioned that they saw films rarely, or that they had not seen six films over the past year. It is notable too that their favourite films included more critical favourites (British war films such as *In Which We Serve* and the documentary *Desert Victory* figured significantly) than popular favourites (Betty Grable's musicals and Tyrone Power's swashbucklers are not mentioned).[93] It is surprising that *Gone with the Wind* registers in this survey at all, given that these respondents were likely to read the quality critics. It is notable, though, that they are somewhat defensive when discussing *Gone with the Wind* (comments include 'it was so much better than I expected it to be', 'much better than I expected', 'it was based on a novel of which I had not heard the best criticisms'), and that both men and women discuss the film in ways that seek to lend legitimacy to their views.[94] Men state that they admire the film for dramatizing an episode of history, thereby suggesting that their enjoyment was intellectual rather than emotional or escapist.[95] By contrast, none of the women mention the film's historical dimension. They focus on another pre-occupation of quality critics: acting. These comments focus almost entirely on Vivien Leigh and the terms of women's admiration for Leigh do not suggest the cool, detached judgements of technique so often found in quality criticism. Rather, words such as 'convincing', 'vivid' and 'beautiful' suggest a visceral response to Leigh's performance.[96]

J.P. Mayer, a University of London academic, sought a broader and more representative sample of cinema-goers when he embarked on his studies of audiences. In advertisements placed in *Picturegoer* in February and August of 1945, Mayer asked the magazine's readers to write to him, revealing whether films had influenced their personal decisions, behaviour, dreams, ambitions, 'temptations' and 'love-making'. These lines of enquiry suited the preoccupations of his research, centred on the harmful impact he believed films had on children and on society as a whole.[97] Yet one need not share his views to find the responses intriguing. They offer a rare glimpse into the attitudes and opinions of the keenest cinema-goers at a time when many went 'to the pictures' as often as two or three times each week. Furthermore, his respondents are less restrained than Mass Observation's; they enjoy popular films and they express their opinions more openly. 'Carry me into the past ... and I am happy,' wrote a 30-year-old housewife, who listed *Gone with the Wind* among the films she had seen recently, admitting that she went to the cinema 'to be taken out of myself, and to forget the cares of housework, rationing and washing baby's nappies!'[98] A 24-year-old stenographer stated that she objected to inaccuracies in historical films only if she was aware of the 'true facts'; otherwise, she admitted, 'I don't really care'.[99] An 18-year-old textile worker remarked that she like period pictures primarily for their costumes, which gave them a 'certain something' that modern films lacked.[100] A 19-year-old woman (whose occupation is not specified) stated that she goes to the cinema 'for the stars [and] not the story'; as a fan of Clark Gable she had seen *Gone with the Wind* three times.[101] All of these responses – the unabashed appreciation of escapism, a disregard for historical accuracy, an enjoyment of period costumes and admiration for stars – would have been regarded as lowly pleasures by the quality critics and their adherents. However, they fit easily within the popular film culture of 1940s, and, as Sue Harper has observed, they were among the chief pleasures that women derived from historical films during this decade.[102]

The enthusiasm of Mayer's respondents should not be confused with a lack of critical standards. The readers of *Picturegoer* may not have been 'Dilysians', but they had their own values and a familiar (if not quite so pronounced) predilection for asserting that their tastes and opinions were valid and informed. An admiration for acting was one value they shared with the Mass Observation respondents, but Mayer's respondents discussed at greater length the impact that a performance had on them. In some cases, the respondents observed the impact on others rather than discussing their own feelings. For example, a 43-year-old housewife asserted that she thought 'the acting was excellent in *Gone with the Wind*' but she preferred to comment on its effects on younger audience members:

> I heard a very strange noise and I discovered two girls in the row in front, arms round one another actually sobbing. Yes, I think most people regardless of sex or age find it difficult to control their emotions when the acting is good.[103]

A more frequent manner of discussing the merits of a performance, while at the same time demonstrating some critical discrimination, was to compare Hollywood stars with British actors. This was a comparison usually made at Hollywood's expense, but admiration for Vivien Leigh blurred the boundaries, and sparked patriotic responses to this Hollywood film. A 24-year-old typist, who thought the film was a 'thrill for any picturegoer', was pleased to see 'our own Vivien Leigh, proving to Hollywood that our stars can act'; while a 23-year-old woman, working as a lab assistant, preferred Leigh's acting ability to the 'more ephemeral charms of a Betty Grable'.[104]

It is striking that in these comments and many more like them, the respondents use the performer's name rather than the character's name when discussing the film. This, too, may be a signal of some critical discrimination – the respondents indicate their knowledge of the production and not just the story – but in many instances it also signals a close identification with the star and the performance. A 17-year-old junior clerk revealed that she dreamed about *Gone with the Wind* more than any other film ('I could see it over and over again and still dream about it'). Her description of her dreams begins with the comment, 'How often did I dream I saw Vivien Leigh as Scarlett O'Hara ...' and she recounts the film's most emotional scenes with herself in Scarlett's position.[105] A 16-year-old clerk reported that for a month after seeing the film, she was 'haunted' by it and particularly its ambiguous ending. This surprised her because 'Clark Gable nor Vivien Leigh aren't [sic] on my "favourites" list', but she often found herself sleepless in the middle of the night and wondering about Leigh's fate: whether '[Gable] would want to go back with her' or if 'Leslie Howard would go with her'.[106] One of the few comments on the film made by a man was also one of the most intense. A 24-year-old farmer had a recurrent dream centred on the scene in which Scarlett falls down the stairs of the Atlanta mansion during an argument with Rhett:

In my dream I see Vivien Leigh hurtling down, clad in that vivid red gown. When she reaches the bottom and is still, I go to touch her and find the red of her gown is of blood. At this point I usually wake up with a horrible sense of morbidity.[107]

An intimate involvement with the film – to the point where the main character's blood is tangible and evokes primal fears – is particularly striking here, but close identification with Scarlett runs throughout the responses to Mayer's surveys.

Few of the responses demonstrate an identification with any other star or character. There is no indication that Leslie Howard's high-minded, idealistic portrayal of Ashley Wilkes summoned a sense of national pride for the British audience; he is mentioned rarely and only in passing. Clark Gable's Rhett Butler drew some comments, partly because a period drama was regarded as a challenge for the Hollywood star ('Clark Gable acting as never before', as one admirer put it) and elsewhere as the object of sexual attraction ('I simply revel in seeing bold, bad men', an 18-year-old woman confided).[108] Most surprisingly, Olivia de Havilland's Melanie Wilkes also drew few comments or strong feelings. Helen Taylor has pointed out that Margaret Mitchell regarded Melanie as the 'true heroine' of her novel, and also that a 1957 survey of American high school girls indicated that they identified with the sweet and genteel Melanie.[109] Taylor's own research, conducted in the 1980s, found that many British women were ambivalent towards the not-so-sweet Scarlett. They admired her for her courage, strength, endurance and adaptability, but also registered an awareness that these characteristics fell outside the parameters of traditional femininity.[110] In the war years that ambivalence did not register so strongly. Only one of J.P. Mayer's respondents, a 14-year-old girl, commented that she preferred Melanie and found Scarlett to be 'rather selfish', but even she acknowledged that 'if I were her then, I might be the same'.[111]

Few of the respondents make a direct connection between the circumstances of the Second World War and Scarlett's circumstances. One exception is the 17-year-old junior clerk, who often dreamt about the film. She wrote that she found some solace in the film when she suffered a bereavement:

Films generally have a happy ending [but] life doesn't always … .When I lost someone very dear to me and I felt the most miserable person in the world, I thought of some of the courageous people I had seen on the screen, and I felt better. I thought of Scarlett O'Hara in *Gone with the Wind* and all she went through. And I thought of the soldiers in *The Way Ahead*. They suffered much more than I did but they never lost face.[112]

This comment is remarkable for the ease with which it links the most opulent of Hollywood films with the semi-documentary, realist British war drama *The Way Ahead* (1944). Two films that now seem poles apart – in terms of style, subject matter and budget – were to this contemporaneous viewer closely related: both offered stories that were relevant to her experience of wartime and its tragedies. This serves as a reminder that, despite its reputation as a lavish romantic melodrama, *Gone with the Wind* has a realist edge of its own, and its depiction of war (as a few reviewers warned) was frank by the standards of the time. Perhaps the most brutal scene is the one in which Scarlett confronts a renegade Yankee soldier at Tara. The soldier is seen in two close-ups: first as he realizes that she has a pistol, and his expression changes from curiosity to horror; and second, after a shot of Scarlett firing the gun, a close-up of his blood-splattered face indicates that she has killed him. Of course, Hollywood films had featured many shootings before this, but few characters were shot in the face or in close-up, and blood was seldom seen.

It is also remarkable, by the standards of the studio era, that Scarlett's appearance deteriorates so markedly and for so long. She wears the same pink dress for a full 56 minutes of the film (from the siege of Atlanta through the Reconstruction period) and it looks increasingly stained and faded as time passes. Over the same period, her hair becomes bedraggled and her face is allowed to appear free of make-up, with circles under her eyes and a slightly ruddy complexion (Figure 14). This was an abrupt break with Hollywood conventions, but it may have reassured some British women that their own, wartime shortages of cosmetics had not yet reached this crisis point.[113] Scarlett's attempt to remedy her appearance, while still living in penury, is the scene in *Gone with the Wind* that modern audiences find the most far-fetched and unrealistic, and one that has inspired memorable parodies. Turning from a mirror, she sees a pair of curtains that have survived the war unscathed (Figure 15). She pulls them down with a single tug, and emerges in the next scene dressed in the green velvet curtain fabric and with the gold

Figure 14   As Mammy (Hattie McDaniel) looks on, Scarlett notes the effect wartime deprivations have had on her appearance

tie-backs wrapped around her as trimming. However outland-ish this scene now appears, it was not quite so unlikely in wartime Britain, when clothes rationing was severe and government regula-tions went so far as to forbid trimmings and restrict the width of hems, collars and sleeves.[114] 'Make do and mend', the Ministry of Information implored would-be consumers from 1941 onward, and

Figure 15   In a demonstration of the principle of 'make do and mend', Scarlett realizes that the curtains will provide her with fabric to make a much needed new dress

regular features in *Picture Show* informed readers on how to copy the fashions they saw in films without 'cheating' or even using clothing coupons, but with recourse to household items such as disused sheets, tablecloths and curtains. One article suggested that draper's shops might also harbour remnants of curtain fabrics that could be patterned into the dresses seen in Hollywood films.[115] Scarlett, it seems, was demonstrating a form of resourcefulness that, when imitated on the British home front, allowed some relief from austerity and shortages.

There are broader parallels between past and present to note, too: the film concerns the impact of war on women and the home front. Men are either away fighting at times of crisis (Ashley and Rhett) or not much use in a crisis (Dr Mead and Scarlett's father). Women must take on masculine roles, fending for themselves in new and challenging ways. Traditional customs and social barriers fall. There are shortages of food and other everyday items previously taken for granted. Homes are razed to the ground (Twelve Oaks) or badly damaged (Tara). Deaths and casualty lists bring misery. A major city is bombed and burned by the enemy, and the threat of invasion looms menacingly. We might wonder, too, whether the film's portrayal of slavery offered audiences some perspective on the acute racial tensions between white and African American GIs stationed in Britain during the war. Certainly, there is more revealed about American race relations in this film than in the wartime feature films that portray the 'yanks' who were 'over-sexed, over-paid and over here'; those films simply avoid the issue.[116]

As a film about 'total war', *Gone with the Wind* represents wartime experiences in a more frank and honest manner than any film made and set during the Second World War. Contemporary war films aimed to uplift and inspire the audience, and their heroines faced challenges that were not quite so overwhelming. Moreover, they faced them with a quiet stoicism that would be hard to match in real life: the wives of *In Which We Serve* (1942) have their grievances but they are always supportive; in *Millions Like Us* (1943), Celia is hardly pleased at being made a 'mobile woman' and sent far away to a war factory, but she accepts her fate almost without complaint; and in *The Way to the Stars* (1945), Toddy's sorrow at becoming a widow is quiet and dignified. These were typical of the role models

British films offered to women in wartime, and Scarlett was in many respects their alter ego. The historical setting therefore appears to be a form of license for women who did not want to connect the dots between their identification with Scarlett and their personal experiences of war on the home front. To bring Scarlett into the present would be to admit to their own minxishness. It was easier to enjoy the film as a story of long ago and far away.

Of course, not all wartime British films were stories of dignified stoicism. The Gainsborough melodramas, and especially *The Man in Grey* (1942) and *The Wicked Lady* (1945), follow the lead of *Gone with the Wind* in presenting dual heroines for the audience to consider: a dutiful and good-natured woman (played in both films by Patricia Roc) and also an immoral, selfish schemer (played in both films by Margaret Lockwood). These films share other qualities with *Gone with the Wind*: period settings, a leading man who is a dashing brute (played in both films by James Mason), and a secondary man who is kind but ineffectual (played in both films by Stewart Granger). With this in mind, it is not difficult to imagine the casting for *Gone with the Wind* had it been made in Britain. The quality critics loathed the Gainsborough films too, but they were very popular with audiences. Tellingly, Margaret Lockwood became a more popular star than Patricia Roc, indicating that in a period setting minxishness was a consistently valuable box office commodity in wartime Britain. It is also telling that the British films present their heroine's selfishness as a form of psychosis, and they are more punitive towards her in the ending. Indeed, her violent death comes as the climax to both films, suggesting that her punishment was not just a necessary corrective to her misdeeds, but an attraction in itself. By contrast Scarlett lives on in the ending of *Gone with the Wind*, surviving the war, dealing with its aftermath, and even looking ahead to the future in the final scene ('tomorrow is another day'). The more balanced treatment of the heroine, together with her happier ending, was likely to be more palatable for British audiences because of the distant time (in the period setting) and the distant setting.

This is an important aspect of Hollywood films for British audiences. The personal and social implications of films are there for the taking, and yet they need not be too close. They can just as easily be overlooked or dismissed as something belonging to a foreign culture. One of J.P. Mayer's respondents, a 23-year-old housewife, expressed this idea quite succinctly in 1945:

> [I] don't mind American films so much as British. When an American film opens with a silk-stockinged leg, it somehow seems quite natural and commonplace, but when a British film does so ... it is merely embarrassing. Probably this is because one can feel superior so long as the film is not one's own nationality, whereas if it is, one feels slightly ashamed.[117]

By the same token, there was no shame in enjoying the selfishness, self-importance, misdeeds and ambitions of Scarlett O'Hara, nor was there any shame in watching an established social order turned upside down, and seeing the more resilient and charismatic characters survive and even prosper from the upheaval. At least, there was no shame so long as the parallels with the present remained unspoken. In this light, *Gone with the Wind* served as a vehicle of expression for feelings about the war that defied the people's war ethos of communality and the quiet acceptance of one's duty, fate and small place in the grand scheme of national survival. Its 220 minutes and its lavish production values can be seen to form a tribute to the audience. The running time suggested that each individual's personal experience of war, and even a woman's experience of war, was worthy of vast and epic treatment, of Technicolor, of crane shots and a soaring musical score.

Over subsequent decades, the film was gradually detached from its original wartime context. It enjoyed six further re-releases in cinemas (1947, 1952, 1957, 1961, 1976 and 1998).[118] This brought the tally of tickets sold in Britain to 35 million.[119] When the BBC and ITV entered into a multi-million pound bidding war for the rights to screen the film on television, there was another outcry about the cost of this oversized film ('millions gone with the wind', one headline read).[120] And ever since it was first shown by the BBC in 1981, television viewings have added significantly to its audience numbers. Along the way, the film has developed new associations and meanings for audiences, and it has been imbued with a considerable measure of nostalgia. Like *Casablanca* (1943) – that other icon of the Hollywood studio era – it has been pulled up from its wartime roots and, in a succession of new contexts, it has found further admirers and significance. Yet in Britain *Gone with the Wind* made its most powerful impact during the war. Its significance was no less meaningful for being figurative rather than literal, and certainly no less compelling for celebrating the experiences of the individual rather than those of a community.

6 'The American Film *Par Excellence*': Domesticating the Western

What can there possibly be to interest Arabs, Hindus, Latins, Germans, or Anglo-Saxons, among whom the western has had an uninterrupted success, about evocations of the birth of the United States, the struggle between Buffalo Bill and the Indians, the laying down of the railroad, or the Civil War? ... [I]t must be a secret that somehow identifies it with the essence of cinema.

Andre Bazin, 'The Western, or the American Film *par excellence*' (1955)[1]

One of the things the western is always about is America rewriting and reinterpreting her own past, however honestly or dishonestly it may be done.

Philip French, *Westerns* (1973)[2]

The cowboy movie was typically the vehicle America used to explain itself to itself...Each Hollywood western, no matter how trite, was a national ritual, a passion play dramatizing and redramatizing the triumph of civilization over 'savage' Indians or outlaws ... [T]he western was our true Fourth of July celebration.

J. Hoberman, 'How the West Was Lost' (1991)[3]

Of all film genres, the western is the most closely associated with the United States. The musical, the melodrama and the screwball comedy – to name but a few prominent alternatives – are not so closely linked to issues of national identity. The western's origins can be located in American culture of the nineteenth and early twentieth century: in Buffalo Bill's *Wild West* shows, the paintings of Frederic Remington and Charles Schreyvogel and the fiction of James Fenimore Cooper, Owen Wister and Zane Grey. Its themes and preoccupations are regarded as peculiar to the American experience, namely the closing of the frontier and the effect that this had on the country's sense of its own direction and purpose. The stories stem from American history, even if the tales they tell of westward expansion, conflicts between settlers and Native Americans and tensions between farmers and ranchers are more often the stuff of legend than faithful accounts of specific historical events and people. It should not surprise us, then, that the influential French film critic Andre Bazin defined the western as 'the American film *par excellence*'. Intriguingly, Bazin also questioned (in the quotation above) what foreign audiences found interesting in these films. Why should the genre travel so widely and easily outside the USA? For all that has been written about the western (and the literature on this genre is extensive, to say the least), this issue has rarely been pursued.[4] Critics and scholars have been more interested in exploring the idea that the western serves as a form of self-reflection for Americans. Philip French (also quoted above), the longstanding film critic for the *Observer* newspaper, was not the only British writer to define the western in this way. Colin McArthur, writing on gangster films, linked the two genres by stating that each represents 'America talking to itself': westerns are preoccupied with the country's 'agrarian past' and gangster films are preoccupied with the 'urban technological present', but both are part of a conversation about national identity.[5] In *The Crowded Prairie*, Michael Coyne has also studied the western as a 'quintessentially American artefact', using the evolution of the genre to chart shifts in national identity.[6] This line of thinking is not peculiar to British writers. American critics also regard the western as a 'national ritual', as J. Hoberman's statement (quoted above) from the *Village Voice* indicates. What is important to note here is that even the most ardent British admirers of the genre (and French and Coyne were keen enough to write books dedicated to it) regard westerns as a distinctly foreign form, and one that offers unique insights into American culture, society and politics.

This chapter returns to Bazin's question – concerning foreign audiences' interest in the western – and focuses on their appeal in Britain. There is no doubt that the western was popular with British audiences. As the first section of this chapter explains, even before the advent of feature films, Britons found western vignettes and imagery fascinating, and Buffalo Bill's *Wild West* show proved to be a landmark attraction when it toured the country in 1887 and 1888. Twenty years later, between 1910 and 1912, early western films were pivotal in establishing the wider popularity of American films. Then, from the 1920s through the 1950s, westerns found a home in a number of different exhibition formats: as fodder for 'flea-pit' cinemas, as the mainstay of children's matinees, as epic historical films playing in picture palaces and, most surprisingly, as a staple of television programming in the post-war period. The second and third sections of this chapter focus on the films of one cowboy who covered much of this terrain. Hopalong Cassidy was the central character in a series of 66 inexpensive and low profile western films made between 1935 and 1948, after which he regularly appeared on television (on both the BBC and ITV). The reception of these 'B' westerns (considered in the second section) and the use of westerns in early television programming (considered in the third section) will be explored in order to reveal how and why the genre found eager audiences in these very specific viewing niches. Finally, the fourth section of the chapter examines the reception of *The Big Country* (1958/59). While no single film can represent an entire genre, *The Big Country* is singled out as a case study because it stands as the most successful western ever released in Britain. Unlike the *Hopalong Cassidy* films, it won critical praise and found a wide audience in plush, first-run, city centre cinemas. While this chapter examines different time periods and exhibition sectors, the common concern throughout is the 'domestication' of the genre in Britain. That is, considering the contexts within which westerns were seen and the relevance that British audiences drew from them. Why should audiences in the world's most urban and industrialized nation be interested in a genre that reflects on the American frontier experience? The answer lies partly in the films themselves, and the pleasures and experiences they offered, but it also lies in the ways in which the conversation of 'America talking to itself' was both overheard and entered into, sparking discussions of Britain's standing in the world and its relationship with the United States.

Capturing the country: Buffalo Bill in Britain

In 1887, William F. Cody, better known as Buffalo Bill, wrote a letter to an American friend describing his reception in London: 'I have captured this country from the Queen down and am doing them to the tune of $10,000 a day.'[7] It was scarcely an exaggeration. Buffalo Bill's *Wild West* show arrived in London that May. The show was by all accounts an extravaganza, with 200 performers and 250 animals (including horses, ponies, elk, deer and a small herd of buffalo). An arena with a circumference of one-third of a mile was needed to stage its rodeo stunts, Indian war dances and exhibitions of shooting. There were also re-enactments of 'phases of Indian life', attacks on pioneer wagon trains, a buffalo hunt and an attack on an Indian village.[8] The narrative arc of the show was, as the subtitle put it, 'The Drama of Civilization'; that is, the progress of Anglo-Saxon 'civilization' and the defeat of 'savages'. Historians Robert Rydell and Rob Kroes have observed that the show promoted a 'shared racial consciousness among whites' and that this had the capacity, among white audiences at least, for 'blurring class distinctions'.[9] The show's wide appeal was certainly apparent in London. At the vast Earl's Court arena, it played to 30,000 people each day, and 2.5 million tickets were sold during a run that lasted from May to October 1887. There were further long-term and large-scale engagements in Birmingham and Manchester, as well as one performance in Hull.[10] It then moved on to France and to Germany, but its success had been significant enough to warrant the return of the *Wild West* to Britain for tours beginning in 1891 and 1902. It was not only a popular success. As a part of the Golden Jubilee, celebrating Queen Victoria's 50-year reign, a royal command performance was held in May, in the presence of the Queen as well as the assembled monarchs of Denmark, Belgium, Saxony and Greece.[11] With such high profile admirers, Cody himself became the toast of the town, and the *Wild West* show received a series of other noteworthy visitors, including Randolph Churchill, William Gladstone, Sir Henry Irving, Ellen Terry and Oscar Wilde.[12] In fact, as the legendary frontiersman and army scout complained privately, he was so sought after in London that he grew weary of the 'society racket, receptions, dinners, etc'.[13]

The success of the *Wild West* show serves as a reminder that British interest in the American West as a form of entertainment did not originate with films. And in fact, long before this extravaganza arrived in London, the foundations for its success had been established in journalism, fiction, paintings and drawings depicting the

West.[14] Indeed, a *Times* journalist commented that, while watching the show, 'Fenimore Cooper and all the many stories one has read of western life come crowding into the memory'.[15] Responses to the show point to the ways in which western films would appeal to British audiences. For example, when the American Exhibition first arrived in London, it was greeted not as a display of foreign achievements and ingenuity but as a welcome reminder of the extended, thriving British presence throughout the world. *The Times* reported on the exhibition by referring to our 'our American cousins' and admiring 'the life and wonderful activity of our old colony'; while the *Illustrated London News* reminded readers that the USA was 'now the largest community of the English race on the face of the earth' and commented that the country's 'progress' was a 'proper subject for congratulation'.[16] In this context, the 'winning of the West' represented the onward march of Anglo-Saxon culture, and the young American nation was bringing new vigour to the cause.[17]

When the *Wild West* moved on to its subsequent engagements in France and Germany, the Native Americans became the subject of extraordinary interest and sympathy, but this was not the case in London.[18] British journalists emphasized their curious attire and their strange and unknowable qualities. The historian Kate Flint has observed that many reporters expressed their 'repulsion' at seeing a demonstration of a 'scalping' by Native American men.[19] A *Times* commentary noted the simplicity of their wigwams and warned readers about their inhabitants: 'some of them [are] hideously ugly, as nature made them, but rendered uglier still by the yellow ochre with which they are smeared'.[20] Queen Victoria expressed her discomfort more privately, in her diary. She confided that she admired the cowboys, but she was not amused by the 'painted Indians, with their feathers, and wild dress (very little of it)'; they were 'rather alarming looking' and had 'cruel faces'.[21] Meetings between the Sioux Chief, Red Shirt, and various dignitaries and officials, including Queen Victoria on one occasion and Prime Minister William Gladstone on another, were reported as though Red Shirt represented an unfathomably primitive way of life. His need for an interpreter, because he did not speak English, and his brief and non-committal replies to all questions added to impressions that the Native Americans were a mysterious, defeated people.[22]

As Rydell and Kroes comment, the Native Americans' very presence in the *Wild West* show, whether as actors in the dramatic vignettes or as ethnographic displays, seems to signal their own demise and the triumph of Anglo-Saxon civilization.[23]

It was the cowboys who were venerated in London.[24] They were not identical to the heroes of the British Empire: their rugged individualism is quite different from the 'stoicism, service [and] duty' that characterizes imperial heroes. Yet the *Wild West* show (and later western films) thrived on the common ground that existed between American and British forms of imperialism. Stories of 'white settlements, tribal uprisings, the exploitation of natural resources' were at the centre of both westerns and British Empire epics made between the 1920s and 1950s, as Jeffrey Richards has observed. In fact, some of the stories were interchangeable (the same plot could be used on a western or eastern frontier) and some of the stars were too; Gary Cooper and Errol Flynn, for example, starred in both settings.[25] In either eastern or western settings, the film's central characters were rugged, chivalrous heroes, and here too there is a common ground between the appeal of films and the appeal of the *Wild West* show. While the show had many attractions, Cody was its most celebrated figure. The view expressed in the *Illustrated London News* was typical of the admiration he inspired:

> He is a perfect horseman, an unerring shot, a man of magnificent presence and physique, ignorant of the meaning of fear or fatigue; his life is a history of hairbreadth escapes, and deeds of daring, generosity, and self-sacrifice, which compare favourably with the chivalric actions of romance.[26]

It may seem odd today to attach the word chivalry to a man such as Cody, who was known primarily for his violent deeds, including scalping a Native American he had killed in battle.[27] In 1887, however, the patrician face he presented to London journalists and his society hosts, together with his physical prowess as a rodeo performer, suggested a winning combination of gentlemanliness and rugged masculinity.[28] Hence, Cody and his bronco-busting cowboys were described as 'magnificent specimens of men' by *The Times*, while the *Observer* urged its readers to see them in action before 'popular favour and superfluous luxury render them civilised and effeminate'.²⁹ This was a common vantage point on the cowboys of the *Wild West*: they offered a useful reminder that masculinity could be corrupted by the trappings of modern, urban life and that it could be renewed by the adventures, conflicts and challenges to be found on the frontier.³⁰ Admiration for the cowboy was thus closely bound up with anxieties about degeneracy and decline: what scope was left for physicality and open air adventure in the urban and industrialized environment of Britain?

The idea that masculinity was better served by life on the frontier than by life in the modern city arises in an early report on the popularity of western films in Britain. In 1910, an editorial in *The Bioscope* explained that western films were the most popular films in London and the provinces. Their appeal, the editorial averred, lay in the 'contrast' between the audience's 'civilised' city life (where 'man is hedged in by habits and customs') and the 'natural' life of the West (where 'once again we are back in a primitive state, when man had to rely upon his own resources'). The 'natural life' of the frontier was clearly beneficial, even if it could only be experienced in films:

> Let us have more of these films, more of the kind which arouses our sympathies, and makes us long to be fighting, and working, and making love as do these cowboys – sturdy, simple men. It does one good to lose the assumed blasé air which fashion now decrees is the correct thing. Lean forward and follow with eager eyes the superb horsemanship, the rough jokes, the stern fighting as depicted by the western film. Applaud, too, at some heroic deed, and do not be afraid to say 'Well done!' when some special feat deserves a word of praise ... Metaphorically speaking, one feels better, cleaner, and brighter for having seen – with one's own eyes – the life and conditions which obtain in the West.³¹

The editor could not have realized how amply his call for more westerns would be met over the next 50 years. Yet the notion that the western could reinvigorate its audience was already apparent in his admiration for the films. For decades to come, the genre would enjoy a reputation as entertainment that was clean and refreshing. Its wide spaces and open skies, together with the simple benevolence of its cowboy heroes, made it seem a wholesome genre, suitable especially for children.

In the early 1910s, when American films were still far from pre-eminent around the world, the international success of westerns was regarded as a curious development. In 1911, a *New York Times* report stated that 'all over Great Britain the American films, particularly those of western life, are the most popular of all', and added the prescient comment that filmmakers were 'exporting an imaginary America' to appreciative foreign audiences.[32] Further comments in 1912 came from the US Vice Consul in Sheffield, who observed that American films were preferred in Britain not because they had superior photography, but because their producers appreciated 'what the public wants to see'. The western, with its 'stirring forceful drama put on in the open [air]' was the public choice.[33] And a key feature of its appeal was the cowboy hero, whose 'magnetic' charm and 'breezy' manner represented a new and distinctively American character type.[34]

The popularity of westerns at this juncture was the crucial first step in establishing American dominance on the world's screens, and in Britain westerns pushed competition from Italian, French and British films to the sidelines. Their popularity in Britain was particularly important because London was the centre of world film distribution at this time, and the high demand for westerns in Britain 'spurred' their distribution further afield.[35] As the film historian Richard Abel has explained, the films of the cowboy star Broncho Billy (played by the actor G.M. Anderson) were central to the growing popularity of westerns, and this in turn solidified the viability of western films built around an individual cowboy star.[36] While some westerns would be high-prestige historical films, telling epic stories of western settlement, a large swathe of more humble westerns would centre on the adventures of individual, charismatic cowboy stars. Broncho Billy was one of the first, but the formula would be perfected in the 1920s by Tom Mix, and Mix's screen persona – marked by dude-ranch clothing and displays of 'riding and roping' skills – borrowed heavily from 'wild west' shows.[37]

In Britain, the appeal of cowboy stars such as Tom Mix was especially apparent in the pages of *Boys' Cinema* (1919–40). Like its sibling publications, *Girls' Cinema* and *Picture Show* (all published by the Amalgamated Press in London), *Boys' Cinema* was an inexpensive weekly paper, sold at a price of just two pennies (in pre-decimal currency) per issue. Unlike the other publications, it had no interest in glamour, and women were seldom seen on its pages. It was an almost exclusively masculine forum. Even the special postcard photographs, offered occasionally as a bonus to an issue, were photographs of men, including shots of well known cowboys or other stars in an athletic pose. Features and news items focused on stunts, technical challenges and anecdotes arising from filmmaking, but the majority of each issue was devoted to short stories, most of which were derived from films. All forms of action and adventure stories were included, but the western was a clear favourite.

Most issues of *Boys' Cinema* included at least one western short story, telling tales in which courage, endurance and friendship were put to the test. In this respect at least, the western stories are similar to other stories in the magazine. Although told against different backgrounds – the Northwest frontier, the football pitch, the boxing ring, or public school playing fields – they are stories of a young man's self-realization. Finding courage, affirming friendship and learning a lesson to carry forward into adulthood were the common threads. The western stories were distinctive, however, in that many were purportedly penned by the cowboy stars themselves, and they began with an introduction in which the star specifically addressed his British fans. These introductions were strikingly casual and friendly. 'To all my British boy friends', began one introduction from William S. Hart.[38] Another from Buck Jones ended with the signature 'your western chum'.[39] Here, and elsewhere in feature articles, the cowboys were attributed with a warm, playful, boyish masculinity. On the cover of one issue, Tom Mix was pictured balancing on one leg as he stood on the saddle horn atop his horse. This did not appear to involve any difficulty; the 'happy-go-lucky cowboy', as he was termed, was all smiles (Figure 16).[40] Another cowboy star of the 1920s, Hoot Gibson, was praised for his abilities to 'ride and fight', and he too always had a wink and a grin for the camera.[41] As the light-hearted and casual tone indicates, the cowboy stars' combination of physical prowess and friendliness was also free of class associations; they held no office or rank and had no place within a recognizable social hierarchy. This made them significantly different from the heroes of other stories and genres,

Figure 16   A 'happy-go-lucky' Tom Mix on the cover of *Boys' Cinema* (12 August 1922, p. 1)

including those of British Empire films, but one type of hero never supplanted the other. Rather, *Boys' Cinema* offered a forum for boys to find a range of heroic figures; the cowboy was but one distinctively informal type.

B westerns: Hopalong Cassidy in British cinemas

Beyond the pages of *Boys' Cinema*, cowboy stars and their films did not have a particularly high profile in Britain. Of course, the high-prestige and quasi-historical westerns had the status of other 'A' films produced by the major studios; that is, they played in metropolitan cinemas and were reviewed by a wide array of critics. But there were relatively few 'A' westerns made in the 1930s, and at any rate the cow-boy stars seldom appeared in them. Instead, both the western and the cowboy stars thrived as a result of the proliferation of 'B' films in the 1930s. Some 'B' westerns were made by major studios and some were made by 'poverty row' outfits, but they were all comparatively inexpensive films (made for less than $100,000), with short running times (less than 70 minutes) and no major stars. They often played on double features: as a second feature to a more important film in the big first-run cinemas, or as one of a pair of 'B' films in smaller cinemas.[42] In the United States they had a particularly strong and consistent following in small towns of the Midwest, South and West, where rural audiences enjoyed these folksy, unpretentious, action-filled 'B' westerns and disliked the 'high society fops' and 'exotic foreign sirens' of mainstream Hollywood films.[43] The film historian Peter Stanfield has argued that these westerns addressed contemporary issues for rural American audiences, including anxieties about the pace of industrialization, failing farms and bank repossessions, and the increasing migration from farms to towns and cities.[44]

Much less is known about the audience for 'B' westerns in Britain, where neither the movement from rural to urban areas, nor the pace of industrialization, was a pressing concern, and the divide between rural and urban audience tastes did not follow an identical pattern. Nevertheless, it is clear that 'B' westerns had a significant following. One sign of this is that, in the mid-1930s, the *Motion Picture Herald* initiated an annual poll, as a part of its wider survey of box office values, which was devoted to ranking 'western stars' on the basis of their popularity. The editor explained:

> While the so-called western motion picture is definitely not a part of British production, that is not true of exhibition. The British theatre owners have come to recognize the peculiar yet definite place which the western has in the public eye and emotion. Hence, the western, as an American production, became a part of [our] questionnaire data.[45]

The poll indicated the wide proliferation of 'B' westerns in Britain: in addition to the top ten ranking of cowboy stars, a further 15 western stars are given an 'honourable mention' for their popularity. Some of these stars were major figures such as Gary

Cooper and Errol Flynn, who made films in a wide variety of genres and appeared in 'A' westerns only occasionally. But most were
the cowboy stars who appeared almost exclusively in 'B' westerns,
including Gene Autry, William Boyd, Dick Foran, Buck Jones, Ken
Maynard, Tim McCoy, George O'Brien, Tex Ritter, Roy Rogers
and (at this point in his career) John Wayne.

What was the 'peculiar place' that the 'B' westerns and these
cowboy stars held in the British exhibition market? The *Motion
Picture Herald* did not elaborate, but the *Hopalong Cassidy* films
clearly held a prominent position within it: their star, William
Boyd, was number one in the 1939 ranking of western stars, and
over the next ten years he vied with Gene Autry and Roy Rogers
for second or third place.[46] British critics shed only a little light on
the issue. They seldom reviewed individual 'B' westerns, and whenever the topic arose the films were clearly demarcated as entertainment for children. In 1933, for example, John Grierson wrote
an admiring piece on Tom Mix. Mix's films were not screened in
London's plush West End cinemas, Grierson noted, and so he had
to travel 'beyond the Elephant and Castle' – that is, south of the
Thames and into the working-class neighbourhoods of Camberwell
– in search of them. There he found three of Mix's films showing
in separate venues. He chose to see *Rustlers' Round Up* (1933) and
his comments about its appeal echoed the comments made about
the western in *The Bioscope* two decades earlier. Grierson found
that the film had the power to transport him 'off the metropolitan pavement [and] into a cool stretch of Wyoming foot-hills'. Yet
his observations on the audience's response to the film – 'the boys
and girls of Camberwell were delighted' – indicated that the audience was composed primarily, if not exclusively, of children.[47] Four
years later, C.A. Lejeune observed that the films in the *Hopalong
Cassidy* series were the most popular of all western films and that
'these light-hearted, straight-fisted westerns … have won the
heart of every schoolboy from San Francisco to Southend', but it
was clear from her comments that she assumed their appeal did
not extend beyond schoolboys.[48] Similarly, in the *Daily Mirror*,
Reginald Whitley discussed the *Hopalong Cassidy* series in a column devoted to examining film tastes beyond his usual West End
haunts. In 1940, after travelling to an unspecified town on the south

coast of England, Whitley attended a matinee at a modest venue that was overrun with children. He noted that the children carried gas masks, but this hardly impeded their enthusiasm for the film:

> You should have just heard those kiddies yell and scream with excitement. They cheered the hero. They warned him of the villain's arrival and greeted his dastardly efforts with hoots of derision and anger. No wonder William Boyd's westerns are a tremendous success outside the sophisticated West End.[49]

Whitley commented that 'for me it was a real tonic to be in that cinema with those kids', thus attributing his enjoyment to the children's enthusiasm, rather than the film itself.[50]

The strong association between 'B' westerns and children stemmed in part from their position as a fixture of the children's matinee, which was a British institution from the 1930s through the 1950s. Held up and down the country, on Saturdays, the matinees were by all accounts packed full of children every week. As Sarah J. Smith has argued, these screenings offered children 'a cinema culture of their own' and an outlet for fantasy, play and aggression.[51] For a very low ticket price (typically two pennies, leading to the nickname of the 'tuppenny rush'), children were able to see a feature film, a shorter serial film and a cartoon. Audience surveys indicate that these matinees were many children's first experiences of the cinema, typically when they were seven or eight years old. The atmosphere was nothing short of raucous: the hero was cheered, the villain was hissed and children became so excited during chase scenes that they would rock in their seats or run down the aisle toward the screen.[52] The children's enthusiasm for westerns was apparent outside the cinema too. Many of the respondents recall re-enacting scenes from these films afterwards, and as a routine part of their play. This must have been one of the most prominent manifestations of Americanization in Britain: children mimicking the gun battles, chases and confrontations of the 'wild west' while playing in fields, on street corners, or among the slag heaps of a Welsh coal mining town.[53] Equally, though, it is important to note that the films, like the play that followed, took place within a context in which both national identity and local identity could scarcely be left behind. The matinees were at once a national phenomenon (the Odeon club song included the lines 'Love of King and Country will always be our song/Loyalty is taught to us at the Odeon') and a highly local affair. The same children and adult supervisors attended each week, and the cinema manager often served as the master of ceremonies for a programme of events that included competitions, community singing, collections for charity and even talks on road safety.[54]

There were practical reasons for showing 'B' westerns at children's matinees. Exhibitors could not show 'A' features at such low admission prices. They looked to 'B' films for an inexpensive alternative and in the westerns they found an ample supply of films (most of the cowboy stars made at least six films in a single year) that were available at a low rental cost. Moreover, the vast majority of these films carried U-certificates, enabling children to see them without an accompanying adult. But practical reasons alone cannot explain the appeal of 'B' westerns, and the *Hopalong Cassidy* series more particularly, to British children. Many different factors made them ideal for the matinees. One was the uncomplicated heroism of the cowboy hero. In this regard Hopalong Cassidy is exemplary, but he was quite unlike the author Clarence Mulford's original character. Mulford's Cassidy – a hard-drinking, tough-talking, quick-tempered man – appeared in a succession of short stories and novels published from 1905. He is like one of the figures in a Remington painting come-to-life: a dusty, grizzled gunman with bad manners and a violent hostility to Native Americans. From the first film in the series, *Hop-along Cassidy* (1935/36), the screen character is very different.[55] He is well mannered, warm-hearted and never swears or drinks. Unusually, he is attired almost entirely in black, a colour that lent a slight edge of danger to the otherwise benevolent and often smiling character (Figure 17). The actor William Boyd, who was a grey-haired 40-year-old when the series began, is also a strikingly paternalistic figure. In the earliest films this is apparent in his struggle to keep his young sidekick, the handsome but rambunctious Johnny (James Ellison), out of trouble. Throughout the series, his paternalism is also apparent in his efforts to save struggling settlers from the ruthless businessmen (and their cowboy henchmen)

Figure 17 In *Hop-along Cassidy*, actor William Boyd made his debut as a smiling, benevolent gunslinger

who seek to exploit them. Native Americans scarcely figure in these films. Instead, conflicts arise because of the aggressive, unfettered form of capitalism found on the frontier. In most of the films, Cassidy is not an official authority figure and his background is not explained. It is simply understood that he is the 'best shot in the West' and that his life is devoted to saving the weak and innocent from the powerful and corrupt.

The films' populist values, and their representation of a beleaguered *petit bourgeoisie* at the mercy of big business, were unlikely to interest British children. Nevertheless, Hopalong Cassidy's form of heroism would have been familiar to them. This cowboy, like many others in 'B' westerns, belongs to what John Fraser has termed the 'family of chivalric heroes' who had roots deep within English culture and dominated American and British popular culture for most of the twentieth century.[56] The terrain may have been different in the *Hopalong Cassidy* films, and the emphasis on gunplay was unusual too, but the hero's purpose and values were remarkably similar to those of Robin Hood and Prince Valiant. There were other points of appeal for children. Westerns were often called 'horse operas' or 'oaters'; terms that highlight the prominence of an alternative set of stars within the films. Most cowboy stars were identified with a individual horse, as William Boyd was with 'Topper', and the appeal of horses is apparent in the prominent place they have on film posters and other publicity materials. Another important factor was the action sequences, which were likely to prevent children's attention from wandering. This was not only a matter of fast pacing, but also the emphasis on visual storytelling over dialogue. Many of the scenes – particularly those filmed outdoors and with the characters on horseback – were shot without dialogue and have thunderous musical accompaniment. Other scenes, including the gunfights, have only slight and inconsequential dialogue. Few close-ups are used; the story is told in broader terms. All of these characteristics suited the low budget constraints that the filmmakers' worked within, but they also meant that the story could be easily enjoyed in the noisy environment of the children's matinee.

The most striking aspect of these films, especially in an era when filmmakers rarely left the confines of the studio, is their location shooting. 'B' westerns were mainly filmed outdoors and amid expansive, bright, natural landscapes. This was done largely as a matter of economy (the expense of using studio space and constructing sets was kept to a minimum) but in the right hands it could also yield stunning outdoor imagery. The *Hopalong Cassidy* series had a number of able directors: Howard Bretherton, Lesley Selander and George Archainbaud had multiple credits across the series. But the consistently high quality of the photography is also attributable to the cameraman, Russell Harlan, who worked on 44 films in the series.[57] Filming was often done in the Alabama Hills of California. The Sierra Nevada mountains form a distant backdrop, with the snow-capped peaks visible in the bright sunshine. The wide, dry valleys beneath the mountains make a perfect racing ground for the chase sequences, while outcrops of boulders serve as the arena for gun battles. Great care is taken with visual composition: tree branches and rock formations serve as framing devices in some shots; low angle shots from the bottom of hills or ravines emphasize the precariousness of horseback chases; and at times the landscape is surveyed in a manner that can only be described as reverential. Admittedly, some dramatic shots were borrowed from prestige films. For a chase sequence in the first film of the series, *Hop-along Cassidy*, Bretherton imitated the famous 'pit shot' of the epic *Ben Hur* (1925/27), in which the camera was placed below ground level, so that when a succession of riders pass over it the horses seem to charge directly at and over the screen. This proved so effective in *Hop-along Cassidy* that the very same shot sequence was used again, in the midst of another chase scene, in the second film of the series, *Eagle's Brood* (1935/36).

The clean, fresh expansiveness of these locations was altogether different from the urban environment in which the films were watched. In Terry Staples' history of children's matinees, *All Pals Together*, there are vivid photographs of children queuing for entry outside their local cinemas. The contrast could not be more stark. The tree-less streets outside the cinemas are cramped with buildings and people; the midday light is dim and the faces are pale; and the coats, scarves and hats suggest the cold and damp climate.[58] No wonder, then, that the notion of the western as a refreshing tonic and a genre that would serve children particularly well endured for so long. It offered children a vast, sunny and natural playground quite unlike their own denuded environment.

It is important to note that adults could appreciate the finer qualities of the 'B' western too, and in fact the children's matinee was likely to represent the end of the exhibition line for these films; a point reached only after they had exhausted their earnings potential at other venues. The trade papers *The Cinema* and *Kinematograph Weekly* described the audience for *Hopalong Cassidy* films with a variety of euphemisms for working-class audiences: they were 'popular bookings'; they appealed to a 'wide audience'; and they had 'everything necessary to please popular taste'. These brief reviews never considered that the films only appealed to children, but unfortunately they did not explain the pleasures these films held for 'popular' audiences. Were the genre's adult audiences merely hungry for action films and gun battles? Did they appreciate a chivalrous hero who was not an officer and a gentleman? Did Hopalong Cassidy reassure viewers – in the years just before, during and after the Second World War – that Americans saw their role in world affairs as defending virtue and defeating evil? The dearth of 'serious' film criticism, together with the fan magazines' disinterest in this male-oriented genre, makes it difficult to move beyond conjecture on these points. The vast majority of critics simply had no interest in these films. The critical values of the era, as we have seen, prized directors with a recognizable style and a distinctive creative vision, acting that demonstrated versatility and range, and stories with some element of social or cultural significance. 'B' westerns met none of these criteria: they were made according to a formula, their directors were unknown, their stars often played the same role in every film they made and the significance of their frontier stories diminished as they moved out of rural areas and across the Atlantic.

In short, the 'B' western was associated with children partly because so many children enjoyed them, but also because the adults who enjoyed them were considered childish in their tastes. This can be demonstrated with reference to two – admittedly anecdotal – pieces of evidence. One is found within the British-made film *The Smallest Show on Earth* (1958). In this half-mocking and half-nostalgic portrait of a dilapidated 'flea-pit' cinema, a middle-class couple inherit a tiny, backstreet cinema and attempt to revive its fortunes. Yet they find the cinema's standard fare – westerns with titles such as *Killer Riders of Wyoming* and *The Mystery of Hell Valley* – to be laughably bad, and they look down upon the audience as well. Tellingly, the first patron to enter the newly re-opened cinema is a young boy, speaking in American slang, who is lured into the cinema by the sound of gunfire. He is soon joined by teenagers and adults, and like the boy, the older patrons are all transfixed by the medium. When the film is fast-paced, they jump in their seats, when it is slow they slump in them, and when the owners turn the heat on full blast during *The Devil Riders of Parched Point*, adults and children alike fall prey to this gambit to sell ice cream. In short, the audience for 'B' westerns is wholly lacking in critical faculties and discernment. The other piece of evidence can be found in Leslie Halliwell's recollections of cinema-going as a child in Bolton during the 1930s. In his memoir, *Seats in All Parts*, Halliwell recalled that the *Hopalong Cassidy* films regularly played at the Rialto, a downmarket cinema on a 'rather dreary' road at the edge of the city centre. He had such a low opinion of these and other 'B' films that he wondered why the Rialto went to the expense of advertising its films. If the Rialto's patrons watched these films, he thought, surely they would turn up to watch anything at all. That they were an 'undiscriminating' audience was demonstrated by their tastes for formulaic action films.[59]

Halliwell also recalls the arrival of *Stagecoach* (1939) in Bolton. He and his mother were avid cinema-goers, but they had mainstream tastes, preferring films that were shown in the town's 'sleek, modernistic' Odeon to the routine fare at the Rialto:

> We had to be talked into seeing [*Stagecoach*] because it was yet another western with John Wayne, and we associated him with second features at the Rialto; what he was doing at our gleaming new Odeon we could not imagine.[60]

Once they saw the film, he admits, they both 'adored it' but, writing 46 years later, he still felt obliged to note that they did not like it simply for its Monument Valley landscapes, but because it offered an interesting story and characters. *Stagecoach* was one of several A-class westerns that emerged at the end of the 1930s, and it drew an especially positive review from the doyenne of 'quality' critics, Dilys Powell. She was so impressed by it that she used her review to reflect on the aesthetic qualities distinctive to the medium, finding these in the film's 'pictorial effects', its 'dazzling' chase sequences and its use of landscape.[61] Like Leslie Halliwell and his mother, Powell appears to have been unaware that these cinematic qualities were already well known beyond the high street Odeons and in the lowly, back street Rialtos. In those humble environs, what Andre Bazin would refer to as the 'essence of cinema' could be found in the 'B' westerns: pace, action and visual splendour. Yet the apparent simplicity of the films ensured that they were regarded as children's fare first and foremost, and that reputation would be reinforced when they found a home on television.

B westerns: Hopalong Cassidy on British television

The 'B' western and the BBC were an unlikely match. When television broadcasting began again in 1946, after a wartime interregnum, audience demographics were skewed by the limited range of transmission (the signal did not extend beyond southeast England for the first few years after the war) and also by the extraordinary costs of television sets. In the late 1940s, average weekly wages for men working in industry hovered around £7, but television sets cost between £70 and £150.[62] Hence, by 1949 only 3 per cent of homes had a television set, and these were the middle-class homes most likely to appreciate the steady diet of dramatic plays (most performed live in the studio), operas, ballets, current affairs programmes and light educational shows that the BBC offered.[63] BBC programmers were eager to include feature films in the schedules because they struggled to provide 50 hours of programming each week.[64] The film industry, however, was deeply suspicious of the new medium, and trade organizations representing both the major Hollywood concerns and the British industry stood firm in their resolution not to provide films for television broadcasts. Whether they were old or new, long or short, films were off limits.[65] In 1946 and 1947 programmers therefore struggled to find *any* films available for screening.[66] But in the following year they arrived at what would prove to be their richest source of films for many years, the 'B' western. These were available in abundance because they had been produced in series, and they were available contractually because their small-time copyright holders had no interest in boycotting the new medium. Thus, 'B' westerns became a fixture of the mid-afternoon television schedules. Indeed, as the media historian Kelly Boyd has documented, the BBC broadcast 57 westerns in 1948 alone, including films in the *Range Busters* and *Renfrew of the Mounties* series and westerns starring Tex Ritter, Ken Maynard and George O'Brien.[67] In September 1949 *Hopalong Cassidy Returns* (1936) marked the debut of that series, even while the last feature films in the series, *Strange Gamble* (1948/49) and *False Paradise* (1948/49), were still in cinemas, and while William Boyd continued to rank among the most popular western stars at the British box office. Altogether, 24 *Hopalong Cassidy* films would be shown on the BBC over the next two years.[68]

'B' westerns were a fixture on American television in the late 1940s too, but their appearance on British television is a more remarkable phenomenon. Although the BBC aimed to offer a variety of entertainment, there was a prevailing assumption that its programmes represented the nation's culture and tastes. The westerns, with their noisy gun battles, long chases and rough-hewn characters, were an odd addition to the line-up. Where they had once played in 'flea-pit' cinemas frequented by working-class audiences, now they were broadcast directly to middle-class homes.

The label attached to them in the *Radio Times* listings, 'For the Children', put them in their place, aesthetically speaking, yet at the same time it prescribed them as a kind of recommended viewing. Kelly Boyd has noted that some readers of the *Radio Times* appreciated the films, including adult men who were at work in the afternoons and therefore requested that the BBC screen the films in the evening.[69] But they did not appeal to everyone. 'Surely nothing could be more unsuitable for children', one mother wrote to the *Radio Times* in 1949, complaining specifically about Tex Ritter's *The Pioneers* (1941).[70] Henceforth, some westerns would carry the label 'For Older Children' in the programming guide, but the flow of westerns was not stemmed. Indeed, they became such a regular feature that by the mid-1950s the BBC packaged its end-of-week, afternoon film as 'The Friday western'. This slot offered little that had not been broadcast before – and *Hopalong Cassidy* was a regular – but the showcase afforded by the title signalled that the 'B' western was now recognized as a cornerstone of BBC programming.

The *Hopalong Cassidy* series received a new lease of life on television. In the United States, William Boyd launched a new television series on the NBC network in 1952. This began with the last 12 feature films of the series (produced between 1946 and 1948), but the films had been drastically edited, from 65 minutes to 26 minutes running time, in order to fit the programming format of commercial television. There were also 40 new 26-minute episodes.[71] In Britain, the series debuted in the very first week that the new commercial network, Independent Television (ITV), began broadcasting in September 1955, and it ran until 1958. The television episodes were significantly different from the feature films. The small television screens of this era were hardly suitable for the original feature films. With most screens ranging in size between nine and 14 inches in diameter, and offering an image that was far from crystal clear, the films' visual aesthetic – with long shots of the landscape oriented for the big screen – was inevitably diminished.[72] It was only logical, then, that when the last 12 *Hopalong Cassidy* features were edited for television, it was the long shots of the landscape and the lengthy chase sequences and gun battles that were cut down to size. Television was a medium for close-ups (rarely used in the original films), dialogue and interiors, and these were the hallmarks of both the re-edited films and the new made-for-television episodes.[73] The stories and the characterization remained the same: Cassidy continued to be the frontier's most virtuous cowboy and each episode was a showcase for his benevolence. But he was indoors more often than outdoors, the chase sequences that once lasted for minutes were abbreviated to mere seconds and, in recognition of the home viewing environment, the gunplay and noise levels were reduced.

William Boyd did not go into television merely to sustain the adventures of Hopalong Cassidy. Boyd's own image had become inextricably linked with this character (the only role he had played since 1936). Realizing the marketing and merchandising opportunities that could be open to him, Boyd bought the non-theatrical rights to the character in 1949 and proceeded to endorse a range of products – including milk, soft drinks, bread and ice cream – suited to his wholesome image.[74] His name was also used for an extensive range of children's toys and clothing, including holsters, cowboy hats, toy pistols and other western gear. In 1950, this array of merchandising generated $70 million in American retail sales.[75] The British press initially looked askance at this phenomenon, discussing it as an example of the faddishness of the American consumer.[76] There was little scope for such frivolous consumerism in austerity Britain. Late in 1951, however, it was announced that the merchandise would be produced in Britain, partly for sale at home but also for sale abroad. Discussion of the merchandise was reframed accordingly: *Hopalong Cassidy* now became a part of Britain's export drive and its economic recovery from the war.[77] Gradually, as the 1950s progressed, the sale of the merchandise became a part of Britain's own gathering consumer boom, and Hopalong Cassidy became a central figure in a new phenomenon in Britain: consumerism for children. The holsters, hats and toy guns were prominent items in department stores such as John Lewis and Selfridges. Radio plays of his adventures were available on long-play records. His smiling face was used in advertisements to sell Spangles sweets, and it also appeared on Timex wristwatches. And from 1954 to 1960, a regular *Hopalong Cassidy* comic strip appeared in the British weekly comic *Knockout*.

If the ubiquitous Cassidy was a symbol of rampant Americanization, few in Britain complained. Parents in the 1950s were likely to remember his films from their own childhood and to recall them as one element within the rituals of the children's matinee, rather than consider him as a specifically American figure. In fact, whichever medium they appeared in, the *Hopalong Cassidy* stories were but one item in a repertoire. In *Knockout*, as in *Boys' Cinema* 20 years earlier, the western stories were situated amid home-grown boys' own adventure stories (including those of Billy Bunter, Sexton Blake and Johnny Wingco). On television, his adventures ran in tandem with those of native heroes in shows such as *Dixon of Dock Green* (1955–76), *The Adventures of Sir Lancelot* (1956–57) and *Robin Hood* (1956–60); all series centred on an idealized hero with a clear sense of right and wrong. Moreover, Boyd recognized the need to alter his message to suit foreign audiences. When he addressed American children, his 'Cowboy Code of Honour' emphasized American exceptionalism, but his message was transformed to the more generic 'be proud of your country and be proud of all the advantages that it offers you' when he spoke over the radio to Scottish children in 1952.[78] Wherever he appeared, then, he was placed within existing frameworks, and in some cases his message was altered, in order to suit local contexts and audiences.

Through sheer persistence, Hopalong Cassidy became a familiar figure within British culture. In 1957, when a controversy erupted over the effect of television violence on children, and the western was cited as a particular problem, the genre as a whole was defended with reference to this most noble of cowboys. Sir Robert Fraser, director general of the Independent Television Authority, argued in *The Times* that the western offered a beneficial moral influence and used 'that modern Knight of the Round Table, Hopalong Cassidy' as his prime example.[79] William Boyd had come a long way since the 1930s. Through scores of films, television episodes, comics and advertising, his character represented the American cowboy as an incorruptible force for order and justice. Of course, for some the cowboy and the western more generally were a marker of the immaturity of American culture. But for others, when the cowboy stood alongside Britain's own chivalrous heroes, it appeared that Britain and the United States had shared values and a shared mission in the world. It was only at the end of the 1950s that a much more critical perspective emerged – on cowboys, on the western genre and on Anglo-American unity – and this is apparent in the reception of *The Big Country* and the wider genre's gradual decline.

The Big Country and the 'adult western' in the 1950s

The western was more prominent than ever before in 1950s Britain. In addition to the comics, the toys and the records, ITV broadcast numerous American-made western television series.[80] By the end of the decade, 50 per cent of households had a television set.[81] At the same time, westerns proved more popular than ever before in cinemas, and they were no longer regarded primarily as films for the 'flea-pit'. This was a result of more ambitious production strategies. In competition with television, Hollywood turned to colour and widescreen formats that the small screen could not match, and a genre so geared to spectacle proved well suited to the age of Technicolor, VistaVision and CinemaScope. Films were also distinguished from television by means of their stories, and many of the big budget westerns of the 1950s were infused with adult themes, political allegories and Freudian psychology, and there was a less celebratory and more reflective representation of the taming of the 'wild west'. As Michael Coyne has observed:

> Before 1950, the western focused largely on the march of civilisation. After 1950, the genre dealt increasingly on roads not taken. Over the ensuing decade, the western's principal theme veered from the glory of pioneer achievement to its awful cost.[82]

While this trend is broadly observable, there were exceptions to it, and audience tastes in Britain did not necessarily move in step with, or even in the same direction as, Hollywood production trends. True, *The Searchers* (1956) offers a prime example of the more challenging, violent and disturbing westerns of the 1950s, and it proved to be one of the most popular films of its year, but so too did Disney's straightforward celebration of a western legend, *Davy Crockett* (1955/56). Meanwhile, the more pronounced trend at the British box office was a preference for westerns that were also generic hybrids, such as the musicals *Annie Get Your Gun* (1950),

Calamity Jane (1953/54), *Oklahoma!* (1955/56) and the comedies *Fancy Pants* (1950) and *Son of Paleface* (1952). The British-made comedy *The Sheriff of Fractured Jaw* (1958) was also a box office hit.[83] Like the later *Carry On Cowboy* (1965), this mild parody of the western hinged on audiences' familiarity with the genre and their openness to seeing its conventions mocked.

The continuing popularity of the western encompassed a wide variety of films, but at the end of the decade one film stood head and shoulders above the rest. *The Big Country* was the most popular western of the decade and, with nine million tickets sold, it still stands as the most popular western of all time in Britain.[84] In terms of production values, *The Big Country* can be placed at the opposite end of the spectrum from the *Hopalong Cassidy* films. The films share a love of the landscape, as witnessed in the lingering shots of carefully framed expanses, but *The Big Country* had a $3 million budget, which provided for filming in Technicolor and the widescreen Technirama format, as well as a starry cast (led by Gregory Peck and Jean Simmons), an Oscar-winning director (William Wyler), a memorable musical score (by Jerome Moross) and a running time of 165 minutes (Figure 18). It can also be placed at the opposite end of the critical spectrum. London's metropolitan film critics were not easily impressed by lavish production values and epic running times – the disdain which greeted *Gone with the Wind* testifies to that – but *The Big Country* was regarded as having a serious and timely

Figure 18   Julie (Jean Simmons) and McKay (Gregory Peck) survey the western landscape in the Technicolor, Technirama epic, *The Big Country*

message, and this justified its size and scale. An early indication of its critical status came in December 1958 when the *Observer*'s theatre critic, Kenneth Tynan, reported approvingly from New York that this new film was 'far more challenging than any of the new Broadway plays' he had recently seen.[85] Tynan dubbed it 'the first pacifist western' and other critics followed a similar line. When the film opened in London the following month, Isabel Quigly's review in *The Spectator* was entitled 'An Adult Goes West'. She deemed the film to be '165 minutes of glory' in comparison with the 'childish and even barbaric' stories found in the 'usual western stuff'.[86] In *Films and Filming*, a magazine initiated in 1954 for 'critical filmgoers', Peter G. Baker explored the 'timely allegory' of the film and also found it 'vastly entertaining'.[87] In the *Sunday Express*, Derek Monsey heartily approved of the film's message, which he read as a 'devastating indictment of the old western code'.[88] And in the *Sunday Times* Dilys Powell commented that she was pleased to see that the western could represent violence as 'pointless', 'odious' and 'in the end self-destructive'.[89]

There is plenty of violence in this 'pacifist' film, including fist fights and gun battles, and the basic story is a familiar one. Two ranching families, the Terrills and the Hannasseys, have a long-standing feud over the water rights to a neighbouring property, the Big Muddy. Neither family's ranch can survive without access to the water and, as a series of tit-for-tat incidents escalates, they are set on course for a blazing showdown. The difference in this version of the story – the revisioning that the critics appreciated – is that it is told from the point of view of an outsider, the easterner James McKay (Peck). This outsider is not treated comically, in the manner of *Ruggles of Red Gap* (1935) or *Fancy Pants*, but proves to be the hero of the film. He arrives in Texas because he has followed his fiancée, Pat Terrill (Carroll Baker), to her father's ranch. As soon as he arrives, a gang of cowboys from the Hannassey ranch attack him, mocking his city clothes and lassoing him with ropes. Life is not much easier for him on the Terrill ranch: a young ranch-hand, Steve Leach (Charlton Heston), is in love with Pat and seeks to belittle and challenge McKay. Yet the high-minded McKay refuses to be drawn easily into fights and remarks upon the futility of the feud between the Terrills and the Hannasseys. This bewilders Pat, who subscribes as faithfully to a code of unfettered machismo as everyone else in her family. Gradually, McKay is drawn into a friendship with the softly spoken schoolteacher Julie Maragon (Simmons), who owns the Big Muddy and seeks to end the feud with a compromise. The families are intent on shooting it out, though, and the bellicose fathers (Charles Bickford and Burl Ives) eventually kill one another. By that time, McKay has bought the Big Muddy and fallen in love with Julie, and in the ending it is implied that they will settle there

The Big Country was a box office failure in the United States and it is not difficult to see why.[90] This is not a story that celebrates the USA's manifest destiny. The Texan town is not an up-and-coming centre of commerce but a dusty and charmless crossroads. The landscape fills the screen, but it appears as arid and unyielding as its inhabitants; this is a western that acknowledges that a frontier can be both vast and empty. The Texans boast about how 'big' their 'country' is, but McKay, whose background is in shipping, deflates them by pointing out that the oceans are bigger. In fact, the easterner proves superior to the westerners in just about every way. McKay is able to tame a wild horse that no one else can get near, and he achieves this through patience and perseverance rather than force. He eventually accedes to Steve Leach's demands for a fist fight, but he refuses to fight in public and for the crowd's pleasure. Instead, they fight in the middle of the night and amid the barren hills. The physical fight itself is a draw (the men leave each other bloody but neither man can claim to have won), but the filming of the scene underscores McKay's perspective. The camera stays back, revealing the fight only in long shots and extreme long shots that, together with the half-light, allow the audience little engagement with the conflict. At the end of the scene, when McKay asks, 'Tell me, Leach, what did we prove?', it is clear that McKay has won a moral victory. He is also the voice of reason regarding the conflict over the Big Muddy. When McKay buys the land, he agrees with Julie that both families should be allowed access to its water, but the families are too bitter and bent on revenge to accept this. They would rather kill one another than compromise.

As the film historian Will Wright has observed, Americans did not like seeing westerners characterized as 'mean or crude' and, in a western context, they disliked an eastern hero 'who hasn't shot a gun in ten years and doesn't in the film'.[91] British audiences were much more likely to feel a strong affinity for the film's sympathetic characters. This stemmed partly from the casting. Gregory Peck was an American star, but his most popular film in Britain prior to *The Big Country* had been the maritime drama *Captain Horatio Hornblower, R.N.* (1951), in which he played the title role.[92] Playing another seafaring Englishman offered an echo of that role and suggested that this easterner had roots that spread all the way across the Atlantic. The London-born Jean Simmons, meanwhile, made her name in high-profile British films such as *Great Expectations* (1946), *Black Narcissus* (1947) and *Hamlet* (1948) before she moved to Hollywood. The contrast between these two sympathetic characters and the film's assortment of western roughnecks accentuates the idea that McKay and Julie are foreigners to the West. McKay's restraint and strong moral sense are utterly at odds with the mean and crude westerners. Similarly, although Julie is meant to have been born and raised in Texas, her softly spoken voice and quiet dignity set her apart from the locals. She is set apart through visual imagery as well: Julie's small cottage in town and her family's grand but derelict home at the Big Muddy are the only locales with any greenery in the otherwise barren terrain.

Class also plays a role in setting McKay and Julie apart from the westerners. They are the only characters who have a family background and history. McKay carries his father's duelling pistols – made in London – which link him with a traditional and gentlemanly form of solving disputes (and several critics referred to him as a 'gent' or 'gentleman'). Julie is introduced as the town's schoolteacher, but later it is revealed that the Big Muddy was bequeathed to her great-grandfather by the King of Spain. By contrast, the Terrills and the Hannasseys have no family heritage apart from their conflict with one another. They are typical westerners in the sense that they have disconnected themselves from traditional social hierarchies and sought to reinvent themselves in a newer, freer society. As many British critics noted, however, the Terrills and the Hannasseys have markedly different financial circumstances and this seems to be the true basis of their feud. In the *Daily Mail*, Fred Majdalany argued that this was one of the 'themes' of the film: 'the unkindness of the haves to the have nots, and their ingenious ways of justifying their attitudes'.[93] Other critics focused on the Terrills' 'extravagant' and 'luxurious' lifestyle, and their 'dog eat dog' outlook, contrasting it with the 'squalor' of the Hannassey's lives.[94] The Hannasseys are termed 'trash' in the film, and this epithet was repeated in reviews.[95] Indeed, British critics were highly attentive to the class dimension they found in this portrait of western life, and especially the notion that a lack of class structure rendered the frontier as a free-for-all, in which decency and order are lost to avarice and self-interest.

Above all, critics focused on the film's depiction of the futility of violence. Here, too, the easterners' values hit close to home, and most critics regarded the question McKay asks at the end of his fist fight with Leach – 'what did we prove?' – as the key moment in the film. McKay's heroic restraint was linked in many reviews with the key conflict of the 1950s, the Cold War, and anxieties about nuclear warfare. The (unnamed) critic for the *Manchester Guardian* stated that the film addressed the issue of 'suicidal warfare among humans'.[96] Jympson Harman of the *Evening News* said that it was about 'warfare between nations' and that it raised the question: 'Just how much violence must a peaceable man use to preserve the peace which he is convinced must never be violated?'[97] Similarly, in the *Evening Standard*, John Waterman pointed out that the story 'invites international interpretation' because 'Gregory Peck portrays an adult in a world where squabbling children threaten war to settle their differences – even today'.[98] If these critics were ready to refer to McKay and Julie as adults seeking sanity in a world ruled by children, they were not quite ready to state an explicit connection between the 'childish' values of the traditional western and America's contemporary role in the Cold War. C.A. Lejeune's review in the *Observer* came the closest. She wrote that she was 'grateful' for having seen *The Big Country* because it reminded her of Andrew Wyeth's painting, *Christina's World*. As Lejeune described it:

[The painting] showed a very young girl lying in a field of long grass, looking up meditatively towards a small, white frame house in the heart of nowhere. I thought it quite beautiful, and it said, with an economy of strokes, everything I have longed to feel assured of about America's size and space and peace.[99]

The obvious resemblance between the painting and the film is in the landscape: wide, treeless, rolling hills of dry grass. Beyond that, *Christina's World* presents an enigmatic scenario, and leaves much to the imagination of the viewer. What has prompted the girl to sit up, after apparently lying in the grass? What makes her look back at the house? We cannot know, because her face is not shown and, apart from a flock of birds on the horizon, the house and surrounding fields appear calm. Yet Lejeune apparently found a peaceful dignity in the girl's repose and in the simplicity of the house. The feminine image and the emphasis on humble domesticity appealed to her, and finding these qualities in a western setting gave her a long sought-after 'assurance' about the United States. If that is linked with the film, it suggests that she welcomed the representation of the country as one capable of quiet meditation, of humility and of turning the other cheek. In short, she sought reassurance that, in the age of nuclear weapons, the calm forbearance of McKay and Julie would hold sway in Washington, and overrule the cowboy values of the Terrills and the Hannasseys.

The immense popularity of *The Big Country* signals that the film appealed to a wide range of audiences and not just to the metropolitan critics and their followers. At a time when cinema admissions were plunging downward, *Kinematograph Weekly* commented on the film's sell-out success at the Odeon, Leicester Square, by observing that 'these days the "horse opera" is about the only form of screen entertainment that invariably appeals to high- and low-brow, young and old, alike'.[100] This suggests that the film could be appreciated for different reasons. Certainly, its political allegory was not essential. Ernest Betts characterized the film to his readers in the *Express* as one offering traditional western elements ('brawls, murders and abductions') and noted that 'the excitement is hot and strong throughout'.[101] Other reviews focused on the film's spectacular dimension. The *Daily Cinema*, for example, welcomed the film as 'a high, wide and handsome box office winner on a scale only the cinema can supply', adding that the film 'makes the biggest TV look like a child's toy'; and *Picturegoer* similarly endorsed the film as one that 'makes TV look pretty small'.[102] Nevertheless, the political reading of the film suggests that, for middle-class audiences at least, attitudes toward the western were in flux by the end of the 1950s.

Cowboys were no longer chivalrous, but could be portrayed as an aggressive, violent and dirty mob ('take a bath sometime', Rufus Hannassey growls at his son when urging him to court Julie). The frontier was no longer necessarily a site for open-air and wholesome adventures; it could be harsh and desolate. And the western itself was no longer identified as a healthy tonic, but was now discussed as a genre that benefited from a revisionist perspective.

These changing perceptions of the western paralleled the changing perceptions (and realities) of the British Empire. For so long a cornerstone of national identity, the Empire's importance had diminished over many years as a result of post-war decolonization (most notably Indian independence in 1947). The Suez Crisis in 1956 offered a further marker of its decline. As the historian Richard Weight has argued, Suez was 'a blow to popular imperialism' and among the young middle classes in particular there was a 'growing revulsion from imperialism'.[103] Thus, one of the cornerstones of British appreciation of the western, the sense of an imperial mission shared between Britain and the USA, was qualified at the very least. The changing perceptions also paralleled Britain's changing relationship with the United States. Until the end of the Second World War there had been a sense of partnership, even if the USA was emerging as the stronger partner. In the Cold War, however, it was clear that Britain had become a secondary power. The conflict was essentially between Washington and Moscow, and yet the advent of nuclear weapons meant that the battlefield was likely to be the whole of Western Europe. In this context, there was a reassessment of Britain's role in the world and its relationship with the United States. For some, including the thousands involved in the launch of the Campaign for Nuclear Disarmament in 1958, this entailed the adoption of a pacifist and anti-American stance.[104] For others, including Prime Minister Harold Macmillan, there was the hope that Britain could 'play Greece to America's Rome'. In this analogy, Macmillan foresaw Britain using its centuries of diplomatic experience and expertise to guide the USA in the development and implementation of foreign policy. Britain would be the elder statesman in the Anglo-American relationship, guiding its less experienced but more powerful ally and restraining its youthful, aggressive tendencies.[105] *The Big Country* expresses similar ideas, admittedly at a more allegorical level, by suggesting that the cowboy era was over and that more civilized values could now tame the wild West. It is an easterner's western, and it found its most appreciative audiences far to the east of the United States – in Britain.

Thinking about the USA

The western has long served as an appealing way for Britons to think about the United States. This is not to suggest that the genre has no other pleasures; as we have seen, even in low budget form, westerns could offer the very 'essence of cinema'. Nor does this indicate that it was a completely foreign form; as we have seen, cowboys were recognized as belonging to the same family as Britain's own mythical heroes. Nevertheless, many westerns represented the USA in a manner that British audiences could turn to their advantage. In this genre, the United States is a young country and therefore a relatively fresh offshoot of Britain. It may be a vast country, with untold resources, but its frontier is fraught with a degree of danger, violence and hardship that does not exist at home. Its heroes may be wholesome and athletic, but they have a childlike simplicity. And of course the films themselves were 'for the children'; this most distinctive of American cultural forms lacked aesthetic complexity and importance. In other words, the genre offered a way of thinking about the United States, as that country grew in power and importance, that softened the blow to British pride. As Philip French observed, the western characteristically 'assumes that young people have a lot to earn from their elders and very little to teach them'.[106] Hence, the mature Hopalong Cassidy would always be accorded more gravitas and screen time than his handsome but immature sidekick and, in *The Big Country*, even the old and embittered Rufus Hannassey could appear wise and reasonable when compared with his overly aggressive son. Yet we must also recognize that if the USA, from a British perspective, was a wild, rambunctious and unsophisticated country, it was nevertheless a fascinating one. Through the western, generations of Britons became acquainted with American folklore, history and myth. Annie Oakley, Davy Crockett, Wyatt Earp, Jesse James and Billy the Kid became as well known as Britain's own historical figures.

Battles at the Alamo and Little Big Horn were rehearsed and re-enacted on playing fields and in back gardens throughout the country. The landscape of Monument Valley was vividly etched in the imagination, while Dodge City, the OK Corral and the Rio Grande were familiar places on the map of popular culture. And the costume of the cowboy hat and holsters was so irresistible to children that it was commonly sold in the major high street shops.

The close association between the West and American national identity was not broken when westerns travelled abroad, but the conversation of 'American talking about itself' took on culturally and politically specific meanings when heard abroad. These changed over time, so that the genre that had seemed so fresh in 1910 was regarded by many as outdated by the 1960s. Old westerns were still revived in repertory cinemas and, after the Hollywood studios sold their back catalogues of films (in the late 1950s), high-profile westerns were showcased as 'classics' for television viewing. But there were fewer new westerns made and the genre was less popular with young cinema-goers. It was much more difficult to believe in myths of American benevolence and chivalry in a decade marked by the Vietnam War, race riots and the assassinations of John F. Kennedy, Robert Kennedy and Martin Luther King. By the 1970s, the term 'cowboy' had taken on a new and tarnished meaning in Britain, referring to 'recklessly unscrupulous and unqualified' builders, plumbers, traders and businessmen.[107] This was diametrically opposed to the responses Buffalo Bill's 'riders and ropers' inspired 100 years earlier, when cowboys were considered 'children of the prairie'. In recent years, westerns have occasionally scored well with British audiences either because of the appeal of their star (for example, Clint Eastwood), or, as with the landmark *Brokeback Mountain* (2005/06), because their revisionist perspective was both startling and welcome. But the genre's steep decline indicates that the myth itself is no longer tenable or compelling. Indeed, a genre that was a cornerstone of British cinema-going for 50 years has faded away to the point that, for many twenty-first-century audiences, it scarcely exists. Of course, gun battles, long chase sequences, spectacular scenery and confrontations between forces of good and evil remain a staple of the mainstream entertainment films, as the *Stars Wars* franchise and more recent science fiction films demonstrate. However, these elements are not deployed in a western setting, but in the vast, empty landscape of outer space. There, in galaxies far, far away, the sound of America talking to itself and about itself is not quite so audible, and among modern British audiences at least, that is apparently a welcome development.

7 'The Sixth Form Was Never Like This': *Grease* (1978) and the American 1950s

I cannot say that flims have ever made me dissatisfied with life but I can safely say flims do make me dissatisfid with my neighbourhood and towns. From what I have seen they are not modern for instance there are no drug stors on the corner of the stree where you can take your girl friend and have some ice-creem or a milk-shake.

Anonymous 14-year-old boy, responding to J.P. Mayer's survey on cinema-going (conducted in 1945, spelling as in the original)[1]

Let the good times roll, live for the day and forget about schools and books – and when everyone stood up and stomped through *Rock Around the Clock*, that was it. The first public demonstration of how our generation felt against our parents' world. No more aping adults, no more dressing like dolls. We were standing up and saying we've arrived: the first of a new tribe – the teenagers – and the world henceforth was to fear and be enthralled by youth.

Ray Gosling's memories of 1956, as recalled in *Personal Copy* (1980)[2]

Ask anyone who was a teenager in the 1950s – the days of pony tails, swinging petticoats and drainpipe trousers – about those halcyon days and they will tell you that it was the best time to be alive. And the reason, they claim, is that everything was 'fun'. Fun is the main ingredient of *Grease*.

Publicity for *Grease* (1978)[3]

Hollywood films have long demonstrated more interest in adolescence than have British films, and particularly in the celebration of adolescence as a distinct and intense phase of life. This stems partly from the industry's competitive drive and its awareness of audience demographics, which have always been skewed towards the young. It also stems from the fact that, for much of the twentieth century, adolescence in the United States was more prolonged, and marked by more distinctive rituals and milestones, than in Britain. From the 1920s, the success of the 'high school movement' ensured that American teenagers stayed in school longer – the majority until the age of 17 or 18 – and shared a quasi-official high school culture of ceremonies and celebrations ('lettering' in a sport, homecoming, the prom, graduation, etc.).[4] Hollywood filmmakers recognized good material in these milestones, for both the teenage audiences experiencing them and the adult audiences revisiting them, but dramatizing them entailed portraying adolescence in a specifically American manner. This might easily have seemed strange or alienating to British audiences, who, for much of the twentieth century, had very different expectations and experiences of youth. However, as the first quotation above indicates, British teenagers could find the lifestyles of their American counterparts intriguingly glamorous rather than alienating. In this case, a 14-year-old boy responding to a question posed in J.P. Mayer's 1945 survey of *Picturegoer* readers ('Do films make you dissatisfied with your way of life or your neighbourhood?'), saw an enviable rather than a strangely foreign way of life. Certainly, some of the restrictions of his own life are apparent in his wider response. He was working class (his father's occupation is listed as 'welder') and, like most working-class boys in the 1940s and 1950s, he expected to leave school and go to work by the age of 15.[5] Moreover, if his spelling is anything to go by, his education had been very limited.[6] His comments indicate that, in Hollywood films, he could see a more pleasurable lifestyle. Ice cream was one form of pleasure, but his reference to a girlfriend suggests that it was not the only form; he imagined that a society geared towards consumer gratification would grant him greater personal status as well. Moreover, from the vantage point of Britain in the 1940s, he saw Hollywood's depiction of American consumerism not as exaggerated or idealized but as 'modern'. It represented a utopian future in which people, places and circumstances would be as attractive and materially bountiful as they were in films.

This 14-year-old's comments serve as a reminder that the appeal of Hollywood films for British adolescents did not originate in the 1950s. In the 1930s and 1940s, the word 'teenager' was not yet in common usage, but stars such as Mickey Rooney and Deanna

Durbin brought so much energy and exuberance to their films that they made youth itself seem vital and empowered rather than immature and marginalized.[7] It was in the 1950s, however, that teenagers were first perceived to be a unique demographic group, with tastes and interests separate from adults. In the second quotation above, Ray Gosling recalls the self-consciousness of his generation and the common cause they found in American rock music and films. Gosling, a journalist and broadcaster in later years, was 16 years old when the film *Rock Around the Clock* (1956) was released. Although the title song was a landmark hit that signalled the beginning of the rock and roll era, the film itself was a cheaply-made vehicle for the American rock band Bill Haley and the Comets, and it is now largely forgotten. Yet Gosling recalls the film's screenings in British cinemas as a pivotal moment for his generation. When teenagers danced in the aisles of their local cinemas, they defied the older generation's codes of restraint and decorum in the public sphere, and in many instances the police were summoned to quell what the newspapers described as 'pandemonium'. For Gosling and his peers, American youth culture offered the means of rejecting propriety, snobbery and their parents' prudence with money:

> I wanted what the American had – wide, open spaces, free style, liberated energy and ready cash. They stood for letting yourself go ... The Americans said go on your guts, it doesn't matter about books and traditions, go on what is inside you: do what you feel.[8]

This new spirit of rebellion lay first and foremost in rock music rather than in films. Indeed, Gosling recalls that 1950s teenagers found many films to be staid and conventional, and cinema-going served mainly as a social activity. It was only exceptional films, and especially those that portrayed young people at odds with authority, that inspired the reverence of the young. *The Wild One* (1953/55), *Blackboard Jungle* (1955) and *Rebel Without a Cause* (1955/56) were prominent among these exceptions, and in subsequent years these films would be recalled as emblematic of their era. It can be surprising, then, to realize how contentious they were when first released. Far from being accepted as a part of mainstream popular culture in the 1950s, the BBFC regarded them as foreign in values and outlook and subjected them to heavy censorship.

Twenty years later, the Hollywood musical *Grease* recycled many of the key elements of these iconic 1950s films, using them to serve a vision of the 1950s as a teenage utopia. As the publicity material written for the British release stated, in the third quotation above, to be a teenager in the 1950s was simply *fun*. In keeping with this, *Grease* mythologizes the period as one of teenage liberation: when teenagers were first able to express their identity (through clothing, hair styles and rock music), when they had spaces outside the home dedicated to their own culture (high school, the drive-in cinema and the diner), and when they had cars as a means of transportation and a symbol of their freedom (from parents, teachers and other authority figures). Of course, the emphasis on high school, cars and consumerism has little relation to the way British teenagers lived in the 1950s.[9] The film's fanciful, unreal approach to the period provoked the derision of British critics, who predicted that any success the film would have would be short-lived and attributed to the intensive marketing campaign that preceded its release. The leading trade magazine, *Screen International*, concurred that such an irrelevant film could only be a 'flash in the pan' success at the box office.[10] This was incorrect: *Grease* was not only the top box office attraction of its year, but it also has gone on to be perennially popular.[11] Furthermore, after a succession of re-releases, its critical reputation has reversed and it is now frequently discussed as a five-star, classic film. This chapter therefore examines the marketing campaign for *Grease* and explores the expectations set for the film and their impact upon the film's meaning and appeal. It also charts the film's changing critical fortunes. The chapter begins, however, in the 1950s – long before *Grease* was made – in order to explore the British perceptions of the films it so freely draws upon.

1950s teen films and 'those wretched young people'

From its very first scene – Danny Zuko (John Travolta) and Sandy Olsson (Olivia Newton-John) frolicking romantically on a sundrenched beach – *Grease* offers a succession of references to 1950s teen films.[12] The first scene recalls *A Summer Place* (1959), a melodrama starring Sandra Dee and Troy Donahue as teenagers in love but kept apart by unsympathetic parents. But where this earlier film is earnestly concerned with teenage romance and approaches the issue of Sandra Dee's virginity with grave solemnity, *Grease* plays it for laughs. As the waves crash on the beach and Danny and Sandy kiss, the lush, string-laden and thoroughly old-fashioned song 'Love is a Many-Splendored Thing' soars on the soundtrack, rendering the scene laughably excessive. 'Is this the end?', Sandy wistfully asks, presumably referring to their chaste summer romance. 'Of course not. It's only the beginning,' Danny replies, and his statement cues the film's opening credit sequence and theme song. The tone of *Grease* is not always so stridently flippant, but its references to earlier films consistently recast their stories as lightweight and harmless entertainment. The high school setting, for example, allows for conflict between teachers and students, but these are treated comically and have none of the malevolence and violence that infuses *Blackboard Jungle*. The students in *Grease* may belong to gangs – the boys in the 'T-birds' and the girls in the 'Pink Ladies' – but gang membership is a matter of close friendships and not the stuff of ethnic tension and violence seen in *West Side Story* (1961/62). The drag racing scene in *Grease* ends without serious injuries or repercussions, whereas in *Rebel Without a Cause* the 'chickie run' ends in tragedy as one of the cars goes over a cliff and its teenage driver is killed. Danny wears the uniform of 1950s 'rebel males' such as Marlon Brando, James Dean and Elvis Presley (jeans, a white t-shirt, a leather jacket and a slicked back 'greaser' hairstyle), and the choreography for his song, 'Greased Lightnin'', echoes the performance of the title song in Presley's *Jailhouse Rock* (1957/58). But while that film cast Presley as a convicted killer, Travolta's winning smile ensures that Danny has no real danger or menace. Indeed, *Grease* steers clear of the associations between youth, deviance and crime that were so prevalent in 1950s films. The staging of 'Greased Lightnin'' can serve as a metaphor for the film's more upbeat, less threatening treatment of the decade. The scene begins in a grubby, run-down garage as Danny and his friends try to polish up a battered old jalopy, but as they sing about the car's potential, the setting transforms into a pristine showroom and the car becomes a gleaming, red convertible hot-rod. Like the showroom and the hot-rod, the film's 1950s are polished to perfection. The film has no interest in a real time or place – hence, neither the year nor the location is actually stated – but instead utilizes a less specific 'Fifties' setting as a realm of fantasy, in which the troubles and limitations of real life can be left behind.[13]

Grease was not always so polished. The original version, first staged at a community theatre in Chicago in 1971, was written by Jim Jacobs and Warren Casey, and about Jacobs' own experiences of attending high school on Chicago's west side during the 1950s. The characters were tough kids from Polish- and Italian-American families, whose ethnicity was a part of their working-class identity. There were songs, and several of Jacobs and Casey's originals are included in both the Broadway and film versions of *Grease*, but there was more drama than music.[14] There was also more sex and swearing in the original. It was when the show moved to New York in 1972 – first as an off-Broadway and then as a Broadway production – that the grit was replaced by nostalgia and the show became a musical mythologizing the 1950s. In the process it lost many of its local Chicago references, almost all of its sex and swearing, and the focus of the story shifted from an ensemble cast to the romance of Danny and Sandy. Jacobs later recalled that the original was an 'in-your-face show about delinquents', and he joked that the Chicago and New York shows were as different as John Gotti and Peewee Herman.[15]

The New York production became the longest running show in Broadway's history, lasting eight years before it closed in 1980, and in the midst of its stage success it was adapted for the screen. For Jacobs, the film adaptation was another step in the process of 'cleaning up' his original.[16] Allan Carr, who adapted the story and produced the film for the Robert Stigwood Organization (RSO), is widely regarded as the guiding light in this process. An article in the *Guardian*, published to mark the film's twentieth anniversary re-release, explained that Carr 'suburbanised [*Grease*] for a wider audience', but Carr's idea of suburbanization was not so much making the film clean or bland as it was making it camp.[17] In this endeavour, his inspiration was undoubtedly the British-made musical *The Rocky Horror Picture Show* (1975), which began its ascent as a cult classic while playing as a 'midnight movie' in New York City in 1976.[18] It is, of course, an understatement to say that *Grease* is not as ribald or transgressive as *Rocky Horror*. However, the two films share an ironic narrative mode, in which Hollywood's familiar generic motifs are 'ransacked', as Justin Smith has argued, in a seemingly 'random' and 'gratuitous' manner.[19] The effect is to offer the audience a distanced perspective on the clichéd material; one that signals the audience's recognition of it and invites them to enjoy it again from a knowing vantage point. Excess and artifice are essential to maintaining this distanced perspective (especially for those who may be too young to recognize the familiarity of these motifs), and in *Grease* the artifice is at times overwhelming. When the 1950s pop star Frankie Avalon sings 'Beauty School Dropout', for example, numerous cues are employed to signal that the performance is both absurd and enjoyable: Avalon is dressed in form-fitting silver lamé; the choreography appears to have been inspired in equal parts by 1930s Busby Berkeley musicals and 1950s science fiction films; and the scene closes with a trio of toga-clad cherubs descending from heaven.

In the United States, nostalgia for the 1950s is often considered in political terms, and as a symptom of longing for the 'mesmerizing lost reality of the Eisenhower era'.[20] However, if we consider *Grease* as a film that recycles 1950s popular culture in the form of parody and pastiche, and not as a representation of a real and locatable 1950s, a different (and more sympathetic) agenda emerges. Films such as *A Summer Place*, *Blackboard Jungle*, *Jailhouse Rock*, *Rebel Without a Cause* and *The Wild One* invest dramatic weight and importance in their teenage characters, as well as a degree of charisma and a vantage point distinct from the adult characters. This is clearly a key part of what made them attractive to teenagers of the time. Yet these films are scarcely free of a judgemental, adult perspective on youth. Teenagers, according to so many 1950s films, may have rotten parents, but they nevertheless need the intervention of adults, who are on hand as social workers, probation officers, psychiatrists or teachers. If the teenagers do not receive their help in time, the consequences can be dire. This is why so many of the 1950s films fall within the 'social problem' genre; the focus on teenagers is prompted by the idea that they are themselves a problem. In *Grease*, however, the values and perspectives of the teenage characters are unchallenged, and the adult characters are marginal and comical. Where once teenage fashions, attitudes and cultural tastes

were bound up with suspicions of criminality and sexual licentious-
ness, in retrospect, and through the re-making of the generation's
most iconic cinematic moments, they appear harmless. In this
light, *Grease* offers a revisioning of the decade's popular culture that
– implicitly at least – serves as a vindication of 1950s teenagers; their
supposed immorality and delinquency was in the minds of narrow-
minded and alarmist adults. The process of adaptation that took
the story further and further away from its original Chicago roots
was therefore crucial to the film's pursuit of a pleasurable, 'fun'
1950s. Within a less specifically located, half-remembered world
of popular culture, the anxious adult perspective on teenagers and
youth culture was mainly overlooked and, if acknowledged at all,
represented as laughably old-fashioned.

In Britain, the film's light-hearted approach to the 1950s and
to the popular culture of that decade was particularly significant.
While rock music and films such as *Blackboard Jungle* and *The Wild
One* raised the hackles of American traditionalists, in Britain the
anxieties were intensified by the perceived foreignness of the new
teenage culture.[21] Its popularity with teenagers fed into post-war
concerns about Britain's declining status in the world (especially
in relation to the United States) and the erosion of authentic and
traditional cultural forms. Richard Hoggart's observations on the
'juke box boys' and the 'American slouch' they developed through
immersion in the 'myth-world' of popular culture offers a prominent example of how these anxieties were expressed within intellectual circles (see Chapter 1).[22] However, as more recent studies by
Dick Hebdige, Dominic Sandbrook and Andrew Caine have demonstrated, it was not only intellectuals who linked youth culture,
Americanization and national decline; the associations had a common currency in the 1950s.[23] As Caine has argued, Americanization
and youth culture were widely perceived to be at the root of the
decade's most inflammatory social problems: 'juvenile delinquency,
the Teddy Boys and perceived immorality'.[24]

In retrospect, it is plain to see that while British youth culture
borrowed from its American counterpart, it was distinctly home
grown. The Teddy Boy phenomenon of the mid-1950s, for example,
involved working-class teenage boys adopting long, velvet-trimmed
suits reminiscent of those once worn by Edwardian dandies.

Although the accessories (notably the 'slim jim' ties worn by cow-boys) were often American, the style itself originated in the dance halls of south London, and it was unknown in the United States.[25] To a disapproving older generation, the Teddy Boys *seemed* American because of the expense their dress code required, its implicit rejec-tion of austerity and its assumption of upper-class ostentation.[26] Outrage over both the Teddy Boy style and the supposed depravity of rock music were fused in the perceptions of the *Rock Around the Clock* 'riots' in 1956. The music in the film prompted teenagers to dance – or, as some newspapers described it, the film caused the 'rhythm crazed teddy boys and teddy girls' to 'jive madly in the gangways' – and the more alarmed cinema managers summoned the police.[27] In some cinemas, teenagers responded by setting off fire extinguishers, but in many instances they were arrested merely because they were singing as they left the cinema and thus causing a disturbance along the high streets of towns and cities.[28] Either way, the press eagerly exaggerated the events. 'Rock'n'Roll mob shocks a city' was a typical headline from the *Daily Express*, which reported on the 'riot' that followed a screening at Manchester's Gaiety Cinema. The accompanying article came close to defining teenagers as sub-human, alien invaders: they were described as moving up Oxford Street in a 'column', 'screaming' and 'swarming' as they went. Yet the disturbance apparently amounted to little more than 'danc-ing round a fountain' and some 'trampled flower beds' outside the cinema.[29] In this report and in reports from other screenings, teen-age exuberance was represented as violent and dangerous criminal behaviour that had been inspired by American popular culture.

Ironically, *Rock Around the Clock* carried a U certificate (for 'uni-versal' admission) from the British Board of Film Censors, indicat-ing that the censors foresaw no potential harm in the film. Most films likely to appeal to teenagers were scrutinized much more care-fully for the influence that they might have on British teens. As Sue Harper and Vincent Porter have argued, the public concern over juvenile delinquency led the BBFC to take 'a repressive and panicky stance' and to apply 'stringent limitations' to British films on the topic.[30] In practice, this meant that British films such as *Good Time Girl* (1948), *The Boys in Brown* (1949), *The Blue Lamp* (1950), *Cosh Boy* (1953) and *Violent Playground* (1958) were acceptable because they portray their teenage delinquents as deviants at odds with the wider, benevolent community. Furthermore, delinquency is punished in the ending and no doubt is left about the rightful authority of the state. By contrast, Hollywood films about juvenile delinquency tend to have more balanced sympathies: they invest a measure of charisma in their delinquents; they cast doubt on the benevolence of the community; and their endings centre on reconciliation rather than punishment. Faced with such films, the BBFC could demand that shots or scenes were cut, as a means of bringing a film more into line with British films on the topic; or, if a film was considered irredeemable, the Board could refuse to grant a certificate to a film.

In 1954, Columbia Pictures' *The Wild One* fell into the irredeemable category. This story of two rival motorcycle gangs who terrorize the inhabitants of an isolated small town could not be cut to the cloth of the British films on juvenile delinquency. The central problem was that the film depicted the activities of young 'hooligans' (as the BBFC described the gangs), and it was exacerbated by Marlon Brando's charismatic performance as one of the gang leaders, Johnny, who comes across as a freewheeling rebel rather than a deviant criminal. In the film's most famous scene, Johnny is asked what he is rebelling against and his reply, 'whaddya got?', suggests that everything in the established order is open to question. His perspective gains credence when the small town community readily turns to vigilante justice as a means of dealing with the gangs, and the community's claim to respectability and lawfulness is therefore lost. Moreover, the film represents authority as ineffective. The local sheriff is weak and the state police ultimately allow Brando to ride away with only a warning. For the BBFC, the film was unacceptable because its hooligans are treated sympathetically, because it leaves them largely unpunished in the ending and because it suggests that adult authority may be questionable.[31] These offences meant that it was unsuitable even for the new X certificate, which prohibited admission to those under the age of 16. A few local authorities allowed it to be shown in 1955, but it was not until 1967 that the film was finally released with an X certificate. By that time, as the BBFC admitted, *The Wild One* had become 'almost a period piece'.[32]

In the midst of the long-running struggle between the BBFC and Columbia over *The Wild One*, the Board frankly explained its intransigent position on this film: it opposed the film because it would serve as 'a dangerous example to those wretched young people who take every opportunity of throwing their weight about'.[33] A similar attitude towards youth, and especially the relationship between youth and authority, informed the censorship of *Blackboard Jungle* and *Rebel Without a Cause* in 1955. MGM's *Blackboard Jungle* was helped by the fact that, at the centre of this story of an inner-city high school, there is an idealistic teacher (Glenn Ford). The students are unruly and violent, and the other teachers are defeated and cowardly, but the film at least has this one clear and legitimate authority figure. Hence, it was granted an X certificate after 20 cuts (totalling six minutes running time) were made. Some cuts were clearly designed to reduce the audience's ability to identify with the youthful transgressors: shots and lines of dialogue showing students defying or challenging their teachers were excised. Other cuts were designed to bolster a sense of adult authority over the young, including the excision of scenes that reveal the teachers' shortcomings.[34] In both respects, the censors struggled to bring *Blackboard Jungle* into line with British films that portray juvenile delinquency.

Rebel Without a Cause was a more difficult case for the BBFC because the teenage delinquents in this film are portrayed much more sympathetically. Far from upholding the authority of adults, the film suggests that juvenile delinquency stems directly from the ineptitude of parents. The BBFC nearly refused to grant a certificate to the film, but the director Nicholas Ray travelled to London to meet with the censors and agreed to a series of cuts that led to an X certificate. Predictably, scenes of criminality were reduced. The knife fight and the tyre slashing that takes place outside a planetarium were cut so extensively that the continuity of these scenes was undermined.[35] The censors also tried to limit the 'spectacle of ridiculous and ineffectual parents' by cutting the scene in which Jim (James Dean) throttles his father and also the scene in which Judy (Natalie Wood) kisses her father and gets a slap in return.[36] There were other cuts that centred on shots or scenes in which the teenagers express strong emotions: Judy's exhilaration as she signals the start of the 'chickie run'; the scream of Buzz (Corey Allen) as his car goes over the cliff during the 'chickie run'; and Jim punching and kicking the desk in the police court.[37] The insistence that the latter scene be cut is especially revealing. Jim has been urged by a youth worker to vent his frustration in this way, so his actions cannot be termed criminal. The censors' objection therefore must have been a response to the intensity of feeling in the scene, which is amplified by Dean's method acting. Certainly, this scene, situated at the beginning of the film, establishes that Jim is the film's most important and sympathetic character; two qualities that the BBFC did not like to see in wayward teenagers.

The BBFC aimed to press upon these films the values of a hierarchical social order, in which the young were expected to treat adults with deference, but even in their altered form the films seemed liberating to teenage audiences in the 1950s. *The Wild One* was scarcely seen before 1967, but it gained a wider currency through its poster, which was available in Britain. The portrait of Marlon Brando – in leather, astride his motorcycle and looking defiant – spoke volumes to his fans.[38] Both *Blackboard Jungle* and *Rebel Without a Cause* were solid box office hits despite their X certificates.[39] *Blackboard Jungle* benefited from its association with the song 'Rock Around the Clock', which plays over its opening credits. It was not the idealistic teacher who made this film attractive to the young, but the song and the story of students who stood up to their teachers.[40] *Rebel Without a Cause* was released in January 1956, just four months after James Dean died and, as Ray Gosling recalled, this gave the film a 'religious' quality. He and his peers watched in awe.[41] The very qualities that made the films objectionable to the BBFC – the voice and importance they gave to teenagers, their willingness to cast doubt on the authority of adults – made them revelatory to a younger generation increasingly aware of its own tastes and values.

These were the feelings that *Grease* sought to recapture 20 years later: the intensity of youthful experience, the newly discovered sense of self, the embrace of teenage customs and attitude. But the 'full-blown moral panic' about 1950s youth culture was over, and teenagers no longer had to be presented as a social problem. In this sense, *Grease* is not quite an example of history being written by the victors, but it is a case of popular culture being rewritten by its admirers. In the 1970s, and as adults themselves, audiences were invited to recall the power and appeal of 1950s popular culture and revisit the exhilaration of seeing these films for the first time, but there was no need to recall the repressive, authoritarian adult perspective surrounding them at the time. Of course, *Grease* could not succeed on the strength of its appeal to adults alone. It would have to be sold to the teenagers who figured so prominently among the remaining cinema-goers. In Britain, this was a particular challenge. Teenagers in the 1970s were far removed from that distinct cultural moment – marked by the arrival of *Rock Around the Clock*, Elvis Presley and James Dean in the mid-1950s – when youth culture was so closely associated with the United States. The moment had passed quickly. By 1960, musicians such as Tommy Steele, Cliff Richard and Adam Faith proved that rock and roll was not inherently American; and later in the decade the Beatles and the Rolling Stones would offer further (and stronger) evidence of this. The 'angry young man' films, such as *Look Back in Anger* (1959), *Room at the Top* (1959) and *Saturday Night and Sunday Morning* (1960), demonstrated that screen rebels did not come from Hollywood alone. By the early 1960s, as Dick Hebdige has observed, continental influences (the motor scooter, the coffee bar and Italian suit) had surpassed American influences among the young.[42] Youth culture became a broader church in the 1960s and 1970s than it had been in the 1950s, and American popular culture did not figure so prominently. Moreover, while nostalgia for the 1950s was a pronounced cultural phenomenon in the USA during the 1970s, it had far less impact in Britain. Hence, Britain's young cinema-goers would have to be convinced that *Grease* was relevant and compelling to them and not just a nostalgia film for their parents.

Selling Grease

In the United States, a 1972 cover story in *Life* magazine celebrated the return of the 'nifty fifties' with reference to pop music, fashion, and the recent arrival of *Grease* on the New York stage.[43] In the following year, the film *American Graffiti* (1973/74) was also recognized as a part of this phenomenon.[44] *American Graffiti* was made on a low budget, but it became one of the 20 top-earning films of the decade in the United States, and a 'spin-off' television series, the long-running situation comedy *Happy Days*, was a prime time ratings success from its launch in 1974. In Britain, by contrast, none of these nostalgic representations of the era had quite the same impact with audiences. *American Graffiti*, for example, was widely admired by British critics for its authentic recreation of the period, but they pointed out that its representation of teenage life would seem distinctly foreign to British teenagers.[45] Audiences apparently agreed insofar as *American Graffiti* was not nearly as successful in Britain as it was in the USA.[46] *Happy Days* did not have the status it had on American television. Beginning in October 1976, ITV scheduled the series early on Saturday evenings, outside of prime time and in a time slot programmed for children. The stage show of *Grease* appeared in the West End in 1973, with the little-known Richard Gere in the role of Danny, but Broadway's biggest hit lasted just six months in the West End before closing. And while 1950s revival bands had some success in the British pop charts in the 1970s, bands such as Showaddywaddy summoned distinctly home-grown memories of the earlier decade. They dressed flamboyantly as Teddy Boys, for example, and they had no crossover success in the USA.

The marketing of *Grease* in Britain therefore needed to address audiences who had no special affinity for the 'nifty fifties'. Setting audience expectations for the film and its treatment of the decade was crucial, but in the late 1970s attracting cinema audiences was a greater challenge than it had been in previous decades. Admissions were just one-fifteenth of what they had been in the 1940s; only two million tickets were sold each week.[47] For the majority of Britons, including the young, cinema-going had ceased to be a habitual or routine leisure-time activity. It was now reserved for seeing the occasional 'blockbuster'. Over the previous year, even as admissions figures dwindled to new lows, a few films – *Star Wars* (1977), *Close Encounters of the Third Kind* (1977/78) and *Saturday Night Fever* (1977/78) – had proven capable of attracting millions of patrons.[48] The hallmarks of the 'blockbuster', according to film historian David Cook, are an aggressive marketing campaign, extensive merchandising 'tie-ins', cross-media promotion and a story that is 'easily reducible to a salient image'.[49] RSO, which produced *Saturday Night Fever* before *Grease,* was no stranger to this approach, and it was widely reported in Britain that the company spent more on marketing than on producing its films.[50] Key components of the promotional campaign were concentrated around the time of the film's release in September 1978. For example, the two leading tab-loid newspapers, the *Mirror* and the *Sun*, declared the week before the release to be '*Grease* week' and ran a succession of features on the film every day, and on prime time television there were adver-tisements every evening for two weeks. But two other strands of promotion were set in motion months before this. One was the advance release of the soundtrack music. The other was the advance release of the film's poster, with a 'salient image' that would also appear on the cover of the soundtrack album and on t-shirts, key-rings, stickers, badges and belt buckles that were widely available for sale.[51] The intensive marketing, in other words, was designed to ensure that *Grease* was regarded as a pop culture phenomenon of here and now and not one relevant only to Americans and those old enough to recall the 1950s.

First 'unveiled' in London in July 1978, the poster for *Grease* is dominated by a head and shoulders photograph of John Travolta and Olivia Newton-John, in an embrace and looking directly into the camera (Figure 19).[52] There are subtle references to the 1950s setting in this image: Travolta's quiff and t-shirt recall the swagger of Marlon Brando and Elvis Presley, while Newton-John's blonde wholesomeness recalls Sandra Dee. But the subtlety signals that the period setting is not a particularly important or demanding aspect of the film. Certainly, neither the title nor the image suggests a film with serious historical pursuits. With the stars gazing into the cam-era, the cartoonish logo of the convertible car and the knowingly nonsensical tagline ('*Grease* is the word'), the poster signals a self-aware, light-hearted, romantic film; more costume party than cos-tume drama. A prominent sticker on the poster, signalling a 'tie-in' with Pepsi and a 'Greased Lightnin' contest' to win a 'whole lotta car', also suggest that the film represents a set of consumer and life-style choices that are available in the present day (at least for the contest winner). The stars are the most prominent feature of the poster, and audiences were likely to recognize them at first glance and to consider them an unlikely match. Newton-John was a popu-lar singer with several easy listening chart hits to her credit. Her background was well known in Britain because she had been born in Cambridge to a prominent academic family; hence, she could be promoted as an 'English rose' even though her family had emigrated

Figure 19   The poster for *Grease* signalled that it is more of a costume party than a costume drama

to Australia when she was six years old.[53] Travolta, by contrast, was known in Britain only for one film, the X-certificate *Saturday Night Fever*, in which he starred as the working-class, Italian-American disco dancer Tony Manero. Together, the image of these two very different stars set up a series of oppositions: middle class and working class, suburban and urban, purity and vulgarity, easy listening and rock and roll. Their embrace on the poster, and even the placement of their names – with Travolta's name situated over Newton-John's face and vice versa – suggests that the film can reconcile these differences. But Newton-John's heavier than usual make-up, her hand on Travolta's shoulder, her red fingernails and teased hair and her black outfit (matching his) suggest that she has changed. The change is not all-encompassing – her wide-eyed expression and gentle smile remain – but nevertheless there is a hint here of her new sexual awareness and maturity.

If the poster offers only hints about Newton-John's transformation in the film, the first single from the soundtrack album, Newton-John and Travolta's duet on 'You're the One That I Want' revealed much more. The single was released in mid-May of 1978, a full four months before the film, and it reached number one on the pop music charts by June and stayed in the top spot for nine consecutive weeks. The song was attributed to the stars and not to the characters and so, like the poster, it shaped perceptions of *Grease* as a star vehicle. It also highlighted the romantic dimension of the film and, through its propulsive disco bass line, it highlighted the film's contemporaneity and its rejection of period authenticity. The idea that the film represented a transformation for Newton-John was apparent, too, in her singing, which abandoned the breathy country crooning of her past hits for a risqué, squawking style more suited to 1970s disco music. Most remarkably, months before the film's premiere, RSO released the scene in which Travolta and Newton-John perform 'You're the One That I Want' as a promotional video for the single. At this time, the early release of a film clip to television was unusual, and it was especially unusual to release such a climactic scene, from the film's ending, before audiences had a chance to see the film in cinemas. But 'You're the One That I Want' played repeatedly on the BBC's prime time *Top of the Pops* programme, which always featured a performance of the week's number one song, and the cumulative effect of weekly screenings of the 'sizzling excerpt' (as it was described by *Screen International*) did 'a power of good' for building interest in *Grease* throughout the summer of 1978.[54]

In the film, the performance of 'You're the One That I Want' serves as a resolution of the film's central conflict, and it solves the problem set up in the first scene (with reference, as mentioned earlier, to *A Summer Place*). In that first scene, Danny and Sandy's chaste summer romance at the beach appears to be at an end. 'Don't spoil it,' Sandy says, as she rebuffs a kiss from him. Then, when she unexpectedly arrives at Rydell High School and finds that Danny is a student there too, the film follows their repeated attempts to rekindle their romance. These are thwarted by a seemingly fundamental incompatibility: Danny is a leather-jacketed greaser, who boasts to his friends about his sexual conquests, while Sandy's prim innocence leads her friends to compare her to Sandra Dee. Finally, on the day of their graduation, Sandy arrives at the celebration dressed in black spandex, red high heels, a leather jacket and with

her hair teased and a cigarette hanging from her lips. The performance of the song ensues and it represents her long awaited rite of
passage from a prim girl-next-door ('lousy with virginity,' as the lyr-
ics to 'Look at Me, I'm, Sandra Dee' say) to a woman able to express
herself sexually ('I need a man to keep me satisfied', she sings in
'You're the One That I Want'). Throughout the clip and scene, she
struts and poses provocatively, and Danny follows behind her with
a loose-hipped swagger. Crucially, though, their performances and
the setting work to contain the sexual implications of the song and
her outfit. At the very beginning of the scene, Sandy looks to her
friends for tips on how to handle her cigarette and so reveals that
her sexy strut is a masquerade. And Danny's swagger seems to have
been inspired more by Jerry Lewis' comical lack of coordination
than by Elvis Presley's brazen sexuality. The setting – a fun fair on
the high school grounds – ensures that desire is expressed only in
an exceptional, carnivalesque context, and also that its consumma-
tion can be expressed, in visual terms at least, as a playful journey
through the fun house. As the couple sing, she leads him through
the entrance, past a sign that says 'danger ahead', and into a laby-
rinth of tunnels and passages (Figure 20). Her lyrical demands ('you
better shape up') prompt his acquiescence ('I better shape up') as
they move toward the 'shake shack', where they are finally able to
sing and dance in unison.

Figure 20   While singing 'You're the One That I Want', Sandy (Olivia
Newton-John) confidently leads Danny (John Travolta) past the warning of
'danger ahead' and into the 'shake shack'

The release of this clip may have revealed the film's resolution, but it clearly intrigued audiences. The fun fair setting, together with the exaggerated zeal of the stars' performances, effectively conveys the wider film's playful approach to the 1950s. The interplay and ultimate unity of Travolta and Newton-John creates a utopian world without social distinctions, in which class and ethnic divisions matter little. Most strikingly, the emphasis on clothing and hair style suggests that sexual liberation is simply a matter of consumer choice. According to Sue Harper and Justin Smith, this was a pervasive idea in British film culture of the 1970s, albeit one that arose in a variety of different forms.[55] Certainly, Newton-John's emergence as a spandex vamp represents one of the more startling examples of this, and her 'makeover' immediately became (and remains) the most frequently discussed aspect of the film. This does not mean that she was the more significant star, and in fact fan magazines and reviews indicate greater interest in Travolta even at the time the film was released, when he was a relative newcomer.[56] Rather, the fascination stems from the scene's ambiguity. On the one hand, Sandy's transformation represents a feminine version of the 'do what you feel' ethos that Ray Gosling admired in 1950s American pop culture. Sandy's rejection of the traditional ideals of feminine propriety, primness and reticence, and her embrace of confidence, expressiveness and sexual maturity, can be viewed as her liberation. In the 1970s, when the women's movement had a particularly high public profile and issues of sexuality and sexual pleasure were discussed with a new openness, ideas of personal and sexual liberation were particularly resonant.[57] On the other hand, her strutting sexual display appears to be performed as a ruse, to attract him, rather than as an expression of her own sexuality. In this light, her transformation is tailored to male desire and the exchange with Danny is far from equal (he wears a white sweater to signal his commitment to her, but he quickly discards it). Her liberation may therefore be merely a mirage of feminine assertiveness and self-realization in a much larger desert of conventional and traditional gender roles. What makes the scene compelling, however, is not that it must be read one way or the other, but that it can be read both ways. It smoothes over a host of contradictory, highly charged ideas about gender roles, sexuality and, especially, sexually empowered women. Hence, the desire to see the scene repeatedly – as an excerpt on television, in cinemas and in subsequent release formats – and to marvel again as a scene so fraught with contentious meanings is rendered as a rollicking, good-natured romp through a fun fair.

The film's ambivalence toward sexually empowered women is also apparent in the character of Betty Rizzo (Stockard Channing). She is as outspoken and adventurous as Sandy is demure and virginal, and for much of the film this is used to mark her as crude and unfeminine. Her friends do not call her Betty but use the masculine nicknames 'Riz' or 'Rizzo'. When the boys try to banter with her, she can easily outdo them. (When Danny wants to put her down, he says, 'Bite the weenie, Riz', and without a moment of hesitation she replies, 'with relish'.) Danny refers to her sexual experience, calling her 'sloppy seconds', when he rejects her come-on. She looks older than the other girls – except perhaps the sultry and similarly assertive Cha Cha (Annette Charles), who also appears to be in her 30s – and so the film suggests an association between her sexual experience and decadence or decline. Most importantly, Betty and her boyfriend, Kenickie (Jeff Conaway), are sexually active and so, when Betty discovers that she may be pregnant, her character and storyline seem designed to serve as a cautionary tale. Yet this is not quite the case. At this point in the film and through her song, 'There Are Worse Things I Could Do', Rizzo asserts her own morality, scorning girls who flirt but then 'refuse to follow through'. Like Sandy's big solo number, the plaintively romantic 'Hopelessly Devoted to You', Rizzo's song is free from the flippancy that is otherwise pervasive in *Grease*. The effect is to suggest that this self-confessed 'trashy and no good' girl is sympathetic and admirable. In keeping with this, the pregnancy scare turns out to be a false alarm, and it is implied that Rizzo and Kenickie will marry. Apart from the happy ending, however, Rizzo's story is remarkable for acknowledging the hypocrisy of the sexual double standard, the limitations of birth control and the stigma attached to unwed mothers in the 1950s. Little wonder, then, that she scarcely figured in the film's publicity and 'There Are Worse Things I Could Do' was not among the six songs from the soundtrack released as a single.[58] *Grease* was sold through images that suggested that sexual liberation held no dangers or challenges and that it need not entail a loss of innocence. Rizzo and Kenickie's more troublesome storyline was therefore left out of the film's marketing campaign.

Responses to Grease

The excitement surrounding the release of *Grease* and the interest in its two leading stars evoked memories of a lost era of Hollywood glamour. The London premiere, on 13 September 1978, brought out thousands of onlookers, who watched the stars arrive in limousines and walk the red carpet into the Empire, Leicester Square. If this was not quite the stately occasion created for *Gone with the Wind*, it was reminiscent of the excitement that accompanied Rudolph Valentino's personal appearances decades earlier. Headlines the next day, such as 'Wild West End', characterized the evening as one of hysterical mayhem, with police holding back thousands of overly eager fans, but it had been so long since a film premiere met with this degree of enthusiasm that the reports were more amused than alarmed. The excitement was not limited to the West End. 'Teenagers faint as fans storm into cinema' was the headline in the *Western Mail*, which reported on crowd control issues at the ABC cinemas in Cardiff and Swansea.[59] The problem was that, at a time when many venues had been subdivided or turned into bingo halls, the reduced seating capacity could not meet the demand for such a popular film. Cinema managers reported that they had thousands of people turning up for venues that had only hundreds of seats. Hence, the film was held over for extended engagements and even after four and five weeks admissions did not diminish in cities across the country.[60] The high attendance levels were partly sustained by children returning to see the film several times. At the Edinburgh ABC, which had become a multi-screen venue, *Grease* ran in the largest theatre but, with only 860 seats, after-school matinees were added in the second week to meet demand. These were attended by children as young as eight years old, whose parents were apparently not deterred by the film's 'A' certificate (indicating that it was 'not recommended for children under 14 years of age'). The Glasgow ABC remained a single-screen venue, with just over 2,000 seats, but the film nevertheless lasted for a 13 week run. Here, too, audiences included a large number of children seeing the film two or three times, mothers were joining their children on the repeat screenings, and the evening performances reportedly drew middle-aged patrons, who were said to be attending the cinema for the first time in years.[61]

While the marketing campaign was successful in attracting audiences, it fuelled disdain for the film among the metropolitan critics. Their annoyed, unsympathetic responses had strong parallels with responses to *Gone with the Wind* nearly 40 years earlier. In both instances, the marketing was regarded as the triumph of commerce over artistry and it led the press to speculate – and apparently to hope – that the public would turn against the film. Even the *Mirror*, which had declared a '*Grease* week' prior to the release, reported after the premiere that 'after all the ballyhoo. ... *Grease* fails to shine'.[62] In the *Guardian*, Derek Malcolm observed that the film had been 'pre-sold to millions' but that it would prove 'a grave disappointment to anyone in search of style or substance'.[63] In the *Sunday Telegraph*, Tom Hutchinson referred to the 'promotional ballyhoo' and found 'nothing but opportunism' in the film; and in the *Spectator*, Ted Whitehead flatly declared that *Grease* was 'not so much a movie as a marketing phenomenon'.[64] In the *Evening Standard*, Alexander Walker followed in Dilys Powell's footsteps by refusing to take an over-hyped film seriously. Where Powell had written a jokey commentary about the endurance needed to sit through the lengthy *Gone with the Wind*, Walker's review took the form of a letter from one middle-class mother to another, reassuring her friend that the film was suitable fare for children ('like most of the junk children consume these days, it will do them no harm').[65]

Another theme common to reviews of both *Grease* and *Gone with the Wind* was the high regard critics placed on realism; a quality both films lacked. With *Grease*, there were two strands to this argument. One was that the film represented a disappointing career move for John Travolta after his breakthrough role in *Saturday Night Fever*. These critics had not admired *Saturday Night Fever* for its music or its dancing, but for its story of a young, working-class man struggling to find fulfilment in a depressed urban environment. Hence, in reviews of *Grease*, Alan Brien of the *Sunday Times* referred to *Saturday Night Fever* as a 'stylish piece of contemporary anthropology' and an 'urban safari into darkest America'. In the *Daily Express* Ian Christie referred to the earlier film as having 'social significance' because it dealt with 'real people', who were 'convincing and contemporary'.[66] And in the *Daily Mail*, Roderick Gilchrist argued that *Saturday Night Fever* 'carried a raw urgency and skilfully exploited and encouraged a highly contemporary subculture – disco dancing and disco music' but *Grease* was merely a 'sickly confection of fifties clichés'.[67] The second strand of comments on realism concerned the film's representation of the 1950s. Many critics applauded the appearance of veteran stars from that decade – Eve Arden as the principal of Rydell High, Sid Caesar as the sports coach, Joan Blondell as a waitress in the diner – but regarded this as the only genuine attempt to capture the period setting. By contrast it was frequently noted that most of the actors playing high school students were far too old ('some of the oldest pupils one is ever likely to see this side of the Open University', Derek Malcolm gibed); that the music did not adhere to 1950s styles; and that the film's many 'dirty jokes' betrayed a 1970s sensibility. All of these shortcomings were symptomatic of a film that, according to David Robinson, was 'so vaguely placed in time that it isn't even a pastiche'.[68] Other critics commented that the film was 'unable to decide whether to recapture the innocence of fifties productions or the realism of the seventies' (Ian Christie); and, along similar lines, that it was 'erratic' (Ted Whitehead), 'a mish-mash' (Madeleine Harmsworth in the *Sunday Mirror*) and 'shamefully unreal' (Alan Brien).[69] The latter comment is the most telling. The idea that the value of films lay in their relevance and authenticity had held sway for so long, and was so entrenched with this generation of critics, that shame could be ascribed to such a wayward film.

The reviews of *Grease* also demonstrate that the auteurism which was beginning to flower in 1940 had fully bloomed by the 1970s, when broadsheet critics considered a director's creative vision as casually as they discussed a film's story and stars. Here, too, *Grease* was woefully inadequate. Its director, Randal Kleiser, was only 31 years old and, although he had experience in television drama, this was his debut in feature films. For some critics, these two factors neatly explained the film's faults. According to Derek Malcolm, Kleiser was too young 'to know what the fifties were about' and

television had left him with only 'the remotest idea of how to handle a widescreen'. David Robinson wrote that his 'timid use of the
camera, his movement of the players, his slight feeling for a musical
number and his cutting style all suggest that his experience must
have been in newscasts'. Philip French, writing in the *Observer*,
found Kleiser to be 'painfully irresolute of purpose'; he had 'no control of mood' and the film's choreography was 'an uneasy mixture
of jitterbug-frenzied and disco-functional'.[70] Richard Barklay in the
Sunday Express also thought the film was 'poorly choreographed',
while William Hall of London's *Evening News* claimed that 'too
much of the choreography is like amateur night at Pebble Mill'.[71]

These prominent reviews may reveal little about the appeal of
Grease to a wider audience, but they serve as a reminder that quality film critics seldom offer a straightforward guide to popular film
tastes. In the 1970s, the gulf between critics and audiences cannot
be attributed primarily to class distinctions. A gender and generation gap had opened as well. The leading critics of the previous generation, Dilys Powell and C.A. Lejeune, had been women, but the
high profile critics of the 1970s – Philip French, Derek Malcolm,
David Robinson and Alexander Walker – were all men. And, at a
time when cinema-going had shifted so heavily towards the young,
they were considerably older than most cinema-goers. Each had
been born in the early 1930s and so they were a little too old to
consider this film as a nostalgic portrait of their own adolescence.
Furthermore, their critical values were rooted in the 1940s and
1950s, when concerns for realism and auteurism offered a means
of taking films seriously, and this meant that none was inclined to
appreciate the flippant and light entertainment of *Grease*. They saw
the film as a form of cinematic bubblegum – defiantly immature,
sugary sweet and more than a little garish – and thought it was their
duty to point out its nutritional deficiencies rather than attempt to
blow a bubble themselves.

In the 1970s, film criticism was seldom written by or for a
younger audience, but the pop music magazines *Record Mirror* and
New Musical Express offered brief reviews which took a more sympathetic view of the film. The (unnamed) critic for *Record Mirror*
commended *Grease* for its 'sharp, rapid and funny' dialogue and
also admonished critics who took the film too seriously by stating

that, 'there is never the suggestion that this is anything more than a tongue-in-cheek comedy'.[72] The *New Musical Express* was aimed at an older teenage readership, and in 1978 much of its writing was devoted to punk-ish rock bands such as The Clash, Talking Heads and Siouxsie and the Banshees. The paper was unlikely, then, to appreciate a film starring Olivia Newton-John, but it was equally unlikely to concur with the views of the older critical establishment. Hence, Monty Smith's review referred to *Grease* as 'ludicrous fluff', but also asserted that the film was a 'pisstake' and that 'you'd have to be as grumpy as a High Court judge not to come out smiling'.[73] It would be many years before views such as these were expanded and developed in print. Indeed, the generation that saw *Grease* as children had to grow up and become critics or journalists themselves before the film was assessed more sympathetically.

The turning point in the critical reception of *Grease* was its twentieth anniversary re-release in 1998, an occasion that prompted several critics and journalists to revisit a favourite film from their childhood. In these reviews and articles, it is clear that the critical values that held sway in 1978 had been soundly defeated. Where the 'shamefully unreal' qualities of *Grease* had been disparaged on its first release, 20 years later it was the film's 'kitsch and clunky' aspects that made it a 'perpetual joy', according to Caroline Westbrook in the popular film magazine, *Empire*. Similarly, where the choreography and Randal Kleiser's direction were once considered dull, Westbrook praised the 'memorable song and dance routines and the all-round exuberance on offer here'.[74] Charlotte O'Sullivan, in the *Observer*, concurred, and explained that the film had been 'ahead of its time' in 1978. She compared Kleiser's humour to the 1990s satirical television series *The Simpsons*, and cited as evidence one of the film's campy sexual innuendoes: at the drive-in theatre, as Danny sings the love song 'Sandy' in the foreground, an advertisement on the screen in the background shows a cartoon of a hot dog eagerly waiting to leap into a reluctant bun (Figure 21).[75] In the *Guardian*, Gaby Wood expressed her surprise at the 'excitement generated in the film' and reported her 'disbelief' at finding it 'so slick, so colourful, so self-mocking' 20 years after first seeing it.[76] These readings were informed by a camp sensibility that emphasized entertainment over artistic value and valued films that

Figure 21   In the 1990s, critics admired the camp humour in *Grease*. Here, Danny sings 'Sandy' as another drama unfolds behind him on the screen

demonstrated an awareness of their own artifice, exaggeration and frivolity. In the 1970s this sensibility had been in the ascendant, especially among the young, but it was at odds with more earnest and long established critical values. As previously noted, it was not just a generational shift in critical values that brought out different perspectives on the film, but also the emergence of women's opinions of the film. In the 1970s, a feminine perspective on *Grease* was scarcely available. Decades later, women led the way in commenting on the film's appeal and significance, and also recounting their own experiences of seeing it in 1978.

Three themes emerge from these retrospective commentaries. One is that *Grease* itself served as a rite of passage for the girls who eagerly awaited its release over the summer of 1978. Eleanor Bailey recalled in the *Independent* that, although she was only eight years old when the film was first released, she and her school friends were enthralled by it. Seeing this A-certificate film became the 'ultimate social distinction' among her classmates, and understanding its 'rude' jokes served as a means of demonstrating sophistication and denying innocence.[77] Both Bailey and Elena Seymenliskya, writing in the *Daily Telegraph*, also referred to the awed fascination that

Sandy's 'makeover' held for their peer group. Considering the scene in this context – as one that appealed to pre-pubescent girls – brings its reassuring qualities to the fore. The scene suggests that sexual maturity is merely a mask, that it can be put on (and taken away) at will and that – amid all the smiles of the 'shake shack' – it cannot hold any real danger or harm. The second theme involves what Gaby Wood referred to as the film's 'kitsch and clunky' qualities. The tongue-in-cheek humour, the age of the actors and the period fashions mark *Grease* as a highly performative film and therefore one that easily inspires imitation. Hence, the film's young fans adopted the clothing and the hairstyles for costume parties, they practised the dance routines and sang the songs, and the 'slumber party' became a new fixture in their social lives. As Bailey recalled, '*Grease* was not just the word, it was the life' in 1978. The third theme centres on a perception of the United States as having an almost other-worldly glamour. This was attributed to the depressing socio-economic realities prevailing at the time of the film's release. Seymenliskya pointed out that when *Grease* arrived in the autumn of 1978, Britain was 'on the verge of the winter of discontent', and the film's 'sunny optimism' served as a tonic to audiences caught up in the sharp economic downturn and escalating labour disputes of the 1970s. Bailey compared *Grease* with *Grange Hill*, which began its long run on the BBC in 1978, noting that this soap opera, centred on a north London comprehensive school, seemed dreary next to its Hollywood counterpart. Similarly, when Seymenliskya concluded her recollections with the statement, 'the upper-sixth form was never like this'. This was not a criticism of the film's unreal qualities but an explanation of how and why her generation was so enthralled by 'the candy-coloured confection' of *Grease*.[78]

These later commentaries on *Grease* are undoubtedly informed by repeated viewings. In fact, judging by these and other commentaries (discussed below) one of the chief pleasures of *Grease* is watching it again, on stage and screen. When it was first screened on television, in December 1982, the *Guardian* listings page described it as 'the 1978 disco cult movie', indicating that it had an avid and active following.[79] *Grease* has some of the qualities identified by Umberto Eco as key components of the 'cult movie' – and not least a 'glorious ricketiness' in its construction and a surfeit of intertextual references – but it was certainly not 'cult' in the sense of being a marginal or fringe film.[80] In fact, its television debut was on BBC1, in prime time, and on the Boxing Day bank holiday no less. This was the first of eight screenings on BBC1 over the next 14 years, most of which were on bank holidays; programming that ensured large audiences and also tacitly acknowledged the film's status as one of the nation's favourite films. When the stage musical returned to the West End in 1993, it was not the original version that had come and gone 20 years earlier. It was a new version based on the film, and this ran for six years at the Dominion Theatre and spawned two national tours. After the film's twentieth anniversary theatrical re-release, there were also a further nine screenings on terrestrial television between 2001 and 2010.[81] In 2003, a Channel Four poll found that *Grease* was the 'nation's favourite musical'.[82] In 2008, the British Video Association reported that the film's VHS and DVD sales reached nearly five million copies, and this data was used to dub the film as Britain's favourite 'chick flick'; a distinction that belatedly recognized the film's strong appeal to women.[83] Most recently, in 2010 there was another theatrical re-release, as *Grease Singalong*, a format that encourages cinema audiences to dress in the film's costumes and sing and dance throughout the screening. These screenings represent the triumph of the *Rock Around the Clock* generation; once vilified for expressing their boisterous enthusiasm in cinemas, they are now encouraged to express it more exuberantly. The advertising for *Grease Singalong* declares that it is an ideal outing for 'hen nights', pointing again to the film's strong following among women.[84] However, comments made on the internet, regarding the purchase of the DVD, indicate that *Grease* is regarded as a family film as well.[85] That is, parents who remember seeing the film when they were young are keen to show it to their own children. As a film about the transition from childhood to adulthood – with children imagining their future and adults remembering their past – it is unusual for representing this difficult phase of life in such utopian terms. Few films about adolescence are so free of angst and full of exuberance (at least, not since Mickey Rooney's heyday in the late 1930s and early 1940s). Fewer still can place burgeoning teenage sexuality so high on the agenda and yet still maintain an aura of family-friendly entertainment (as well as the current PG rating). Seeing the film has become a rite of passage for successive generations, and one almost uniquely suited to keeping both parents and children amused.

Looking back on *Grease* and the 1950s

Over the course of its many screenings, revivals and re-releases, *Grease* has become 'embedded' in British culture: a process that involves not only repeated and high-profile screenings over many years, but also the accumulation of new meanings and significance.[86] This process has taken the film far away from its references to 1950s pop culture and to a much wider audience than those who would recall the original impact and significance of the decade's youth culture. Its performative nature and its sly, tongue-in-cheek humour have made it ripe for the ritualistic and participatory viewing that has become so central to popular film culture in recent years. Hence, journalists refer to the film's songs as 'karaoke favourites' and use terms such as 'comforting' to describe the experience of seeing it again.[87] Clearly, the film's camp sensibility has been crucial to its acceptance and popularity in Britain. A film that recalled the 1950s in more specific terms (as Jim Jacobs and Warren Casey's original stage show did), or that took a semi-realist approach to representing time and place (as in *American Graffiti*), would be less pliable and less likely to travel so well through time and across national borders. In the ending, when Danny and Sandy drive the 'greased lightnin'' hot rod into the sky and wave farewell (to Rydell High School and to the audience) from the clouds, few viewers could be left with the impression that this is a film concerned with an exact time and place. The knowing, ironic humour of this scene also points to a key part of the film's appeal for British audiences. Irony offers audiences a distance from and a superiority over the film. The distance might be very different for separate audience groups, but it nevertheless represents a mode in which audiences are able to enjoy American culture on their own terms and from their own vantage point. It invites audiences to mock *Grease*, however gently, even as they sing along to it.

It could be said, then, that *Grease* has been 'appropriated' by British audiences; that is, that audiences have taken their own meanings and pleasures from the film, shaping it for their own purposes. Yet it must also be acknowledged that, whether mocked or not, the popularity of the film has made aspects of American culture and adolescence seem familiar as well as desirable. The film represents the high school and its customs, the culture of the automobile, the affluence of the characters and the free and easy social relations among students (and with teachers) as part of everyday life. Most of all, it lends a glamour and importance to teenagers that is seldom matched in real life, and could scarcely be realized in a more specific or realistic setting.[88] Little wonder, then, that in Britain girls wanted to have slumber parties and 'pink lady' jackets, that the 'high school prom' has gradually overtaken the 'school leaver's disco' as an annual custom and that, in the wake of *Grease*, theme restaurants based on the 1950s American diner suddenly appeared alongside pubs and chip shops on British high streets.[89] The film represents the 1950s as a fun fair of popular culture, in which every attraction celebrates the mythic, empowered teenager of that decade. Yet it is American popular culture, and an American teenage lifestyle, that the film foregrounds. In the process, elements of the 1950s that were specific to British society and culture may be eclipsed. Teenage fans of *Grease* are more likely to know the rituals and customs of the 1950s American high school than they are to know about Teddy Boys, or milk bars, or that, as recently as the 1950s, the vast majority of their forebears left education and went into full-time work by the tender age of 15.

The film can serve, then, as an example of Hollywood's tendency to naturalize American culture, and to portray the American past as a universal past and a part of the march of progress towards the present day. Equally, the enthusiasm of British audiences for this vision of the American 1950s can be taken as evidence of Hollywood's powerfully Americanizing influence. Through the appeal of its stars and the power of its marketing, Hollywood can make the American culture seem vibrant and compelling, and in the process push Britain's own past and culture to the margins. However, this does not mean that an American perspective or the American values of Hollywood films are always appealing. *Grease* offers a vision of the past that is useful and flattering for audiences in the present. That is, it suggests that the 1950s represent a wider rite of passage, or liberation, from old-fashioned and laughable innocence to assured and glamorous modernity. The film's retrospective view and its ironic humour allow audiences to feel that they have made this transition and moved on. Furthermore, the climactic scene makes the transition seem easy and painless. As we will see in the next chapter, though, films with an American perspective and values are not always so pleasing to British audiences. When audiences do not feel that a film has anything to offer them, or indeed that it may even be an affront to them, they are clearly able to reject and refute it. The power of *Grease*, by contrast, lies in its ability to reassure audiences that they have outgrown the American 1950s even as it allows them to revisit the American 1950s over and over again.

8

'The Wrong Side of the Special Relationship': *The Patriot* (2000) and the War of Independence in Films

That no single French, English or other troops took part in the war is perhaps the impression of many Americans – the film seems to point this way. But it does nothing for the cause of Anglo-American amity to insist, as *The Big Parade* does, on this point.

Review of *The Big Parade* in the *Spectator* (1926)[1]

[*Objective, Burma!*] was rejected, not by a censorship, or by the intervention of highly placed persons, but by *public opinion* expressing itself through the trained observers of the Press. More power to their elbows. Cinema audiences too often have to take whatever dope is given to them. It is important that the distinction between entertainment and propaganda should be constantly emphasised.

Editorial in the *Daily Mirror* (1945)[2]

With *The Patriot*, Hollywood seems about to unleash yet another offensive against our honour. If so, in the name of historical truth, and justifiable national pride, let's, at last, fight back.

Andrew Roberts, commentary in the *Daily Express* (2000)[3]

The preceding chapters have considered the extent to which Hollywood films have suited the tastes and preferences of British audiences over many decades, and particularly films that have appealed to a broad swathe of cinema-goers or to specific niche audiences. Either way, the emphasis has been on exploring the extent to which Hollywood films have not seemed to be foreign films, or, in some cases, why their foreign qualities have proved to be more appealing than alienating. This chapter, however, explores films that have seemed foreign and have caused offence by emphasizing an American perspective over and above a British one. Whereas most Hollywood films are accepted as a part of ordinary, every-day entertainment, there are occasionally some that are narrowly nationalistic in their values and outlook. The chapter will focus on war films – the genre most likely to cause offence – and more specifically on films made about the War of Independence. But it is worth acknowledging first that it is not only films about this war, fought between Britain and the United States in the eighteenth century, that have given rise to controversies. Britain and the USA may have fought side by side and as allies in the First and Second World Wars, and remained the staunchest of allies thereafter, but films about these conflicts have at times highlighted imbalances and differences in the relationship rather than unity and common purpose.

The review of MGM's *The Big Parade* (1925/26) that appeared in the *Spectator* (quoted in the first excerpt above) was one of many that objected to this First World War drama. The film arrived in London riding a wave of its critical and commercial success in the United States, and the London critics had to admit that it was skilfully made and highly entertaining. But the critics were aghast that Hollywood would make a film about the war that centres entirely on American soldiers, and they questioned whether British audiences would accept a war film that does not even acknowledge the involvement of British or French troops. In stating that the film would do 'nothing for the cause of Anglo-American amity' the (unnamed) critic for the *Spectator* also betrayed a common and persistent assumption. That is, films are not simply the creation of a team of filmmakers or a single studio, but can be regarded as quasi-official ambassadors that express an entire nation's views and outlook.[4] This is an assumption often ascribed to Hollywood and one that, especially where war films are concerned, is capable of stirring anti-American feeling abroad.

Nearly 20 years later, Warner Brothers' *Objective, Burma!* (1945) caused much greater offence. As the editorial in the *Daily Mirror* demonstrates (in the second excerpt above), the objections to this Second World War combat drama were vehement. The critics protested because the film centres on a (fictional) group of American paratroopers operating behind enemy lines in Burma and it implies that they were a decisive factor in victory, when actually British and

Commonwealth troops played a major role in the long, brutal Burma campaign. The hostile commentary in the *Daily Mirror* was typical of the press responses, which regarded *Objective, Burma!* not just as an insult to veterans of the Burma campaign, but as a 'propaganda' film designed to bolster the USA's standing in the world and to do this at Britain's cost. It is notable, too, that the editorial asserts that public opinion 'expresses itself through the press'. There is hardly evidence to confirm that this was the case with *Objective, Burma!* In fact, the press campaign was so fierce that Warner Brothers withdrew the film after it had screened for just one week in a single West End cinema.[5]

When they emphasized a singularly American perspective on world events, films such as *The Big Parade* and *Objective, Burma!* were considered to have committed crimes of oversight and self-aggrandizement. By contrast, *The Patriot* was regarded as much more aggressive in its intent. This was partly because in the past Hollywood had approached the War of Independence so rarely and with great pains taken to avoid offence. But it was also because the filmmakers set out to tell their story in the idiom of the modern Hollywood action film – with clear demarcations of good and evil and ample violence and bloodshed – and this required them to portray the British as unabashed villains. When it was released in the summer of 2000, *The Patriot* provoked an uproar in the press, where it was discussed as one of several recent films with an anti-British slant. In the *Daily Express*, the historian Andrew Roberts (quoted in the third excerpt above) listed Hollywood's other, recent insults to the country. Chief among them were two recent Second World War films. *Saving Private Ryan* (1998) tells the story of D-Day without mentioning British involvement, apart from an offhand reference to General Montgomery as 'overrated'; and *U-571* (2000) portrays the US Navy capturing the first German Enigma machine, when actually this was accomplished by the Royal Navy before the USA entered the war. For Roberts, *The Patriot* was a leading example of a recent anti-British trend in Hollywood films, and he called for a boycott of the film. But do British audiences actually take offence at Hollywood films that misrepresent the nation's history, and portray its people as villains? Or are outcries such as these merely talking points for journalists, commentators and politicians?

This chapter pursues these questions by considering a range of critical and audience responses to *The Patriot*. It begins, however, by examining the extraordinary sensitivities surrounding films about the American War of Independence, and the extent to which *The Patriot* marked the end of the longstanding cinematic 'special relationship' between Hollywood and Britain.

The cinematic 'special relationship'

When *The Patriot* was released, Hollywood's longstanding reluctance to portray the revolutionary period was widely discussed in the American press. In *The New York Times*, a feature article asked why Gary Cooper had never been cast as George Washington, why Errol Flynn had played so many historical characters but never a revolutionary figure such as Paul Revere and why in the 1960s 'screen rebels' such as Peter Fonda and Dennis Hopper had not played 'the rebels of 1776'.[6] This article and others like it put forth a variety of explanations. One was that the period is considered unattractive and remote to modern viewers, who cannot fathom a time in which American men wore powdered wigs and stockings and wrote with quill pens. Another theory was that the reverence attached to the 'founding fathers' in modern times made them unsuitable subjects for popular films; they are the stuff of school lessons rather than entertainment. It was also said that they are known for political ideas rather than action, and so their heroism is too abstract for popular filmmaking. And, when considering the studio era, some journalists argued that Hollywood's studio moguls were ardent Anglophiles, and so they were reluctant to dramatize a war in which the British would be seen in an unflattering light.[7] All of these explanations have an element of truth in them, but they overlook one overriding factor. Hollywood had long relied on Britain for the majority of its foreign earnings, and foreign earnings were crucial to the studios' profit margins. This was the basis of the cinematic 'special relationship', and it was established long before Churchill and Roosevelt established the military and political 'special relationship'. It was not Anglophilia that made Hollywood producers wary of insulting the British, but the size and value of the Britain's lucrative exhibition market.

The relationship was at its height in the 1930s and 1940s, and its significance was apparent in the large Hollywood British community of stars, character actors, producers, directors and scriptwriters who forged their careers in California rather than London. It was apparent, too, in the large number of Hollywood 'British' films made by the studios.[8] In the 1930s, these included literary adaptations such as *Treasure Island* (1933), *David Copperfield* (1934), *A Tale of Two Cities* (1936) and *Wuthering Heights* (1939); as well as historical films ranging from *Mutiny on the Bounty* (1935) to *The Adventures of Robin Hood* (1938) and *Stanley and Livingstone* (1939). Stories such as these represented a shared culture and heritage for American and British audiences, and on both sides of the Atlantic they were among the most high-profile and popular films of their decade. Hollywood's British interests were even more apparent during the war years. Early war films such as *Foreign Correspondent* (1940), *The Sea Hawk* (1940) and *A Yank in the RAF* (1941) were released before the United States had entered the war, and *Mrs Miniver* (1942) and *This Above All* (1942) were already in production when Pearl Harbor was attacked. Far from remaining neutral, Hollywood demonstrated its pro-British stance from the beginning of the war in Europe. If there is an undercurrent of Anglophobia in these films, it can be detected in the representation of class. Aristocratic characters are often unsympathetic, or, in the wartime films, they are used to demonstrate the beneficial, democratizing effects of the war. But the films emphasize Britain's fortitude most of all, and American audiences were intrigued and heartened by them. In Britain, critics often scoffed at the films' anachronisms, but audiences appreciated seeing themselves – or at least their country – mythologized by Hollywood. Some of these films – and especially *Mrs Miniver* – were more popular with British audiences than Britain's own war films.[9]

If the war years represent the apex of the cinematic 'special relationship', it is important to note that it had a long legacy, and not only in further historical and literary dramas but also in postwar war films. For example, Twentieth Century-Fox's *The Longest Day* (1962) is a kaleidoscopic view of D-Day that features a host of British actors in roles as RAF officers and pilots. Films such as *Where Eagles Dare* (1968) and *A Bridge Too Far* (1977) recall the war in collaborative terms as well. *The Bridge on the River Kwai* (1957) and *The Great Escape* (1963) place American stars at the front of their stories as a means of ensuring an audience in the United States, but they nevertheless tell tales of Anglo-American cooperation in the war. It is this vantage point that links them to the wider transatlantic film culture that peaked in wartime and then diminished very gradually over the decades that followed.

Earlier films on the War of Independence

Hollywood's long reluctance to make films about the War of Independence attests to the strength and endurance of the cinematic 'special relationship'. For Americans, the founding fathers have never lost their currency. Their stories and deeds have been kept alive in the country's classrooms, from elementary school lessons through university level courses. Their views continue to be cited by liberals and conservatives alike in debates on contemporary issues. They are the subjects of a continuous stream of bestselling biographies and historical studies. And of course their achievements and the events of 1776 are commemorated enthusiastically in annual Independence Day celebrations. The dramatic stories associated with the revolutionary period would seem to offer vivid cinematic material: the Boston Tea Party, Paul Revere's ride, the first shots fired in Lexington, the signing of the Declaration of Independence and Washington crossing the Delaware, to name but a few. Equally, it is easy to envisage biopics in which a young George Washington admits to having chopped down a cherry tree, Thomas Jefferson writes the Declaration of Independence, or Benjamin Franklin experiments with electricity. Yet despite their iconic status, and the centrality of the founding myth within American culture, Hollywood's reluctance to cause offence in Britain ensured that films along these lines have been few and far between.

The earliest known feature film to dramatize the War of Independence provided filmmakers with a remarkable and cautionary tale. *The Spirit of '76* (1917) was made by an independent American producer, Robert Goldstein, who had the idea of making a spectacular, patriotic epic along the lines of D.W. Griffith's *The Birth of a Nation*, but using the nation's true 'birth', rather than the Civil War, as the subject matter. However, Goldstein released his film just after the United States entered the First World War as Britain's ally. In this context, *The Spirit of '76* appeared to be a slur against the British, and one that was designed to stoke anti-war feeling in the USA. It did not help that the film dramatized one of the most contested episodes in the War of Independence, the Cherry Valley Massacre of 1778, in which British troops (in what is now upstate New York) are alleged to have killed civilians and burned their homes. Nor did it help that Goldstein chose Chicago, with its large German- and Irish-American populations, as the site of the film's premiere. It was when he defied the demands of local censorships boards and reinserted scenes that they had insisted must be cut from the film that Goldstein was arrested and tried under the newly passed Espionage Act. In April 1918, he was found guilty and sentenced to ten years in a federal penitentiary.[10]

No other film would portray British villainy in the War of Independence so blatantly as *The Spirit of '76* until *The Patriot* was released more than 80 years later. In the meantime, Hollywood film-makers were more likely to produce films that would appeal to both of their principal markets – the United States and Britain – than they were to produce films that would divide them. Hence, the War of Independence was avoided, and when the subject was broached it was handled with great care. D.W. Griffith's *America* (1924) was a pivotal film in establishing just how careful filmmakers needed to be. Griffith was defensive about the arguments surrounding the historical accuracy of *The Birth of a Nation*, and so he was intent on portraying as many uncontested historical vignettes in *America* as possible.[11] The film dramatizes Paul Revere's ride, the signing of the Declaration of Independence, the Continental Army's winter at Valley Forge and the British surrender at Yorktown, and it is these scenes which make *America* a distinctive film today. It portrays a wider range of actual revolutionary events than any other feature film. It also set several precedents that would be followed in future films on the subject. Griffith was careful not to offend British sensi-bilities. Thus, Anglo-American enmity is downplayed in the open-ing titles, which declare that the war was 'a civil war between two groups of English people', thereby indicating that it was not a war between the British and the Americans. The 'two groups of English people' are represented in the story by the aristocratic Montague family and by the commoner Nathan Holden (Neil Hamilton), a dispatch rider. Their differences are easily reconciled when young Nancy Montague (Carol Dempster) falls in love with Nathan.

Villainy is attributed solely to Captain Butler (Lionel Barrymore), an American Tory who plots to attack and burn a fort protecting civilians. It is made clear, however, that Butler is a renegade, not acting under orders, and that his troops are neither colonists nor Redcoats but Native Americans. A brief scene that portrays George III as a mad, bad monarch is immediately counter-balanced by one showing William Pitt arguing on behalf of the over-taxed colonists in the House of Commons. And, while the ending does depict the British surrender at Yorktown, this is followed by intertitles that proclaim the strength of the friendship between the 'English-speaking peoples'.

America was not a success. Critics complained that its story and especially its ending – which has a nick of time, ride to the rescue ending like the one in *The Birth of a Nation* – was old fashioned and overly familiar. Audiences apparently agreed, because the film failed to cover its costs in the United States.[12] Worse, the BBFC refused to grant a certificate to *America*. Griffith had renamed the film *Love and Sacrifice* for the British release, attempting to downplay its nationalism for British audiences.[13] He also travelled to Britain to protest against the notion that his film was anti-British, but his attempts to gain favour with the press and the public backfired.[14] The two leading British trade papers, *The Bioscope* and *Kinematograph Weekly*, published full-page editorials denouncing the director and his attempt to interfere with Britain's censorship policy.[15] The censors held firm, and Griffith was required to cut and re-cut the film. When it finally met with the censors' approval, it had become infamous and it faced derisory reviews.[16]

Griffith had been careful with *America* but not careful enough. He apparently did not realize that the BBFC was particularly protective of the monarchy and the reputation of British soldiery. Even if the monarch was George III and the soldier was a renegade, the BBFC did not allow films that cast the nation's venerated institutions in a disreputable light. The fact that a foreign filmmaker had breached these principles only added to the offence. Yet while the film and the filmmaker suffered, *America* nevertheless proved to be a strong influence on later films set in this period. Nearly all of these would define the War of Independence as a civil war, as Griffith had, but they took additional steps to ensure British audiences were not offended. Rather than labelling the war as one between 'two groups of English people', later films would portray it as a war between two groups of Americans. Archly aristocratic Tories and rough-and-ready Whigs became the stock characters of the later films, too. As in *America*, a romance involving the younger members of these representative groups would point the way toward the reconciliation of differences and toward the future classlessness of American society. Native Americans would continue to take the blame for any atrocities. Overt statements of Anglo-American unity and friendship would be made, and the credits of many of the films that followed would offer real evidence of Anglo-American cooperation. Most were assigned to British directors, as a means of ensuring that the films did not have – and were seen not to have – a purely American outlook.

The subsequent films came mainly in two waves. Remarkably, the first wave arrived in the early years of the Second World War. This may seem an odd time for Hollywood to portray conflict between Britain and the United States, but as the historian John E. O'Connor has explained, the hardships of the Depression and the spread of fascism in Europe led Americans to reflect on their country's origins, recalling both the hardships of pioneer struggles and the country's democratic ideals.[17] In the early war years, interventionists rallied American interest in the European war by representing it as a 'fight for freedom' that had parallels in the country's own experience; the rallying cry of the American revolution – Patrick Henry's 'give me liberty or give me death' – could also serve as a rallying cry against Nazism.[18] In 1943 the United States wartime propaganda agency, the Office of War Information, endorsed this line of thinking when it produced a poster combining the images of the Continental Army of 1778 at Valley Forge and the modern American army of 1943. The by-line – 'Americans will always fight for their liberty' – makes the parallel clear, but, given that the USA was fighting against Britain in 1778 and alongside Britain in 1943, there was an impolitic dimension to the message. Posters, however, could be produced for domestic consumption alone, while feature films rarely were. Hence, just as D.W. Griffith had taken it for granted that he would release *America* in Britain, with only a change of title to mark its passage outside the United States, the producers of *Allegheny Uprising* (1939/40), *Drums Along the Mohawk* (1939/40) and *The Howards of Virginia* (1940/41) assumed that their films would naturally be shown in Britain. In this respect, Hollywood was seeking to have its cake and eat it too; that is, the studios sought to make films about the War of Independence that would stir American pride and yet also prove palatable to the British.

This difficult balancing act met with varying results. RKO's *Allegheny Uprising* (1939/40), renamed *The First Rebel* in Britain, was the least successful in all respects. This story, set in the backwoods of Pennsylvania, is ostensibly about the struggle between frontier settlers and the Native Americans who attack their homes. But by casting the rough-and-ready John Wayne as the leading settler, and the refined George Sanders as a British Army captain who does little to help the settlers, the film suggests that the cultural differences between the Americans and the British are profound. Twentieth Century-Fox's *Drums Along the Mohawk* (1939/40) also concerns the conflict between settlers and Native Americans on the frontier, but the story centres squarely on the hardships of a newlywed couple (played by Henry Fonda and Claudette Colbert) rather than the political context for the violence. It is clear that a shadowy American Tory (John Carradine) prompts the raids on the settlers' homes by the Iroquois, but with the director John Ford at the helm the film has the look and feel of a Western, albeit one filmed in brilliant Technicolor and with a setting in upstate New York. Indeed, the story was so vaguely placed in terms of period and location that when it was showcased in the fan magazines *Boys' Cinema* and *Picture Show* the War of Independence was scarcely mentioned.[19] Columbia's *The Howards of Virginia* (1940/41) was produced and directed by Frank Lloyd, a British filmmaker who spent much of his career in Hollywood, and the film stars the British-born actor Cary Grant in his most unlikely role, as a buckskinned pioneer who marries into a socially prominent Tory family. But historical figures such as Patrick Henry, Thomas Jefferson and George Washington feature as minor characters, and location filming in Williamsburg, Virginia, further enhances the film's sense of period and purpose. Interestingly, the studio gambled in its marketing campaign by drawing attention to the historical conflict rather than downplaying it. For the British release, the film was renamed *The Tree of*

Liberty (with reference to Thomas Jefferson's words, 'The tree of liberty must be refreshed from time to time with the blood of patriots and tyrants.').[20] The story was described as a struggle for 'liberty and democracy', and parallels were drawn with 'the critical times in which we are now living'.[21] It was a bold but unsuccessful strategy, and this film, like the others before and after it, made little impact at the British box office.[22]

The second and less significant wave of films arrived in the 1950s. This is an odd collection of films, and each fell into obscurity soon after its release. MGM's *The Scarlet Coat* (1955/56) promises at the outset to tell the story of the infamous American traitor Benedict Arnold, but the focus soon shifts from this potentially divisive subject to the more harmonious story of the friendship and respect that develops between a British officer (Michael Wilding) who hides Arnold's identity and the American counter-agent (Cornel Wilde) who seeks it.[23] Disney's charming but low-key *Johnny Tremain* (1957) was directed by Robert Stevenson, another British director who was a Hollywood veteran. This boy's-eye-view of the Boston Tea Party was offered within a familiar story of down-to-earth rebels and snobbish Tories. *John Paul Jones* (1958) is a biopic of America's first naval hero and it was directed by John Farrow, an Australian-born director who had served with the Royal Navy during the Second World War. In the title role, Robert Stack lends a vigorous American tone to Jones' declaration 'I have not yet begun to fight', but the film uses a prologue and epilogue to set this defiant spirit within a Cold War context. The revolution itself is explained as Americans 'seeking liberty according to English ideas and principles', while the war is portrayed in the most sportsman-like manner. After one sea battle, Jones even invites the defeated British to join his men on their ship so that a joint burial service can be held for those killed in battle. The earnest and stirring tone is in direct contrast to the satire of *The Devil's Disciple* (1959). George Bernard Shaw's play was adapted for the screen by Burt Lancaster's production company and filmed at Elstree by the British director Guy Hamilton. Its story is carefully balanced between the British soldiers who fight only to advance their careers (represented by Laurence Olivier as a world-weary General Burgoyne) and the colonists whose sympathies lie with whichever side is winning at the moment. The stars of the film, Lancaster and Kirk Douglas, clearly relish their parts, but the film was too cynical and dialogue-bound to find a wide audience.

Subsequently, only *1776* (1972/73) and *Revolution* (1985/86) attempted to fill the void of films on the topic.[24] *1776* is a musical centred on the writing of the Declaration of Independence, and it is the only feature film to portray the founding fathers as flesh and blood characters rather than rarefied, unknowable beings. It represents an enormous leap in this respect; not only are John Adams, Benjamin Franklin and Thomas Jefferson in the front and centre of the film as its main characters, but they sing and dance their way through the second Continental Congress. The Broadway stage version was a modest success in the West End, but the film held little interest for either British or American cinema audiences. *Revolution* (1985) was made by the British company Goldcrest, which had scored a run of international box office hits, but this story of the War of Independence proved to be the company's downfall. *Revolution* does not stray far from the narrative formula laid down by *America*: the colonists are earthy everymen, the Tories are arrogant and antiquated and there is a romance between the main character, a penniless trapper (Al Pacino) and a woman who rebels against her stuffy Tory family (Nastassja Kinski). The film is unique, though, for its refusal to romanticize the past. The war is not a struggle for progressive ideals but a brutal conflict that the main character tries (in vain) to avoid. The story is set among the urban poor and the film highlights the squalor of their existence. In keeping with this, the director Hugh Hudson shot the film in bleak and murky hues, using long takes and hand-held cameras.[25] Together with a pair of stars who seemed woefully miscast, these qualities ensured that *Revolution* became a colossal box office failure.[26] In its wake, no other feature film would portray the War of Independence for another 15 years.

Re-writing the War of Independence

The Patriot broke with almost all of the traditions of the earlier films that took the revolutionary period as their subject or setting. Its main character is not an idealistic backwoodsman who has no interest in the war, but an affluent, middle-aged plantation owner who becomes enraged by the British and seeks to defeat them by means of guerrilla warfare. Unlike previous films, there is little romance in *The Patriot* – indeed, women scarcely figure in the film at all – and there is certainly not a romance that bridges the opposing forces of the revolution. The war is not portrayed as one between 'two groups of Englishmen', nor as one between American Whigs and Tories, and there are no statements attesting to Anglo-American unity or even shared principles. Unlike *Revolution*, it is filmed for maximum visual appeal; the lush green landscapes and glowing candlelit interiors render the past in vivid, pristine terms. Unlike most of the films centred on this period, the filmmaking team was not Anglo-American, but included a trio of American producers, an American scriptwriter and a German director. Most importantly, in terms of the film's reception in Britain, *The Patriot* portrays the war as a violent conflict in which peaceful Americans were roused to fight against tyrannical British rule. Indeed, the violence is represented with such gruesome spectacle that the BBFC granted a 15 certificate, indicating that it was suitable only for audiences over the age of 15.

The story centres on Benjamin Martin (Mel Gibson), a veteran of the French and Indian War who, in 1776, is a widower seeking a quiet life on his plantation. He is pushed into the War of Independence not out of patriotism, as the title would suggest, but because it arrives, in the form of Colonel Tavington (Jason Isaacs), at his front door (Figure 22). Tavington – a sneeringly haughty Englishman – is a caricature that only an Anglophobe could create.

Figure 22   Colonel Tavington (Jason Isaacs) takes aim in *The Patriot*

Where Hollywood 'British' films once suggested that aristocratic, superior airs and graces were merely inegalitarian, in Colonel Tavington they are an expression of his psychotic disregard for human life. When he arrives at Martin's plantation, he orders his troops to kill the rebel soldiers who are injured and recuperating there. He orders them to burn Martin's house. He seeks to execute Martin's older son (Heath Ledger) as a spy and when a younger son (Gregory Smith) intervenes, he kills the younger boy without a moment's hesitation or regret. The latter sequence, shot in slow motion for extra emotional impact, serves as Martin's reawakening as a warrior. In the scene that follows, he ambushes and slaughters a score of British soldiers, and this rampage leaves him dripping with their blood. Henceforth, he is known as the 'the ghost', and he leads lightning raids against the British troops and then disappears into the swamps where he cannot be found. Colonel Tavington takes revenge by ordering a local community to gather in their church, which is then barricaded and burned to the ground, killing them all (Figure 23). Martin meets with a forlorn General Cornwallis (Tom Wilkinson) to discuss a prisoner exchange, and outsmarts him. Eventually, the two sides meet in a conventional battle, Martin leads the rebels to victory and, in the film's climax, he savagely kills Colonel Tavington. An epilogue portrays the American victory at Yorktown and briefly acknowledges France's role in the war.

Historians delighted in pointing out the many distortions in this story.[27] Benjamin Martin is a figure similar to Francis Marion, who

Figure 23   British troops watch as the church they have set alight, with the parishioners barricaded inside, burns to the ground

used guerrilla tactics to harass British troops in his home state of South Carolina; and Tavington is reminiscent of Banastre Tarleton, the commander of the British Legion, who pursued the elusive Marion through the back roads of his home state and dubbed him the 'swamp fox'.[28] However, Francis Marion did not kill Banastre Tarleton (who actually survived the war and lived for another 50 years). Although he was a notoriously ruthless warrior in battle, Tarleton was never accused of committing atrocities against women and children.[29] The troops led by Tarleton were American Loyalists, who were effectively engaged in a civil war with their rebel neighbours, but the film acknowledges only one Loyalist (Captain Wilkins) and represents the war in the starker terms of peaceful American settlers imperilled by occupying British forces.[30] The depiction of slavery is also highly misleading. In the film, it is said that the slaves who work on Benjamin Martin's plantation are free, waged labourers, but this is a very unlikely scenario in South Carolina at this time. In fact, Francis Marion was a slave owner and, as a colonel in the Continental Army, he was dispatched by the governor of South Carolina to pursue and if necessary kill any slaves who aided or joined the British cause.[31] It is notable, too, that a subplot in the film indicates that slaves who enlisted in the Continental Army would be freed at the end of the war; indeed, the filmmakers suggest that the War of Independence was fought in order to grant liberty to *all* Americans. Yet the vast majority of African Americans did not gain their freedom until slavery was ended in the wake of the Civil War, nearly 100 years later.

This new perspective on the War of Independence fitted well with what the film historian Albert Auster has referred to as Hollywood's '*fin de siècle* American triumphalism'. Fuelled, in Auster's view, by victory in the Cold War and in the first Gulf War, the patriotic films of the late 1990s glorify American history, values and achievements in unfettered terms.[32] The screenwriter of *The Patriot*, Robert Rodat, and its director, Roland Emmerich, were already well known for films in this vein. Rodat had written the screenplay for Steven Spielberg's *Saving Private Ryan*, which, through means of both extraordinary violence and sentimentality, single-handedly revived the war film in the late 1990s. Emmerich was not known for historical films, but for high-concept action films packed with special effects. His most successful film, *Independence Day* (1996), is a tongue-in-cheek science fiction film about an alien invasion of earth, but it also has some surprisingly bombastic patriotic moments. At its climax, set on American Independence Day, the US president (Bill Pullman) embarks on an expedition to destroy the aliens and so save the world. But first, in a heartfelt speech, he declares that when victory is achieved, 'The fourth of July will no longer be known as an American holiday', thereby suggesting that the USA's new global supremacy will inspire every nation to celebrate this day.

Saving Private Ryan and *Independence Day* were two of the most commercially successful films of the 1990s, but the box office power of *The Patriot* rested primarily with its star, Mel Gibson. In recent years, and largely because of revelations about his private life, Gibson's popularity has plummeted.[33] In 2000, however, he had been one of Hollywood's top stars for 15 years and *The Patriot* fitted well with his established screen persona. In his most popular films, Gibson plays an ordinary man driven to manic despair and crazed violence by circumstances beyond his control. The revenge scenarios at the centre of his films often render him emotionally unstable as well as violently enraged. This persona is not associated exclusively with historical films, as Gibson's very successful contemporary action film *Lethal Weapon* (1987) and its sequels demonstrate. But over the years he has had career defining moments in historical dramas that cast him as an ordinary man driven to extremes by corrupt and arrogant authority figures whose standing stems from class privilege rather than ability or achievements. That the actor himself is an American (despite a childhood spent in Australia) and the authority figures are English imbues these films with a sense that a virile new world machismo is righteously overthrowing an effete and corrupt old world order. In *Gallipoli* (1981), for example, Gibson plays a reluctant young Australian recruit, sent during the First World War to Turkey, where he witnesses the horrific incompetence of the British command. In *The Bounty* (1984), he portrays the mutineer Fletcher Christian as an angry young man who cannot abide the repressive, authoritarian Captain Bligh (Anthony Hopkins). And in *Braveheart* (1995), he depicts the Scots nationalist William Wallace as an initially peaceful man who is compelled to fight against Scotland's merciless, sadistic English oppressors.

There was nothing new in Hollywood films that pit a plain-speaking everyman against a high-ranking, arrogant Englishman. John Wayne and George Sanders enact this conflict in *The First Rebel*. Clark Gable and Charles Laughton go through similar paces in MGM's *Mutiny on the Bounty*, and (the Australian-born) Errol Flynn lends a new world urgency to his struggle with Basil Rathbone in *The Adventures of Robin Hood*. If these films betray an Anglophobic perspective, it is a subtle one and, because it was associated with class distinctions, it was one that the majority of British audiences were more likely to sympathize with than resent. The difference with Gibson's films, and especially *Braveheart*, which he also produced and directed, is that English arrogance serves as a springboard not just for rebellion, but for a prolonged, violent pursuit of vengeance.

As far as *Braveheart* and international audiences were concerned, there was nothing wrong in this. *Braveheart* was a box office hit throughout the world, with earnings of $210 million, and it won Academy Awards for the 'best picture' and 'best director' of the year. Remarkably, it was also a box office success in the UK, where $17 million of that sum was derived. The film was of course especially popular in Scotland, where teenage audiences reportedly 'cheered every time Wallace killed an Englishman'.[34] Yet the enthusiasm of the Scots cannot fully explain the strong UK earnings. The wider acceptance of the film south of the border may have stemmed simply from English audiences' willingness to accept *Braveheart* as a genre film. Importantly, though, national sensitivities may have been assuaged by the fact of Wallace's defeat (seen in the film when he is tortured and killed) and by the knowledge that Scotland ultimately joined the union (in the wider sweep of history). *The Patriot*, by contrast, would offer English audiences little to alleviate the prevailing sense of bias and hostility.

Release and reception

When *The Patriot* was released in Britain on 14 July 2000 it had already been the subject of discussion on the news and opinion pages of the major, national newspapers for many weeks. The

Guardian was the first to raise the alarm with a news item in April that informed readers *The Patriot* would be in the 'same Brit-bashing vein' as *Braveheart*.[35] By 4 June, a lengthy opinion piece in the *Sunday Times*, headlined 'damned lies', denounced *The Patriot* as a '160-minute polemic against Britain'.[36] On 14 June, when Andrew Roberts urged *Daily Express* readers to boycott the film, the head-line was 'Hollywood's racist lies about Britain and the British'. On 19 June, the *Daily Telegraph* weighed in with an extended analysis of the film's treatment of history entitled, 'Truth is the first casualty of Hollywood's war'.[37] On the day the film was released, the conserva-tive commentator Peter Hitchens reminded readers of the *Daily Express* to 'shun this pack of celluloid lies'.[38] And a few days later, the liberal commentator David Aaronovitch's commentary on the film in the *Independent* was headlined, 'cynical, demeaning and violent rubbish'.[39] Rarely has any one issue, cause or event united such a broad swathe of the press (from the *Guardian* on the left to the *Telegraph* on the right) and the controversy was not limited to the newspapers alone. A panel was convened to discuss the film on the BBC-Two television programme, *Newsnight*. On BBC Radio Four's *Today* programme, the American Ambassador to London, Philip Lader, was pressed to comment on whether the film was 'damaging' to UK–US relations.[40] And the government's Culture Secretary, Chris Smith, announced in July that on an upcoming visit to the United States he would 'complain to film directors and producers about their portrayal of the British as bullies, villains and racists'.[41]

According to many of these commentaries, *The Patriot* alone was not the problem. It was the latest and worst example of the anti-British bias observable in many recent Hollywood films. *Saving Private Ryan*, *U-571* and *Braveheart* were the other commonly cited examples.[42] It was noted, too, that an English accent had come to serve as a shorthand for villainy in Hollywood films and that British actors were routinely cast as villains, even if the villainous charac-ter was not British. For example, Gary Oldman plays the American assassin Lee Harvey Oswald in *JFK* (1991), Dracula in *Bram Stoker's Dracula* (1992) and the terrorist in *Air Force One* (1997). Anthony Hopkins is the psychopath Hannibal Lecter in *The Silence of the Lambs* (1991) and Richard Nixon in *Nixon* (1995/96). Dougray Scott is the terrorist in *Mission: Impossible II* (2000). Charles Dance is the psychotic hit man in *The Last Action Hero* (1995). Ralph Fiennes is the concentration camp commander in *Schindler's List* (1993/94). Alan Rickman is the South African terrorist Hans Gruber in *Die Hard* (1988). Jeremy Irons is Simon Gruber, his vengeful brother, in the sequel, *Die Hard With a Vengeance* (1995), and also the voice of the evil lion, Scar, in Disney's *The Lion King* (1994).[43] In this context, Jason Isaacs' sneering performance as Colonel Tavington was taken as the culmination of a long line of cinematic insults.

There were, however, very specific objections to *The Patriot*. One was the film's misleading representation of slavery. The American filmmaker Spike Lee's public criticism of the film as a 'racist white-wash of history' and 'pure, blatant Hollywood propaganda' was often cited in the British press to bolster claims that the film takes a determinedly blinkered and biased view of American history.[44] The other, more frequently discussed aspect of the film was the character of Colonel Tavington, and especially the scene in which he gives an order for men, women and children to be barricaded in their church and burned alive. As numerous commentators pointed out, there is no record of an event such as this during the War of Independence, but a very similar atrocity was perpetrated by the Nazi SS during the Second World War in the French village of Oradour sur Glane. The film therefore seems to draw an equivalency between the British and the Nazis, at least as far as wartime conduct is concerned, and this left many commentators spluttering. 'This is the kind of thing that British troops prevent, rather than the sort of thing they do,' Peter Hitchens insisted; while Jonathan Foreman asserted in the *Daily Telegraph* that *The Patriot* is 'exactly the movie you would expect' to be made about the War of Independence 'if the Nazis had won the war in Europe'.[45]

The controversy and accusations surrounding the film did not stop it from opening in 361 cinemas across the UK, and it was not withdrawn, as *Objective, Burma!* had been in 1945, after its first week of release. In fact, by contrast with the political commentators and columnists, the majority of film critics were surprisingly open-minded about *The Patriot*. They were willing to consider its aesthetic and entertainment value rather than judge it on the grounds of historical accuracy alone. In *Screen International*, Sheila Johnston led the way when she observed that *The Patriot* is 'more of a red-blooded action movie than a stuffy costume epic' and praised its 'opulent' production values and battle scenes. Johnston noted the wider, hostile press response to the film but predicted that 'Gibson's name and the picture's spectacular elements' would overcome the negative coverage of the film.[46] The marketing campaign was built on this assumption too. The UK poster, which was also used for most print advertisements, foregrounds Mel Gibson and downplays the film's historical concerns (Figure 24). It is dominated by a large, close-up shot of Gibson's face, and this portrait is so tightly framed that no signs of period dress (hat, haircut or clothing) are visible. With his steely blue eyes looking directly into the camera, this confrontational image could represent any of his contemporary action films. The vast blue sky and colourful sunset behind him hint at the film's spectacle and its attractive cinematography, but this too has no period connotations. It is only on the lower left hand side, where a blurred and partial image of a flag appears, and the lower right hand side, where a man on horseback carrying an obscured flag appears, that the film's historical setting is signalled. Arguably,

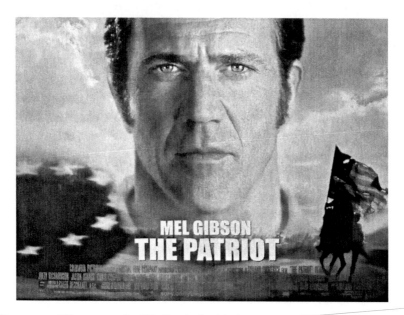

Figure 24   The poster for *The Patriot* highlighted its star, Mel Gibson, above all else

though, specialist knowledge would be needed to identify the flag and there is certainly no indication anywhere on the poster that the film involves Britain in any way.

Many film critics were willing to consider the film almost entirely as the poster defines it, as an action film with a vague historical background. They referred briefly to the controversy surrounding it and then moved on to other, more cinematic concerns. In the leading fan magazine, *Empire*, Colin Kennedy acknowledged that *The Patriot* was 'sure to annoy *Daily Mail* readers', but he praised Gibson's 'deep and dark, brutal and bloody' performance, admired director Roland Emmerich's capacity for 'shamelessly manipulating the emotions' and referred to the film's 'rousing action' scenes and 'powerful moments'.[47] Tabloid critics were not quite so dismissive of the film's treatment of the British – at the very least they warned their readers about it – but they too judged the film's entertainment value above all else. The *Daily Mail* readers referred to by Kennedy were told by Christopher Tookey that if they could leave behind their 'national pride and sense of the historically absurd' they would find the film to be 'an impressive display of cinematic fireworks'.[48] In the *News of the World*, Mariella Frostup informed readers that *The Patriot* is 'big on theatrics and clichés, [and] low on historical accuracy' but promised that it would nevertheless provide 'a great night out'.[49] Nick Fisher admitted in the *Sun* that the film makes 'the Brits look like inbred spineless twits', but he also concluded 'You'd be mad not to go and see it. It's the sort of movie very big screens were made for.'[50] In the *Daily Star*, Alan Frank dismissed the controversies surrounding the film with the question, 'How many people go to the movies for a history lesson?', and stated admiringly that *The Patriot* 'pounds your senses with stunning and gorily realistic battle scenes'.[51]

Elsewhere, some critics explored the issue of whether or not audiences *should* be offended by the film. Philip French admitted in the *Observer* that the film is 'undeniably entertaining', and he took a post-colonial view of its representation of the British, commenting that, 'It is perhaps salutary for English audiences to experience what our filmmakers have so often handed out to Germans, Japanese, Zulus, Aborigines – seeing the British blown away by a picture's heroes.'⁵² Sebastian Faulks in the *Mail on Sunday* took a similar perspective when he observed:

> Popular history is written by the victors: control of the 'facts' is the greatest spoil of battle. After all, how many British children grew up believing the decisive moments of the Second World War were the retreat from Dunkirk and the Battle of Britain, rather than Stalingrad and Hiroshima?

Faulks did not like the film, even as an action film, but he argued that, 'whatever its bias, *The Patriot* seems to me a perfectly legitimate, if unsuccessful, stab at popular entertainment.'⁵³ Only Andrew O'Hagan of the *Daily Telegraph* and Andrew Pulver of the *Guardian* argued that this was not legitimate entertainment. O'Hagan bemoaned the film's nationalism ('must everything be a national anthem these days?') and observed with exasperation that the British are portrayed as 'worse than the Nazis'.⁵⁴ Pulver took the opportunity to refer to the United States as 'the most powerful and self-regarding of modern nations' and labelled the film's portrayal of slavery as 'nauseating', but he was more concerned with making the case that *The Patriot*, like *U-571* before it, is another film 'in which we Brits come out on the wrong side of the special relationship'.⁵⁵

Audience responses

Apart from the reviews written by O'Hagan and Pulver, the overwhelming impression offered by critical responses to *The Patriot* is that historical accuracy matters little within popular film culture. The majority of critics focused on filmic elements: visual spectacle, action sequences, music, special effects and star performance. They judged the film for the visceral impact that it makes – for its merits as a form of fairground ride with thrills and spills – and on this score most found the means to recommend it. In these reviews it was taken for granted that for the purposes of entertainment complex historical events and issues must be reduced to simple notions of good and bad; that heroes must be suitable for cheering and villains for hissing. It was taken for granted, too, that audiences would not mind if Britons were cast as history's villains; indeed, some critics felt that a critical perspective on British history was overdue.

Research into audience responses, however, indicates that these assumptions were incorrect, and that a large portion of the audience had very different concerns from the critics.

Audience responses are available on many internet sites, but for the purposes of this analysis the Internet Movie Database (IMDb) is the most useful source. Since 1998, when it was purchased by Amazon, this website (www.imdb.com) has become 'ingrained into the contemporary cinematic culture', with some 57 million visits each month from around the world.[56] Like film fan magazines, the IMDb offers film industry news and reports on current and upcoming releases. Unlike film fan magazines, it has the capacity to offer a database of film credits and other factual information relating to 220,000 films. Crucially, for the purpose of gauging audience responses, it also has the capacity to provide a forum for audiences to rate, review and discuss each of these films. This participatory dimension is a pivotal part of internet-based film culture, and one that thrives on the IMDb.

On the IMDb pages for *The Patriot*, over 117,000 people have rated the film, using the website's one-to-ten star ratings system.[57] The discussion forum for the film remains active 12 years after its release, still receiving several messages every day on dozens of different discussion threads. The reviews section is also extensive, with over 1,100 user reviews of the film submitted between June 2000 and June 2012.[58] The reviewers are identified by a name or an email address, but it is often impossible to determine their gender, age or other characteristics from this; this, of course, limits the usefulness of the reviews for reception studies. Importantly, though, unlike other film websites the IMDb requires its reviewers to indicate where they live, and so it is possible to identify responses from Britain. We can also observe that the majority write in the informal, hasty style common to internet user forums and discussion boards, and many make allusions to other contemporary films when discussing *The Patriot*. This suggests that the reviewers are film fans, writing as a matter of routine, rather than people who have visited the site simply to log a protest against a single film.[59] In total, there are 74 reviews of *The Patriot* written by contributors living in Britain. These range in length from a few sentences to several paragraphs and, although they were written over a 12-year period, and from reviewers who saw the film in the cinema, on VHS, DVD, or broadcast television, the views of the film are strikingly consistent over time. British reviewers are much less enthusiastic about the film than the IMDb's wider, international contributors. The average British rating for *The Patriot* is just 4.4 stars; far lower than the average rating of 6.9 stars that the international users grant the film. The British average, however, belies strong opinions both for and against the film.

Only 27 of the 74 British reviewers awarded the film a generally positive rating of six, seven, eight, nine or ten stars. In these reviews, and especially in the eight reviews that awarded the film the strongest, ten-star rating, the film's historical inaccuracy was acknowledged, but the issue was dismissed as irrelevant. 'If I wanted a history lesson about the War of Independence I would watch the History Channel,' one observed, while others commented 'who cares if it is inaccurate', 'it's a movie not a history lesson' and 'it's not a documentary'.[60] These reviewers were much more interested in Gibson's performance and the emotional impact of the film; two qualities that went hand in hand. Gibson was described as 'charismatic and captivating', and his admirers were particularly impressed that an action hero could also convey 'emotional distress'.[61] He was proclaimed 'one of the few modern day movie actors capable of [expressing] believable grief' and, unusually for an action film, viewers were left 'crying their eyes out' and 'on the verge of tears all the way through the film'.[62] In keeping with this, there was some praise, too, for Jason Isaacs' performance as Colonel Tavington. These reviewers admired the actor especially for his excessive villainy; they found him 'deliciously vile', 'a baddie that you really hate' and 'brilliant' because 'I wanted to kill him from the start'.[63] The computer generated special effects and violent spectacle were also praised. A sequence in which a cannonball is fired and then seen in slow motion, racing through the air and taking a soldier's head off, was a highlight for several reviewers. One referred to this as 'one of the best special affects [sic] i [sic] have ever seen', while others praised not only this specific sequence but the battle scenes more generally.[64] Thus, the positive reviewers appreciated the film on very similar terms to those employed by the film critics, as an action film and as an enthralling experience, and to varying degrees they considered its entertainment value more important than the issue of historical accuracy.

Of the 74 British reviews, 21 awarded the lowest ranking of one star and a further 26 gave ratings of two, three, four or five stars. Overwhelmingly, these negative reviews cited historical inaccuracy and bias as their main objections to the film. Many listed the film's inaccuracies, pointing out that Britain ended slavery decades before the United States did, that Francis Marion was actually a slave owner and that Banastre Tarleton was not as despicable as Colonel Tavington.[65] The vast majority highlighted the church burning scene as evidence that the film purposefully misrepresents the British. In reviews written at the time of the film's release and for years afterward, IMDb reviewers expressed varying degrees of dismay, resentment and outrage that a wartime atrocity should be transposed from the Germans in the Second World War to the British in the War of Independence. That so many reviewers were able to discuss the film's representation of history may lend some credence to Mel Gibson's defence of The Patriot, and of films taking liberties with historical accuracy more generally. 'It's a good thing that historians are going to harangue this and say, "it's not accurate",' Gibson commented about The Patriot in 2000, adding, 'Good. It'll make somebody pick up a book.'[66] However, the film's representation of history had another effect on many reviewers. They were highly attuned to the representation of nation and culture in this film (some noted, for example, that the British soldiers are entirely English and that no Scottish or Welsh accents are heard) and they were aggrieved by what they considered to be an anti-English bias. Some attributed this bias to Mel Gibson and referred to Braveheart as earlier evidence of this, but others saw the film as representative of a peculiarly American outlook. The Patriot, for these reviewers, was not just anti-English, but also a 'flag-waving' and 'nationalistic' film on behalf of the United States, and this kind of 'propaganda' raised acute resentments among British reviewers:[67]

As an Englishman, I find myself deeply insulted ... Are American audiences so gullible and shallow that they actually believe this?[68]

Let's see Europe release a film depicting Americans as stupid, savage, brutal, dishonorable and evil and then see how it is received in the US???[69]

Once again we are subjected to yet another piece of rewritten history, especially in order to make American history more noble at the expense of other nations.[70]

What concerns me is that all of these inncuracies [sic] in many films are ALL pointed against the British. They form a steady drip, drip of anti-Britishness which can hardly be warranted.[71]

The only purpose of this movie seemed to be to make insecure Americans feel good about themselves.[72]

The film was selfishly made for an American audience.[73]

The film was offensive from start to finnish [sic], Mel Gibson is to me the worst thing that ever came from Hollywood, i [sic] would love to see his films banned in England.[74]

The patriotism in this film is sickening. Gibson clearly hates the English for some reason, but with films like this he is only making America look stupid.[75]

Over here are [sic] buffoonish politicians always remind us of the 'special relationship' we are supposed to have with America and how we've been allies since W.W.II, etc. Well gee, honey, with allies like these who needs enemies?!?[76]

This last, ironic comment offered a rare glimpse of humour. Most of the reviewers, as the other examples indicate, wrote in a quarrelsome tone. Throughout all of these comments, and many more like them, the film is regarded not simply as inaccurate but also as offensively nationalistic. The comments plainly indicate an underlying resentment and condescension towards the USA, but there is also an underlying assumption that Hollywood films should have an international rather than a strictly national outlook. Thus, this film is criticized for being 'at the expense of other nations' and 'selfish', and Americans are labelled as 'gullible and shallow', 'insecure' and 'stupid' for finding its narrow nationalism appealing.

Some of the political columnists who condemned *The Patriot* before its release may have been surprised to find that many film fans concurred with their view of the film. When Andrew Roberts raised the alarm about the film prior to its release, he justified his concerns with remarks that suggested audiences are unable to resist Hollywood films:

> As educational standards decline, British schoolchildren learn a greater and greater proportion of history from movies. Yet most of the ones Hollywood currently produces seriously misrepresent the motivations and achievements of our forefathers.[77]

Similarly, in their *Sunday Times* article, John Harlow and Nicholas Hellen wrote that:

> There is a growing concern that in a 'post-literate' society, where children get more information from films and television than from books, the routine distortion of history in Hollywood films is becoming pernicious. Films are no longer mere entertainments: they are a prime and often sole source of information for many young minds.[78]

These arguments place *The Patriot* and other recent Hollywood historical films within a wider narrative of national decline, in which educational standards are falling, literacy is a thing of the past and influence over the nation's children has been lost to a foreign entertainment industry. Yet the reviews on the IMDb indicate that the popular film culture of the internet era is hardly 'post-literate'. True, many of its participants may not heed every rule of grammar, syntax and spelling when expressing their views. Nevertheless, they read and write avidly on websites such as the IMDb. It is clear, too, that many question what they see in films and bring wider knowledge to bear on the way history is represented on screen. And while the internet serves as a medium for marketing films, it also offers audiences access to alternative viewpoints on heavily marketed, high-profile releases. Thus, the commentators were wrong to herald a new age of ignorance, but their observations continued the long tradition of elitist concerns over impressionable audiences and insidious films.

The end of the special relationship?

Given the many objections to *The Patriot*, it is not surprising that it fared poorly at the UK box office. Its earnings reached $6 million, a dismal sum for a high-profile film, and *Variety* attributed this failure to 'much chatter over its historical accuracy and the way it portrays the Brits'.[79] Interestingly, the biggest box office hit in Britain during the summer of 2000 turned out to be the animated *Chicken Run* (2000), which earned $48 million in the UK alone.[80] *Chicken Run* is an affectionate parody of a much-loved, often-revived post-war war film, *The Great Escape*. Its story of American and British prisoners escaping from a Nazi prison camp offers a definitive example of the way popular memory of the war was centred on the triumph of British pluck and ingenuity over German tyranny and malevolence. As a descendant of *The Great Escape*, *Chicken Run* was appreciated all the more for having been made by the British animation company Aardman Entertainment. Audiences offended by *The Patriot* also may have appreciated the casting of Mel Gibson in *Chicken Run* as the voice of 'Rocky the Rooster', a boastful and vainglorious American flyer who turns out to be utterly incompetent.

Of course, the producers of *The Patriot* were not relying on strong British box office results. Success in the United States was more important, and there the film was released over the Fourth of July holiday weekend to maximize its topicality. An American box office gross of $113 million marks it as a successful film, but it was controversial in the USA, too, and in ways that apparently diminished rather than heightened its appeal.[81] Even over the Fourth of July holiday, *The Patriot* fell into second place in the box office rankings, behind *The Perfect Storm* (2000).[82] Interestingly, though, the film made its best box office showings beyond the UK and the USA. During its opening week, it was number one in the box office rankings in Austria, Brazil, Denmark, Germany, Italy, Spain and Sweden, and 'strong results' were also reported in Belgium, France, Holland, Lebanon, Russia, Slovenia and Turkey.[83] In these non-English-speaking countries, *The Patriot* could be accepted much more readily as a Mel Gibson action film, and on this level it found favour. An exception was Australia, where it was the number one film for three weeks, but this was attributed to national pride in stars Mel Gibson and Heath Ledger.[84] Altogether, the tally of foreign earnings reached $102 million, and this provides a clear demonstration of why the cinematic 'special relationship' had waned.[85] Britain remained a potentially lucrative exhibition market, as the earnings of *Chicken*

Run indicate, but there are now many more markets.[86] It was only in the 1990s, after the Cold War had ended, that Hollywood attained a truly global outlook, and it was perhaps inevitable that some films would reflect the industry's changing orientation.

Did this signal the end of the cinematic 'special relationship'? As far as British audiences were concerned, *The Patriot* was almost unique in its capacity to cause offence. The Second World War, as the historian Mark Connelly has explained, remained a 'vital prop' in the nation's sense of identity as the twentieth century came to a close. It separated Britain from a defeated Europe and allowed it to stand proudly alongside the United States as a victor nation.[87] The historian Richard Weight has emphasized the war's importance to English national identity in particular.[88] The film's depiction of English officers committing atrocities associated with Nazi Germany thus struck at the very heart of English national identity. That this blow to national pride should take place in a film centred on the War of Independence only added to the sense of insult. For much of its history, Hollywood had celebrated and promoted British culture, but *The Patriot* signalled what seemed to be the end of the cinematic 'special relationship', and this in itself was taken as a symptom of national decline and the ever-increasing imbalance in the Anglo-American relationship. In the years after the film's release, perceptions of this imbalance were magnified. The Iraq War (2003–11) brought another alliance between the two countries, but the idea that Britain was the weaker, subservient partner in the alliance was pervasive, as indicated by frequent public assertions that Prime Minister Tony Blair was the 'poodle' of President George W. Bush.[89] Public opinion toward the USA declined sharply during the early years of the war.[90] In this context, it is not surprising that IMDb reviews of *The Patriot* continued to sound notes of alienation and resentment for many years after the film was released. Attitudes toward American patriotism and self-aggrandizement had only hardened in that time.

Nevertheless, in their heated response to *The Patriot*, British journalists, critics and some audiences seem to have forgotten that British actors relish playing arch villains, and it is a sign of the esteem with which they are regarded in Hollywood that they are so often cast in these parts. They seem to have forgotten, too, that Hollywood still has some attractive and sympathetic British stars;

that the annual Academy Awards often highlight the American reverence for British actors and films; and that, as far as action films are concerned, James Bond remains a hero closely identified not just with Britain but with England. Furthermore, one need only look to the year after *The Patriot*, and to the release of *Harry Potter and the Philosopher's Stone* and *Lord of the Rings: The Fellowship of the Rings* in 2001, to find evidence that the cinematic 'special relationship' had not died. In some respects, these films hark back to the heyday of Hollywood's 'British' films: they are based on well known British novels and, as in the studio era, they feature the work of a plethora of British stars and character actors. Their success and popularity quickly put an end to the hand-wringing over Hollywood's Anglophobia and it established that, while Britain may no longer be the most lucrative foreign market in the world, its cultural importance remains unrivalled.

The Patriot, in this context, appears to be an anomaly. It represents a fleeting moment: when Hollywood lost Britain. But for the larger purposes of this book it serves as a useful case study in several respects. As a reception study, it demonstrates the need to engage with the widest array of evidence available. The determination of most film critics to emphasize aesthetic and entertainment values over historical accuracy was representative of some but not all audience views. While journalists and political commentators put forth views closer to the majority of audience responses expressed on the internet, the terms in which they framed their argument indicate that this was probably an unusual coincidence, stemming from the nature of the film under consideration. The internet, meanwhile, offers a multitude of audience responses, but a means must be found of isolating responses relevant to the priorities of the research. For this study being able to locate British responses was crucial, even if the age, gender and region of respondents could not be identified. Nevertheless, issues of authenticity and identity will always be a concern when using the internet as a source for reception studies and the responses will always have to weighed alongside a range of other forms of evidence. In this case, the box office figures lend credence to the finding that audiences were – largely but not entirely – hostile to the film, while the responses themselves help us to understand the terms on which the film was found acceptable or objectionable.

The reception of *The Patriot* also demonstrates the persistence of the concept of feature films as powerfully persuasive and of audiences as uncritical sponges, who simply absorb what they see on screen. The most anxious commentators expressed views in line with the age-old argument that film is an insidious means of propaganda, and one that has the potential to overwhelm audiences and strip them of their national identity. Yet Hollywood films were always less powerful and more diverse than British critics have supposed. It is not America that audiences have sought in the cinema, or indeed any specific nationality. Rather, Hollywood's appeal has rested in its international qualities, in its ability to transport audiences beyond the confines of nationality, beyond the constraints of everyday life, and into realms at least one step removed from everyday life (and often far, far removed). This should be regarded as an aesthetic choice, and one actively made by British audiences, rather than as a sign of the seductive appeal of the United States. Undoubtedly, British audiences have become overwhelmingly familiar with the USA through watching Hollywood films. Some have felt varying degrees of envy and admiration in response to the idealized representation of American life seen in so many Hollywood films, while many have adopted aspects of American culture (in the form of customs, language, fashions, etc.) that they found appealing. But it is important to acknowledge, too, that audiences have been alienated by aspects of American culture that they found unappealing or irrelevant. They have delighted in mocking mores, manners and expressions that they found odd and unappealing, and films that strike a note of strident patriotism have given rise to indignation not too far removed from that expressed by Sydney Smith in 1820. *The Patriot* is an extreme example of Hollywood's ability to inspire anti-American feeling, but its reception serves as a reminder that the Hollywood films that have been most successful with British audiences are those that are not peculiarly or narrowly national in tone and flavour. It shows, too, that the audiences are more than capable of accepting such a film as entertainment, or rejecting it and expounding on its flaws. If these were the descendants of G.A. Atkinson's 'temporary American citizens', many were remarkably unpatriotic towards their adopted country, and they certainly did not 'talk America, think America and dream America' in quite the way that Hollywood's critics had feared for so long.

Notes

Introduction

1. See, for example, Genevieve Abravanel, *Americanizing Britain: The Rise of Modernism in the Age of the Entertainment Empire* (Oxford: Oxford University, 2012); Margaret Dickinson and Sarah Street, *Cinema and State: The Film Industry and the British Government* (London: British Film Institute, 1985); Ian Jarvie, *Hollywood's Overseas Campaign: The North Atlantic Movie Trade, 1920–50* (Cambridge: Cambridge University Press, 1992); Tom Ryall, *Britain and the American Cinema* (London: Sage, 2001); Paul Swann, *The Hollywood Feature Film in Postwar Britain* (London: Croom Helm, 1987); John Trumpbour, *Selling Hollywood to the World: US and European Struggles for Mastery of the Global Film Industry* (Cambridge: Cambridge University Press, 2002); and Duncan Webster, *Looka Yonder: The Imaginary America of Populist Culture* (London: Routledge, 1988).

2. Sean Perkins relates that in 1946, the peak year of cinema-going in Britain, 1.6 billion cinema tickets were sold, which represents an average of 36 tickets per person in that year. In 2010, feature films were watched on 4.6 billion occasions, which represents an average of 81 films watched per person in that year. The comparison should be regarded as a rough one, though, especially as cinema-goers often saw more than one feature film in a single visit to the cinema in the 1940s. See Sean Perkins, 'Film in the UK, 2001–10: A Statistical Overview', *Journal of British Cinema and Television* 9/3 (2012), pp. 310–12.

3. Geoffrey Nowell-Smith, 'But Do We Need It?', in Martyn Auty and Nick Roddick (eds), *British Cinema Now* (London: British Film Institute, 1985), pp. 151–52.

4. Ryan Gilbey (ed.), *The Ultimate Film: The UK's 100 Most Popular Films* (London: British Film Institute, 2005).

5. See especially Melvyn Stokes and Richard Maltby (eds), *Hollywood Abroad: Audiences and Cultural Exchange* (London: British Film Institute, 2004); and Sarah Street, *Transatlantic Crossings: British Feature Films in the USA* (London: Continuum, 2002).

6. Andrew Higson, 'The Concept of National Cinema', *Screen* 30/4 (1989), p. 37.

7. Victoria de Grazia, 'Mass Culture and Sovereignty: The American Challenge to European Cinemas, 1920–60', *Journal of Modern History* 61/1 (1989), p. 53.

8. For a wider examination of ideas of national decline, and one that traces the concept back to the nineteenth century, see the essay entitled 'Statecraft: The Haunting Fear of National Decline', in David Cannadine, *In Churchill's Shadow: Confronting the Past in Modern Britain* (London: Allen Lane, 2002), pp. 26–44.

9. Helen Taylor, *Scarlett's Women:* Gone with the Wind *and its Female Fans* (London: Virago, 1987); and Jackie Stacey, *Star Gazing: Hollywood Cinema an Female Spectatorship* (London: Routledge, 1994).

10. Annette Kuhn, *An Everyday Magic: Cinema and Cultural Memory* (London: I.B.Tauris, 2002).

11. Another book that might be considered here is Thomas Austin's *Hollywood, Hype and Audiences: Selling and Watching Popular Films in the 1990s* (Manchester: Manchester University Press, 2002). Like Taylor and Stacey, Austin also used questionnaires to seek British audience responses to popular Hollywood films, albeit of a much more recent vintage. But while Austin's research highlights important aspects of reception study (notably the impact of marketing and publicity on audience responses), he is largely unconcerned by the transnational dimensions of his study.

12. Janet Staiger, *Interpreting Films: Studies in Historical Reception of American Cinema* (Princeton, NJ: Princeton University Press, 1992).

13. This argument is made most forcefully in Janet Staiger, '"The Handmaiden of Villainy": Methods and Problems in Studying the Historical Reception of a Film', *Wide Angle* 8/1 (1986), p. 21. It is also made, with less specific reference to audience research, in Staiger's *Interpreting Films*, pp. 79–80.

14. See, for example, Richard Weight, *Patriots: National Identity in Britain, 1940–2000* (London: Macmillan, 2002), p. 88.

15. Staiger: *Interpreting Films*, p. 93; and Barbara Klinger, 'Film History Terminable and Interminable: Recovering the Past in Reception Studies', *Screen* 38/2 (1997), pp. 107–28.

16. Klinger: 'Film History Terminable and Interminable', p. 111.

17. Richard Maltby, 'Introduction: The Americanisation of the World', in Melvyn Stokes and Richard Maltby (eds), *Hollywood Abroad: Audiences and Cultural Exchange* (London: British Film Institute, 1994), pp. 2–3.

18. Michael Hammond, *The Big Show: British Cinema Culture in the Great War, 1914–1918* (Exeter: Exeter University Press, 2006), p. 4.

19. Harper's studies concern the Regent Cinema, Portsmouth, in the 1930s and 1940s; see 'A Lower Middle-Class Taste Community in the 1930s: Admissions Figures at the Regent Cinema, Portsmouth, UK', *Historical Journal of Film, Radio and Television* 24/4 (2004), pp. 565–87; and 'Fragmentation and Crisis: 1940s Admissions Figures at the Regent Cinema, Portsmouth, UK', *Historical Journal of Film, Radio and Television*

26/3 (2006), pp. 361–94. Poole's study concerns the Majestic Cinema, Macclesfield; see Julian Poole, 'British Cinema Attendance in Wartime: Audience Preference at the Majestic, Macclesfield, 1939–1946', *Historical Journal of Film, Radio and Television* 7/1 (1987), pp. 15–34. Sedgwick's study is a wider study of the 1930s; see John Sedgwick, *Popular Filmgoing in 1930s Britain: A Choice of Pleasures* (Exeter: University of Exeter, 2000).

Chapter 1 Temporary American Citizens

1. Sydney Smith, *The Edinburgh Review* 33 (January 1820), pp. 69–80.
2. W.T. Stead, *The Americanisation of the World, or The Trend of the Twentieth Century* (London: The Review of Reviews, 1902).
3. G.A. Atkinson, '"British" Films Made to Please America', *Daily Express*, 18 March 1927, p. 6.
4. Smith: *The Edinburgh Review* 33, p. 78.
5. Stead: *The Americanisation of the World*, p. 135.
6. See the discussion in Robert E. Spiller, 'The Verdict of Sydney Smith', *American Literature* 1/1 (March 1929), p. 6.
7. For further discussion of Atkinson's view, and the use of this phrase by historians, see Mark Glancy, 'Temporary American Citizens? British Audiences, Hollywood Films and the Threat of Americanization in the 1920s', *Historical Journal of Film, Radio and Television* 26/4 (2006), pp. 461–84.
8. *Variety* considered Atkinson the world's most powerful film critic because he had the dual role of commenting on films for both the BBC (in a regular Friday evening broadcast) and the *Express* newspapers. He was profiled in a response to his views that 'American films menace decent British homes'. See *Variety*, 1 July 1925, pp. 1 and 3.
9. James R. Barrett, 'Americanization From the Bottom Up: Immigration and the Re-Making of the Working Class in the United States, 1880–1930', *The Journal of American History* 79/3 (December 1992), p. 997.
10. Rob Kroes, 'Americanization: What Are We Talking About?', in R. Kroes, R.W. Rydell and D.F.J. Bosscher (eds), *Cultural Transmissions and Receptions: American Mass Culture in Europe* (Amsterdam: VU University Press, 1993), p. 303.
11. *Times*, 28 September 1849, p. 4.
12. Kathleen Burk, *Old World, New World: The Story of Britain and America* (London: Little, Brown, 2007), pp. 414–15.
13. *Times*, 21 August 1868, p. 6.
14. The earliest anxiety registered regarding Australia was that, once the telegraph had reached California, American newspapers could reach Australia much more quickly via a Pacific Ocean crossing than British newspapers could be brought via the Indian Ocean (*Times*, 14 May 1862, p. 6). Concerns about Canada were registered as early as 1869 (*Times*, 22 March 1869, p. 8) and later included one of the first reports on Americanization through the cinema (*Times*, 30 October 1911, p. 6).

15. F.A. Mackenzie, *The American Invaders* (London: Grant Richards, 1902), p. 1.

16. Mackenzie: *The American Invaders*, p. 47.

17. Stead: *The Americanisation of the World*, p. 138.

18. *Times*, 23 June 1920, p. 13.

19. *Express*, 11 September 1921, p. 1.

20. *Express*, 11 September 1921, p. 6.

21. Ian Jarvie, *Hollywood's Overseas Campaign, The North Atlantic Movie Trade, 1920–50* (Cambridge: Cambridge University Press, 1992), p. 107.

22. See the discussion in Nicholas Reeves, *The Power of Film Propaganda: Myth or Reality?* (London: Continuum, 1999).

23. Griffith's comments can be found in 'Looking Forward to a World Americanized' in *Kinematograph Weekly*, 3 January 1924, p. 105. Hays' comments are considered in E.J. MacDonald, 'Los Angelising Europe', *Kinematograph Weekly*, 4 September 1924, p. 49. They are also discussed in Richard Maltby: 'The Americanization of the World', in Melryn Stokes and Richard Maltby (eds) *Hollywood Abroad Audiences & Cultural Exchange* (London: British Film Institute 1994), p. 1.

24. Ruth Vasey, *The World According to Hollywood, 1918–1939* (Madison: University of Wisconsin Press, 1997), p. 42.

25. Jarvie: *Hollywood's Overseas Campaign*, p. 108; and T.J. Hollins, 'The Conservative Party and Film Propaganda Between the Wars', *The English Historical Review* 96/379 (1981), p. 359.

26. Jarvie: *Hollywood's Overseas Campaign*, p. 109.

27. *Times*, 22 March 1927, p. 15.

28. The Prince of Wales endorsed the notion that 'trade follows the film' when he gave his backing to the British National Film League at its inaugural event in November 1923; *Times*, 15 November 1923, p. 10. The Liberal MP Geoffrey Le Mander cited the trade 'corollary' in a House of Commons debate on film; *Kinematograph Weekly*, 24 July 1930, p. 29. Documentary filmmaker John Grierson also cited the corollary in an editorial; John Grierson, 'One Foot of Film Equals One Dollar of Trade', *Kinematograph Weekly*, 8 January 1931, p. 87.

29. *Parliamentary Debates (Lords)*, 14 May 1925, volume 61, column 275. Also discussed in Jarvie: *Hollywood's Overseas Campaign*, p. 111.

30. *The Bioscope*, 22 November 1923, p. 41.

31. Duncan Webster, *Looka Yonder! The Imaginary America of Popular Culture* (London: Routledge, 1988), p. 24.

32. See the discussion of the Leavises in D.L. LeMahieu, *A Culture For Democracy: Mass Communication and the Cultivated Mind in Britain Between the Wars* (Oxford: Clarendon, 1988), pp. 294–304; Webster: *Looka Yonder!*, pp. 179–83; and John Docker, *Postmodernism and Popular Culture: A Cultural History* (Cambridge: Cambridge University Press, 1994), pp. 15–35.

33. F.R. Leavis, *Mass Civilisation and Minority Culture* (Cambridge: Minority, 1930), pp. 9–18.

34. Richard Hoggart, *The Uses of Literacy* (London: Penguin, 1965 [1957]), pp. 190–1.
35. Hoggart: *The Uses of Literacy*, p. 188.
36. Hoggart: *The Uses of Literacy*, p. 324.
37. Hoggart: *The Uses of Literacy*, p. 248.
38. Webster: *Look Yonder!*, p. 187.
39. George Orwell, 'The Decline of the English Murder', in *Essays* (London: Penguin, 2000), pp. 345–7.
40. John Storey (ed.), *Cultural Theory and Popular Culture: An Introduction*, 4th edn (Harlow: Pearson, 2006), p. 9.
41. Jessica C.E. Gienow-Hecht, 'Shame on US? Academics, Cultural Transfer, and the Cold War – A Critical Review', *Diplomatic History* 24/3 (2000), pp. 465–94.
42. Richard Pells, *Not Like Us: How Europeans Have Loved Hated and Transformed American Culture Since World War Two* (New York: Basic Books, 1997), pp. 280–1.
43. Annette Kuhn, *An Everyday Magic: Cinema & Culture Memory* (London: I.B.Tauris, 2002), p. 100.
44. Rachael Low, 'The Implications Behind the Social Survey', in *The Penguin Film Review* 7 (London: Penguin, 1948), pp. 107–12.
45. A.J.P. Taylor, *English History, 1914–1945* (Oxford: Oxford University Press, 1992 [1965]), p. 313.
46. Christine Geraghty, *British Cinema in the Fifties: Gender, Genre and the 'New Look'* (London: Routledge, 2000), pp. 5–6.
47. Maltby: 'Introduction: The Americanization of the World', p. 2.
48. Richard Collins, 'National Culture: A Contradiction in Terms?', *Canadian Journal of Communication* 16/2 (1991), p. 5.
49. Collins: 'National Culture'.
50. Neal Gabler, *An Empire of their Own: How the Jews Invented Hollywood* (New York: Knopf, 1989), pp. 5–6.
51. Victoria de Grazia, *Irresistible Empire: America's Advance Through Twentieth Century Europe* (Cambridge, MA: Harvard University Press, 2005), pp. 304–5.
52. See, for example, the comments in David L. Goodrich, *The Real Nick and Nora* (Carbondale: Southern Illinois University Press, 2001), p. 54; and Gregory Paul Williams, *The Story of Hollywood: An Illustrated History* (Los Angeles: B.L. Press, 2008), pp. 124 and 129.
53. Lord Newton is quoted in Jarvie: *Hollywood's Overseas Campaign*, p. 111.
54. The description and identity of each venue is taken from the analysis of the survey offered by Jeffrey Richards and Dorothy Sheridan (eds), *Mass Observation at the Movies* (London: Routledge, 1987), pp. 32–3.
55. Richards and Sheridan: *Mass Observation at the Movies*, pp. 32–136. Richards and Sheridan offer an authoritative overview of the survey and also reprint the replies in full.
56. Richards and Sheridan: *Mass Observation at the Movies*, pp. 32–136. The specific comments, in the order they appear in the text, are no. 71, p. 51;

no. 75, p. 52; no. 6, p. 59; no. 86, p. 119; no. 23, p. 43; no. 47, p. 84; no. 103, page 122.

57. Richards and Sheridan: *Mass Observation at the Movies*, pp. 32–136, no. 30, p. 44; no. 73, p. 52; no. 15, p. 61.

58. Richards and Sheridan: *Mass Observation at the Movies*, pp. 32–136, no. 45, p. 47.

59. Richards and Sheridan: *Mass Observation at the Movies*, pp. 32–136, no. 112, p. 97; no. 14, page 108; no. 109, page 97.

60. Richards and Sheridan: *Mass Observation at the Movies*, pp. 32–136, no. 114, p. 98; no. 26, p. 74; no. 65, p. 88; no. 113, p. 97; no. 29, p. 75.

61. Richards and Sheridan: *Mass Observation at the Movies*, pp. 32–136, no. 24, p. 110.

62. Richards and Sheridan: *Mass Observation at the Movies*, pp. 32–136, no. 47.

63. Richards and Sheridan: *Mass Observation at the Movies*, pp. 32–136, no. 74, p. 89; no. 158, p. 104; no. 85, p. 119.

64. Richards and Sheridan: *Mass Observation at the Movies*, pp. 32–136, no. 76, p. 90; no. 101, p. 95; no. 143, pp. 100–1.

65. Richards and Sheridan: *Mass Observation at the Movies*, pp. 32–136, no. 17, p. 79; no. 119, p. 98.

66. Richards and Sheridan compiled the list of favourite films and discuss them. Richards and Sheridan: *Mass Observation at the Movies*, pp. 32–136, pp. 39–40.

67. File Report 1095, 'Report on Opinion on America', 16 March 1942, Mass Observation Archive, University of Sussex, UK.

68. The report indicates that 53 per cent of people said that they got their ideas about the USA from newspapers and magazines, 32 per cent cited the radio and 30 per cent cited 'personal experience' (e.g., knowing an American, having visited the USA or knowing someone who had visited the USA). Only 16 per cent cited the cinema as a source of ideas. 'Report on Opinion on America', 16 March 1942, p. 16.

69. 'Favourable' opinion towards the USA remained at 60 per cent in the study's most recent survey, conducted in February 1942, while 'unfavourable' opinion stood at 24 per cent. 'Report on Opinion on America', 16 March 1942, pp. 3 and 10.

70. 'Report on Opinion on America', 16 March 1942, p. 16. The report states that Mass Observation's view of the limited influence of cinema has grown directly from its studies of audience responses to wartime films. These studies are reprinted in Richards and Sheridan: *Mass Observation at the Movies*, pp. 299–380.

71. David Reynolds takes a more sceptical view of Mass Observation's argument about the limited influence of the cinema, pointing out that polling methods were in their infancy at this time, that Mass Observation's questions were posed 'to the more articulate' Britons, and that films were likely to propagate visual 'images' subliminally even if they did not convey intellectual 'ideas' directly. His argument, however, does not take into

account wider audience surveys of this era, such as the 'Worktown' study, which demonstrate the public's awareness of the artifice of films. See the discussion in David Reynolds, *Rich Relations: The American Occupation of Britain, 1942–1945* (London: HarperCollins, 1996 [1995]), pp. 36–40.

72. See the discussion of the film's impact in Annette Kuhn, '*Snow White* in 1930s Britain', *Journal of British Cinema and Television* 7/2 (2010), pp. 183–99.

73. Kuhn: '*Snow White*', pp. 189–93.

74. The method and data used to compile this chart are explained (very briefly) by the researchers. Ryan Gilbey, *The Ultimate Film: The UK's 100 Most Popular Films* (London: British Film Institute, 2005), p. 326.

75. Gilbey: *The Ultimate Film*, p. 165.

76. Gilbey: *The Ultimate Film*, pp. 98–9.

Chapter 2   For the Purpose of Pleasing Women

1. Iris Barry, *Let's Go to the Pictures* (London: Chatto and Windus, 1926), p. 59.

2. Marjorie Williams, 'The Woman Patron', *Kinematograph Weekly*, 3 December 1925, p. 47.

3. Dorothy M. Richardson, 'Continuous Performance', *Close Up*, July 1927, pp. 34–7.

4. The general trend in admissions over the decade was upward, and it was hastened in 1924 by the lifting of taxes on seats costing less than sixpence. See Nicholas Hiley, '"Let's Go to the Pictures": The British Cinema Audience in the 1920s and 1930s', *The Journal of Popular British Cinema* 2 (1999), pp. 40–1.

5. Hiley: '"Let's Go to the Pictures"', p. 47.

6. Barry later became the first curator of the film library at New York's Museum of Modern Art in the 1930s. In that capacity, she played an integral role in establishing a canon of revered films. Her views on Hollywood had softened by then, but in *Let's Go to the Pictures*, she complains about the mediocrity of most films by saying, 'I am blaming all of this on the American films and I think with good reason'. Barry: *Let's Go to the Pictures*, p. 61.

7. Lejeune wrote a weekly column for the *Manchester Guardian* from 1922 to 1928. She then moved to the *Observer*, where she wrote weekly film reviews until 1960. Her early views on film are expressed in a book published in 1931. C.A. Lejeune, *Cinema* (London: Alexander Maclehose, 1931), p. 4.

8. Williams: 'The Woman Patron', p. 47.

9. Richardson: 'Continuous Performance', pp. 34–7.

10. A.J.P. Taylor, *English History 1914–1945* (Oxford: Oxford University Press, 1992 [1965]), p. 181.

11. Virginia Woolf, 'The Movies and Reality', *New Republic*, 4 August 1926, pp. 308–10.

12. Richardson's article 'The Film Gone Male' first appeared in the March 1932 issue of *Close Up*. As Anne Friedberg later commented, for the film

to have 'gone male', 'there had to be a film once female'. For her discussion of Richardson's work, and a reprint of 'The Film Gone Male', see *Framework* 20 (1982), pp. 6–8. Richardson and Woolf are also discussed in Miriam Hansen, *Babel and Babylon: Spectatorship in American Silent Film* (Cambridge, MA: Harvard University Press, 1991), p. 327.

13. Cynthia L. White, *Women's Magazines, 1693–1968* (London, Michael Joseph, 1970), pp. 96–9.

14. 'Stay Where You Are', *Picturegoer*, April 1921, p. 7.

15. 'Without the Cane', *Picturegoer*, June 1921, p. 7.

16. 'Why I Go to the Pictures', *Girls' Cinema*, 29 December 1923, p. 10.

17. 'All the World's A Film', *Picturegoer*, May 1921, p. 7.

18. Rachael Low, *The History of the British Film, 1918–1929* (London, George Allen and Unwin, 1971), pp. 47–53.

19. Jeffrey Richards, *The Age of the Dream Palace* (London: Routledge and Kegan Paul, 1984), p. 19.

20. Francois Truffaut with Helen G. Scott, *Hitchcock: The Definitive Study* (London, Paladin, 1986 [1968]), p. 21.

21. White: *Women's Magazines*, p. 113.

22. 'Anything But The Truth', *Picturegoer*, March 1921, p. 7.

23. W.N. Coglan, *The Readership of Newspapers and Periodicals, 1936* (London: Incorporated Society of British Advertisers, 1936), pp. 272–3.

24. Coglan: *The Readership of Newspapers and Periodicals*. The 1936 survey found that only 9 per cent of *Picturegoer* readers were in the survey's lowest income group (annual earnings of less than £125 per year), 62 per cent had earnings in a range of £125 to £249, 24 per cent had earnings between £250 and £499, 4 per cent had earnings of £500 to £999 and 1 per cent had earnings over £1,000. This was at a time when, according to John Stevenson, average salaried earnings were approximately £200 per year, and 'the great majority of the population' earned less than £250. John Stevenson, *British Society: 1914–45* (London: Penguin, 1984), p. 122.

25. Ross McKibbin, *Classes and Cultures: England, 1918–1951* (Oxford: Oxford University Press, 1998), p. 527.

26. The 'schoolboy shape' describes long dresses that have a low waistline, or none at all, and a cut that minimizes curves. Charles Loch Mowat, *Britain Between the Wars, 1918–1940*, (London: Methuen, 1968 [1955]), p. 212.

27. The advertisement for the Chas. E. Dawson Home Study Course, for example, promises that a course in 'commercial art' or 'fashion drawing' will allow entry into a 'profession' and provide a 'big income'. See the ads in the January 1921 (p. 51) and February 1921 (p. 47) issues of *Picturegoer*.

28. *Picturegoer*, April 1923, p. 63.

29. J.B. Priestley, *English Journey* (London: Folio Society, 1997 [1934]), pp. 325–6.

30. Christine Gledhill, *Reframing British Cinema, 1918–28: Between Restraint and Passion* (London: British Film Institute, 2003), p. 79.

31. *Picturegoer*, October 1921, p. 21.

32. *Picturegoer*, December 1921, pp. 8–9.

33. In a typical piece, Gloria Swanson's home is said to be 'as gorgeous as the star herself'. She is said to have designed the 'ornate' mantelpieces, to have dresses that match each room in the house. *Picturegoer*, June 1923, pp. 36–7.

34. The most expensive clothes advertised in *Picturegoer* were usually those seen in advertisements for the department stores Debenham & Freebody and Harvey Nichols, which emphasized high style and low prices.

35. *Picturegoer*, April 1921, p. 57.

36. *Picturegoer*, April 1924, p. 36.

37. *Picturegoer*, August 1921, p. 24.

38. *Picturegoer*, April 1927, p. 18.

39. *Picturegoer*, March 1923, p. 66.

40. *Picturegoer*, May 1925, p. 74.

41. The circulation data from 1936 indicates that *Picture Show* had fewer readers in the middle to upper income groups; 9 per cent of its readers earned less than £125 per year, 74 per cent earned between £125 and £249, 15 per cent earned between £250 and £499, 2 per cent earned between £500 and £999, and less than 1 per cent earned over £1,000. It also had a slightly stronger presence in Wales and the southwest of England than *Picturegoer*. Coglan: *The Readership of Newspapers*, pp. 272–3.

42. *Picture Show*, 23 September 1922, p. 9.

43. Gledhill: *Reframing British Cinema*, p. 40.

44. *Picture Show*, 15 September 1923, p. 1.

45. Jenny Hammerton reveals that the 'doubles' competition coincided with a talent-scouting contest in the *Daily Sketch* newspaper in 1922. Jenny Hammerton, 'Screen Struck: The Lure of Hollywood For British Women in the 1920s', in Alan Burton and Laraine Porter (eds), *Crossing the Pond: Anglo-American Film Relations Before 1930* (Trowbridge: Flicks, 2002), p. 102.

46. White: *Women's Magazines*, p. 96.

47. *Girls' Cinema*, 28 July 1923, p. 14.

48. *Girls' Cinema*, 9 June 1923, p. 8.

49. *Girls' Cinema*, 16 June 1923, p. 8.

50. *Girls' Cinema*, 13 October 1923, pp. 3–4.

51. *Girls' Cinema*, 1 September 1923, p. 14.

52. The judgement on popularity has been made on the basis of the length of the initial playing dates on their first release and how many times the films were revived in the immediate aftermath of Valentino's death. Reports in *Kinematograph Weekly* indicate that the six films cited in the text circulated throughout Britain in the autumn of 1926 and drew large crowds once again.

53. See, for example, the review of *The Sheik* in the *News of the World*, 28 January 1923, p. 12; or the article entitled 'Sheiky Women' in the *Daily Mail*, 3 August 1925, p. 6.

54. See the letter from Margaret P. Johnson of Harborne (Birmingham); *Picture Show*, 21 July 1923, p. 20. Similar praise can be found in the letters pages of *Picturegoer*. See, for example, a letter from Bristol praising his 'good looks, good acting and good *dress*' [my emphasis]. *Picturegoer*, November 1924, p. 66.

55. For an astute comparison of these two stars, see Gavin Lambert, 'Fairbanks and Valentino: The Last Heroes', *Sequence* 8 (Summer 1949), pp. 77–80.

56. Miriam Hansen has pointed out (with specific reference to Valentino's films) that 'whenever a woman initiates the look, she is invariably marked as a vamp'. Nevertheless, the films present him as an object of the gaze and, especially in the case of *Blood and Sand*, as a grateful recipient of the gaze. See Miriam Hansen: *Babel and Babylon*, p. 269.

57. The advertisement can be seen in the *Hull Daily Mail*, 26 February 1923, p. 6.

58. These portraits appeared in *Picture Show*, 14 July 1923, p. 11; and 5 April 1924, pp. 12–13.

59. Williams referred to *The White Sister* (1923) rather than this particular photograph, but her point applies to both. *Kinematograph Weekly*, 3 December 1925, p. 47.

60. See, for example, an article attributed to the British actress June, in which she ponders 'who will be the screen hero of 1924' and decides that no one can take Valentino's place; *Picture Show*, 3 November 1923, p. 17.

61. 'Hercules, London', *Picturegoer*, March 1923, p. 66.

62. 'Rudolph Valentino Fan, Birmingham', *Picturegoer*, February 1923, p. 66.

63. *Picturegoer*, November 1924, p. 66.

64. See Hansen: *Babel and Babylon*; and also Gaylyn Studlar, *This Mad Masquerade: Stardom and Masculinity in the Jazz Age* (New York: Columbia University Press, 1996).

65. Emily W. Leider, *Dark Lover: The Life and Death of Rudolph Valentino* (London: Faber, 2004), pp. 122–4.

66. For example, see the interview in *Picturegoer*, September 1923, pp. 39–42; and the obituaries in the *Hull Daily Mail*, 24 August 1926, p. 3; and in the *Bolton Evening News*, 24 August 1926, p. 4.

67. See the discussion in Leider: *Dark Lover*, p. 211; and also in Hansen: *Babel and Babylon*, p. 261.

68. The film's release is recounted in *Films and Filming*, May 1956, p. 15. The 'super film' was a much-discussed phenomenon in the early 1920s. See *Kinematograph Weekly*, 18 January 1923, p. 47.

69. The review originally appeared in the *Tatler* issue dated 19 August 1922 and it is reprinted in James Agate, *Around Cinemas: First Series* (London: Home and Van Thal, 1946), pp. 17–19.

70. *Picturegoer*, February 1923, p. 66.

71. *Picturegoer*, February 1923, p. 66. See also the letters published in *Picturegoer*, June 1923, p. 66; December 1925, p. 98; and July 1926, p. 66.

72. *Girls' Cinema*, 24 March 1923, pp. 8–9.

73. Gledhill: *Reframing British Cinema*, pp. 62–3.

74. *Times*, 20 November 1922, p. 18.

75. Gledhill: *Reframing British Cinema*, p. 67.

76. Leider: *Dark Lover*, p. 305.

77. *Picturegoer*, April 1925, p. 18.

78. See, for example, the letters published in *Picturegoer*, December 1924, p. 102; and February 1925, p. 82.

79. *Scotsman*, 25 August 1924, p. 8; *Daily Mirror*, 4 September 1924, p. 2.

80. Even the trade paper *Kinematograph Weekly* (26 January 1922, p. 46) felt obliged to inform its readers that *The Sheik* was 'frankly an insult to the intelligent public'.

81. *Bioscope*, 18 January 1923, p. 45.

82. *Times*, 2 December 1924, p. 17; and *Daily Mirror*, 28 November 1925, p. 9.

83. Leider: *Dark Lover*, p. 353.

84. Hansen: *Babel and Babylon*, p. 264.

85. *News of the World*, 12 August 1923, p. 12.

86. See, for example, the coverage in *Picture Show*, 6 October 1923, pp. 3–4; and in *Picturegoer,* September 1923, p. 7.

87. *Sunday Express*, 5 August 1923, p. 4.

88. *London Evening News*, 24 November 1925, p. 1.

89. The journalist Marjorie Williams discussed events at the Marble Arch Pavilion with nothing but disdain for fans who were 'hysterically minded' and let their 'feelings to run riot and obscure their judgement'. *Kinematograph Weekly*, 3 December 1925, p. 47.

90. *Daily Express*, 3 August 1923, p. 9.

91. See, for example, the stories in the *Daily Mail*, the *London Evening Standard* and the *Daily Telegraph* on the 25, 26 and 27 August 1926.

92. See, for example, the stories in the *Daily Mail*, the *London Evening Standard* and the *Daily Telegraph* on the 25, 26 and 27 August 1926.

93. A Pathé Newsreel story on Valentino's death includes some scenes filmed outside the funeral home. The newsreel is included as an 'extra' on the [region 1] DVD of *The Sheik* and *The Son of the Sheik* released by Image Entertainment in 2002. Much more footage can be seen on the Getty Images website. Online. Available at <http://www.gettyimages.co.uk/detail/video/news-footage/2011-446> (accessed 3 January 2010).

94. *Bolton Evening News*, 24 August 1926, p. 4.

95. *News of the World*, 29 August 1926, p. 11.

96. This article, originally printed in the *Yorkshire Evening Post*, appeared as a syndicated feature in the *Hull Daily Mail*, 24 August 1926, p. 5.

97. Douglas was the editor of the *Sunday Express*. *Daily Express*, 25 August 1926, p. 8.

98. Unusually, *Kinematograph Weekly* ran box office reports during the summer and autumn of 1926, and Valentino's films feature prominently in these after his death. See, for example, 'What the Box Office Says', 7 October 1926, p. 58.

99. See the microfiche file on Rudolph Valentino in the British Film Institute Library, which has a large number of posthumous articles, including coverage of the two memorial associations.
100. *Picturegoer*, 2 July 1949, p. 17.
101. Kenneth Anger, *Hollywood Babylon* (New York: Dell, 1991), pp. 166–70.

Chapter 3   Two Countries Divided by a Common Language

1. Oscar Wilde, 'The Canterville Ghost', collected in *Lord Arthur Savile's Crime and Other Stories* (London: Penguin, 1995 [1891]), p. 33.
2. *Daily Mirror*, 5 October 1928, p. 13.
3. Elizabeth Knowles (ed.), *The Oxford Dictionary of Quotations* (Oxford: Oxford University Press, 1999), p. 521.
4. Of course, film historians have offered more complex, less linear and less romantic accounts of the transition from silent to talking films. See, for example, Donald Crafton, *The Talkies: America's Transition to Sound, 1926–1931* (Berkeley: University of California, 1997); and Douglas Gomery, *The Coming of Sound* (New York: Routledge, 2005).
5. David Reynolds, *Rich Relations: The American Occupation of British, 1942–1945* (London: HarperCollins, 1996 [1995]), pp. 4–5.
6. A writer for the *Times*, commenting on 'sound pictures', noted this with the observation that 'the wave of ebullient enthusiasm which swept America has not found its counterpart in this country'. *Times*, 19 March 1929, p. 7.
7. Joel Finler, *The Hollywood Story* (London: Octopus, 1988), p. 288.
8. See Robert Murphy, 'The Coming of Sound to the Cinema in Britain', *Historical Journal of Film, Radio and Television* 4/2 (1984), p. 151.
9. See the figures in Nicholas Hiley, '"Let's Go to the Pictures" The British Cinema Audience in the 1920s and 1930s', *Journal of Popular British Culture* 2 (1992), pp. 41–2.
10. Crafton: *The Talkies*, pp. 516–31; Gomery: *The Coming of Sound*, pp. 55–61. Also see the discussion in Robert C. Allen and Douglas Gomery, *Film History: Theory and Practice* (New York: Knopf, 1985), pp. 195–7.
11. Gomery: *The Coming of Sound*, pp. 56–7.
12. See Crafton: *The Talkies*, ch. 12, which discusses films released in the 1928–9 season.
13. *Variety*, 5 December 1928, p. 6.
14. In Leicester and Nottingham, for example, the first talkies were shown in June 1929. See the discussion in M. Jancovich and L. Faire with S. Stubbings, *The Place of the Audience: Cultural Geographies of Film Consumption* (London: British Film Institute, 2003), pp. 92–4.
15. See the reports on CEA meetings in the following issues of *Kinematograph Weekly*: 27 September 1928, pp. 40–1; 18 October 1928, p. 43; 25 October 1928, p. 37.
16. *Bioscope*, 19 September 1928, p. 40.
17. *Kinematograph Weekly*, 6 December 1928, p. 31.

18. See, for example, the review in *The Times* (28 September 1928, p. 12) and in *The Bioscope* (3 October 1928, p. 22).

19. *Kinematograph Weekly*, 1 November 1928, p. 52.

20. A report on the London premiere can be found in *Variety*, 31 October 1928, p. 3.

21. *New York Times*, 18 November 1928, p. X7; also discussed in Alexander Walker, *The Shattered Silents: How the Talkies Came to Stay* (London: Elm Tree, 1978), pp. 87–9.

22. *Times*, 28 September 1928, p. 12.

23. *Kinematograph Weekly*, 1 November 1928, p. 50; *Bioscope*, 31 October 1928, p. 33.

24. Agate's comments referred to the trailer that was shown for *The Terror* at a screening of *The Jazz Singer*. His column was originally published in the 17 October 1928 issue of the *Tatler*, and it is reprinted in James Agate, *Around Cinemas* (London: Hane and Van Thal, 1946), pp. 29–30.

25. Lejeune's autobiographical essay, 'My Story', is reprinted in a collection of her film criticism, and so too is her review of *The Terror*, which was originally published in the *Observer* on 4 November 1928. See Anthony Lejeune (ed.), *The C.A. Lejeune Film Reader* (Manchester: Carcanet, 1991), pp. 23–38 and 54–5, respectively.

26. *Daily Mirror*, 29 October 1928, p. 27.

27. *Sunday Express*, 2 September 1928, p. 8; 9 September 1928, p. 8; 4 November 1928, p. 4; and 16 December 1928, p. 4

28. *Times*, 30 July 1929, p. 13.

29. These comments were reported in articles entitled 'Notes of London's Screen World' and 'English Survey of Sound' in the *New York Times*, 4 August 1929, p. X5.

30. *Kinematograph Weely*, 14 March 1929, p. 38; and 25 April 1929, p. 20.

31. *Bioscope*, 1 May 1929, p. 20.

32. *Kinematograph Weekly*, 14 February 1929, p. 68.

33. See the small news items in *Kinematograph Weekly*: 28 February 1929, p. 47; 14 March 1929, pp. 48 and 91; 21 March 1929, p. 42; 28 March 1929, p. 62.

34. *Bioscope*, 26 June 1929, p. 4.

35. The *New York Times* observed the 'cleavage' between British critics who 'condemn' the talkies and 'the public [which] flocks to see and hear them'. The films cited are indicated as having 'long lines to gain admission'. See *New York Times*, 17 March 1929, p. X7; and also 7 April 1929, p. X8.

36. Gomery: *The Coming of Sound*, p. 107.

37. Michael Balcon, *Michael Balcon Presents … A Lifetime of Films* (London: Hutchinson, 1969), p. 34.

38. *Kinematograph Weekly*, 4 April 1929, p. 21.

39. The emphasis is in the original. Crafton: *The Talkies*, p. 509.

40. *Picturegoer*, September 1927, pp. 46–8.

41. *Picturegoer*, June 1928, p. 28.

42. For the comparative circulation figures, see W. N. Coglan, *The Readership of Newspapers and Periodicals in Great British 1936* (London: Incorporated Society of British Advertisers, 1936), pp. 272–3.

43. *Picturegoer*, May 1929, pp. 8–9.

44. *Film Weekly*, 15 July 1929, p. 5.

45. *Picturegoer*, May 1929, p. 60; and June 1929, p. 60.

46. Letter from E.S., *Picturegoer*, August 1929, p. 60.

47. See the letters in *Picturegoer*, July 1929, p. 62; and August 1929, p. 62.

48. See, for example, the letters in *Picturegoer* from H.H., Junior (July 1929, p. 62) and M.E. (September 1929, p. 80).

49. Letter from 'Leatherface', *Picturegoer*, July 1929, p. 60.

50. Letter from 'Filma', *Picturegoer*, August 1929, p. 62.

51. Letter from Miss Rona Green (Crouch End, London), *Picturegoer*, October 1929, p. 78.

52. Letter from Jack Buchanan, Banbridge, *Film Weekly*, 1 July 1929, p. 16.

53. Letter from Peggie Ferguson, Eastbourne, *Film Weekly*, 23 December 1929, p. 12.

54. Letter from Robert Greaves (Walthamstow, London) in *Picturegoer*, October 1929, p. 77.

55. 'The applause at the end [of the trade screening] was loud, long and sincere', according to *The Daily Film Renter*, 24 June 1929; clipping included in the *Blackmail* Clippings Scrapbook, Alfred Hitchcock Collection, Margaret Herrick Library, Academy of Motion Pictures Arts and Sciences, Beverly Hills, California (hereafter HC/AMPAS).

56. British Lion's *The Clue of the New Pin*, which was first shown to the trade in March 1929, is now reckoned to be the first British talkie. See the discussion in Rachael Low, *The History of the British Film 1918–29* (London: George Allen and Unwin, 1971), pp. 204–5.

57. Kenneth Macpherson, 'As Is', *Close Up* 5/4 (October 1929), pp. 257–63.

58. See also Mark Glancy, 'Hitchcock, *Blackmail* and Film Nationalism', in J. Chapman, M. Glancy and S. Harper (eds), *The New Film History: Sources, Methods, Approaches* (London: Palgrave, 2007), pp. 185–200.

59. *Daily Chronicle*, 24 June 1929; HC/AMPAS.

60. *Daily Mirror*, 24 June 1929; and *Newcastle Chronicle*, 24 June 1929; both HC/AMPAS.

61. *Kinematograph Weekly*, 27 June 1929, p. 43. *Morning Post*, 24 June 1929; and *Evening Standard*, 22 June 1929; both HC/AMPAS.

62. *Sunday Dispatch*, 23 June 1929; HC/AMPAS.

63. *Picturegoer*, September 1929, p. 13.

64. *Film Weekly*, 8 July 1929, p. 10.

65. Letter from Mr Overbury, *Picturegoer*, November 1929, p. 76.

66. *Picturegoer* letters from Miss Molly Lambert (Sheffield), November 1929, p. 76; and E.K. (Bournemouth), January 1930, p. 71.

67. *Picturegoer*, August 1929, p. 14.

68. *Glasgow Herald*, 24 June 1929, p. 15.

69. *Sunday Express*, 28 July 1929, p. 4.
70. Gomery: *The Coming of Sound*, p. 107.
71. The (intentional) misspellings are in the original. *Picturegoer*, 29 August 1931, p. 4.
72. John Ellis, 'Victory of the Voice?', *Screen* 22/2 (1981), p. 71.
73. Letter from Miss J. Fisher (Bethnal Green, London), *Picturegoer*, 14 November 1931, p. 30.
74. Letter from A.E. Gorman (Cleveland, Yorkshire), *Picturegoer*, 7 November 1931, p. 29.
75. Letter from David D. Jolly (Angus), *Picturegoer*, 28 November 1931, p. 30.
76. Letter from Maitland M. Shearer (Glasgow), *Picturegoer*, 14 May 1932, p. 29.
77. Letter from T.M. (Edinburgh), *Film Weekly*, 29 April 1932, p. 66.
78. Letter from E.Wm Ellis (Penarth, Cardiff), *Film Weekly*, 28 March 1931, p. 20.
79. See, for example, *Film Weekly*, 18 April 1931, p. 8; and *Picturegoer*, 7 November 1931, p. 29.
80. Glasgow *Evening Times*, 3 November 1932, p. 3.
81. *World Film News*, February 1937, p. 6. This survey included replies from 66 exhibitors throughout the country, but in previous and subsequent issues, specific towns and neighbourhoods were profiled.
82. These comments were made in a separate survey of East End exhibitors. *World Film News*, January 1937, pp. 8–9.
83. *World Film News*, February 1937, p. 6.
84. *World Film News*, July 1937, p. 15.
85. See, for example, the responses numbered 14, 23, 29 and 103; Jeffrey Richard and Dorothy Sheridan, *Mass Observation at the Movies* (London: Routledge, 1987), pp. 43, 81, 108 and 122.
86. See, for example, the responses numbered 74, 101, 119, 134, 158; Richards and Sheridan: *Mass Observation at the Movies*, pp. 89, 95, 101, 119 and 131.
87. *Picturegoer*, 20 June 1931, p. 11.
88. *Film Weekly*, 7 June 1930, p. 10; and 24 January 1931, p. 3.
89. *Picturegoer*, April 1928, p. 11.
90. See the discussion of Colman in A. Scott Berg, *Goldwyn* (London: Sphere, 1990), p. 177; and Crafton: *The Talkies*, pp. 460–1.
91. Crafton: *The Talkies*, p. 461.
92. See, for example, the letters to *Picturegoer* from 'Leatherface' and from D.W.S., both July 1929, p 60; and the letter from B.H.H., August 1929, p. 63.
93. See, for example, the reviews in *Kinematograph Weekly*, 13 June 1929, pp. 41 and 45; and *The Bioscope*, 12 June 1929, p. 34.
94. *Sunday Times*, 16 June 1929, p. 6.
95. Allen Eyles and Keith Skone, *London's West End Cinemas* (Sutton: Premier Bioscope, 1984), pp. 24–5.
96. Letter to *Picturegoer* from Miss Rona Green (Crouch End, London) and from Jimmy (SW10, London), both October 1929, p. 78

97. The advertising is compiled in the British pressbook for *Bulldog Drummond* (author's own collection).

98. The findings of the 1928 Bernstein Questionnaire are discussed in *Picturegoer*, May 1929, p. 11. The 1932, 1934 and 1937 reports are held as special collections at the British Film Institute Library.

99. See the annual box-office review in *Kinematograph Weekly*, 13 January 1938, p. 49.

100. In 1928, Bernstein found that 50 per cent of men and 70 per cent of women were 'against talking pictures', although it was admitted that many of the respondents would not have experienced a talkie yet. *Picturegoer*, May 1929, p. 11.

101. *The Bioscope*, 13 April 1932, p. 8.

102. David Sutton, *A Chorus of Raspberries: British Film Comedy, 1929–39* (Devon: University of Exeter Press, 2000), p. 101.

103. See the discussion of national cinema in Sutton: *A Chorus of Raspberries*, pp. 7–22.

104. See John Sedgwick, *Popular Filmgoing in 1930s Britain: A Choice of Pleasures* (Exeter: University of Exeter, 2000), p. 111.

105. Margaret Dickinson and Sarah Street, *Cinema and State: The Film Industry and the British Government* (London: British Film Institute, 1985), p. 42.

Chapter 4   Nothing Ever Happens in England

1. *Parliamentary Debates (Commons)*, 15 April 1932, volume 264, column 1141.

2. Commission on Educational and Cultural Films, *The Film in National Life* (London: George Allen and Unwin, 1932), p. 10.

3. Elizabeth Bowen, 'Why I Go to the Cinema', in C. Davy (ed.), *Footnotes to the Film* (London: Lovat Dickson, 1938), p. 205.

4. See, for example, John Springhall, *Youth, Popular Culture and Moral Panics: Penny Gaffs to Gangsta Rap, 1830–1996* (New York: St Martin's Press, 1998), pp. 115–16.

5. See the wider discussion in Sarah J. Smith, *Children, Cinema and Censorship: From Dracula to the Dead End Kids* (London: I.B.Tauris, 2005), pp. 84–7.

6. See, for example, the observations made in the *Manchester Guardian*, 6 January 1933, p. 13; and in *Picture Show*, 7 May 1932, pp. 18–19.

7. *Picturegoer*, for example, regularly used 'sez you' as a headline on its letters pages during 1932, above short, sharp excerpts from readers' letters.

8. *Kinematograph Weekly*, 21 May 1931, p. 48.

9. *Manchester Guardian*, 6 January 1933, p. 13.

10. *Kinematograph Weekly*, 1 June 1933, p. 3.

11. Smith: *Children, Cinema and Censorship*, pp. 79–104.

12. The delegation was calling for greater censorship of films but it was eager not to be seen to be critical of the British Board of Film Censors; hence the finger of guilt was pointed at American films and the practice of block booking. *The Times*, 16 January 1935, p. 8.

13. *Parliamentary Debates (Commons)*, 4 November 1937, volume 328, columns 1234–5.
14. Daniel LeMahieu, *A Culture For Democracy: Mass Communication and the Cultivated Mind in British Between the Wars* (Oxford: Clarendon, 1988), p. 273. As Valeria Camporesi points out, the policy of educating the public and lifting its tastes was so entrenched that the BBC did not begin to conduct audience research in a systematic way until 1936. Valeria Camporesi, *Mass Culture and National Traditions: The BBC and American Broadcasting, 1922–1954* (Fucecchio, Italy: European Academic Press, 2000), pp. 69–74.
15. Asa Briggs, *The History of Broadcasting in the United Kingdom*, Vol. 1: *The Birth of Broadcasting* (London: Oxford University Press, 1961), p. 292.
16. Ross McKibben, *Classes and Cultures: England, 1918–51* (Oxford: Oxford University Press, 1998), pp. 459–60.
17. Asa Briggs, *The History of Broadcasting in the United Kingdom*, Vol. 2: *The Golden Age of the Wireless* (London: Oxford University Press, 1965), p. 109.
18. Briggs: *The Golden Age of the Wireless*, pp. 350–3.
19. See the discussion of the Board's origins and its outlook in Jeffrey Richards, *The Age of the Dream Palace Cinema and Society in British, 1930–1939* (London: Routledge, 1984), pp. 89–107.
20. *Kinematograph Weekly*, 7 January 1926, p. 50.
21. 'O'Connor's 43' is reprinted in Smith, *Children, Cinema and Censorship*, pp. 179–80.
22. *Ibid*, p. 31.
23. *Ibid*, pp. 181–3.
24. See the discussion of 'Domestic Policy' in Richards: *The Age of the Dream Palace*, and, for a discussion of crime films, see pp. 113–14.
25. A useful list of films refused a certificate can be found in the appendices of James C. Robertson, *The British Board of Film Censors: Film Censorship in Britain, 1896–1950* (London: Croom Helm, 1985), pp. 185–8.
26. Smith: *Children, Cinema and Censorship*, pp. 65–73.
27. Smith: *Children, Cinema and Censorship*, p. 47.
28. Richard Maltby, 'The Production Code and the Mythologies of "pre-Code" Hollywood', in Steve Neale (ed.), *The Classical Hollywood Reader* (London: Routledge, 2012), pp. 237–48.
29. Arthur Marwick, *A History of the Modern British Isles, 1914–99* (Oxford: Blackwell, 2000), pp. 68–71.
30. Stevenson John, *British Society, 1914–45* (London: Penguin, 1984), p. 373.
31. Martin Pugh, *We Danced All Night: A Social History of Britain between the Wars* (London: Bodley Head, 2008), p. 102.
32. Andrew Davies, 'The Scottish Chicago? From "Hooligans" to "Gangsters" in Inter-war Glasgow', *Cultural and Social History* 4/4 (2007), pp. 511–27.
33. Davies: 'The Scottish Chicago?', p. 512.
34. Stevenson: *British Society, 1914–45*, p. 375.

35. The Home Secretary reviewed the reasons in a statement to the House of Commons. See *Parliamentary Debates (Commons)*, 15 April 1932, volume 264, column 1141. See also the editorial in the *Times*, 8 February 1932, p. 13.

36. A letter to *The Times*, entitled 'Criminality and the Film', disagreed with Herbert Samuels' view that cinema-going was more likely to prevent crime than to cause it. *Times*, 27 April 1932, p. 15.

37. *Parliamentary Debates (Commons)*, 15 April 1932, volume 264, column 1171.

38. The idea that gangster films tutored boys in criminal ways was so strong in Britain that the Warner Brothers film *Crime School* (1938) was regarded as particularly inflammatory, even though, as Springhall has observed, the story was essentially about the reformation of juvenile delinquents and it 'did not recommend or glamorize crime'. Springhall: *Youth, Culture and Moral Panics*, pp. 104–5.

39. His speech was reported in *Kinematograph Weekly*, 1 June 1933, p. 3.

40. In 1929, and largely as a result of the problems posed by the talkies, the BBFC urged filmmakers to submit scenarios for proposed films before filming actually began. The Scenario Reports are among the few BBFC documents from this era that are now available to historians (most were destroyed when the Board's offices were destroyed by bombing in the Second World War) and they are held as a special collection at the British Film Institute in London. Report dated 5 August 1932, *Speed King*, BBFC Scenario Reports, 1930–32, British Film Institute, London (hereafter BBFC/BFI).

41. Robert Murphy, 'Riff-Raff: British Cinema and the Underworld', in C. Barr (ed.), *All Our Yesterdays* (London: British Film Institute, 1986), p. 287.

42. Report dated 3 November 1932, *When the Gangs Came to London*, BBFC Scenario Reports, 1930–32, BBFC/BFI. Also discussed in Richards: *The Age of the Dream Palace*, p. 114.

43. Report dated 28 April 1933, *The Mail Bag Murder*, BBFC Scenario Reports, 1933, BBFC/BFI; and Report dated 5 November 1935, *Public Enemy*, BBFC Scenario Reports, 1935, BBFC/BFI.

44. Report dated 14 June 1933, *Tiger Bay*, BBFC Scenario Reports, 1934, BBFC/BFI. Also discussed in Richards: *The Age of the Dream Palace*, p. 112.

45. These quotations are taken from the opening of Gill Plain's study of John Mills. See Gill Plain, *John Mills and British Cinema: Masculinity, Identity and Nation* (Edinburgh: Edinburgh University Press, 2006), p. 1.

46. As Murphy comments, there was a 'flowering of low-life movies' at the end of the 1930s. See Murphy: 'Riff-Raff', p. 290.

47. For a discussion of post-war crime films, see James Chapman, '"Sordidness, Corruption and Violence Almost Unrelieved": Critics, Censors and the Post-war British Crime Film', *Contemporary British History* 22/2 (2008), pp. 181–201.

48. Jeffrey Richards, *Swordsmen of the Screen: From Douglas Fairbanks to Michael York* (London: Routledge, 1977), pp. 218–23.

49. Report dated 6 August 1931, *The Devil Man*, BBFC Scenario Reports, 1930–32, BBFC/BFI.
50. Report dated 5 February 1932, *The Anatomist*, BBFC Scenario Reports, 1930–32, BBFC/BFI.
51. Report dated 24 June 1932, *The Lodger*, BBFC Scenario Reports, 1930–32, BBFC/BFI.
52. Jeffrey Richards, 'Tod Slaughter and the Cinema of Excess', in J. Richards (ed.), *The Unknown 1930s: An Alternative History of the British Cinema, 1929–1939* (London: I.B.Tauris, 1998), p. 147.
53. These comments were made in an interview entitled 'The Censor and Sidney Street', *World Film News* 2/12 (March 1938), pp. 4–5. The article is reprinted in Sidney Gottlieb (ed.), *Hitchcock on Hitchcock: Selected Writings and Interviews* (London: Faber and Faber, 1997), pp. 192–5.
54. 'The Censor Wouldn't Pass It', *Film Weekly*, 5 November 1938, pp. 6–7; reprinted in Gottlieb: *Hitchcock on Hitchcock*, pp. 196–201.
55. Although Hitchcock's origins are often traced to Leytonstone, on the northeastern fringe of London, he actually lived there only for the first seven years of his life. Then (in late 1906 or early 1907) his family moved back into the city's East End and lived above their fish-and-chip shop on Salmon Lane. Patrick McGilligan, *Alfred Hitchcock: A Life in Darkness and in Light* (London: HarperCollins, 2003), p. 13.
56. The BBFC's annual reports listed its reasons for banning films over the course of the year, as a warning to filmmakers for the future. The reference to machine guns is included in the report for 1930. *Bioscope*, 18 March 1931, p. 23.
57. The reports indicate that the film was initially entitled *The Hidden Hand*, but at this stage it was a thriller based around H.C. McNiele's fictional detective 'Bulldog Drummond' and the BBFC had no significant objections to the script. Report dated 27 February 1934, *The Hidden Hand*, BBFC Scenario Reports, 1934, BBFC/BFI. The revised and more problematic scenario was submitted three months later. See the reports dated 10 May 1934, 16 May 1934 and 5 June 1934, *The Man Who Knew Too Much*, BBFC Scenario Reports, 1934, BBFC/BFI.
58. For a fuller account of this film's development, see Mark Glancy, '*The Man Who Knew Too Much* (1934): Alfred Hitchcock, John Buchan and the Thrill of the Chase', in D. Boyd and R.B. Palmer (eds), *Hitchcock at the Source: The Auteur as Adapter* (Albany: State University of New York, 2011), pp. 77–87.
59. Richards: *The Age of the Dream Palace*, p. 114.
60. *New York Times*, 1 May 1932, p. 5.
61. Robertson: *The British Board of Film Censors*, pp. 78–9.
62. *Times*, 4 May 1931, p. 12.
63. *Kinematograph Weekly*, 7 May 1931, p. 26.
64. *Film Weekly*, 28 November 1931, p. 26.
65. *Picturegoer*, 28 November 1931, p. 20.

66. *Picturegoer*, 30 April 1932, p. 18. The same reviewer commented that *The Front Page* 'obviously approximates very closely to what newspaper life is in America'. *Film Weekly*, meanwhile, stated that *Five Star Final* 'ruthlessly exposed … the inside workings of the American "yellow press"'. *Film Weekly*, 29 April 1932, p. 75.

67. *Picturegoer*, 31 October 1931, p. 22.

68. The review in *Picturegoer*, for example, defined *Little Caesar* as 'a brilliant character study' by Edward G. Robinson. *Picturegoer*, 7 November 1931, p. 20.

69. *Film Weekly*, 16 May 1931, p. 24; and 7 November 1931, p. 27.

70. *Kinematograph Weekly*, 16 April 1931, p. 76.

71. *Kinematograph Weekly*, 26 May 1932, p. 59.

72. *Daily Express*, 28 June 1932, p. 3.

73. *Manchester Guardian*, 12 July 1932, p. 13.

74. Robertson: *The British Board of Film Censors*, p. 79.

75. The film's prologue is discussed in a review in *The Times*, 20 September 1930, p. 8.

76. Sydney Carroll, the critic for the *Sunday Times*, observed that, 'It has upon good authority been asserted that it was this picture [*The Big House*] that provided the English convicts with inspiration for their outburst'; *Sunday Times*, 31 January 1932, p. 7. Months later, an article in *Picture Show* reflected that 'It is not for me to say that the recent epidemic of bag snatching and daylight robberies in this country has been inspired by the gangster type of films, nor that the revolt at Dartmoor was suggested by *The Big House*, but it is quite obvious that these and other types of American pictures have greatly changed the general outlook on life of thousands of people in Great Britain today'. *Picture Show*, 7 May 1932, pp. 18–19.

77. *Daily Mail*, 25 January 1932, p. 14.

78. Simon Dell, *Mutiny on the Moor: The Story of the Dartmoor Prison Riot of 1932* (Newton Abbot: Forest, 2006).

79. See the editorial in *The Times*, 8 February 1932, p. 13; and the letter to the editor published two weeks later; *Times*, 24 February 1932, p. 13. See also the coverage in the *Sunday Express*, 24 January 1932, p. 1; *Daily Mail*, 25 January 1932, p. 14; *News of the World*, 31 January 1932, p. 1; *Sunday Times*, 24 January 1932, p. 7; and *Picture Show*, 7 May 1932, pp. 18–19.

80. Robertson: *The British Board of Film Censors*, pp. 78–9.

81. *Sunday Express*, 19 June 1932, pp. 20–1.

82. The longer ending is indicated in the script reprinted in Henry Cohen (ed.), *The Public Enemy* (Madison: University of Wisconsin, 1981).

83. *Picture Show*, 12 November 1932, p. 28.

84. Robertson: *The British Board of Film Censors*, p. 78.

85. *Sunday Times*, 10 January 1932, p. 6.

86. *Sunday Times*, 19 June 1932, p. 6.

87. *Observer*, 3 January 1932, p. 12.

88. *Observer*, 10 January 1932, p. 13.

89. *Observer*, 19 June 1932, p. 12.

90. In his *Sunday Express* columns, Belfrage praised Cagney's performances in *Taxi!* (3 January 1932, p. 16) and *Larceny Lane* (10 January 1932, p. 17) and *The Crowd Roars* (22 May 1932, p. 18).

91. *Sunday Express*, 19 June 1932, pp. 20–1.

92. The review appeared in the January 1938 issue of *World Film News*, and it is reprinted in Forsyth Hardy (ed.), *Grierson on the Movies* (London: Faber and Faber, 1981), pp. 104–5.

93. This review originally appeared in the 2 July 1932 issue of the *New Clarion*, and it is reprinted in Hardy: *Grierson on the Movies*, pp. 82–4.

94. *Daily Express*, 20 June 1932, p. 8; *Daily Telegraph*, 20 June 1932, p. 3; *Film Weekly*, 4 November 1932, p. 26.

95. *Kinematograph Weekly*, 23 June 1932, pp. 49 and 51.

96. John Sedgwick, *Popular Filmgoing in 1930s Britain: A Choice of Pleasures* (Exeter: University of Exeter, 2000), pp. 262–4.

97. *Film Weekly*, 20 May 1932, p. 31.

98. *Bernstein Questionnaire 1934 Report*, pp. 1 and 4.

99. *Bernstein Questionnaire 1937 Report*, pp. 1 and 6.

100. *Bernstein Questionnaire 1934 Report*, p. 4; and *Bernstein Questionnaire 1937 Report*, p. 6.

101. See, for example, the reviews of *Taxi!*; *Kinematograph Weekly*, 31 December 1931, pp. 21 and 23; and of *The Crowd Roars*; *Bioscope*, 20 April 1932, p. 13; and *Kinematograph Weekly*, 21 April 1932, p. 35.

102. The editor of *Film Weekly* printed a photo of Edward G. Robinson brandishing a machine gun beneath the headline 'Stop this crude sensationalism!'; *Film Weekly*, 5 December 1931, p. 3. *Picturegoer* took the opportunity to print the letter from Leeds beneath the headline, 'Stop this gangster business!'; letter from J.G. Melrose (Leeds), *Picturegoer*, 30 May 1931, p. 26. See also the letters from R.R. Bushell (Westminster, London), *Picturegoer*, 20 June 1931, p. 26; and G. Bertolini (Glasgow), *Picturegoer*, 15 August 1931, p. 26.

103. See the editors' discussion of the audience preferences; Jeffrey Richards and Dorothy Sheridan, *Mass Observation at the Movies* (London: Routledge, 1987), pp. 32–41.

104. Richard Carr, 'People's Pictures and People's Palaces', *World Film News*, January 1937, pp. 8–9.

105. Robert James, *Popular Culture and Working Class Taste in Britain, 1930–39: A Round of Cheap Diversions?* (Manchester: Manchester University Press, 2010).

106. Kennedy's comments were reported in *The Times*, 19 May 1939, p. 17.

107. See the discussion of 'working class comedy' in David Sutton, *A Chorus of Raspberries: British Film Comedy, 1929–39* (Exeter: Exeter University Press, 2000), pp. 103–55.

108. Gill Plain makes some interesting comparisons between Mills and Cagney. Plain: *John Mills and British Cinema*, pp. 27–8 and 33–4.
109. Winifred Holtby, *South Riding* (London: Virago, 2005 [1936]), p. 17.

Chapter 5   The Minx's Progress

1. *Observer*, 8 September 1940, p. 4.
2. *Kinematograph Weekly*, 26 September 1940, p. 12.
3. Guy Morgan, *Red Roses Every Night: An Account of London Cinemas Under Fire* (London: Quality, 1948), pp. 75–6.
4. Hazel Wheeler, *Huddersfield at War* (Gloucestershire: Alan Sutton, 1992), pp. 35, 109, 146 and 207.
5. *Observer*, 6 September 1942, p. 2.
6. For comments on the book's success in Britain, see the *Manchester Guardian*, 18 January 1940, p. 6; the *Scotsman*, 12 March 1940, p. 9; and the *New Yorker*, 26 April 1941, p. 11.
7. See, for example, the *Daily Mirror*, 11 February 1939, p. 15, and 22 May 1939, p. 18; the *Bystander*, 10 April 1940, pp. 48–9; and *Cavalcade*, 13 January 1940, p. 17.
8. Only Fleming receiving credit for directing. *Manchester Guardian*, 30 June 1939, p. 12.
9. For an authoritative account of the film's exhibition, and the related controversy, see Allen Eyles, 'When Exhibitors Saw Scarlett: The War Over *Gone with the Wind*', *Picture House* 27 (2002), pp. 23–32.
10. See the reports in the *Motion Picture Herald*, 27 April 1940, p. 51; and *Today's Cinema*, 24 April 1940, p. 9.
11. This advertisement appeared in several national newspapers. See, for example, the *Daily Mail*, 19 April 1940, p. 9; the London *Evening Standard*, 19 April 1940, p. 9; and *The Times*, 16 April 1949, p. 10.
12. George Pitman of *Reynolds' News* put it most succinctly when he wrote, 'Everything about the Film Event of All Time, as its proud begetters call it, is the longest, the largest, or the highest ever'. *Reynolds' News*, 21 April 1940, p. 10.
13. *Picturegoer and Film Weekly*, 6 April 1940, p. 3. Of course, the editor's disapproval did not stop him from using one of the film stills, featuring Gable and Leigh in an embrace, on the cover of the magazine a few weeks later; 27 April 1940, p. 1.
14. The headlines are listed in the order the articles appeared; *Picturegoer and Film Weekly*, 7 October 1939, p. 3; 27 January 1940, pp. 6–7; 2 March 1940, pp. 6–7; 23 March 1940, pp. 3–4; 11 May 1940, pp. 3 and 11.
15. See, for example, the *Daily Telegraph*, 19 April 1940, p. 6; *Picturegoer and Film Weekly*, 11 May 1940, p. 11; and *Kinematograph Weekly*, 27 June 1940, p. 21.
16. *Picturegoer and Film Weekly*, 27 January 1940, pp. 6–7.
17. *Picturegoer and Film Weekly*, 2 March 1940, p. 3.
18. *Picturegoer and Film Weekly*, 23 March 1940, p. 4.

19. Hicks issued the letter to the press and it received wide coverage in the USA. See, for example, the *New York Times*, 24 May 1940; *Time*, 10 June 1940; and *Variety*, 29 May 1940, p. 52. In Britain, it was discussed in an article published in one of the country's leading tabloid newspapers under the headline 'Stars Who Ran Away'; *Sunday Pictorial*, 9 June 1940, p. 5. Hicks also recalled in his memoirs that the letter gained him 'immense popularity' at the time. Seymour Hicks, *Hail Fellow Well Met* (London: Staples, 1949), pp. 174–5.

20. Eyles: 'When Exhibitors Saw Scarlett', p. 24.

21. Ticket prices are discussed in Fred Russell, 'Home Truths', *The Performer*, 23 May 1940, p. 6.

22. Eyles: 'When Exhibitors Saw Scarlett', p. 27.

23. See James Chapman, *The British at War: Cinema, State and Propaganda, 1939–1945* (London: I.B.Tauris, 1998), p. 17.

24. *Today's Cinema*, 3 May 1940, p. 1.

25. This argument was linked to the American companies' 'blocked earnings' in Britain. In wartime, the companies were allowed to remit only a portion of their British earnings to the USA. The rest could be held or spent in Britain. The CEA suspected that the companies would choose to spend what they could not remit on theatres. See *Kinematograph Weekly*, 25 April 1940, p. 4.

26. *Kinematograph Weekly*, 23 May 1940, p. 11.

27. See the reports on CEA branch meetings in *Kinematograph Weekly*, 20 June 1940, p. 8.

28. *Kinematograph Weekly*, 25 April 1940, p. 5.

29. *Evening News*, 22 April 1940, p. 3.

30. The *Daily Mirror*, for example, commented about the advanced ticket prices: 'We think Hollywood is a bit optimistic in expecting Britain to pay out what is saved after it's had a glass of beer and a fag, on four hours of the American Civil War, particularly when this country's got a war of its own.' *Daily Mirror*, 14 May 1940, p. 11. Sympathetic coverage of the CEA campaign can also be found in the *Bystander*, 1 May 1940, p. 257; *Cavalcade*, 27 April 1940, p. 12; the *Daily Mirror*, 26 April 1940, p. 13; and the *People*, 5 May 1940, p. 3.

31. *Kinematograph Weekly*, 6 June 1940, p. 9.

32. Hansard, House of Commons Debates, 30 April 1940, 360/516. See also the reports in the *Hollywood Reporter*, 1 May 1940, p. 1; *New York Times*, 1 May 1940, p. 23; *Today's Cinema*, 1 May 1940, p. 1.

33. *Evening News*, 22 April 1940, p. 3.

34. Eyles: 'When Exhibitors Saw Scarlett', p. 32.

35. *Daily Film Renter*, 17 June 1940, p. 9.

36. *The Daily Film Renter*, 29 May 1940, p. 1; 30 May 1940, p. 1; and 17 June 1940, p. 1.

37. Audrey Field describes the interior of the Empire and comments, 'Yes, I well remember that carpet … You felt as if you were sinking in up to the ankles. Most of us thought, before, during and after the Second World

War, that, just for a change, exuberance could not go too far'. Audrey Field, *Picture Palace: A Social History of the Cinema* (London: Gentry, 1974), pp. 81–2.

38. *Daily Express*, 4 November 1944, p. 4.
39. Eyles: 'When Exhibitors Saw Scarlett', p. 30.
40. C.A. Lejeune, 'Tensely London Waits', *New York Times*, 30 June 1940.
41. Eyles: 'When Exhibitors Saw Scarlett', p. 29.
42. Morgan: *Red Roses Every Night*, pp. 76–7.
43. Allen Eyles and Keith Skone, *London's West End Cinemas* (Sutton: Premier Bioscope, 1984), p. 45.
44. The minimum ticket price of three shillings and six pence was waived in Blackpool, where it was thought local patrons could not pay that price. Tickets there ranged from nine pence to three shillings. *Kinematograph Weekly*, 4 July 1940, p. 1; 29 August 1940, p. 9; and 12 September 1940, p. 6.
45. Eyles: 'When Exhibitors Saw Scarlett', pp. 27–30.
46. *Kinematograph Weekly*, 1 August 1940, p. 8.
47. *Kinematograph Weekly*, 30 May 1940, p. 5; 18 July 1940, p. 18; 25 July 1940, p. 7; 17 October 1940, p. 12; also *The Daily Film Renter*, 29 May 1940, p. 1; 30 May 1940, p. 1; and 17 June 1940, p. 1.
48. Eyles: 'When Exhibitors Saw Scarlett', p. 31.
49. Eyles: 'When Exhibitors Saw Scarlett', p. 31.
50. Ballots for the survey were issued two months before the results were printed and thus preceded the general release on 6 September 1942. *Picturegoer*, 17 October 1942, p. 7.
51. See, for example, the *Daily Mirror*, 20 March 1942, p. 7; and 17 July 1942, p. 7.
52. *Daily Mirror*, 23 May 1942, p. 5.
53. Leslie Halliwell claims that it lasted for a full year in Bolton, where he grew up, but this is likely to be an exaggeration. Leslie Halliwell, *Seats in all Parts: Half a Lifetime at the Movies* (London: Granada, 1985), p. 101.
54. *Picturegoer*, 19 September 1942, p. 2.
55. *Kinematograph Weekly*, 14 January 1943, p. 47; and 13 January 1944, p. 51.
56. *Kinematograph Weekly*, 25 April 1940, p. 22; *Today's Cinema*, 24 April 1940, p. 9.
57. *Daily Mail*, 19 April 1940, p. 4, and 20 April 1940, p. 9; *Sunday Pictorial*, 21 April 1940, p. 19; *Sunday Express*, 21 April 1940, p. 8; *Evening News*, 19 April 1940, p. 4.
58. For an early survey of audience preferences on colour, see the 1937 Bernstein Questionnaire, which revealed that 40 per cent of the respondents disliked colour films. *Bernstein Questionnaire 1937 Report*, p. 19.
59. *Daily Express*, 18 April 1940, p. 7; *Daily Herald*, 18 April 1940, p. 4; *Daily Mirror*, 19 April 1940, p. 13; *Evening Standard*, 18 April 1940, p. 10, and 20 April 1940, p. 8.
60. Jympson Harman, 'Don't Smother the Child', *Sight and Sound* 10/40 (Spring 1942), pp. 67–9.

61. For an analysis of the 'quality' critics in wartime, see John Ellis, 'The Quality Film Adventure: British Critics and the Cinema, 1942–1948', in A. Higson (ed.), *Dissolving Views: Key Writings on British Cinema* (London: Cassell, 1996), pp. 66–93.

62. For an example of Powell's thoughts on 'people who bring the book with them' to the cinema, see her review of *Wuthering Heights*, originally printed in the *Sunday Times* in April 1939 and reprinted in Dilys Powell, *The Golden Screen: Fifty Years of Films* (London: Headline, 1990 [1989]), pp. 11–12.

63. Dilys Powell, 'Credo of a Critic', *Sight and Sound* 10/38 (Summer 1941), pp. 26–7.

64. For views similar to Powell's, see P.L. Mannock, 'We Critics Have Our Uses', *Sight and Sound* 10/39 (Autumn 1941), pp. 40–2; and Roger Manvell, *The Cinema and the Public* (London: Army Bureau of Current Affairs, 1944), pp. 8–9.

65. Others agreed. Technicolor was 'a distraction' for George Pitman, of *Reynolds' News*, and thought it 'added nothing' to the film (*Reynolds' News*, 21 April 1940, p. 10), while James Agate sneered that the film was so 'bathed in colour' that it looked like a 'picture postcard' (*Tatler*, 24 April 1940, p. 124).

66. *Sunday Times*, 21 April 1940, p. 5.

67. Powell was banned after writing a flippant review of another MGM film, *Flight Command* (1940/41). See Melanie Selfe, '"Intolerable Flippancy": The Arnot Robertson v. MGM Libel Case (1946–1950) and the Evolution of BBC Policy on Broadcast Film Criticism', *Historical Journal of Film, Radio and Television* 31/3 (2011), p. 376.

68. James Agate, writing in the *Tatler*, used the term 'Dilysians' to describe Powell's influence as a critic when he reviewed *In Which We Serve* (1942). This is reprinted in James Agate, *Around Cinemas, 2nd Series* (Amsterdam: Home and Van Thal, 1948), pp. 215–17.

69. *Picturegoer and Film Weekly*, 13 July 1940, p. 16.

70. *Bystander*, 1 May 1940, p. 145.

71. *Illustrated London News*, 27 April 1940, p. 574.

72. Of the critics surveyed, only George Pitman of *Reynolds' News* took issue with the film's historical accuracy. Referring to it as 'a reactionary distortion of history from the Southern viewpoint', Pitman was particularly aggrieved by the film's depiction of slavery. *Reynolds' News*, 21 April 1940, p. 10.

73. *The Daily Mirror* reported that the Colored People's Association was planning the protest, with predictions that 300 people would picket the three London cinemas showing the film, but no follow-up articles reported on this. *Daily Mirror*, 24 April 1940, p. 3.

74. *Daily Telegraph*, 22 April 1940, p. 4.

75. *Manchester Guardian*, 28 May 1940, p. 6.

76. *Monthly Film Bulletin* 7/76 (30 April 1940), p. 56.

77. *Punch*, 8 May 1940, p. 504.
78. *Reynolds' News*, 21 April 1940, p. 10.
79. *Sketch*, 1 May 1940, p. 146.
80. *Spectator*, 26 April 1940, p. 594.
81. *Sunday Chronicle*, 21 April 1940, p. 9.
82. *Tatler*, 24 April 1940, p. 124.
83. *Time and Tide*, 27 April 1940, p. 452.
84. Lejeune reviewed films for both the weekly newspaper the *Observer* and the monthly magazine the *Sketch*. These comments are taken from the *Observer*, 21 April 1940, p. 9. For a discussion of critical attitudes toward the 'woman's film', see M. Bell and M. Williams (eds), *British Women's Cinema* (London: Routledge, 2009).
85. For a broader discussion of the difference between the historical film and the costume drama, see James Chapman, *Past and Present: National Identity and the British Historical Film* (London: I.B.Tauris, 2005), pp. 2–5.
86. Tom Brown, 'Spectacle/gender/history: the case of *Gone with the Wind*', *Screen* 49/2 (Summer 2008), p. 158.
87. The headline on A.E. Wilson's review defined the film as 'Mammy's big hit'; London *Star*, 19 April 1940, p. 2. James Agate remarked that McDaniel 'very nearly redeems the picture'; while the *Monthly Film Bulletin* critic referred to her performance as 'unforgettable'. Even Dilys Powell admitted that McDaniel was 'excellent'. But these are just a few examples of the praise reserved for her. As George Campbell remarked, 'Unanimous, whatever they think of the film as a colossal whole, are the critics about Hattie McDaniel as the Tara household Mammy'; *Bystander*, 1 May 1940, p. 145.
88. Mass Observation's 1943 survey is reprinted in full in Richards and Sheridan: *Mass Observation at the Movies*, pp. 220–91; Mayer's research into cinema-going is spread over two volumes: *Sociology of Film* (London: Faber, 1946) and *British Cinemas and their Audiences* (London: Dobson, 1948).
89. Richards and Sheridan: *Mass Observation at the Movies*, p. 241.
90. Mayer: *Sociology of Film*, p. 67.
91. Mayer: *Sociology of Film*, p. 70.
92. This information is drawn from the Wartime Social Survey (1943), conducted for the Ministry of Information, and based on a sample of 5,639 people. The findings are reprinted as an appendix to Mayer: *British Cinemas and their Audiences*, pp. 250–75. The survey is discussed in Mark Glancy, '*Picturegoer*: The Fan Magazine and Popular Film Culture in Britain During the Second World War', *Historical Journal of Film, Radio and Television* 31/4 (2011), pp. 456–7.
93. See the editors' introduction to the survey for an overview of the findings. Richards and Sheridan: *Mass Observation at the Movies*, pp. 220–1.

94. Richards and Sheridan: *Mass Observation at the Movies*, pp. 227, 238 and 241.

95. Richards and Sheridan: *Mass Observation at the Movies*, pp. 222, 227, 238, 240, 241 and 243.

96. Richards and Sheridan: *Mass Observation at the Movies*, pp. 259, 261–4, 268, 269, 277.

97. For a wider discussion of Mayer's work, see Sarah Street, *British Cinema in Documents* (London: Routledge, 2000), pp. 139–58.

98. Mayer: *British Cinemas and their Audiences*, pp. 29–31.

99. Mayer: *British Cinemas and their Audiences*, p. 218.

100. Mayer: *British Cinemas and their Audiences*, p. 184.

101. Mayer: *British Cinemas and their Audiences*, p. 129.

102. Sue Harper, *Picturing the Past: The Rise and Fall of the British Costume Film* (London: British Film Institute, 1994), pp. 139–41.

103. Mayer: *British Cinemas and their Audiences*, p. 62.

104. The emphasis is in the original document; Mayer: *British Cinemas and their Audiences*, pp. 47 and 213.

105. Mayer: *Sociology of Film*, pp. 213–14.

106. Mayer: *Sociology of Film*, p. 183.

107. Mayer: *Sociology of Film*, p. 209.

108. Mayer: *British Cinemas and their Audiences* pp. 73 and 213.

109. Helen Taylor, *Scarlett's Women,* Gone with the Wind *and its Female Fans* (London: Virago, 1987), p. 78.

110. Taylor: *Scarlett's Women*, pp. 91–102.

111. Mayer: *Sociology of Film*, pp. 94–5.

112. Mayer: *Sociology of Film*, p. 216.

113. Hollywood had long required female stars to appear flawless even in the most unlikely circumstances. Just a few years earlier, in the MGM melodrama *Camille* (1936), Greta Garbo performed a deathbed scene, dying from tuberculosis no less, and her hair and make-up remained pristinely intact throughout.

114. Angus Calder, *The People's War: Britain 1939–1945* (London: Pimlico, 1969), pp. 279–80. See also Ina Zweiniger-Bargielowska, *Austerity in Britain: Rationing, Controls and Consumption, 1939–1955* (Oxford: Oxford University Press, 2000), pp. 120–1.

115. See the 'Make Do and Mend' column written by 'Gillian' in *Picture Show* during 1944, and also columns appearing in *Picture Show*, 12 July 1941, p. 16; 29 January 1944, p. 14; and 27 July 1944, p. 14.

116. On racial tensions among the GIs, see Graham A. Smith, *When Jim Crow Met John Bull: Black GIs in World War II Britain* (London: I.B.Tauris, 1987); and David Reynolds, *Rich Relations, The American Occupation of Britain, 1942–1945* (London: HarperCollins, 1996 [1995]), pp. 302–24.

117. Mayer: *British Cinemas and their Audiences*, p. 205.

118. Eyles: 'When Exhibitors Saw Scarlett', pp. 31–2.

119. Ryan Gilbey: *The Ultimate Film: The UK's 100 Most Popular Films* (London: British Film Institute, 2005), pp. 10–13.

120. *Guardian*, 22 November 1980, p. 24.

Chapter 6   The American film *par excellence*

1. Andre Bazin, 'The Western, or the American Film *par excellence*', in Hugh Grey (ed. and trans.), *What is Cinema: Volume Two* (Berkeley: University of California, 1971), p. 140.

2. Philip French, *Westerns* (Manchester: Carcanet, 2005 [1973]), p. 13.

3. J. Hoberman, 'How the West Was Lost', in Jim Kitses and Gregg Rickman (eds), *The Western Reader* (New York: Limelight, 1998), p. 85.

4. For a concise and authoritative overview of key writings about the genre, see Steve Neale, *Genre and Hollywood* (London: Routledge, 2000), pp. 133–49.

5. Colin McArthur, *Underworld USA* (London: British Film Institute, 1972), p. 18.

6. Michael Coyne, *The Crowded Prairie: American National Identity in the Hollywood Western* (London: I.B.Tauris, 1997), p. 15.

7. The contents of the letter were made public and revealed in the *Manchester Guardian*, 23 August 1887, p. 3.

8. Paul Reddin, *Wild West Shows* (Chicago: University of Illinois Press, 1999), pp. 90–1.

9. Robert W. Rydell and Rob Kroes, *Buffalo Bill in Bologna: The Americanization of the World, 1869–22* (Chicago and London: University of Chicago Press, 2005), p. 109.

10. Kate Flint, *The Transatlantic Indian, 1776–1930* (Princeton: Princeton University Press, 2009), p. 230. The show's success is also discussed in Reddin: *Wild West Shows*, p. 95.

11. Rydell and Kroes: *Buffalo Bill in Bologna*, pp. 107–8.

12. Duncan Andrew Campbell, *Unlikely Allies: Britain, America and the Victorian Origins of the Special Relationship* (London: Hambledon Continuum, 2007), pp. 230–3.

13. *Manchester Guardian*, 23 August 1887, p. 3.

14. As Joy S. Kasson has observed, the success of the Wild West show lay in its ability to 'assemble the tropes and images of the American West into a convincing and popular entertainment form … [which] filmmakers could adapt and embellish'. Joy S. Kasson, 'Life-like, Vivid, and Thrilling Pictures: Buffalo Bill's Wild West and Early Cinema', in Janet Walker (ed.), *Westerns: Films Through History* (London: Routledge, 2001), p. 117.

15. *Times*, 27 April 1887, p. 6. Kate Flint also observes that Cooper's name frequently arose in press commentaries on the show. Flint: *The Transatlantic Indian*, p. 233.

16. Flint: *The Transatlantic Indian*, p. 233; *Illustrated London News*, 16 April 1887, p. 440.

17. Rydell and Kroes: *Buffalo Bill in Bologna*, p. 109.

18. Rydell and Kroes: *Buffalo Bill in Bologna*, pp. 109 and 112. The authors indicate that, when the 'Wild West' show reached France and Germany, the Native Americans were received with more sympathy.
19. Flint: *The Transatlantic Indian*, p. 230.
20. *Times*, 27 April 1887, p. 6.
21. Quoted in Reddin: *Wild West Shows*, p. 94.
22. See the report in *The Times*, 29 April 1887, p. 10.
23. Rydell and Kroes: *Buffalo Bill in Bologna*, p. 109.
24. Flint observes that the Native Americans 'invariably attracted the most attention' from reporters and presumably from audiences too. This is not quite the same, however, as attracting sympathy and admiration, which was directed primarily toward Cody and his cowboys. Flint: *The Transatlantic Indian*, p. 233.
25. Jeffrey Richards, 'Imperial Heroes for a Post-Imperial Age: Films and the End of Empire', in Stuart Ward (ed.), *British Culture and the End of Empire* (Manchester: Manchester University Press, 2001), p. 129.
26. *Illustrated London News*, 16 April 1887, p. 440. See also further references to Cody and his fellow cowboys as chivalrous figures in Reddin: *Wild West Shows*, p. 93.
27. Reddin: *Wild West Shows*, p. 58.
28. Reddin: *Wild West Shows*, p. 92.
29. *Times*, 27 April 1887, p. 6; The *Observer* quotation is from Reddin: *Wild West Shows*, p. 87.
30. Abel considers the conception of the frontier in the American context. See Richard Abel, *The Red Rooster Scare: Making Cinema American, 1900–1910* (Berkeley: University of California Press, 1999), pp. 158–9.
31. *Bioscope*, 18 August 1910, pp. 4–5; also discussed in Richard Abel, *Americanizing the Movies and 'Movie-Mad' Audiences, 1910–1914* (Berkeley: University of California Press, 2006), p. 106.
32. *New York Times*, 30 July 1911, p. SM4.
33. The Vice Consul was quoted in the *New York Times*, 30 June 1912, p. X8.
34. The references to the characterization of the cowboy are from a *Bioscope* review of a Broncho Billy film published in 1912. This is discussed in Abel: *Americanizing the Movies*, p. 108.
35. *New York Times*, 30 July 1911, p. SM4.
36. Abel: *Americanizing the Movies*, p. 108.
37. Richard Koszarski, *An Evening's Entertainment: The Age of the Silent Feature Picture* (Berkeley: University of California Press, 1994), p. 290.
38. *Boys' Cinema*, 24 January 1920, p. 6.
39. *Boys' Cinema*, 17 September 1921, p. 12.
40. *Boys' Cinema*, 12 August 1922, p. 1.
41. *Boys' Cinema*, 28 October 1922, pp. 14–15.
42. Brian Taves, 'The B Film: Hollywood's Other Half', in Tino Balio (ed.), *Grand Design: Hollywood as a Modern Business Enterprise, 1930–1939* (Berkeley: University of California, 1995 [1993]), pp. 315–28.

43. Kathryn H. Fuller-Seeley, '"What the Picture Did for Me": Small Town Exhibitors' Strategies for Surviving the Great Depression', in Kathryn H. Fuller-Seeley (ed.), *Hollywood in the Neighbourhood: Historical Case Studies of Local Movie-Going* (Berkeley: University of California Press, 2008), pp. 186–206. Cross and Waller also attest to the western's popularity with small town audiences; Gregory A. Waller, 'Hillbilly Music and Will Rogers: Small Town Picture Shows in the 1930s', in Melvyn Stokes and Richard Maltby (eds), *American Movie Audiences: From the Turn of the Century to the Early Sound Era* (London: British Film Institute, 1999), p. 169; Robin Cross, *The Big Book of B Movies* (London: Frederick Muller, 1981), p. 72.

44. Peter Stanfield, *Hollywood, Westerns and the 1930s: The Lost Trail* (Exeter: University of Exeter Press, 2001), pp. 91–2.

45. Terry Ramsaye (ed.), *The 1939–40 Motion Picture Almanac* (New York: Quigley, 1939), p. 852.

46. The 1939 chart appears in Ramsaye: *The 1939–40 Motion Picture Almanac*, p. 852. In 1947, Boyd was still in the top three, placing below Roy Rogers and Gene Autry; Terry Ramsaye (ed.), *The 1948–49 Motion Picture Almanac* (New York: Quigley, 1948), p. 919.

47. The article first appeared in *New Britain* (2 August 1933). It is reprinted in Forsyth Hardy (ed.), *Grierson on the Movies* (London: Faber and Faber, 1981), pp. 78–9.

48. *Observer*, 12 September 1937.

49. Whitley's account has a parallel in John Boorman's film *Hope and Glory* (1987), in which the lead character, 9-year-old Billy, attends a riotous children's matinee on the eve of the Second World War. It is only when the *Hopalong Cassidy* feature begins that the children settle into their seats, transfixed by the action.

50. Whitley does not specify the town or the title of the film. He says of the cinema, 'It wasn't what you'd call a flea pit, nor was it up to West End luxury standard'. *Daily Mirror*, 5 January 1940, p. 12.

51. Sarah J. Smith, *Children, Cinema and Censorship: From Dracula to the Dead End Kids* (London: I.B.Tauris, 2005), p. 172.

52. See, for example, the accounts in Mayer, *British Cinemas and their Audiences*, pp. 43, 62, 65 and 88.

53. Mayer: *British Cinemas and their Audiences*, pp. 17, 50, 52, 53, 80, 104, 114 and 117. Also see the discussion of children re-enacting westerns as a part of their play in Annette Kuhn, *An Everyday Magic: Cinema and Cultural Memory* (London: I.B.Tauris, 2002), pp. 101–3.

54. Terry Staples, *All Pals Together: The Story of Children's Cinema* (Edinburgh: Edinburgh University Press, 1997), p. 53.

55. He is shot in the leg in the first film, but his subsequent limp (which explains his name) disappears after one scene. The hyphen was dropped from the film titles thereafter too.

56. Fraser points out that Owen Wister, author of the seminal Western novel *The Virginian* (1902), 'traced the Code of the Cowboy back to Middle English chivalry' and conceived of the cowboy hero as a 'a knight at arms, the Anglo-Saxon tradition come to flower again'. John Fraser, *America and the Patterns of Chivalry* (Cambridge: Cambridge University Press, 1982), p. 12. Fraser's work is also discussed in Jeffrey Richards, *Films and British National Identity: From Dickens to Dad's Army* (Manchester: Manchester University Press, 1998), p. 170.

57. As Miller comments, there was a 'remarkable continuity' to the personnel for this series. Don Miller, *'B' Movies: An Informal Survey of the Low-budget Film* (New York: Curtis, 1973), p. 72.

58. Staples: *All Pals Together*, pp. 26, 34–5, 36, 68–9 and 74–5.

59. Leslie Halliwell, *Seats in All Parts: Half a Lifetime at the Movies* (London: Granada, 1985), p. 67.

60. Halliwell: *Seats in All Parts*, p. 63.

61. Powell's review of *Stagecoach* originally appeared in her weekly column in the *Sunday Times*. It is reprinted in Dilys Powell, *The Golden Screen: Fifty Year of Films* (London: Headline, 1990 [1989]), pp. 14–15.

62. See Asa Briggs, *The History of Broadcasting in the United Kingdom*, Vol. 4: *Sound and Vision* (Oxford: Oxford University Press, 1995 [1979]), p. 181.

63. Briggs: *Sound and Vision*, p. 242.

64. Briggs: *Sound and Vision*, p. 253. See also Asa Briggs, *The History of Broadcasting in the United Kingdom*, Vol. 5: *Competition* (Oxford: Oxford University Press, 1995), p. 186.

65. Briggs: *Sound and Vision*, p. 190.

66. For example, the film historian Roger Manvell presented a series of programmes on silent cinema, which included screenings of Charlie Chaplin's early films and an abbreviated version of *The Birth of a Nation*. Other films screened in 1946 and 1947 include wartime documentaries made by the Crown Film Unit, such as *Coastal Command* (1943) and *A Diary for Timothy* (1945).

67. Kelly Boyd, 'Cowboys, Comedy and Crime: American Programmes on BBC Television, 1946–1955', *Media History* 17/3 (2011), pp. 233–51 [240].

68. The BBC reportedly paid £4,000 for the licence to show these 24 films; *Times*, 17 October 1953, p. 3.

69. Boyd: 'Cowboys, Comedy and Crime', p. 241.

70. *Radio Times*, 11 February 1949, p. 25.

71. Michael Kackman, '"Nothing On But Hoppy Badges": *Hopalong Cassidy*, William Boyd and Emergent Media Globalization', *Cinema Journal* 47/4 (Summer 2008), pp. 76–101.

72. Screen sizes are discussed in Briggs: *Sound and Vision*, p. 235.

73. For a discussion of the different visual aesthetics of film and television westerns, see William Boddy, '"Sixty Million Viewers Can't Be Wrong": The Rise and Fall of the Television Western', in Edward Buscombe and

Roberta E. Pearson (eds), *Back in the Saddle Again: New Essays on the Western* (London: British Film Institute, 1998), pp. 119–40.

74. Kackman: 'Nothing on but Hoppy Badges', pp. 84–5.

75. Oliver Jensen, 'Hopalong Hits the Jackpot', *Life*, 12 June 1950, pp. 63–70.

76. See the articles in the British Film Institute's microfiche file on William Boyd: *Daily Mail*, 10 February 1950; *Daily Herald*, 12 May 1951; *News Chronicle*, 31 May 1951.

77. *Daily Mirror*, 5 December 1951, p. 8.

78. Quoted in Kackman: '"Nothing On But Hoppy Badges"', p. 90.

79. *Times*, 7 December 1957, p. 57.

80. In addition to *Hopalong Cassidy* (1955–58) other series broadcast on ITV included *Roy Rogers* (1955–57), *Gunsmoke/Gun Law* (1955–73), *Gene Autry* (1956), *Annie Oakley* (1956–60), *Wyatt Earp* (1956–60), *The Cisco Kid* (1957–60), *Cheyenne* (1958–63), *Wagon Train* (1958–61), *Maverick* (1959–61) and *Rawhide* (1959–65). These programme dates were found in the database of ITV programmes compiled by the British University Film and Video Council, and are available online at <http://tvtip.bufvc.ac.uk/> (last accessed 30 June 2012).

81. Sue Bowden and Avner Offner, 'Household Appliances and the Use of Time: the United States and Britain since the 1920s', *Economic History Review* 47/4 (1994), p. 729.

82. Coyne: *The Crowded Prairie*, p. 66.

83. The references to box office and popularity trends in this paragraph are taken from *Kinematograph Weekly*, which published an annual summary of box office results in the last issue of each year.

84. *The Big Country* was the only Western included in the BFI's tally of the top 100 films at the UK box office. Gilbey: *The Ultimate Film*, pp. 244–5.

85. *Observer*, 14 December 1958 (BFI microfiche).

86. *Spectator*, 16 January 1959 (BFI microfiche).

87. *Films and Filming*, February 1959, p. 23. Curiously, Baker argues that the feud between the Terrills and the Hannasseys is a 'timely allegory' for the conflict between Fascism and Communism. As Michael Coyne has pointed out, this would hardly be timely in 1958, and the filmmakers were far more likely to have the Cold War in mind. Coyne: *The Crowded Prairie*, pp. 92–3.

88. *Sunday Express*, 11 January 1959 (*The Big Country*, BFI microfiche).

89. *Sunday Times*, 11 January 1959 (BFI microfiche).

90. Will Wright, *Six Guns and Society: A Structural Study of the Western* (Berkeley: University of California, 1975), pp. 13–14.

91. Wright: *Six Guns and Society*, pp. 13–14.

92. Although it was produced by Warner Brothers, *Captain Horatio Hornblower, R.N.* was filmed in England. This meant that it was marketed in Britain

as a British-made film. Its box office success is reported in *Kinematograph Weekly*, 20 December 1951, p. 5. Many of Peck's other films scored well with British audiences, but none placed so high in the annual rankings until *The Big Country* was released at the end of the decade.

93. *Daily Mail*, 10 January 1959 (BFI Microfiche).

94. In addition to the other reviews discussed, see the review in *The Times*, 8 January 1959 (BFI microfiche).

95. C.A. Lejeune, for example, described the Hannasseys as 'local trash: they live in unrelieved squalor and delight in horseplay'; *Observer*, 11 January 1959 (BFI Microfiche). John Waterman describes the Hannasseys as a 'poor family of cattleman who live in shacks'. In the *Star*, Ivon Adams referred to the 'Hannasseys boys' as the 'Teds of Texas', indicating that they were juvenile delinquents; *Star*, 8 January 1959 (BFI Microfiche).

96. *Manchester Guardian*, 10 January 1959 (BFI Microfiche).

97. *Evening News*, 8 January 1959 (BFI Microfiche).

98. *Evening Standard*, 8 January 1959 (BFI Microfiche).

99. Lejeune commented that she had seen the painting once before when it featured in a London exhibition, but she did not name the artist and she misremembered the title (as 'Joanna's World'). She also did not seem to be aware that the subject of the painting, Christina, was not able to walk. Wyeth painted her crawling toward the house, using her arms rather than her legs to propel herself. Of course, this does not in any way invalidate Lejeune's interpretation of a painting which suggests a great deal and gives away very little.

100. *Kinematograph Weekly*, 29 January 1959, p. 11.

101. *Express*, 10 January 1959 (BFI Microfiche).

102. *Daily Cinema*, 7 January 1959, p. 6; *Picturegoer*, 10 January 1959, p. 10.

103. Richard Weight, *Patriots: National Identity in Britain, 1940–2000* (London: Macmillan, 2002), pp. 284–6.

104. Arthur Marwick, *The Sixties: Cultural Revolution in Britain, France, Italy and the United States, c. 1958–1974* (Oxford: Oxford University Press, 1998), p. 65.

105. Kathleen Burk, *Old World New World The Story of Britain and America* (London: Little, Brown, 2007), pp. 499 and 563. See also Weight: *Patriots*, p. 165.

106. French: *Westerns*, p. 43.

107. The term 'cowboy' had been used metaphorically in previous decades. In the 1950s, for example, 'coffee bar cowboys' were the 'teenagers with black jackets and fast motor cyclists who gather in cafés'. But the term was not used in such stridently negative terms until the 1970s. See the entry in *The Oxford English Dictionary* (Oxford: Clarendon, 1989), p. 1084.

Chapter 7   The Sixth Form Was Never Like This

1. J.P. Mayer, *British Cinemas and their Audiences* (London: Dobson, 1948), p. 35.
2. Ray Gosling, *Personal Copy: A Memoir of the Sixties* (London: Faber and Faber, 1980), p. 39.
3. This comment appeared in the ABC cinema chain's in-house magazine, which featured an eight-page section on *Grease* while it was on release in ABC cinemas. *Film Review*, October 1978, pp. 29–36.
4. Claudia Goldin and Lawrence F. Katz, *The Race Between Education and Technology* (Cambridge, Harvard University Press, 2008), pp. 195–6.
5. The 1951 census revealed that 73 per cent of the population had no full-time education beyond the age of 14 and fewer than 3 per cent had been educated to the age of 17. David Wardle, *English Popular Education, 1780–1970* (Cambridge, Cambridge University Press, 1976), p. 141.
6. Mayer: *British Cinemas and their Audiences*, pp. 31–3.
7. According to polls conducted by the *Motion Picture Herald*, Durbin and Rooney were the most popular stars in Britain during the years 1939, 1940 and 1941. For a study of Durbin's popularity in Britain, see Annette Kuhn, 'Cinema Culture and Femininity in the 1930s', in Christine Gledhill and Gillian Swanson (eds), *Nationalising Femininity: Culture, Sexuality and British Cinema in the Second World War* (Manchester: Manchester University Press, 1996), pp. 177–92. On Rooney, see David Eldridge, 'Britain Finds Andy Hardy: British Cinema Audiences and the American Way of Life in the Second World War', *Historical Journal of Film, Radio and Television* 31/4 (2011), pp. 499–521.
8. Gosling: *Personal Copy*, p. 30.
9. The Education Act of 1944 had raised the school leaving age to 15, and throughout the 1950s students increasingly stayed in education longer, but the change was very gradual. By the end of the decade – the time in which *Grease* is set – just 7 per cent of 17- and 18-year-olds were in full-time education. Wardle: *English Popular Education, 1780–1970*, p. 141.
10. *Screen International*, 2 September 1978, p. 17.
11. In the BFI's ranking of the country's all-time box office attractions, *Grease* is in twelfth place with an estimated 17.2 million tickets sold. The tally presumably includes tickets sold during the 1998 re-release. Ryan Gilbey, *The Ultimate Film: The UK's 100 Most Popular Films* (London: British Film Institute, 2005), pp. 52–3.
12. Doherty has argued that the 'teenpic' originated 'around 1955' and as a result of the 'decline of classical Hollywood cinema and the rise of the privileged American teenager'. See Thomas Doherty, *Teenagers and Teenpics: The Juvenilization of American Movies in the 1950s* (Philadelphia: Temple University Press, 2002), p. 12.
13. For a discussion of the 'nostalgic construct' of the 'Fifties', see Christine Sprengler, *Screening Nostalgia: Populuxe Props and Technicolor Aesthetics in Contemporary American Film* (Oxford: Berghahn, 2009), pp. 39–43.

14. Jim Jacobs later explained that when the show moved from Chicago to New York, 'We turned it from a three-fourths book, one-fourth music show to the opposite – one-fourth book and three-fourths music.' See Robert Simonson, '*Grease* Returns to Its R-Rated Roots in New Chicago Production', *Playbill*, 30 March 2011.

15. Simonson: '*Grease* Returns'. See also Chris Jones, '*Grease* Gets Back Its Original Chicago Grit', *Chicago Times*, 23 April 2011.

16. Simonson: '*Grease* Returns'.

17. *Guardian*, 3 July 1998, p. 31.

18. Justin Smith, *Withnail and Us: Cult Films and Film Cults in British Cinema* (London: I.B.Tauris, 2010), pp. 26–7.

19. Smith: *Withnail and Us*, p. 15.

20. Frederic Jameson initiated this line of argument in his wider discussion of 1970s nostalgia for the 1950s; see Jameson, *Postmodernism, or, The Cultural Logic of Late Capitalism* (London: Verso, 1991), pp. 19–21. The issue is discussed with particular reference to *Grease* in M. Keith Booker, *Postmodern Hollywood: What's New in Film and Why it Makes us Feel so Strange* (London: Praeger, 2007), p. 65; and Vera Dika, *Recycled Culture in Contemporary Art and Film: The Uses of Nostalgia* (Cambridge: Cambridge University Press, 2003), pp. 122–42.

21. See the discussion in Jerold Simmons, 'Violent Youth: The Censoring and Public Reception of *The Wild One* and *Blackboard Jungle*', *Film History* 20/3 (2008), pp. 381–91.

22. Richard Hoggart, *The Uses of Literacy* (London: Penguin, 1957), pp. 246–50.

23. Dick Hebdige, *Hiding in the Light* (London: Routledge, 1998), pp. 52–8; Dominic Sandbrook, *Never Had It So Good: A History of Britain From Suez to the Beatles* (London: Abacus, 2006 [2005]), pp. 409–53; Andrew Caine, *Interpreting Rock Movies: The Pop Film and its Critics in Britain* (Manchester: Manchester University Press, 2004), pp. 42–50.

24. Caine: *Interpreting Rock Movies*, p. 43.

25. Sandbrook: *Never Had It So Good*, pp. 442–3.

26. Steve Chibnall refers to the Teddy Boy style as a 'blasphemous mixture of orthodox British dandyism and Yank style'. See Chibnall, 'Whistle and Zoot: The Changing Meaning of a Suit of Clothes', *History Workshop Journal* 20/1 (1985), pp. 56–81 [74].

27. *Daily Express*, 3 September 1956, p. 1.

28. See also the reports in *The Times*, 12 September 1956, p. 4; 13 September 1956, p. 6; and 15 September 1956, p. 4.

29. *Daily Express*, 10 September 1956, p. 9. A similar report appears in the *Mirror*, 10 September 1956, p. 5.

30. Sue Harper and Vincent Porter, *British Cinema of the 1950s: The Decline of Deference* (Oxford: Oxford University Press, 2003), p. 228.

31. The BBFC's handling of *The Wild One* is discussed in James Robertson, *The Hidden Cinema: British Film Censorship in Action, 1913–1975* (London, Routledge, 1989), pp. 104–10; and also in Tom Dewe Matthews, *Censored* (London: Chatto and Windus, 1994), pp. 128–31.

32. Robertson: *The Hidden Cinema*, p. 108.
33. This explanation was offered by John Trevelyan (the new Secretary of the BBFC) to Columbia Pictures in 1959, when the latter asked yet again for the censors to reconsider the film. See Matthews: *Censored*, p. 130.
34. The cuts are detailed in Robertson: *The Hidden Cinema*, 116.
35. Daniel Biltereyst, 'Youth, Moral Panics, and the End of Cinema: On the Reception of *Rebel Without a Cause* in Europe', in J. David Slocum (ed.), Rebel Without a Cause: *Approaches to a Maverick Masterwork* (Albany: State University of New York Press, 2005), pp. 171–89 [178–82].
36. Matthews: *Censored*, p. 133.
37. Details of the censorship of this film were reported in *Variety*, 23 November 1955 (*Rebel Without a Cause*, BFI Microfiche).
38. Ray Gosling: *Personal Copy*, p. 40.
39. The films are ranked among the most popular films of the respective years by *Kinematograph Weekly*. See *Kinematograph Weekly*, 15 December 1955, pp. 4–9; and 13 December 1956, pp. 6–10.
40. Gosling: *Personal Copy*, p. 34; Matthews: *Censored*, pp. 132–3.
41. Gosling: *Personal Copy*, pp. 33–4.
42. Hebdige: *Hiding in the Light*, pp. 74–5.
43. *Life*, 16 June 1972, pp. 38–46. See also the discussion in Sprengler: *Screening Nostalgia*, pp. 43–4.
44. Although it is set in 1962, its representation of teenagers cruising in cars, gathering at diners and listening to Bill Haley and Buddy Holly was redolent of a 'long 1950s' that ended with the assassination of President Kennedy in 1963.
45. Cecil Wilson of the *Daily Mail* was particularly struck by the centrality of cars in the film and commented that 'You really need to be an American teenager to get the best out of this picture'. In London's *Evening News*, Felix Barker observed that 'British youth may well look back on their 1962 American counterparts as creatures from another planet'. And in the *New Statesman*, John Coleman answered the question posed in the film's tagline – 'where were you in '62?' – with the rejoinder, 'well, actually, I was "here", reviewing Fellini'. See the reviews in the *Daily Mail*, 29 March 1974; *Evening News*, 28 March 1974; and *New Statesman*, 5 April 1974; all *American Graffiti*/BFI Microfiche.
46. In 1974, *American Graffiti* ranked in twentieth place at the British box office. By contrast, it was the third most popular film of 1973 in the USA. For the American box office figures, see Joel Finler: *The Hollywood Story*, pp. 277–8. For the British figures, see Sue Harper and Justin Smith, *British Film Culture in the 1970s: The Boundaries of Pleasure* (Edinburgh: Edinburgh University Press, 2012), pp. 270–1.
47. For UK admissions figures, see the BFI's Screen Online website. Available at <http://www.screenonline.org.uk/film/facts/fact1.html> (last accessed 21 July 2010).

48. Each of these three films figures in the list of the 100 all-time box office hits in Britain. Gilbey: *The Ultimate Film*, p. 5.

49. David Cook, *Lost Illusions: American Cinema in the Shadow of Watergate and Vietnam* (Berkeley: University of California Press, 2000), pp. 40–3.

50. See the discussion of the marketing campaign in the *Daily Mail*, 26 August 1978 (*Grease*/BFI Microfiche).

51. *Screen International*, 23 September 1978, p. 4.

52. *Screen International*, 15 July 1978, p. 10.

53. See, for example, the article in *Record Mirror*, 23 September 1978, p. 8.

54. *Screen International*, 22 July 1978, p. 4.

55. Harper and Smith: *British Film Culture in the 1970s*, pp. 140–1 and 153–4.

56. The girls' magazines *Blue Jeans* and *Jackie* demonstrated a high level of interest in John Travolta during the summer of 1978. This is remarkable given that, at this stage in his career, Travolta was known in Britain only for *Saturday Night Fever*, and the young readers of these magazines would not have been able to see that X certificate film. But Travolta was the 'pin-up' of the moment, as the photographs in these magazines demonstrate, and *Grease* offered a first chance to see him in a film.

57. See the discussion in Harper and Smith: *British Film Culture in the 1970s*, p. 229.

58. The singles were 'You're the One That I Want' (released in May 1978), 'Grease' (August 1978), 'Summer Nights' (September 1978), 'Hopelessly Devoted To You' (November 1978), 'Greased Lightnin'' (December 1978) and 'Sandy' (January 1978).

59. *Western Mail*, 2 October 1978 and 9 October 1978 (*Grease*/BFI Microfiche).

60. See the reports entitled 'UK Provincial Box Office' in each weekly issue of *Screen International*; for example, *Screen International*, 4 November 1978, 20–1.

61. The film's runs in Glasgow and Edinburgh were reported in the *Glasgow Herald*, 9 October 1978 (*Grease*/BFI Microfiche).

62. *Mirror*, 14 September 1978 (*Grease*/BFI Microfiche).

63. *Guardian*, 14 September, 1978 (*Grease*/BFI Microfiche).

64. *Sunday Telegraph*, 17 September 1978; and *Spectator*, 23 September 1978 (*Grease*/BFI Microfiche).

65. *Evening Standard*, 14 September 1978 (*Grease*/BFI Microfiche).

66. *Sunday Times*, 17 September 1978; *Mirror*, 13 September 1978 (*Grease*/BFI Microfiche).

67. These comments were made prior to the film's release, and in an article commenting on the film's American success and the scale of the marketing campaign in Britain. *Daily Mail*, 26 August 1978 (*Grease*/BFI Microfiche).

68. *Times*, 15 September 1978, p. 10.

69. *Sunday Mirror*, 17 September 1978 (*Grease*/BFI Microfiche).

70. *Observer*, 17 September 1978 (*Grease*/BFI Microfiche).

71. *Sunday Express*, 17 September 1978; *Evening News*, 12 September 1978 (*Grease*/BFI Microfiche).

72. *Record Mirror*, 22 September 1978, p. 19.
73. *New Musical Express*, 23 September 1978, pp. 36–7.
74. *Empire*, August 1998, p. 37.
75. *Observer*, 5 July 1998, p. 152.
76. *Guardian*, 3 July 1998, p. 31.
77. *Independent*, 24 May 1998, p. 14.
78. *Daily Telegraph*, 11 June 2004, p. 21.
79. *Guardian*, 28 December 1982, p. 14.
80. Umberto Eco, '*Casablanca*: Cult Movies and Intertextual Collage', in Howard Koch (et al.), Casablanca: *Script and Legend* (New York: Overlook, 1992), pp. 253–66.
81. The television screening dates can be found on the BIDS database in the British Film Institute Library.
82. '*Grease* Tops "Best Musical" Poll', BBC News, 30 October 2005, Online. Available at <http://news.bbc.co.uk/1/hi/entertainment/4390526.stm> (last accessed 30 June 2012).
83. 'Top Ten Chick Flick Best Sellers To Date', British Video Association, Online. Available at <http://www.bva.org.uk/news-press-releases/dancing-weddings-and-love-football-season-full-swing> (last accessed 30 June 2012).
84. The advertising for *Grease Singalong* reveals an audience consisting mainly of middle-aged women. See the 'Grease Singalong' website. Online. Available at <http://www.singalonga.net/grease> (last accessed 30 June 2012).
85. The internet comments referred to in the text appear on Amazon's UK website, where the most frequent comment customers make is that they purchased the DVD in order to show the film to children or grand-children. '*Grease* Customer Reviews' Online. Available at <http://www.amazon.co.uk/*Grease*-DVD-JohnTravolta/dp/B00006FI2Z/ref=cm_cr_pr_product_top> (last accessed 30 June 2012).
86. I am using this term in the sense that it was used in a discussion of the frequently televised film *The Great Escape* (1963) in Mark Connelly, *We Can Take It!: Britain and the Memory of the Second World War* (London: Pearson, 2004), p. 233.
87. See, for example, the comments on the television screening in the *Guardian*, 22 December 1996, p. 115; and the comments about the release of a 'collector's edition' DVD in *The Times*, 4 November 2006, p. 18.
88. A more culturally specific portrayal of teenage life is offered by the very popular British television series *The Inbetweeners* (2008–10) and the subsequent feature film *The Inbetweeners Movie* (2011). But these demonstrate that cultural specificity entails a much less glamorous and empowered view of youth; the comedy derives from the extraordinary awkwardness, insecurity and ignorance of its four misfit characters.
89. Susan Marling (ed.), *American Affair: The Americanisation of Britain* (London: Bath Press, 1993), pp. 7–22.

Chapter 8   The Wrong Side of the Special Relationship

1. *Spectator*, 5 June 1926, pp. 946–7.
2. *Daily Mirror*, 27 October 1945, p. 6. This quotation is also discussed in I.C. Jarvie, 'Fanning the Flames: Anti-American Reaction to Operation Burma (1945)', *Historical Journal of Film, Radio and Television* 1/2 (1981), pp. 117–37.
3. Andrew Roberts, 'Hollywood's Racist Lies about Britain and the British', *Daily Express*, 14 June 2000, p. 11.
4. See the discussion in the *Daily Express*, 24 May 1926, p. 1. See also the review in the *Daily Express*, 22 May 1926, p. 3.
5. The film was given a full release in 1951. For a full account of the controversy surrounding *Objective, Burma!*, see Jarvie: 'Fanning the Flames', pp. 117–37.
6. Jamie Malanowski, 'The Revolutionary War is Lost on Hollywood', *New York Times*, 2 July 2000, p. 9.
7. See also Bill Desowitz, 'The Battle behind *The Patriot*', *The Los Angeles Times*, 27 June 2000, p. 1f; and Richard Willing, 'The Colonies won the war but rarely can conquer Hollywood's heart', *USA Today*, 3 July 2000, p. 1a.
8. For further discussion of Hollywood's 'British' films, and the industry's dependence on earnings from the British exhibition market, see H. Mark Glancy, *When Hollywood Loved Britain: The Hollywood 'British' Film, 1939–45* (Manchester: Manchester University Press, 1999).
9. *Mrs Miniver* was number one in the box office ranking for films released in 1942; *Kinematograph Weekly*, 14 January 1942, pp. 46–8.
10. For a full account of this film, see Anthony Slide (ed.), *Robert Goldstein and The Spirit of '76* (Metuchen, NJ: Scarecrow Press, 1993).
11. Robert M. Henderson, *D.W. Griffith: His Life and Work* (Oxford: Oxford University Press, 1972), p. 246.
12. Richard Schickel indicates that the box office was 'disappointing'; Schickel, *D.W. Griffith: An American Life* (New York: Limelight, 1996 [1984]), pp. 488–92. Henderson reports that the film did eventually recoup its costs, but only after 'years of distribution, re-issue, and the sale of stock footage for other films'; Henderson: *D.W. Griffith*, p. 249.
13. 'Mr. Griffith's new film banned', *Times*, 11 August 1924, p. 8.
14. Griffith invited the press to a private screening of the film and gave a speech in which he declared, 'The picture, *Love and Sacrifice*, is of no consequence. It is the fact that I, who love Britain and the British, have been called anti-British that has brought me here today.' *Pictures and Picturegoer*, 24 October 1924, p. 51.
15. *The Bioscope*, 11 September 1924, p. 23. This referred to Griffith's 'colossal egotism' and characterized his arguments on behalf of the film as 'sanctimonious bluff and sentimental'. *Kinematograph Weekly*, 11 September 1924, p. 53. This mocked Griffith's claim that he was an Anglophile and that his film was not anti-British; these were 'the tearful protests of a crocodile accused of being carnivorous'.

16. *The Times*, for example, stated that 'there is much in this film that cannot be forgiven' but also argued that its artistic shortcomings were a greater offence than its depiction of the War of Independence. 'Two New American Productions', *Times*, 8 September 1924, p. 10. The trade papers commented on its limited box office prospects. *Bioscope*, 11 September 1924, pp. 38–9; *Kinematograph Weekly*, 2 October 1924, p. 46.

17. John E. O'Connor, 'A Reaffirmation of American Ideals: *Drums Along the Mohawk* (1939)', in J.E. O'Connor and M.A. Jackson (eds), *American History/American Film: Interpreting the Hollywood Image* (New York: Ungar Publishing, 1988), p. 102.

18. Eric Foner, *The Story of American Freedom* (New York: W.W. Norton, 1998), pp. 219–21.

19. *Boy's Cinema* featured *Drums Along the Mohawk* as a short story and used images from the film on its cover; 4 May 1940, pp. 1–3. *Picture Show* offered a 16-page supplement devoted to images and plot details from the film; the supplement was offered with the 11 May 1940 issue.

20. *The Tree of Liberty* is the title of Elizabeth Page's novel, on which the film is based.

21. The pressbook for *The Tree of Liberty* is held at the British Film Institute library.

22. The poor box office performance of these three films is indicated in the annual reports compiled by *Kinematograph Weekly*, which appeared in either the first or last issue of each year.

23. *The Scarlet Coat* was one of the few films on this subject to be directed by an American. But this film was made in Cinemascope and Eastmancolor, and Sturges had experience with both formats.

24. Other films that could be considered in this category include *Alexander Hamilton* (1931), in which George Arliss plays the first US Treasury Secretary. However, the film's story begins after the revolution. Similarly, *Jefferson in Paris* (1995) depicts only the post-Revolutionary years that Thomas Jefferson spent as the American Ambassador in Paris. *Sweet Liberty* (1986) is a comedy set mainly in the present that depicts an author's travails as he watches a Hollywood production team ruin his historical novel, set during the War of Independence.

25. Hudson remains proud of the film, and its critical reputation has improved through the release of DVD and Blu-ray editions. See, for example, Jason Solomons, 'Pacino Has Never Been More Moving', *Observer*, 22 March 2009. Online. Available at <http://www.guardian.co.uk/film/2009/mar/22/revolution-al-pacino-hugh-hudson?INTCMP=SRCH> (last accessed 30 June 2012).

26. *Revolution* had a production budget of $28 million, but it earned less than $360,000 in North America. See the data on the Box Office Mojo website: <http://boxofficemojo.com/movies/?id=revolution.htm> (last accessed 30 June 2012).

27. As one commented in the *New York Times*, '*The Patriot* is to history what *Godzilla* is to biology'. David Hackett Fischer, 'Hubris, But No History', *New York Times*, 1 July 2000, p. 13.

28. Marion was portrayed by Leslie Nielsen and Tarleton by John Sutton in a 1959 television mini-series produced by Disney and entitled *The Swamp Fox*.

29. William Ross St George Jr, 'Review of *The Patriot*', *Journal of American History* 87/3 (December 2000), pp. 1146–8.

30. St George Jr: 'Review of *The Patriot*'.

31. Jeffrey Robert Young, *Domesticating Slavery: The Master Class in Georgia and South Carolina, 1670–1837* (North Carolina: University of North Carolina, 1999), p. 74.

32. Albert Auster, '*Saving Private Ryan* and American Triumphalism', *Journal of Popular Film and Television* 30/2 (2002), pp. 98–104.

33. According to one report, Gibson's popularity has been hit hardest among viewers outside the United States. See Michael Cieply and Brooks Barnes, '"Bad Boy" Star Loses Support Abroad', *New York Times*, 21 July 2010, p. C1.

34. The British reception of *Braveheart* is discussed in Colin McArthur, *Brigadoon, Braveheart and the Scots: Distortions of Scotland in Hollywood Cinema* (London: I.B.Tauris, 2003), pp. 123–36.

35. 'Gibson Blockbuster Baits the Censors', *Guardian*, 13 April 2000. Online: <http://film.guardian.co.uk/News_Story/Exclusive/0,160530,00.html> (last accessed 30 June 2012).

36. John Harlow and Nicholas Hellen, 'Lies, Damned Lies and Hollywood', *Sunday Times*, 4 June 2000, p. 13.

37. Ben Fenton, 'Truth is the First Casualty of Hollywood's War', *Daily Telegraph*, 19 June 2000, p. 3.

38. Peter Hitchens, 'We Should All Be Patriots and Shun This Pack of Hollywood Lies', *Express*, 14 July 2000, p. 13.

39. David Aaronovitch, 'Cynical, Demeaning and Violent Rubbish', *Independent*, 19 June 2000, p. 3b.

40. The programmes are discussed in Hugh Davies, 'US Envoy Wages War on *The Patriot*, *Daily Telegraph*, 15 July 2000, p. 9.

41. Jon Craig, 'Minister Goes to War Over Gibson's *Patriot*', *Sunday Express*, 30 July 2000, p. 27.

42. *Michael Collins* (1996), a sympathetic biopic of the eponymous IRA leader, was also mentioned in some accounts and so too was *Titanic* (1997/98). See, for example, Fenton, 'Truth is the First Casualty', *Daily Telegraph*, 19 June 2000, p. 3; and Roberts, 'Hollywood's Racist Lies', *Daily Express*, 14 June 2000, p. 11.

43. Andrew Roberts offered the most examples of this widely noted phenomenon; Roberts, *Daily Express*, 14 June 2000, p. 11.

44. Lee commented on *The Patriot* in a letter to the *Hollywood Reporter*, but his comments were reported in most British newspapers. See, for example,

Ben Fenton, 'Mel Gibson movie "is a racist whitewash"', *Daily Telegraph*, 8 July 2000, p. 8.

45. Foreman is the British-born film critic for *The New York Post*. Jonathan Foreman, 'The Film That Says We're Nazis', *Daily Telegraph*, 6 July 2000, p. 16.

46. *Screen International*, 30 June 2000, p. 20.

47. *Empire*, August 2000, p. 56.

48. *Daily Mail*, 14 July 2000, p. 60.

49. *News of the World*, 16 July 2000, p. 42.

50. *Sun*, 15 July 2000, p. 40.

51. *Daily Star*, 14 July 2000, p. 27.

52. *Observer*, 16 July 2000, (Review) p. 8

53. *The Mail on Sunday*, 16 July 2000, p. 17.

54. *Daily Telegraph*, 14 July 2000, p. 25.

55. *Guardian*, 14 July 2000, p. 5b.

56. Alex Fischer, '"IMDb Helps Me Sleep at Night": How a Simple Database Changed the World of Film', in Dina Iordanova and Stuart Cunningham (eds), *Digital Disruption: Cinema Moves On-line* (St Andrews: St Andrews Film Studies, 2012), pp. 143–52.

57. <http://www.imdb.com/title/tt0187393/ratings>. Online (last accessed 30 June 2012).

58. <http://www.imdb.com/title/tt0187393/reviews>. Online (last accessed 30 June 2012) (hereafter IMDb/*The Patriot*).

59. The IMDb allows readers to see all of the reviews written by a single reviewer. It is therefore possible to see that most of the reviewers for *The Patriot* had written between ten and 20 reviews.

60. The reviews are locatable on the IMDb reviews pages for *The Patriot* by the date they were submitted, and, in the interests of preserving the reviewers' anonymity, they will be identified here by date rather than by name or email address. The quotations in the sentence cited were published on 1 July 2001, 26 December 2000, 30 October 2008 and 16 August 2006, respectively; IMDb/*The Patriot*.

61. IMDb/*The Patriot*, 24 November 2000.

62. IMDb/*The Patriot*, 1 August 2009; 4 February 2005; 28 July 2006.

63. IMDb/*The Patriot*, 1 August 2009, 10 August 2000, 30 October 2008.

64. IMDb/*The Patriot*, 28 January 2001.

65. IMDb/*The Patriot*, 26 February 2006 and 9 April 2009.

66. Gibson is quoted in St George Jr: 'Review of *The Patriot*', p. 1148.

67. IMDb/*The Patriot*, 23 May 2002, 23 February 2008 and 29 March 2006.

68. IMDb/*The Patriot*, 18 July 2000.

69. IMDb/*The Patriot*, 24 August 2000.

70. IMDb/*The Patriot*, 24 July 2001.

71. Emphasis is in the original; IMDb/*The Patriot*, 12 January 2002.

72. IMDb/*The Patriot*, 17 January 2002.

73. IMDb/*The Patriot*, 29 March 2006.

74. IMDb/*The Patriot*, 8 April 2006.

75. IMDb/*The Patriot*, 21 April 2007.

76. IMDb/*The Patriot*, 22 September 2007.

77. Roberts: *Daily Express*, 14 June 2000, p. 11.

78. Harlow and Hellen: *Sunday Times*, 4 June 2000, p. 13.

79. Don Groves, 'Patriot Misses at O'Seas B.O.', *Variety*, 24 July 2000.

80. The international earnings of *Chicken Run* are available from the *Variety* website: <http://www.variety.com/index.asp?layout=filmsearch_exact&d ept=Film&movieID=10742>.

81. The controversy surrounding *The Patriot* in the USA is discussed in Mark Glancy, 'The War of Independence in Feature Films: *The Patriot* (2000) and the Special Relationship Between Hollywood and Britain', *Historical Journal of Film, Radio and Television* 24/4 (2005), pp. 523–45.

82. By contrast, the most successful historical film of the year, *Gladiator* (2000), earned $188 million in North America, and *The Perfect Storm* earned $183 million. The figures are available at <http://boxofficemojo.com/yearly/chart/?yr=2000&p=.htm>.

83. See the weekly international box office reports in the *Hollywood Reporter*, 1–7 August 2000, pp. 86–7; 8–14 August 2000, pp. 54–5; 22–8 August 2000, pp. 146–7; and 29 August–4 September 2000, pp. 78–9.

84. *Hollywood Reporter*, 25–31 July 2000, p. 106.

85. The international earnings of *The Patriot* are available from the *Variety* website: <http://www.variety.com/index.asp?layout=filmsearch_ exact& dept=Film&movieID=40957>.

86. The two most lucrative markets for Hollywood films in the late 1990s were Japan and Germany. By contrast, in the 1930s these countries had banned Hollywood films and, in doing so, strengthened Hollywood's reliance on Britain. *Hollywood Reporter*, 11–17 July 2000, p. 8.

87. Mark Connelly, *We Can Take It!: Britain and the Memory of the Second World War* (London: Pearson, 2004), pp. 294–7.

88. Richard Weight, *Patriots: National Identity in Britain, 1940–2000* (London: Macmillan, 2002), p. 729.

89. As John Dumbrell has observed, the phrase 'special relationship' has become 'almost as associated with British weakness and dependency as with transatlantic mutuality'. See John Dumbrell, 'The US–UK "Special Relationship" in a World Twice Transformed', *Cambridge Review of International Affairs* 17/3 (2004), p. 438.

90. A YouGov poll conducted in June 2006 asked 1,962 Britons, 'What has happened to your overall opinion of the USA in recent years?' Sixty-nine per cent of the respondents said 'it has gone down'; 20 per cent said 'it has gone up' and 11 per cent said that they did not know. The link between this decline and US foreign policy was apparent in other findings: 77 per cent rated George W. Bush as a 'poor' or 'terrible' world leader; 72 per cent thought that his foreign policies were 'merely a cover for American interests'; and 58 per cent thought that the USA was 'essentially an imperial power'. See Anthony King, 'Britain Falls Out of Love with America', *Daily Telegraph*, 3 July 2006, p. 10.

Select Bibliography

Articles and chapters

Auster, Albert, '*Saving Private Ryan* and American Triumphalism', *Journal of Popular Film and Television* 30/2 (Summer 2002), pp. 98–104.

Bakker, Gerben, 'Building Knowledge about the Consumer: The Emergence of Market Research in the Motion Picture Industry', *Business History* 45/1 (2003), pp. 101–27.

Barr, Charles, 'Deserter or Honored Exile? Views of Hitchcock from Wartime Britain', *Hitchcock Annual* 13 (2004–05), pp. 1–24.

Biltereyst, Daniel, 'Youth, Moral Panics, and the End of Cinema: On the Reception of *Rebel Without a Cause* in Europe', in J. David Slocum (ed.), Rebel Without a Cause: *Approaches to a Maverick Masterwork* (Albany: State University of New York Press, 2005), pp. 171–89.

Boddy, William, '"Sixty Million Viewers Can't Be Wrong": The Rise and Fall of the Television Western', in Edward Buscombe and Roberta E. Pearson (eds), *Back in the Saddle Again: New Essays on the Western* (London: British Film Institute, 1998), pp. 119–40.

Bowen, Elizabeth, 'Why I Go to the Cinema', in C. Davy (ed.), *Footnotes to the Film* (London: Lovat Dickson, 1938), pp. 205–20.

Bowden, Sue and Avner Offner, 'Household Appliances and the Use of Time: the United States and Britain since the 1920s', *Economic History Review* 47/4 (1994), pp. 725–48.

Boyd, Kelly, 'Cowboys, Comedy and Crime: American Programmes on BBC Television, 1946–1955', *Media History* 17/3 (2011), pp. 233–51.

Brown, Tom, 'Spectacle/gender/history: The Case of *Gone with the Wind*', *Screen* 49/2 (2008), pp. 157–78.

Burton, Antoinette, 'When was Britain? Nostalgia for the Nation at the End of the "American Century"', *The Journal of Modern History* 75 (2003), pp. 359–74.

Chapman, James, 'Celluloid Shockers', in Jeffrey Richards (ed.), *The Unknown 1930s: An Alternative History of the British Cinema, 1929–1939* (London: I.B.Tauris, 1998), pp. 75–98.

—— '"Sordidness, Corruption and Violence Almost Unrelieved": Critics, Censors and the Post-war British Crime Film', *Contemporary British History* 22/2 (2008), pp. 181–201.

Chibnall, Steve, 'Whistle and Zoot: The Changing Meaning of a Suit of Clothes', *History Workshop Journal* 20/1 (1985), pp. 56–81.

—— 'Counterfeit Yanks: War, Austerity and Britain's American Dream', in Philip John Davies (ed.), *Representing and Imagining America* (Keele: Keele University Press, 1996), pp. 150–9.

Chow, Karen, 'Popular Sexual Knowledges and Women's Agency in 1920s England: Marie Stopes's *Married Love* and E.M. Hull's *The Sheik*', *Feminist Review* 63 (1999), pp. 64–87.

Clarke, John, 'Pessimism versus Populism: The Problematic Politics of Popular Culture', in Richard Butsch (ed.), *For Fun and Profit: The Transformation of Leisure Into Consumption* (Philadelphia, Temple University Press, 1999), pp. 28–46.

Collins, Richard, 'National Culture: A Contradiction in Terms?', *Canadian Journal of Communication* 16/2 (1991). On line. Available <http://www.cjcn-line.ca/index.php/journal/article/view/603/509> (last accessed 30 June 2012).

Davies, Andrew, 'Glasgow's "Reign of Terror": Street Gangs, Racketeering and Intimidation in the 1920s and 1930s', *Contemporary British History* 21/4 (2007), pp. 405–27.

—— 'The Scottish Chicago? From "Hooligans" to "Gangsters" in Inter–war Glasgow', *Cultural and Social History* 4/4 (2007), pp. 511–27.

De Grazia, Victoria, 'Mass Culture and Sovereignty: The American Challenge to European Cinemas, 1920–60', *Journal of Modern History* 61/1 (1989), pp. 53–87.

Dyer, Richard, 'Entertainment and Utopia', in Bill Nichols (ed.), *Movies and Methods*, Vol. 2 (Berkeley: University of California, 1985), pp. 220–32.

Eco, Umberto, '*Casablanca*: Cult Movies and Intertextual Collage', in Howard Koch et al., *Casablanca: Script and Legend* (New York: Overlook, 1992), pp. 253–66.

Eldridge, David, 'Britain Finds Andy Hardy: British Cinema Audiences and the American Way of Life in the Second World War', *Historical Journal of Film, Radio and Television* 31/4 (2011), pp. 499–521.

Ellis, John, 'Art, Culture and Quality: Terms for a Cinema in the Forties and Seventies', *Screen* 19/3 (1978), pp. 9–50.

—— 'Victory of the Voice?', *Screen* 22/2 (1981), pp. 69–72.

Eyles, Allen, 'Hits and Misses at the Empire', *Picture House* 13 (1989), pp. 25–47.

—— 'When Exhibitors Saw Scarlett: The War Over *Gone With the Wind*', *Picture House* 27 (2002), pp. 23–32.

Fischer, Alex, '"IMDb Helps Me Sleep At Night": How a Simple Database Changed the World of Film', in Dina Iordanova and Stuart Cunningham (eds), *Digital Disruption: Cinema Moves On-line* (St Andrews: St Andrews Film Studies, 2012), pp. 143–52.

Fox, Jo, 'Millions Like Us? Accented Language and the "Ordinary" in British Films of the Second World War', *Journal of British Studies* 45 (2006), pp. 819–45.

Fuller-Seeley, Kathryn H., '"What the Picture Did for Me": Small Town Exhibitors' Strategies for Surviving the Great Depression', in Kathryn H. Fuller-Seeley (ed.), *Hollywood in the Neighbourhood: Historical Case Studies of Local Movie-Going* (Berkeley: University of California Press, 2008), pp. 186–206.

Gans, Herbert J., 'Hollywood Films on British Screens: An Analysis of the Functions of American Popular Culture Abroad', *Social Problems* 7/4 (1961), pp. 324–9.

Geraghty, Christine, 'Cinema as Social Space: Understanding Cinema-going in Britain, 1947–63', *Framework*, 42 (2000). Online. Available at <http://www.frameworkonline.com/Issue42/42cg.html> (last accessed 30 June 2012).

Gienow-Hecht, Jessica C.E., 'Shame on US? Academics, Cultural Transfer, and the Cold War—A Critical Review', *Diplomatic History* 24/3 (2000), pp. 465–94.

Glancy, Mark, 'The War of Independence in Feature Films: *The Patriot* (2000) and the Special Relationship Between Hollywood and Britain', *Historical Journal of Film, Radio and Television* 24/4 (2005), pp. 523–45.

——— 'Temporary American Citizens? British Audiences, Hollywood Films and the Threat of Americanization in the 1920s', *Historical Journal of Film, Radio and Television* 26/4 (2006), pp. 461–84.

——— 'Hitchcock, *Blackmail* and Film Nationalism', in James Chapman, Mark Glancy and Sue Harper (eds), *The New Film History: Sources, Methods, Approaches* (London: Palgrave, 2007), pp. 185–200.

——— '"What Would Bette Davis Do?", British Reactions to Bette Davis in the 1940s: A Case Study of *Now, Voyager*', *Screen* 49/1 (2008), pp. 77–85.

——— 'The Hollywood Woman's Film and British Audiences: A Case Study of Bette Davis and *Now, Voyager*', in Melanie Bell and Melanie Williams (eds), *British Women's Cinema* (London: Routledge, 2010), pp. 49–61.

——— '*The Man Who Knew Too Much* (1934): Alfred Hitchcock, John Buchan and the Thrill of the Chase', in D. Boyd and R.B. Palmer (eds), *Hitchcock at the Source: The Auteur as Adapter* (Albany: State University of New York, 2011), pp. 77–87.

——— '*Picturegoer*: The Fan Magazine and Popular Film Culture in Britain During the Second World War', *Historical Journal of Film, Radio and Television* 31/4 (2011), pp. 453–78.

Hammerton, Jenny, 'Screen Struck: The Lure of Hollywood For British Women in the 1920s', in Alan Burton and Laraine Porter (eds), *Crossing the Pond: Anglo-American Film Relations Before 1930* (Trowbridge: Flicks, 2002), pp. 72–80.

Hammond, Michael, 'A Great American Sensation: Thomas Ince's *Civilisation* at the Palladium, Southampton, 1917', in Melvyn Stokes and Richard Maltby (eds), *Hollywood Abroad: Audiences and Cultural Exchange* (London: British Film Institute, 2004), pp. 35–50.

Harper, Sue, 'A Lower Middle-Class Taste Community in the 1930s: Admissions Figures at the Regent Cinema, Portsmouth, UK', *Historical Journal of Film, Radio and Television* 24/4 (2004), pp. 565–87.

——— 'Fragmentation and Crisis: 1940s Admissions Figures at the Regent Cinema, Portsmouth, UK', *Historical Journal of Film, Radio and Television* 26/3 (2006), pp. 361–94.

Harper, Sue and Vincent Porter, 'Moved to Tears: Weeping in the Cinema in Post-war Britain', *Screen* 37/2 (1996), pp. 152–73.

——— '"Throbbing Hearts and Smart Repartee": The Reception of American Films in 1950s Britain', *Media History* 4/2 (1998), pp. 175–93.

——— 'Cinema Audience Tastes in 1950s Britain', *Journal of Popular British Cinema* 2 (1999), pp. 66–82.

Hawkins, Leslie K., 'Iris Barry, Writer and Cineaste, Forming Film Culture in London, 1921–24', *Modernism/Modernity* 3/3 (2004), pp. 488–515.

Higson, Andrew, 'The Concept of National Cinema', *Screen* 30/4 (1989), pp. 36–47.

Hiley, Nicholas, '"Let's Go to the Pictures": The British Cinema Audience in the 1920s and 1930s', *Journal of Popular British Cinema* 2 (1999), pp. 39–53.

Hill, John, 'British Cinema as National Cinema: Production, Audience and Representation', in Robert Murphy (ed.), *The British Cinema Book* (London: British Film Institute, 1997), pp. 244–54.

Hill, Steven, 'Lost in the Seventies: *Smash Hits* and the Televisual Aesthetics of British Pop', in Laurel Fortster and Sue Harper (eds), *British Culture and Society in the 1970s* (Newcastle Upon Tyne: Cambridge Scholars Publishing, 2010), pp. 175–85.

Hollins, T.J., 'The Conservative Party and Film Propaganda Between the Wars', *English Historical Review* 96/379 (1981), pp. 359–69.

Jarvie, I.C., 'Fanning the Flames: Anti-American Reaction to Operation Burma (1945)', *Historical Journal of Film, Radio and Television* 1/2 (1981), pp. 117–37.

Kackman, Michael, '"Nothing On But Hoppy Badges": *Hopalong Cassidy*, William Boyd and Emergent Media Globalization', *Cinema Journal* 47/4 (2008), pp. 76–101.

Kasson, Joy S., 'Life-like, Vivid, and Thrilling Pictures: Buffalo Bill's Wild West and Early Cinema', in Janet Walker (ed.), *Westerns: Films Through History* (London: Routledge, 2001), pp. 109–30.

Klinger, Barbara, 'Film History Terminable and Interminable: Recovering the Past in Reception Studies', *Screen* 38/2 (1997), pp. 107–28.

Krämer, Peter, 'Hollywood and its Global Audiences: A Comparative Study of the Biggest Box Office Hits in the United States and Outside the United States since the 1970s', in Richard Maltby, Daniel Biltereyst and Philippe Meers (eds), *Explorations in New Cinema History: Approaches and Case Studies* (Oxford: Wiley-Blackwell, 2011).

Kuhn, Annette, 'Cinema Culture and Femininity in the 1930s', in Christine Gledhill and Gillian Swanson (eds), *Nationalising Femininity: Culture, Sexuality and British Cinema in the Second World War* (Manchester, Manchester University Press, 1996), pp. 177–92.

—— 'Snow White in 1930s Britain', *Journal of British Cinema and Television* 7/2 (2010), pp. 183–99.

Kuisel, Richard, 'Americanization for Historians', *Diplomatic History* 24/3 (2000), pp. 509–15.

Lacey, Joanne, 'Seeing Through Happiness: Hollywood Musicals and the Construction of the American Dream in Liverpool in the 1950s', *Journal of Popular British Cinema* 2 (1999), pp. 54–65.

Lambert, Gavin, 'Fairbanks and Valentino: The Last Great Heroes', *Sequence* 8 (Summer 1949), pp. 77–80.

Maltby, Richard, 'Introduction: The Americanisation of the World', in Melvyn Stokes and Richard Maltby (eds), *Hollywood Abroad: Audiences and Cultural Exchange* (London: British Film Institute, 1994), pp. 1–20.

—— 'D is for Disgusting: American Culture and English Criticism', in Geoffrey Nowell-Smith and Steven Ricci (eds), *Hollywood and Europe: Economics, Culture, National Identity* (London: British Film Institute, 1998), pp. 104–15.

—— 'The Production Code and the Mythologies of "pre–Code" Hollywood', in Steve Neale (ed.), *The Classical Hollywood Reader* (London: Routledge, 2012), pp. 237–48.

Maltby, Richard and Ruth Vasey, 'The International Language Problem: European Reactions to Hollywood's Conversion to Sound', in David W. Ellwood, Rob Kroes and Gian Piero Brunetta (eds), *Hollywood in Europe: Experiences of a Cultural Hegemony* (Amsterdam: VU University Press, 1994), pp. 68–93.

Murphy, Robert, 'The Coming of Sound to the Cinema in Britain', *Historical Journal of Film, Radio and Television* 4/2 (1984), pp. 143–60.

—— 'Riff-Raff: British Cinema and the Underworld', in Charles Barr (ed.), *All Our Yesterdays* (London: British Film Institute, 1986), pp. 286–305.

Nowell-Smith, Geoffrey, 'But Do We Need It?', in Martyn Auty and Nick Roddick (eds), *British Cinema Now* (London: British Film Institute, 1985), pp. 147–58.

O'Connor, John E., 'A Reaffirmation of American Ideals: *Drums Along the Mohawk* (1939)', in J.E. O'Connor and M.A. Jackson (eds), *American History/American Film: Interpreting the Hollywood Image* (New York: Ungar Publishing, 1988), pp. 97–112.

Perkins, Sean, 'Film in the UK, 2001–10: A Statistical Overview', *Journal of British Cinema and Television* 9/3 (2012), pp. 310–12.

Poole, Julian, 'British Cinema Attendance in Wartime: Audience Preference at the Majestic, Macclesfield, 1939–1946', *Historical Journal of Film, Radio and Television* 7/1 (1987), pp. 15–34.

Richards, David A., 'America Conquers Britain: Anglo-American Conflict in the Popular Media During the 1920s', *Journal of American Culture* 3/1 (1980), pp. 95–103.

Richards, Jeffrey, 'Tod Slaughter and the Cinema of Excess', in Jeffrey Richards (ed.), *The Unknown 1930s: An Alternative History of the British Cinema, 1929–1939* (London: I.B.Tauris, 1998), pp. 139–60.

—— 'Imperial Heroes for a Post–Imperial Age: Films and the End of Empire', in Stuart Ward (ed.), *British Culture and the End of Empire* (Manchester: Manchester University Press, 2001).

Roodhouse, Mark, 'In Racket Town: Gangster Chic in Austerity Britain, 1939–53', *Historical Journal of Film, Radio and Television* 31/4 (2011), pp. 523–41.

St George Jr, William Ross, 'Review of *The Patriot*', *Journal of American History* 87/3 (December 2000), pp. 1146–8.

Sedgwick, John, 'Cinema-going Preferences in Britain in the 1930s', in Jeffrey Richards (ed.), *The Unknown 1930s: An Alternative History of the British Cinema, 1929–1939* (London: I.B.Tauris, 1998), pp. 1–36.

Selfe, Melanie, '"Intolerable Flippancy": The Arnot Robertson v. MGM Libel Case (1946–1950) and the Evolution of BBC Policy on Broadcast Film Criticism', *Historical Journal of Film, Radio and Television* 31/3 (2011), pp. 373–98.

Semati, M. Mehdi and Patty J. Sotirin, 'Hollywood's Transnational Appeal: Hegemony and Democratic Potential?', *Journal of Popular Film and Television* 26/4 (1999), pp. 176–88.

Shingler, Martin, 'Interpreting *All About Eve*: A Study in Historical Reception', in Melvyn Stokes and Richard Maltby (eds), *Hollywood Spectatorship:*

Changing Perceptions of Cinema Audiences (London: British Film Institute, 2001).

Simmons, Jerold, 'Violent Youth: The Censoring and Public Reception of *The Wild One* and *Blackboard Jungle*', *Film History* 20/3 (2008), pp. 381–91.

Sontag, Susan, 'Notes on "Camp"', in *Against Interpretation and Other Essays* (London: Penguin, 2009 [1966]), pp. 275–92.

Spiller, Robert E., 'The Verdict of Sydney Smith', *American Literature* 1/1 (1929), pp. 3–13.

Staiger, Janet, '"The Handmaiden of Villainy": Methods and Problems in Studying the Historical Reception of a Film', *Wide Angle* 8/1 (1986), pp. 19–28.

Stead, Peter, 'Hollywood's Message for the World: The British Response in the 1930s', *The Historical Journal of Film, Radio and Television* 1/1 (1981), pp. 19–31.

Stokes, Melvyn, 'Introduction: Historical Hollywood Spectatorship', in Melvyn Stokes and Richard Maltby (eds), *Hollywood Spectatorship: Changing Perceptions of Cinema Audiences* (London: British Film Institute, 2001).

Strinati, Dominic, 'The Taste of America: Americanization and Popular Culture in Britain', in D. Strinati and S. Wagg (eds), *Come on Down? Popular Media Culture in Post-War Britain* (London: Routledge, 1992), pp. 46–81.

Studlar, Gaylyn, 'Discourses of Gender and Ethnicity: The Construction and De(con)struction of Rudolph Valentino as Other', *Film Criticism* 13/2 (1989), pp. 18–35.

Taves, Brian, 'The B Film: Hollywood's Other Half', in Tino Balio (ed.), *Grand Design: Hollywood as a Modern Business Enterprise, 1930–1939* (Berkeley: University of California, 1995 [1993]), pp. 315–28.

Waller, Gregory A., 'Hillbilly Music and Will Rogers: Small Town Picture Shows in the 1930s', in Melvyn Stokes and Richard Maltby (eds), *American Movie Audiences: From the Turn of the Century to the Early Sound Era* (London: British Film Institute, 1999), pp. 153–66.

Wasson, Haidee, 'Writing the Cinema Into Daily Life: Iris Barry and the Emergence of British Film Criticism in the 1920s', in Andrew Higson (ed.), *Young and Innocent? The Cinema in Britain, 1896–1930* (Exeter: Exeter University Press, 2002), pp. 321–37.

Waters, Chris, 'Beyond "Americanization": Rethinking Anglo-American Cultural Exchange Between the Wars', *Cultural and Social History* 4/4 (2007), pp. 451–9.

Williams, Melanie and Ellen Wright, 'Betty Grable: An American Icon in Wartime Britain', *The Historical Journal of Film, Radio and Television* 31/4 (2011), pp. 543–59.

Books

Abel, Richard, *The Red Rooster Scare: Making Cinema American, 1900–1910* (Berkeley: University of California Press, 1999).

—— *Americanizing the Movies and 'Movie-Mad' Audiences, 1910–1914* (Berkeley: University of California Press, 2006).

Abravanel, Genevieve, *Americanizing Britain: The Rise of Modernism in the Age of the Entertainment Empire* (Oxford: Oxford University, 2012).

Allen, Robert C. and Douglas Gomery, *Film History: Theory and Practice* (New York: Knopf, 1985).

Altman, Rick (ed.), *Sound Theory, Sound Practice* (London: Routledge, 1992).

Anderson, Benedict, *Imagined Communities: Reflections on the Origin and Spread of Nationalism* (London: Verso, 1986).

Ang, Ien, *Watching Dallas: Soap Opera and the Melodramatic Imagination* (London: Routledge, 1989 [1985]).

Austin, Thomas, *Hollywood, Hype and Audiences: Selling and Watching Popular Film in the 1990s* (Manchester: Manchester University Press, 2002).

Bamford, Kenton, *Distorted Images: British National Identity and Film in the 1920s* (London: I.B.Tauris, 1999).

Barker, Martin, *A Haunt of Fears: The Strange History of the British Horror Comics Campaign* (London: Pluto, 1984).

Barry, Iris, *Let's Go to the Movies* (New York: Payson and Clarke, 1926).

Basinger, Jeanine, *A Woman's View: How Hollywood Spoke to Women, 1930–1960* (New York: Alfred A. Knopf, 1993).

Bell, Melanie and Melanie Williams (eds), *British Women's Cinema* (London: Routledge, 2009).

Bernstein, Matthew and Gaylyn Studlar (eds), *Visions of the East: Orientalism in Film* (London: I.B.Tauris, 1997).

Bigsby, C.W.E. (ed.), *Superculture: American Popular Culture and Europe* (London: Paul Elek, 1975).

Booker, M. Keith, *Postmodern Hollywood: What's New in Film and Why It Makes Us Feel So Strange* (London: Praeger, 2007).

Briggs, Asa, *The History of Broadcasting in the United Kingdom*, Vol. 1: *The Birth of Broadcasting* (London: Oxford University Press, 1961).

—— *The History of Broadcasting in the United Kingdom*, Vol. 2: *The Golden Age of the Wireless* (London: Oxford University Press, 1965).

—— *The History of Broadcasting in the United Kingdom*, Vol. 4: *Sound and Vision* (Oxford: Oxford University Press, 1995 [1979]).

—— *The History of Broadcasting in the United Kingdom*, Vol. 5: *Competition* (Oxford: Oxford University Press, 1995).

Burk, Kathleen, *Old World, New World: The Story of Britain and America* (London: Little, Brown, 2007).

Caine, Andrew, *Interpreting Rock Movies: The Pop Film and its Critics in Britain* (Manchester: Manchester University Press, 2004).

Calder, Angus, *The People's War: Britain, 1939–45* (London: Jonathan Cape, 1969).

—— *The Myth of the Blitz* (London: Pimlico, 1991).

Campbell, Duncan Andrew, *Unlikely Allies: Britain, America and the Victorian Origins of the Special Relationship* (London: Hambledon Continuum, 2007).

Campbell, Neil, Jude Davies and George McKay, *Issues in Americanisation and Culture* (Edinburgh: Edinburgh University Press, 2004).

Camporesi, Valeria, *Mass Culture and National Traditions: The BBC and American Broadcasting, 1922–1954* (Fucecchio, Italy: European Press Academic Publishing, 2000).

Chapman, James, *The British at War: Cinema, State and Propaganda, 1939–1945* (London: I.B.Tauris, 2001).

—— *Past and Present: National Identity and the British Historical Film* (London: I.B.Tauris, 2005).

Chapman, James, Mark Glancy and Sue Harper (eds), *The New Film History: Methods, Sources, Approaches* (London: Palgrave, 2007).

Chibnall, Steve, *Quota Quickies: The Birth of the British 'B' Film* (London: British Film Institute, 2007).

Coglan, W.N., *The Readership of Newspapers and Periodicals in Great Britain, 1936* (London: Incorporated Society of British Advertisers, 1936).

Cohen, Stanley, *Folk Devils and Moral Panics: the Creation of the Mods and Rockers* (New York: St Martin's Press, 1980 [1972]).

Cohen, Henry (ed.), *The Public Enemy, Wisconsin/Warner Bros. Screenplay Series* (Madison: University of Wisconsin Press, 1981).

Connelly, Mark, *We Can Take It!: Britain and the Memory of the Second World War* (London: Pearson, 2004).

Cook, David, *Lost Illusions: American Cinema in the Shadow of Watergate and Vietnam* (Berkeley: University of California Press, 2000).

—— (ed.), *World Cinema's 'Dialogues' with Hollywood* (London: Palgrave, 2007).

Coyne, Michael, *The Crowded Prairie: American National Identity in the Hollywood Western* (London: I.B.Tauris, 1997).

Crafton, Donald, *The Talkies: American Cinema's Transition to Sound, 1926–1931* (Berkeley: University of California, 1997).

Cross, Robin, *The Big Book of B Movies* (London: Frederick Muller, 1981).

Davies, Philip John, *Representing and Imagining America* (Staffordshire: Keele University Press, 1996).

De Grazia, Victoria, *Irresistible Empire: America's Advance through Twentieth Century Europe* (Cambridge, MA: Harvard University Press, 2005).

Dickie, John, *'Special' No More, Anglo–American Relations: Rhetoric and Reality* (London: Weidenfeld and Nicolson, 1994).

Dickinson, Margaret and Sarah Street, *Cinema and State: The Film Industry and the British Government* (London: British Film Institute, 1985).

Dika, Vera, *Recycled Culture in Contemporary Art and Film: The Uses of Nostalgia* (Cambridge, Cambridge University Press, 2003).

Docherty, David, David Morrison and Michael Tracey, *The Last Picture Show? Britain's Changing Film Audience* (London: British Film Institute, 1987).

Docker, John, *Postmodernism and Popular Culture: A Culture History* (Cambridge: Cambridge University Press, 1994).

Dodds, Klaus, 'Popular Geopolitics and Audience Dispositions: James Bond and the Internet Movie Database', *Transactions of the Institute of British Geographers* 31/2 (2006), pp. 116–30.

Doherty, Thomas, *Teenagers and Teenpics: The Juvenilization of American Movies in the 1950s* (Philadelphia: Temple University Press, 2002).

Dyer, Richard, *Only Entertainment* (London: Routledge, 2002).

Ellwood, David W., Rob Kroes and Gian Piero Brunetta (eds), *Hollywood in Europe: Experiences of a Cultural Hegemony* (Amsterdam: VU University Press, 1994).

Eyles, Allen and Keith Skone, *London's West End Cinemas* (Sutton: Premier Bioscope, 1984).

Field, Audrey, *Picture Palace: A Social History of the Cinema* (London: Gentry, 1974).

Finler, Joel, *The Hollywood Story* (London: Octopus, 1988).

Flint, Kate, *The Transatlantic Indian, 1776–1930* (Princeton: Princeton University Press, 2009).

Foner, Eric, *The Story of American Freedom* (New York: W.W. Norton, 1998).

Forster, Laurel and Sue Harper (eds), *British Culture and Society in the 1970s* (Newcastle Upon Tyne: Cambridge Scholars Publishing, 2010).

Fraser, George MacDonald, *The Hollywood History of the World* (London: Penguin, 1988).

Fraser, John, *America and the Patterns of Chivalry* (Cambridge: Cambridge University Press, 1982).

French, Philip, *Westerns* (Manchester: Carcanet, 2005 [1973]).

Geraghty, Christine, *British Cinema in the Fifties: Gender, Genre and the 'New Look'* (London: Routledge, 2000).

Gienow-Hecht, Jessica C.E. (ed.), *Decentering America* (Oxford: Berghahn, 2007).

Gilbey, Ryan (ed.), *The Ultimate Film: The UK's 100 Most Popular Films* (London: British Film Institute, 2005).

Glancy, Mark, *When Hollywood Loved Britain: The Hollywood 'British' Film, 1939–45* (Manchester: Manchester University Press, 1999).

—— *The 39 Steps: A British Film Guide* (London: I.B.Tauris, 2003).

Gledhill, Christine, *Reframing British Cinema, 1918–28: Between Restraint and Passion* (London: British Film Institute, 2003).

Gledhill, Christine and Gillian Swanson (eds), *Nationalising Femininity: Culture, Sexuality and British Cinema in the Second World War* (Manchester: Manchester University Press, 1996).

Goldstein, Philip and James L. Machor (eds), *New Directions in American Reception Study* (Oxford: Oxford University Press, 2008).

Gomery, Douglas, *The Coming of Sound* (New York: Routledge, 2005).

Halliwell, Leslie, *Seats in all Parts: Half a Lifetime at the Movies* (London: Granada, 1985).

Hammond, Michael, *The Big Show: British Cinema Culture in the Great War, 1914–1918* (Exeter: Exeter University Press, 2006).

Hansen, Miriam, *Babel and Babylon: Spectatorship in American Silent Film* (Cambridge, MA: Harvard University Press, 1991).

Hanson, Stuart, *From Silent Screen to Multi-Screen: A History of Cinema Exhibition in Britain since 1896* (Manchester: Manchester University Press, 2007).

Harper, Sue, *Picturing the Past: The Rise and Fall of the British Costume Film* (London: British Film Institute, 1994).

—— *Women in British Cinema: Mad, Bad and Dangerous to Know* (London: Continuum, 2000).

Harper, Sue and Vincent Porter, *British Cinema of the 1950s: The Decline of Deference* (Oxford: Oxford University Press, 2003).

Harper, Sue and Justin Smith, *British Film Culture in the 1970s: The Boundaries of Pleasure* (Edinburgh: Edinburgh University Press, 2012).

Hebdige, Dick, *Hiding in the Light* (London: Routledge/Comedia, 1988).

Heindel, Richard Heathcote, *The American Impact on Great Britain, 1898–1914* (Philadelphia: University of Pennsylvania Press, 1940).

Higson, Andrew (ed.), *Dissolving Views: Key Writings on British Cinema* (London: Cassell, 1996).

—— *Waving the Flag: Constructing a National Cinema in Britain* (Oxford: Oxford University Press, 1997).

Higson, Andrew and Richard Maltby (eds), *'Film Europe' and 'Film America': Cinema, Commerce and Cultural Exchange, 1920–39* (Exeter: University of Exeter Press, 1999).

Hill, John, *British Cinema in the 1980s* (Oxford: Clarendon, 1999).

Hitchens, Christopher, *Blood, Class and Nostalgia: Anglo–American Ironies* (London: Chatto and Windus, 1990).

Hjort, Mette and Scott Mackenzie (eds), *Cinema and Nation* (London: Routledge, 2000).

Hoggart, Richard, *The Uses of Literacy* (London: Penguin, 1957).

Horn, Adrian, *Juke Box Britain: Americanisation and Youth Culture, 1945–60* (Manchester: University of Manchester Press, 2009).

James, Robert, *Popular Culture and Working Class Taste in Britain, 1930–39: A Round of Cheap Diversions?* (Manchester: Manchester University Press, 2010).

Jameson, Frederic, *Postmodernism, or, The Cultural Logic of Late Capitalism* (London: Verso, 1991).

Jancovich, Mark and Lucy Faire with Sarah Stubbings, *The Place of the Audience: Cultural Geographies of Film Consumption* (London: British Film Institute, 2003).

Jarvie, Ian, *Hollywood's Overseas Campaign: The North Atlantic Movie Trade, 1920–50* (Cambridge: Cambridge University Press, 1992).

Klinger, Barbara, *Melodrama and Meaning: History, Culture, and the Films of Douglas Sirk* (Bloomington: Indiana University Press, 1994).

Koszarski, Richard, *An Evening's Entertainment: The Age of the Silent Feature Picture* (Berkeley: University of California Press, 1994).

Kroes, Rob, Robert W. Rydell and Doeko F.J. Bosscher (eds), *Cultural Transmissions and Receptions: American Mass Culture in Europe* (Amsterdam: VU University Press, 1993).

Kuhn, Annette, *Cinema, Censorship and Sexuality, 1909–25* (London: Routledge, 1988).

—— *An Everyday Magic: Cinema and Cultural Memory* (London: I.B.Tauris, 2002).

Lant, Antonia, *Blackout: Reinventing Women for Wartime British Cinema* (Princeton: Princeton University Press, 1991).

LeMahieu, D.L., *A Culture For Democracy: Mass Communication and the Cultivated Mind in Britain Between the Wars* (Oxford: Clarendon, 1988).

Leider, Emily W., *Dark Lover: The Life and Death of Rudolph Valentino* (London: Faber, 2004 [2003]).

Lewis, Lisa A. (ed.), *The Adoring Audience: Fan Culture and Popular Media* (London: Routledge, 1992).

Low, Rachael, *The History of the British Film, 1918–29* (London: George Allen and Unwin, 1971).

McArthur, Colin, *Underworld USA* (London: British Film Institute, 1972),

—— *Brigadoon, Braveheart and the Scots: Distortions of Scotland in Hollywood Cinema* (London: I.B.Tauris, 2003).

McKibben, Ross, *Classes and Cultures: England, 1918–51* (Oxford: Oxford University Press, 1998).

Malchow, H.L., *Special Relations: The Americanization of Britain?* (Stanford: Stanford University Press, 2011).

Marling, Susan, *American Affair: The Americanisation of Britain* (London: Boxtree, 1993).

Marwick, Arthur, *The Sixties: Cultural Revolution in Britain, France, Italy and the United States, c. 1958–1974* (Oxford: Oxford University Press, 1998).

——*A History of the Modern British Isles, 1914–1999* (Oxford: Blackwell, 2000).

Matthews, Tom Dewe, *Censored* (London: Chatto and Windus, 1994).

Mayer, J.P., *Sociology of Film: Studies and Documents* (London: Faber, 1946).

——*British Cinemas and their Audiences* (London: Dobson, 1948).

Medved, Michael, *Hollywood vs. America: Popular Culture and the War on Traditional Values* (New York: HarperCollins, 1992).

Melling, Phil and Jon Roper (eds), *Americanisation and the Transformation of World Cultures: Melting Pot or Cultural Chernobyl?* (Lampeter: Edwin Mellor Press, 1996).

Miller, Jeffrey S., *Something Completely Different: British Television and American Culture* (Minneapolis: University of Minnesota Press, 2000).

Miskell, Peter, *A Social History of the Cinema in Wales, 1918–1951: Pulpits, Coal Pits and Fleapits* (Cardiff: University of Wales Press, 2006).

Mowat, Charles Loch, *Britain Between the Wars, 1918–1940* (London: Methuen, 1968 [1955]).

Murphy, Robert (ed.), *The British Cinema Book* (London: British Film Institute, 1997).

—— *Realism and Tinsel: Cinema and Society in Britain, 1939–49* (London: Routledge, 1989).

Neale, Steve, *Genre and Hollywood* (London: Routledge, 2000).

Nowell-Smith, Geoffrey and Steven Ricci (eds), *Hollywood and Europe: Economics, Culture, National Identity, 1945–95* (London: British Film Institute, 1998).

Orwell, George, *Essays* (London: Penguin, 2000).

Pells, Richard, *Not Like Us: How Europeans Loved, Hated and Transformed American Culture Since World War Two* (New York: Basic, 1997).

Plain, Gill, *John Mills and British Cinema: Masculinity, Identity and Nation* (Edinburgh: Edinburgh University Press, 2006).

Powell, Dilys, *The Golden Screen: Fifty Years of Films* (London: Headline, 1990 [1989]).

Pugh, Martin, *We Danced All Night: A Social History of Britain between the Wars* (London: Bodley Head, 2008).

Reddin, Paul, *Wild West Shows* (Chicago: University of Illinois Press, 1999).

Reeves, Nicholas, *The Power of Film Propaganda: Myth or Reality?* (London: Continuum, 1999).

Reynolds, David, *Rich Relations: The American Occupation of Britain, 1942–1945* (London: HarperCollins, 1996 [1995]).

Richards, Jeffrey, *Swordsmen of the Screen: From Douglas Fairbanks to Michael York* (London: Routledge and Kegan Paul, 1977).

—— *The Age of the Dream Palace: Cinema and Society in Britain, 1930–1939* (London: Routledge, 1984).

——*Films and British National Identity: From Dickens to Dad's Army* (Manchester: Manchester University Press, 1997).

——*Hollywood's Ancient Worlds* (London: Continuum, 2008).

Richards, Jeffrey and Dorothy Sheridan (eds), *Mass Observation at the Movies* (London: Routledge, 1987).

Rixon, Paul, *American Television on British Screens: A Story of Cultural Interaction* (London: Palgrave, 2006).

Robertson, James C., *The British Board of Film Censors: Film Censorship in Britain, 1896–1950* (London: Croom Helm, 1985).

——*The Hidden Cinema: British Film Censorship in Action, 1913–75* (London: Routledge, 1989).

Ryall, Tom, *Britain and the American Cinema* (London: Sage, 2001).

Rydell, Robert W. and Rob Kroes, *Buffalo Bill in Bologna: The Americanization of the World, 1869–1922* (Chicago: University of Chicago Press, 2005).

Sandbrook, Dominic, *Never Had It So Good: A History of Britain from Suez to the Beatles* (London: Little, Brown, 2006).

Sedgwick, John, *Popular Filmgoing in 1930s Britain: A Choice of Pleasures* (Exeter: University of Exeter, 2000).

Segrave, Kerry, *American Films Abroad: Hollywood's Domination of the World's Movie Screens* (Jefferson, NC: McFarland, 1997).

Seitz, Raymond, *Over Here* (London: Weidenfeld and Nicolson, 1998).

Slide, Anthony (ed.), *Robert Goldstein and The Spirit of '76* (Metuchen, NJ: Scarecrow Press, 1993).

Smith, Graham A., *When Jim Crow Met John Bull: Black GIs in World War II Britain* (London: I.B.Tauris, 1987).

Smith, Justin, *Withnail and Us: Cult Films and Film Cults in British Cinema* (London: I.B.Tauris, 2010).

Smith, Sarah J., *Children, Cinema and Censorship: From Dracula to the Dead End Kids* (London: I.B.Tauris, 2005).

Sprengler, Christine, *Screening Nostalgia: Populuxe Props and Technicolor Aesthetics in Contemporary American Film* (Oxford: Berghahn, 2009).

Springhall, John, *Youth, Popular Culture and Moral Panics: Penny Gaffs to Gangsta Rap, 1830–1996* (New York: St Martin's Press, 1998).

Stacey, Jackie, *Star Gazing: Hollywood Cinema and Female Spectatorship* (London: Routledge, 1994).

Staiger, Janet, *Interpreting Films: Studies in Historical Reception of American Cinema* (Princeton, NJ: Princeton University Press, 1992).

——*Perverse Spectators: The Practices of Film Reception* (New York: New York University Press, 2000).

Stanfield, Peter, *Hollywood, Westerns and the 1930s: The Lost Trail* (Exeter: University of Exeter Press, 2001).

Staples, Terry, *All Pals Together: The Story of Children's Cinema* (Edinburgh: Edinburgh University Press, 1997).

Stead, Peter, *Film and the Working Class* (London: Routledge, 1989).

Stevenson, John, *British Society: 1914–45* (London: Penguin, 1984).

Stokes, Melvyn and Richard Maltby (eds), *American Movie Audiences: From the Turn of the Century to the Early Sound Era* (London: British Film Institute, 1999).

—— *Hollywood Spectatorship: Changing Perceptions of Cinema Audiences* (London: British Film Institute, 2001).

—— *Hollywood Abroad: Audiences and Cultural Exchange* (London: British Film Institute, 2004).

Storey, John (ed.), *Cultural Theory and Popular Culture: A Reader*, 4th edn (Harlow: Pearson, 2006).

Street, Sarah, *British National Cinema* (London: Routledge, 1997).

—— *British Cinema in Documents* (London: Routledge, 2000).

——*Transatlantic Crossings: British Feature Films in the USA* (London: Continuum, 2002).

Studlar, Gaylyn, *This Mad Masquerade: Stardom and Masculinity in the Jazz Age* (New York: Columbia University Press, 1996).

Sutton, David, *A Chorus of Raspberries: British Film Comedy, 1929–1939* (Exeter: University of Exeter Press, 2000).

Swann, Paul, *The Hollywood Feature Film in Postwar Britain* (London: Croom Helm, 1987).

Taylor, A.J.P., *English History, 1914–1945* (Oxford: Oxford University Press, 1992 [1965]).

Taylor, Helen, *Scarlett's Women:* Gone with the Wind *and its Female Fans* (London: Virago, 1987).

Thompson, Kristin, *Exporting Entertainment: America in the World Film Market, 1907–34* (London: British Film Institute, 1985).

Trumpbour, John, *Selling Hollywood to the World: US and European Struggles for Mastery of the Global Film Industry* (Cambridge: Cambridge University Press, 2002).

Tunstall, Jeremy, *The Media Are American: Anglo-American Media in the World* (London: Constable, 1977).

Vasey, Ruth, *The World According to Hollywood, 1918–1939* (Madison: University of Wisconsin Press, 1997).

Walker, Alexander, *The Shattered Silents: How the Talkies Came to Stay* (London: Elm Tree, 1978).

Webster, Duncan, *Looka Yonder: The Imaginary America of Popular Culture* (London: Routledge, 1988).

Weight, Richard, *Patriots: National Identity in Britain, 1940–2000* (London: Macmillan, 2002).

White, Cynthia L., *Women's Magazines, 1693–1968* (London: Michael Joseph, 1970).

Worpole, Ken, *Dockers and Detectives: Popular Reading, Popular Writing* (London: Verso, 1983).

Wright, Will, *Six Guns and Society: A Structural Study of the Western* (Berkeley: University of California, 1975).

Zweiniger-Bargielowska, Ina, *Austerity in Britain: Rationing, Controls and Consumption, 1939–1955* (Oxford: Oxford University Press, 2000).

Index

All italicised titles refer to films unless otherwise indicated. Dates placed into brackets refer to film titles that have been made more than once. Italicised page references refer to illustrations.